The Japanese Period Film

The Japanese Period Film

A Critical Analysis

S.A. THORNTON

Foreword by Donald Richie

McFarland & Company, Inc., Publishers
Jefferson, North Carolina, and London

A translation from the *Kōnodai kōki* in "Thematic Composition in the Japanese Epic: On the Type Scene" and other parts first appeared in "*Kōnodai senki:* Traditional Narrative and Warrior Ideology in Sixteenth-Century Japan," *Oral Tradition* 15, no. 2 (2000): 306–376, http://journal.oraltradition.org/issues/15ii.

Translations from the *Kōnodai senki* in "The Buddhist Background of Popular Narrative: The Japanese Epic as Buddhist Sermon" first appeared in "*Kōnodai senki*: Traditional Narrative and Warrior Ideology in Sixteenth-Century Japan," *Oral Tradition* 15, no. 2 (2000): 306–376, http://journal.oraltradition.org/issues/15ii.

A translation from the *Meitokuki* in "The Buddhist Background of Popular Narrative: The Japanese Epic as Buddhist Sermon," "Thematic Composition, Formulaic Diction and Cinema," and "Thematic Composition in the Japanese Epic: On the Type Scene" first appeared in "From Warrior to Holy Man," *Parabola* 12, no. 1 (spring 1987):43–49.

Translations from the *Ōtō monogatari* in "The Buddhist Background of Popular Narrative: The Japanese Epic as Buddhist Sermon" and "Thematic Composition in the Japanese Epic: On the Type Scene" first appeared in "The Tale of [The Battle of] Ōtō: The Japanese Epic and Religious Propaganda Traditions from the Ippen School of Pure Land Buddhism," in *Religions of Japan in Practice*, edited by George Tanabe (Princeton University Press, 1999).

"The Shinkokugeki and the Zenshinza: Western Representational Realism and the Japanese Period Piece" first appeared in *Asian Cinema* 7, no. 2 (winter 1995): 46–57.

Unless otherwise noted, all photographs are from the author's collection.

LIBRARY OF CONGRESS CATALOGUING-IN-PUBLICATION DATA

Thornton, Sybil Anne.
The Japanese period film : a critical analysis / S.A. Thornton ; foreword by Donald Richie.
p. cm.
Includes bibliographical references and index.

ISBN-13: 978-0-7864-3136-6
softcover : 50# alkaline paper ♾

1. Historical films — Japan — History and criticism. I. Title.
PN1995.9.H5T46 2008
791.43'0909358 — dc22 2007034257

British Library cataloguing data are available

Cover photograph: Bandō Tsumasaburō (center) in the 1925 silent *Orochi (Serpent)*, directed by Futagawa Buntarō (courtesy of Matsuda Film Productions)

Manufactured in the United States of America

McFarland & Company, Inc., Publishers
Box 611, Jefferson, North Carolina 28640
www.mcfarlandpub.com

To Inna Gens-Katanyan

Acknowledgments

I am most indebted to the many people who have made this book possible through their kindnesses and generosity. In the seventies and eighties, there were Americans and Europeans, already well established in their careers, who were doing research and publishing on Japanese film, but there were not many virtual nobodies like me. Luckily, I was a volunteer at the Pacific Film Archive, where I catalogued the Nikkatsu collection, typed the first card catalogue of the entire collection, and organized two series of screenings. Therefore, I was introduced to the Japanese filmmakers and others who came through; one introduction led to the other. They all took very good care of me while I was in Japan, for one month in 1977 and for over two years in 1980 through 1982: they took me out to dinner, invited me home, and arranged interviews for me. The first draft of the book was written while I was in Japan. Work on the book was interrupted by some twenty years' researching and writing a Ph.D., finding a permanent job, and getting tenure. Nevertheless, I have always felt grateful for the help I received in Japan and would like to express my deepest thanks here to the following:

The Kawakita Memorial Film Institute (formerly the Japan Film Library Council): Kawakita Kashiko (Mme. Kashiko Kawakita), Shimizu Akira, my legal guarantor, and the friendly and welcoming staff;

The National Museum of Modern Art Tokyo Film Center: Maruo Sadamu, director, and the staff, especially Okajima Hisashi, Ōba Masatoshi, and Chiba Nobuo; Misono Kyōhei, a major collector of film ephemera (posters, stills, etc.) heard about me from them and gave me a very rare copy of his book on period films illustrated with stills from his collection;

Matsuda Film Productions: Matsuda Shunsei, the late *benshi* (narrator) and collector of silent films, screened many important silent films for me and I always went to his monthly performances;

The directors and actors who were kind enough to grant me interviews in offices or over lunch or permitted me to view rehearsals or sets during filming: Hasegawa Kazuo, Ichikawa Utaemon, Inagaki Hiroshi, Kumai Kei,

Nakamura Kan'emon, Nomura Yoshitarō, Shinoda Masahiro, and Tsuruta Kōji; Yoda Yoshikata welcomed me at his home several times, and Mrs. Yoda read my horoscope;

Kuriyama Tomio (*Shukuji* [Congratulatory Speech, 1985], *Ho–mu sui–to ho–mu* [Home Sweet Home, 2000]), whom I met when he was an assistant director spending his sabbatical at the archive, introduced me to Yamada Yōji, who introduced me to Asama Yoshitaka (co-scripted *Tasogare Seibei* [*Twilight Samurai*, 2002]). They were all very kind to me;

Donald Richie, who often acted as my mentor and provided much-needed encouragement;

Muragishi Kiyoko, *okami-san* of the Kingen Ryōkan in Akasaka, who took me in as "a relative from the country."

I would also like to acknowledge the three people most important in my development as a scholar and writer: Ernest "Chick" Callenbach, who published my first book review in *Film Quarterly* ("You *can't* write like *that*!"); Douglas Gallez, my M.A. thesis supervisor at San Francisco State ("Give it back to me when it's one-tenth the size!"); and Carmen Blacker, my Ph.D. thesis supervisor at Cambridge ("This sentence belongs at the beginning of the paragraph, *not* at the end!"). They were all, of course, right, as they were in everything else.

Table of Contents

Foreword

by Donald Richie

Alexis de Tocqueville, looking back at the *ancien régime*, observed that "history is a gallery of pictures in which there are few originals and many copies." True, but copies are valuable. They connect the parts of the past; they indicate a path through which the present is reached. History stacks one version on top of another, and it is by sifting through these strata that we learn something about ourselves.

How we got here, for example. This is one of the tasks undertaken by Sybil Thornton in her valuably iconoclastic essays on Japan's relation to its past. To this end she studies Japanese legend, epic, and chronicle, turning these pages of history and indicating how the copies differ or how they remain the same. From early myth through recent film and nightly television, she shows that the major use of the past, Japan's *ancien régime*, is to illuminate the present.

To find out where we are is to look at where we came from and then to use this knowledge. For those of us who complain that later Japanese historical films are studded with anachronisms, Thornton points out that they always have been, that indeed "anachronism is the essence of the period film, whose function is to discuss the present."

Moreover, the period film itself constitutes a "matching of present and past, combining Tokugawa-period iconography with purely modern use of narrative and language," resulting in a double-edged "criticism of society," both past and present.

The principal concern of this Tokugawa regime was, as Thornton interprets it, "to classify the population and to organize it into a hierarchy with the military class on top." Thus, the principal concern of society was a graded organizational structure, and a major concern of the resident individual was for status within that structure.

Cinematic criticism of such ambitions began early. As Thornton demonstrates, "the function of a Japanese period piece, in print, on stage, or in film, is to discuss politically sensitive material and, at the same time, to evade government censorship." The means of such evasion she then examines, and these in turn become the markings of the modern period film or TV program.

Among these means are Western borrowings, new roles for modern "realism," and for the traditional evasive methods of *mitate*. To follow these uses is to recreate the history of the period film, which is what Thornton admirably does. From Sawada Shōjirō, Itō Daisuke, Inagaki Hiroshi, through Yamanaka Sadao, Kurosawa Akira and Kobayashi Masaki, we watch influences continue, learned lessons repeated, and the creation of new images from old forms as the period piece morphs to meet the demands of today and tomorrow.

Contemporary foreign writings on the Japanese film take a variety of means, many of which are theoretical and most of which base themselves on the idea that film is a universal medium transparent to everyone. The idea of a "national" cinema is discouraged.

Yet, universal as film may be, it has its specifics. Transparency is to be achieved through instruction. Here, Thornton is culturally specific. It is the Japanese film and the Japanese narrative and theatrical traditions which concern her. It is through their elucidation that her valuable conclusions are reached.

One of them is found in Thornton's demonstration of the uses which Japan has found for its past. Others, forming an historical nexus, take us back to the medieval epic, to the Buddhist popular narrative, and to other themes tangential to the major concern of the writing and rewriting of Japanese history.

All of them constitute an informed investigation of the specifics of the Japanese genius for discovering uses for the findings of copies of the past.

Introduction

In 1967, when I was sixteen, San Francisco's public television station KQED broadcast Ichikawa Kon's (1915–) multi-part television series *Genji monogatari* (*The Tale of Genji*).[1] Entranced, I watched it week after week: a woman dipped the little finger of her right hand in candle soot and drew a line high on her forehead; another lay in her bed with her long hair neatly rolled up in a shallow box; poor Genji was forced to stay the night with the wrong woman because he was too genteel to disappoint her.

KQED later broadcast a series of Japanese films, which of course I enjoyed very much. Moreover, as I entered Berkeley in 1972, an enormous boom in Japanese films hit the Bay Area: what with Japanese films playing at the Pacific Film Archive, the Berkeley repertoire theaters, and the theater in San Francisco's Japan Town, it was at times possible to see eight different films a week. Japanese filmmakers like Okamoto Kihachi, Kurosawa Akira, and Yoda Yoshikata came to Berkeley. I left the graduate program in Latin to study film at San Francisco State.

In the beginning, when I first started studying Japanese film, all I wanted was to find out why the samurai always got killed at the end of the movie. Thirty years later, the problem now engaging me is how the medieval Japanese epic made the transition from oral composition to literary composition. Is there a relationship between the two quests? Indeed, yes! The modern yakuza and samurai films are both cognates of the medieval epic and share the same composition techniques. This is what the book is about, and this is what makes this book about Japanese cinema different from others.

Because this study proposes that there is indeed a relationship between past and present in the narrative tradition of this nation, distinguished by its cultural development under conditions of near hermetic seclusion, it affirms the notion that Japanese cinema is indeed distinctively — if not exclusively — Japanese. The most recent generation of American film scholars and critics have assumed, certainly on the basics of film language and film techniques, that there is little difference between American and Japanese cinema. Even

Donald Richie, the dean of Western criticism of Japanese cinema, has recently written, "Now, my ideas of film style have broadened and I am no longer so confident that such a thing as national character can be said to exist."[2] That may very well be true if one focuses on the problem of moving image media (pre-production, post-production, and whatever comes in between).

In discussing Japanese film as film, there are several approaches to take and most of them have already been ventured: auteurist, historical, Jungian, generic, literary, semiotic, etc. There is more, however, to consider in a film than film techniques. This study, thus, relies less on any one analytical method or combination of methods than on what seems a foregone conclusion: that Japanese period films, those films set in the past, belong to a discrete, national narrative tradition and must be understood, not exclusively, but first and foremost as such. Focusing on a comparison of the narrative strategies of the Japanese period film with those in traditional theater and popular literature, not to speak of religious rituals, is likely to be regarded with some skepticism by those who maintain, like Aaron Gerow, that "[i]nsisting on only seeing Japanese film through the narrow looking glasses of Zen, ukiyo-e, kabuki and other 'traditional' arts is not only self-delusion (and a problematic form of self-construction), but also a refusal to engage in a dialogue with film makers and audiences of other cultures. It is myopic and deeply disturbing."[3] I take his point about "only." Even so, the hostility animating this comment can be seen as a reaction, not to the analysis of the place of Japanese cinema in the tradition of Japanese performance and narrative, but to the orientalism informing some criticism of Japanese film, a western and patronizing representation of the exotic East whose principal purpose is self-aggrandizement for both its producers and its consumers. The persistence of this perspective in discussions of Japanese cinema, however, whether dominant or attenuated, has less to do with ulterior motives than with the surprisingly low level of expertise of so many of those fascinated by the idea of Japanese cinema as a vehicle of Japanese culture. This innocent orientalism, then, inasmuch as it does expose the problem of expertise, requires not abjuring the study of the relationship of Japanese cinema to other Japanese narrative and performance arts but rectifying that study.

This book offers such a re-examination, the product of some thirty years' study and teaching of Japanese cinema, religion, history, and epic. It is the synthesis of a master's thesis, a bachelor's dissertation, a doctoral thesis, papers presented at academic conferences, publications in academic and other journals, and thousands of hours spent watching plays at the theater (big and little, classical and modern) and films at the Pacific Film Archive, in front of the TV in a traditional inn *(ryōkan)*, at the Steenbeck of the Tokyo Modern Museum of Art Film Center, in tiny but sometimes charming cinema boutiques, at monthly showings of silent films narrated by septuagenarian and older *benshi* (narrators), and at all-night screenings at Shinjuku and Asakusa movie houses.

Although the Japanese period film is the focus of this book, other topics covered concern narrative in Japanese epic, religion, theater, and modern popular literature. It is easy to point out the breaks and discontinuities in Japanese culture. It is true that in the nineteenth century, Japan was nearly overwhelmed by foreign influences; it is also true that it was the performers of traditional narrative arts who made the foreign influences comprehensible to the public. The government enlisted the entertainment world — stage actors, tellers of didactic stories, and others — to translate western culture to the masses. Kabuki actors cut their hair and played at going up in a balloon. Professional raconteurs of the better sort sat on a chair at a table and read the newspapers to their illiterate audiences. Politicians registered with the government as these raconteurs in order to make speeches and wrote novels on the western model to popularize their western liberal politics. The western form of mass media, the newspaper, first served as the chief vehicle for narrative in modern Japan: western translations, transcriptions of story-tellers' performances, political novels, and descriptions and critiques of plays all found their places (side by side, cheek by jowl) in the newspapers. Even the film camera — cinema — was introduced in 1897 "as the most appropriate device for introducing contemporary Western culture to [Japan]."[4] Japan did undergo enormous changes in the nineteenth century; one can rightly point to obvious discontinuities between the Tokugawa period and the modern period. Nevertheless, there were continuities in society and continuities in narrative.[5]

As this study demonstrates, the narrative in the Japanese period film has cognates in Buddhist preaching, rituals for the pacification of angry spirits of the dead, and rhetorical devices for evading censorship, among others. The form and function of this narrative tradition were fixed more or less in the eighteenth century.

The narrative is comprehensible only when one understands the basic assumptions of how the world works upon which the narrative itself is premised. These basic assumptions are what make up the intangible mental culture of the Japanese: their memories, values, aspirations, fears, loyalties, priorities, and sense of place in the pattern of relationships that make up everyday life and the sense of place in the cosmos. A *Weltanschauung* (ideology) defines the individual and the group; it varies according to environment, time, class, sex, religion, position in the family, and individual psychological state within a culture and from culture to culture. As long as the view or perception of the world differs from community to community, from ethnic of their local tutelary deities.[7] Folklorists, still influenced by theories current a generation and more before, expounded on the differentiation of performing arts from age-old religious ritual; to Nō, especially, they ascribed shamanic functions and a real transformation into a divinity with the wearing of the *okina* (old man) mask.[8] With all this in the air, it should come as no surprise that film reflected these trends, consolidated them, and even intensified them throughout the fifties and sixties. This was most apparent in the work of Hashimoto Shinobu (1918–), whose scenario for Kurosawa Akira's 1950 *Rashōmon* established the flashback as a standard narrative technique in Japanese film: the flashback, as a story about the past, reflects the post–World War II appropriation of spirit possession as a form of individual or group legitimation.[9]

The fourth and fifth chapters expand on the theme of criticism of the present through the past. "Sixteenth Century Japan in Film" examines the representations of different levels of society characterized by social mobility in an era of warfare. Whether samurai, peasant, artisan, or millionaire aesthete, any and all caught up in the warfare of the period suffer enormously. The most distinctive development in films about the sixteenth century was the ninja film which stressed the resistance of the common people (that is, they are not samurai) against the unification by military conquest of ruthless warlords such as Oda Nobunaga (1534–1582) and Toyotomi Hideyoshi (1536–1598). In these films, the unification period can be seen as analogous to the first half of the twentieth century, the period of Japan's attempt to expand by military conquest into Korea, China, and Southeast Asia. The theme of the resistance of the common man is carried through by chapter 5, "The Yakuza Film," which focuses on the *ninkyō eiga* (chivalry film) of the 1960s. Although set in the modern period (after 1867), they, along with the ninja film, are counterpoints to the critical period films of the same time: while the samurai cannot strike back at his immediate superiors, the common man can and does.

Part Two, "Realism in the Narrative," is made up of three chapters on the topic of realism. The first, "The Shinkokugeki and the Zenshinza: Western Representational Realism and the Japanese Period Film,"[10] analyzes the roles of two theater troupes, the Shinkokugeki (New National Theater) and Zenshinza (Progressive Troupe), in introducing the representational realism of the nineteenth century European theater, that of Ibsen and Chekhov, to Japanese theater and film. "Historical Realism," chapter 7, traces the development of antiquarianism, a preoccupation with the physical details and authentic speech patterns of a particular historical period, from the Kabuki stage of Ichikawa Danjūrō (1839–1903) to the period films of Kurosawa Akira (1910–1998). This preoccupation was the result of the government's insistence on the reform of the popular theater as part of its plans to make it a wing of its propaganda machine. Kurosawa's obsession with historical detail reflected an upper-class and Confucian background (his father was a former military officer) and a concern very different from that of most filmmakers, historical (rather than political) didactism.

The third, chapter 8, "From Stage Realism to Film Realism," compares the stage techniques of Kabuki with film techniques to demonstrate that the experience of watching a play in a Kabuki theater offered pretty much the same experience as watching a film — depending on one's seat. The actor, however, understood exactly how he was seen by all the members of the audience above, below, far from, and near to him — and often sitting on the stage itself. This put traditional Kabuki actors at an advantage, compared with actors from the modern theater, in making the transition to film and its multiple points of view.

Part Three, "The Scene in Japanese Narrative," is made up of three individual essays which analyze the scene in film and its medieval precursor, the epic. Chapter 9, "Thematic Composition, Formulaic Diction and Cinema," offers an introduction to the way oral tradition studies would analyze cinema. The essay identifies the scenes which make up the genre of the Western, the scenes which identify John Ford as an "auteur," and the scenes from Ford's films which Kurosawa, in his films, was permitted by his culture. Chapter 10, "The Japanese Epic as Buddhist Sermon," compares through oral tradition methods the form and function of the epic, fixed in the fourteenth century, with those of the Buddhist sermon. Each of the three sections of the epic, the background, the battle, and the aftermath, is shown to contain scenes which typify the section. The addendum examines a precursor of realistic depictions of violence in the period film: battles and their aftermaths in medieval Japanese epic. The terrible, sometimes gruesome descriptions define the battlefield as the realm of hatred and jealousy or the realm of the fighting titans (*shura* or *asura*) of Hindu and Buddhist mythology, who are constantly at war with the gods (*devas*). They also prefigure the realistic depiction of violence in Kabuki, where heads are lopped off and blood is spattered on *shōji* (sliding doors of lattice and rice paper) and, of course, in film. It is too easy, however, seeing the fighting and killing in Japanese period films, to characterize Japan and the Japanese as violent[11]; In fact, the realistic depiction of violence is a rhetorical tactic of Buddhist preaching, which attempts to persuade people to reject the world and its evils. The use of realistic violence is a narrative strategy of the Buddhist picture of hell.

Chapter 11, "Thematic Composition in the Japanese Epic: On the Type Scene," analyzes a single type scene. In the original fictional story, a seasoned, middle-aged soldier kills a young aristocrat, an act which later leads to his

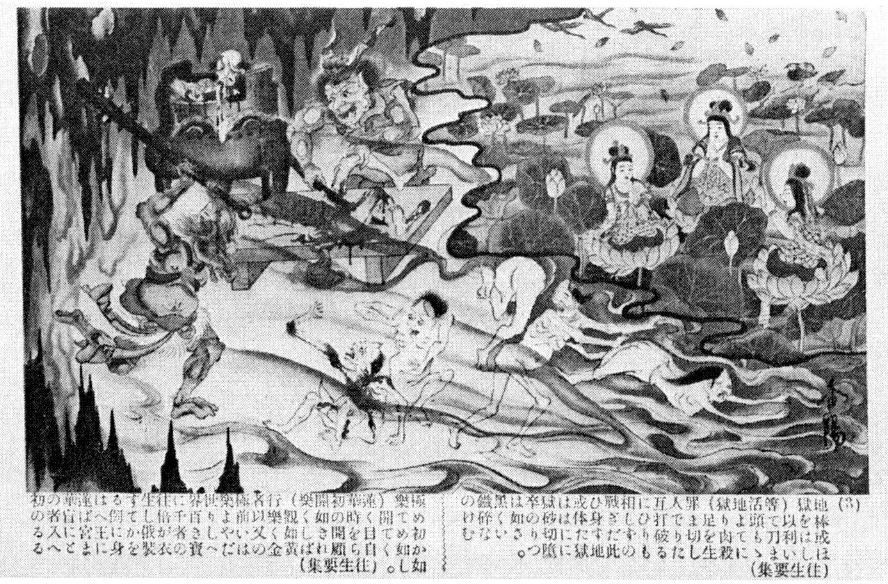

This prewar illustration, one of a series, follows a long tradition of illustrating the *Ōjōyōshū* (*The Teachings Essential for Rebirth*, 985) of Genshin (942–1017). Much popular narrative — and popular film — can be seen as falling in the Buddhist preaching tradition of illustrating the pleasures of heaven and the horrors of hell.

taking the tonsure; the scene came to be used as a model for later epics in which a boy is killed in battle or by execution. The chapter traces its origins and permutations in four later epics.

The final chapter, "Traditional Narrative and Yamada Yōji," examines the use of traditional narrative techniques in Yamada's two most recent films, *Tasogare Seibei* (*The Twilight Samurai*, 2002) and *Kakushiken: oni no tsume* (*The Hidden Blade*, 2004). At a time when the period film seems to have all but disappeared from Japanese cinema (as opposed to television), Yamada and Asama Yoshitaka, his collaborator on the script, have demonstrated that traditional narrative is not dead — not only not dead but still adept at mesmerizing an audience and even bringing it to tears. The *bakumatsu-mono* is still relevant; the period film is still the genre of choice to criticize modern society. There is nothing new in this film; traditional Japanese narrative and its techniques still, as they always have, facilitate limitless variation and creativity if the performer — the scriptwriter, the director, even the actor — has sufficient experience in using them. In Japan, as in other societies with still-viable indigenous narrative traditions, creativity is evidenced not by the degree of difference, but by the degree of excellence in a given performance.

Part One

The Narrative Set in the Past

1

The Japanese Period Film

A Definition of the Term *Period Film*

With the publication in 1959 of Anderson and Richie's *The Japanese Film*,[1] the West was introduced to the classification of Japanese films into *gendai-geki* (contemporary-life plays), films set in the modern period, and *jidai-geki* (period plays), films set in the feudal past. Also accepted as standard is the year 1868 as the line of demarcation between the two: 1868 marks the end of feudal Japan and the beginning of modern Japan.

This classification system, as convenient as it is, tends to be prescriptive (how things ought to be) rather than descriptive (how things are).

First, the term *gendai-geki* is not used for all the contemporary life plays produced in Japan since 1868. Kabuki plays about contemporary Japan produced early in the Meiji period (1868–1912) by the traditional stage are called *zangiri-mono* (cropped-hair pieces) and those produced later by the independent stage are called Shinpa ("new school" as opposed to "old school" or Kabuki, the popular stage of the Tokugawa Japan). Plays set between 1868 and 1912 can also be called *Meiji-mono* (Meiji pieces, because they are set in the years of the reign of the Meiji emperor) and those set 1912–1926 *Taishō-mono* (Taishō pieces, because set in the years of the reign of the Taishō emperor). The term *gendai-geki* refers only to those films produced since the end of World War I, and strictly to films modeled on the light comedies and films about ordinary life of the West — especially of the United States.

Moreover, the term *jidai-geki* does not include all the period films produced in Japan. It does not include the filmed *kyūgeki* (old theater from Kabuki and Kōdan, didactic story-telling) of Japan's first film star, Onoe Matsunosuke (1875–1926), or other films of various degrees of film realism produced at the same time. Nor does it include some important period films made later. Yoda Yoshikata (1909–1991), scenarist, has made it clear that the films he wrote for Mizoguchi Kenji (1898–1956) are not *jidai-geki* (period films) but *rekishi eiga* (history films).[2] There are also films by other Japanese film directors well known in the West, such as Inagaki Hiroshi (1905–1980), which must be classified as history films rather than as period pieces.

Interesting enough, both the contemporary film (*gendai-geki*) and the period film (*jidai-geki*) have a common antecedent. The *gendai-geki* movement was established in the late nineteenth and early twentieth centuries by leaders of the Shingeki (new theater) stage movement, which was opposed to old theater, Kabuki and Shinpa, and dedicated to the western representational realism of Ibsen and Chekhov. The Shingeki movement was also responsible for the creation of the period film. The first period films produced under the auspices of the Shingeki movement were produced, like the *gendai-geki*, at Shōchiku Studio.[3]

Of these Shōchiku period films, Nomura Hōtei's (1880–1934) 1923 *Kunisada Chūji: kari no mure* (*Chūji from Kunisada: A Flock of Wild Geese*) was the first to be publicized as a *shin jidai-geki* (new period play). The term was chosen to identify the film with both the Shingeki movement and the period pieces of classical Kabuki, the *jidai-mono* (period piece). The term was later contracted to *jidai-geki*, with which the West is now familiar.[4]

The problems posed by this lack of perfect agreement on the term *jidai-geki* will be addressed in the course of the study. *Gendai-geki* and *jidai-geki* are both terms from the early twenties which distinguish certain films being produced at that time. Despite the fact that they no longer correspond exactly to all the films they are supposed to cover, these terms have been retained — if for no other reason than for their convenience. I personally use the term *jidai eiga* for films set in the past, but *jidai-geki* is fine. "Samurai film" is not: not all the protagonists of all the films are samurai. Zatoichi is not a samurai; Kunisada Chūji is not a samurai; Shimizu Jirōchō is not a samurai.

1868

Convenience dictates the choice of the year 1868 as the dividing line between the categories of films, *jidai-geki* and *gendai-geki*. In 1868, due to both internal and external factors, the Tokugawa shogunate (1603–1867) collapsed, the system of government of rule by military commander (shogun, or general) was abolished, and the emperor assumed the position of ruling as well as of reigning monarch (he had become emperor in 1866).

The year 1868 marks Japan's transition to the modern as defined by the western powers. Between 1868 and 1912, the Meiji period, the Neo-Confucian moral order, the political order as a police state with feudal trappings, and even the entertainment world of the Tokugawa period were adapted and mobilized to send the country hurtling toward industrialization, militarism, and colonialism — meeting contemporary requirements of a modern state.

With the defeat of a major European power in the Russo-Japanese War (1904–05), Japan secured that status in the eyes of the world.

The question is, of course, how much Japan and the Japanese really changed after 1868 and whether the terms *jidai* and *gendai* correspond to a period of change in Japan. It is certainly beyond the scope of this book to discuss the whole of the question. Nevertheless, something can be said about what it is that happened in or after 1868 that determines the difference between *jidai* and *gendai* in film.

In 1876, the military caste,[5] the *bushi*, were stripped of their two swords and men of all ranks began to cut off their topknots. The transition to modern is best represented by this, the most superficial and, at the same time, most symbolic level. The iconography of class distinction developed during the Tokugawa period was abandoned. It corresponds directly in significance to the bobbed hair and short skirts for women that mark the beginning of the modern era in the West.

What distinguishes a Japanese period film from a contemporary film, *jidai* from *gendai*, is the men's iconography, especially the two swords and the topknot. Since at least ninety percent of Japanese period films are set in the Tokugawa period, it is Tokugawa-period iconography that dominates the period film. Before one can properly understand a period film, one has to be able to make some sense out of what one is actually looking at on the screen.

Tokugawa-Period Iconography

In order to understand a Japanese period film, it is necessary to be able to "read it," and the principal reading skill is a grasp of the iconography, the ability to identify and to interpret the signs carried by the characters in the films: what they wear, how they style their hair, how they speak, move, and their relative arrangements in space communicate certain information about them.

Most of the iconography in film is the conventionalized and stylized iconography of Tokugawa-period theater, Kabuki and Bunraku (puppet theater). Some elements, usually details, were adapted and developed later—such as the black mask, white horse, and pistols, apparently borrowed from Zorro by Kurama Tengu, the fictional Restoration hero made famous in the silents by actor Arashi Kanjūrō (1903–1980) first in 1927.[6]

What makes traditional Japanese iconography so difficult is that the differences are of degree rather than of kind. There is no difference in the cut of the robe *(kimono)* of a princess and that of a fishmonger's wife. However, sumptuary laws of the period were explicit to the last detail about the quality of materials allowed to members of each caste. The theater had no trouble in adapting and exaggerating the conventions of dress, but it is still evident that colors, patterns, length, and styles of wearing the sash (*obi*) constitute the only differences. In the case of men, the differences between commoners and *bushi* are obvious enough, but the differences amongst the military of different rank are barely to be recognized at all — even though they were as jealously guarded as were the differences in rank.[7]

Iconography — costumes, movement, space, speech pattern, and even conduct — is a shorthand for communicating the context of the narrative; it provides certain information about the characters upon which the development of the plot depends. The information communicated by the individual character is his place in society. And the context of the narrative indicated is that society, the society of the Tokugawa period (1603–1867), during which the country was ruled by the Tokugawa family.

I do not intend here to duplicate Ruth Shaver's *Kabuki Costume*,[8] a marvelous and complete study of Tokugawa theater costume. However, some interpretation of the meaning of Tokugawa iconography and its application in the period film might be in order.

Absolute Status

There are two kinds of status in traditional Japanese society: absolute and relative. Absolute status is based on caste, the social identity and function acquired by birth. Traditionally, the most significant line was that drawn between those of the *bushi* and everyone below. Thus, only a *bushi*, rich or poor, in service (samurai) or not (ronin), was permitted to wear two swords, to have a proper name, and to wear his top-knot high and flipped forward straight over the crown of the head. On the other hand, in films it is sometimes difficult to tell the wives and daughters of the military houses, who may be very poor, from those of the commoners: however, their robes tend to be flowered and fairly sober and their underwear white, while the robes of the wives and daughters of commoners usually have black collars, geometric patterns, stripes and checks, and red underwear peeking out at the collar. In the eighties, one began to see a distinction in the way the sash was worn: the modern flat bag in the back for commoner women, the single knot with short ends for the women of *bushi* houses.

Relative Status

Although there is an absolute value assigned to an individual based on one's caste, there is also a relative value assigned based on one's position within a particular group. The individual, whether *bushi* or townsman (*chōnin*), is evaluated according to how closely he matches a preconceived model, an ideal. The problem is that the model shifts according to whether the individual is with a superior, an equal, or an inferior. This will result in a change of language, of physical movement, and of space.

Arrangement in space is based on a few simple rules. For example, the most important man (or woman) will sit at one end of a room with people of decreasing importance seated farther and farther away — sometimes speaking from outside the room altogether. This is true of a lord sitting next to a decorative alcove (*tokonoma*) with his lady or chief concubine beside him, his chief advisers a few feet away with positions angled about forty-five degrees (the back is never fully turned on a superior), and so on. It is equally true of a shopkeeper sitting behind his brazier (*hibachi*) with his wife beside him, his chief clerk facing him from a few feet away, and the apprentices listening at the open door.

But it can all change in a flash. In Mizoguchi Kenji's 1954 *Chikamatsu monogatari* (*A Story from Chikamatsu*), the artisan with his semi-samurai status (as calendar-maker to the emperor) lords it over family, staff, and acquaintances in one moment, and, in the next, kneels with his face in the dirt of the garden until invited to enter his own house by a government inspector.

A man is a *bushi* by the way he wears his hair, the way he dresses, and the way he sits — with his knees apart. But depending on the rank of the person with whom he is speaking, he will touch his fan to the knee or to the floor, touch his fingertips, knuckles, or the flat of the palm to the floor. There is almost no element of the character's iconography which does not indicate caste status and relative place in a hierarchy. Iconography is a shorthand for communicating the context of a narrative — all those things one has to take for granted before one can accept the premises of the plot, the logic of the sequence of events. The iconography of the Japanese period film is social iconography. This means that the subject, the theme of the films is Japanese society. And the principal concern of this society is hierarchy, and of the individual, status.

Insiders and Outsiders

The principal function of Tokugawa sumptuary laws and, therefore, of Tokugawa iconography was to indicate the difference between insider and outsider. In actuality, there were three definitions of insider versus an outsider.

First, theoretically, the insiders were the four recognized components of society: samurai, farmers, artisans, and merchants.[9] Everyone above (court noble) or below (pariah) was technically an outsider. In films, this is easily recognized by the treatment of hair. Insider status for men is indicated by hair, usually a ponytail, stiffened with camellia oil and flipped over the shaven crown. Buddhist monks, masseurs, and those who have taken nominal Buddhist vows completely shave their heads: they have "left home"; they have left society. Teachers, doctors, and Kyoto noblemen do not shave the crown, an indication of irregular status. Young boys — minors — who have not yet held coming-of-age ceremonies (*genpuku*) wear forelocks.

Second, a line was drawn between the *bushi* and the other three components of society, and in films this, too, can be seen in the hairstyles. The *bushi* (whether lords, vassals, or unemployed), as well as doctors, teachers, and Kyoto noblemen wear the hair drawn straight off the sides and back. Commoners (and in older films, boys of all classes) wear the hair fanned out behind the ears to look like a little bag (the way *sumo* wrestlers do now).

A third line was drawn between the upper and lower ranks of the samurai. The insider-outsider problem became critical during the Meiji period and had repercussions throughout the modern period. The frustrations of the former Tokugawa vassals and other samurai kept out of the centers of power in government and the military were vented in the Christian, socialist, anarchist, pacifist, environmental, and literary movements of the Meiji period. Their followers and spiritual heirs were the intellectuals, especially the newspaper journalists, who had been prevented by lack of money and, therefore, higher education, from climbing the ladder of the strictly controlled hierarchy of the modern meritocracy. Among these were the young filmmakers of the twenties and thirties (late Taishō and early Shōwa periods), who projected their frustration onto the silent screen.

The tension between insiders and outsiders was nowhere so explicitly represented as in the period film: unemployed and low-ranking men among the *bushi* exploded in furious and bloody rages against their oppressors, abusers, and betrayers, and the social distinctions of Tokugawa iconography were extended to give a psychological and even political meaning. An overgrown crown used to mean only that the man had been unable, usually because

Opposite: *Saikaku ichidai onna* (*The Life of Oharu*, 1952), directed by Mizoguchi Kenji. Oharu (Tanaka Kinuyo) is importuned by Katsunosuke (Mifune Toshirō); she faints in assent and he whisks her off. The two are dressed in the flamboyant style of the Genroku period (1688–1704). Oharu also wears the dagger of a samurai's daughter in her sash while Katsunosuke's hair is in the fashion of a townsman rather than that typical of a samurai. These subtle but unmistakable signs indicate the predicament of their unequal social status. As punishment for their transgression, Katsunosuke is beheaded for seducing a woman of superior status, and, for failure to maintain order in the house, Oharu's family is banished from the imperial capital (photograph courtesy of the Kawakita Memorial Film Institute).

of illness, to see a barber. In films, however, hair on the crown allowed to grow out marked the outsider: impoverished ronin fighting vassals of the shogun to save a girl and their self-respect; a gang boss running from the police and betrayers among his own men; and a direct vassal to the shogun (*hatamoto*) who prefers the company of commoners.[10] In the early twenties, the young, outsider ronin (such as the lead characters played by Bandō Tsumasaburō in Futagawa Buntarō's 1924 *Gyakuryū* [*Retaliation*] and 1925 *Orochi* [*Serpent*]) had both the overgrown crown and the bag of the commoner, but that particular combination was later used *almost* exclusively for the outsider commoner, specifically the outsider traveling gambler (*toseinin*). In the sixties, for example, a ronin like Nemuri Kyōshirō, played by Ichikawa Raizō in the *Sleepy Eyes of Death* series (twelve films 1963–1969), wears his hair off the sides and back.

The iconography of the hairstyles indicating the line between the insiders and the outsiders can be very important to understanding the plot of a film. For example, in Mizoguchi's 1952 *Saikaku ichidai onna* (*The Life of Oharu*), the tragic hero Katsunosuke (played by Mifune Toshirō), executed for seducing the daughter Oharu (Tanaka Kinuyo) of a higher-ranking samurai, has a shaven crown to indicate his adult and, perhaps, his samurai status, while the bag of the commoner indicates his very low status as a page at the imperial court. Westerners may fail to recognize Mifune in this hairstyle, just as they may fail to recognize the extent of his character's transgression in seducing Oharu, because they fail to recognize the difference in status indicated by his hairstyle. The seduction is not the problem; crossing the barrier between the ranks of the samurai is, and for Mifune's character, the punishment is death.

The Inviolability of Caste and Iconography

The line between the *bushi* and the commoners was the most important one. In Tokugawa Japan, social identity — for a man especially — was established at birth and could be changed only by adoption and only within limits set by law. Social identity prescribed one's clothes, names, and occupation. Clothes, names, and occupation indicated one's social identity. It was a closed system no one thought of violating without considering the rather fearsome consequences (one Kyoto merchant had his property confiscated because his wife, in a heated competition for first place on the best-dressed list, wore in public a back silk sash beaded with coral[11]). Furthermore, it was a system no one thought anyone else could successfully violate: the attempt would entail changing not just one's hair and clothing, but one's speech, posture, table manners, and musical or martial accomplishments. Anyone capable of doing such a thing was a man more to be feared than admired. One might as well change skin color.

There were two responses to the man who violated the iconography. The first, in historical reality and in narratives, was to mete out punishment. In one film, a commoner is cut down for wearing wooden clogs in the rain, a prerogative of the warrior class. In Shinoda Masahiro's 1964 *Ansatsu* (*Assassination*), the ambitious farmer's son who had bought both his *bushi* status and his seven-star sword is assassinated. And in Kobayashi Masaki's 1962 *Seppuku* (*Harakiri*), a horrible fate is dealt young Chijiwa for selling his swords to buy food and medicine for his wife and child, for cheating the iconography and pretending to be a *bushi* when he was carrying only bamboo blades: he is asked to commit suicide with them. In order to reestablish his status, to punish himself for this transgression, he spares himself an easy but shameful death and does it. Rigor in the maintenance of the direct correspondence between iconography and identity is incumbent upon all members of the warrior class.

Iconography is not an empty formalism. Chijiwa's swords are not "worthless symbols." They correspond directly to function in society, status in society, identity. That he does give them up means that he has a set of values which does not correspond to his iconography, his identity: that as husband and father. For his family, he gives up his iconography (he sells his two swords), his status, his social function or *yaku*: he turns to anti-social behavior when he tries to extort money from the Ii house, whose vassals would rather, he supposes, pay him than allow him to commit suicide on the premises. When he is found out, he tries to regain his identity and status as a member of the hereditary military elite by disembowelment with a bamboo blade; the ignominious alternative, allowing himself to be beheaded, is unacceptable.

The second response to the basic assumption that it is practically impossible to violate the iconography is the run of "the hero in disguise" narratives about high-ranking officials who walk among the commoners to ensure their safety and protection, which themselves have their antecedents in old Buddhist propaganda stories about bodhisattvas (those on the way to becoming buddhas) working their miracles in this world (like Kannon, Skt. Avolekiteshvara) and in hell (like Jizō, Skt. Kshitigarbha) to save humans from their sins. These men, however, are not villains, but heroes. Indeed, the climax is the moment the hero reveals his true identity (known in Kabuki as *jitsu wa* or "really"[12]).

For example, the city magistrate Tōyama Kagemoto — Kin-san[13] to his friends — has had himself tattooed — which is illegal — with an elaborate and distinctive cherry blossom design so that he can pass in the lowest ranks of society and there root out crime and corruption. After all, who would expect a gentleman to do such a thing? And who would suspect a man with a tattoo of being a gentleman, let alone city magistrate? He hauls the evildoers into his court and testifies against them. But no one recognizes him until he pulls his right arm out of his robe (he wears the *nagakamishimo* [formal costume of matching top and bottom with long legs] so that he can strike a thrilling pose with the trailing leg of the *hakama* rippling down the steps of his garden veranda), shows his tattoo (whereupon the villains collapse in the dust), and declares himself in the rough, working-class argot of his a.k.a.[14] Mito Kōmon is just an old farmer on a journey until he (or one of his companions) whips out his tobacco case with the most familiar crest in the country and reveals himself as Mitsukuni (1628–1701), the head of the Tokugawa house of Mito (whereupon — again — the villains collapse in the dust — this is, after all, what the audience is waiting for).[15]

The tension of the narrative is created by putting off as long as possible the moment the disguise is revealed. For example, in Kurosawa Akira's 1980 *Kagemusha* (*Shadow Warrior*), Lord Takeda Shingen's pages relax and sit cross-legged in front of the double, a former thief. But when the fake Shingen gives the signal that identifies him as the real Shingen (personal iconography: he takes an armrest, leans forward on it, and strokes his beard), the pages are forced to respond with a corresponding signal — they get back on their knees. The double sails over every hurdle, each one more dangerous than the last, until he is thrown by Shingen's horse, knocked unconscious, and exposed by Shingen's concubines. Now worthless as a double, he is paid off and sent on his way. The characterization of the warrior class as exploitive and callous, however, is mitigated by having the lowest-ranking soldiers do the dirty work of "escorting" the double through the gates.

Iconography and Identity

The tension between personal identity and social iconography is played upon in a variety of ways. Physical features do not seem to matter. No one recognizes Kinshirō's face, only his tattoo; identity can be changed by a change in iconography. The priority of iconography over physical features in determining identity upon which the success of Kinshirō's disguise depends is revealed in Shinoda Masahiro's 1969 *Shinjū ten Amijima* (*Double Suicide*): Shinoda, in casting one woman (Iwashita Shima) to play both wife and courtesan, is following the Tokugawa puppet theater convention of using the same head for all women of the same age.

Many films use the technique of violating the direct correspondence of iconography and identity to criticize a principal assumption of traditional Japanese society — principally that of the samurai — that an individual's capacity for intellectual and moral achievement is determined by his caste and rank; that, in effect, an individual's identity is reduced to that of a member of a certain social group, which is determined by birth, i.e., predetermined by fate (karma or *inga*/*innen*). Indeed, the line between the upper and lower ranks of samurai was as rigid as that between the hereditary military and the commoners. For example, Itami Mansaku's 1932 *Kokushi musō* (*Peerless Patriot*) presents a poor ronin who steals the right clothes from a second-hand shop and gets his dinner by impersonating a famous swordsman and charging it to his bill. When he is challenged to prove his identity with the sword, he beats the swordsman and, logically, takes his place, and the real swordsman is forced to go into the mountains to train for a return match.

Again, in the Japanese society of the Tokugawa period, identity was one's function in society which was portioned out according to one's place in society, one's lot (*bun*).[16] This meant that because of his birth and the implacable laws of nature, a farmer's son could not have the intellectual or moral capacity that would entitle him to serve in the government. Only those born to be samurai had that capacity. This basic assumption on the part of Tokugawa-period samurai is the basis for discussion of a very obvious problem in the Japanese period film: the lack of direct correspondence between iconography and identity. Intellectually and morally qualified men are not content with their lot; the brilliant but low-ranking are frustrated in their attempts to move up, to express their identities through corresponding functions in society and corresponding status.

An example of the resistance to accepting qualified outsiders is seen in Suganuma Kanji's 1941 *Kenkō sakura fubuki* (*Flash of a Sword, Snow Storm of Cherry Blossoms*). An impoverished but erudite and morally upright ronin is taken on as tutor to the heir of the shogun. Humiliated beyond endurance by the seven (corrupt) samurai of the office to which he has been assigned, he finally draws his sword in the palace, cuts them down, and then commits suicide.

There is always this feeling that even if the hero can demonstrate intellectual equality, he can never demonstrate moral capacity equal to that of his social superiors. Shinoda's *Assassination* offers an interesting turn on the theme. Kiyokawa Hachirō (Tanba Tetsurō) bought his seven-star sword (impossible! a samurai, no matter how desperate, would never sell his sword!) just as he bought his right to carry it. He wants to be a samurai, he wants a position with the Tokugawa government or with any domainal government that will give him the status he craves and thinks he deserves: he is brilliant, he runs his own school, and he is an expert swordsman. But it is because he was not born and bred a samurai that he is assassinated. Kiyokawa's two swords tell us — and his assassin, Sasaki — that he is one kind of man, and the film reveals that he is another: he is afraid of killing, he is emotionally dependent on a woman, and he is committed more to his own advancement in the world than to any principle or to any master (i.e., he is not capable of loyalty, the ultimate expression of the samurai and the highest expression of morality, of humanity[17]). Sasaki is afraid of Kiyokawa because Kiyokawa plays the samurai so well; he has mastered the iconography. But when Sasaki reads the diary of the woman who died for Kiyokawa, he learns of his personality traits, which are not those of a samurai (certainly not as a samurai idealizes himself) and for the first time realizes that he can kill him — not fairly, of course, but that is not the point (and fairness has nothing to do with being a samurai). Kiyokawa gets drunk, and a "real" samurai would not. The assassination is a vicious version of *kirisute gomen*, the right of the *bushi* to cut down a commoner who has insulted him — in this case, by assuming the *bushi*'s prerogative — the iconography, the function, the status — which does not belong to him. Kiyokawa cannot change his identity by changing his iconography; he cannot change his values reflected in his obsessions, fears, and emotional dependencies. According to *Assassination*, then, iconography is not identity, and the sympathy of the audience lies with Kiyokawa, who, in the end, could not become completely one of the samurai, obviously not very nice people.

Although most films treat of the perils faced in trying to rise to or in the military ranks, some actually look at what it takes to choose demotion. In Makino Masahiro's 1952–54 series *Jirōchō Sangokushi* (*Jirōchō and the Record of the Three Kingdoms*), gang boss Jirōchō's most important lieutenant is a former low-ranking samurai, Ōmasa: no longer able to endure the humiliation he suffers in his position, he leaves not only his domain (*han*) but his samurai status in order to join the boss (*oyabun*) Jirōchō as his second-in-command. It is not merely that he would rather be a big fish in a little pond than a little fish in a big one; the problem is that he could never realize his full potential as a low-ranking samurai. Nevertheless, the experience of giving up his swords and having his hair rearranged in the commoner's style is devastating: he goes on a drunk (singing the Kuroda *bushi* drinking song), only to collapse in tears on arriving home.

Ōmasa, the former samurai, like Kiyokawa, must change his function, his status, and his iconography in order to make them correspond with what he perceives as his identity. As far as the people about him are concerned — the wife he leaves, the clan he leaves, and the men he joins — Ōmasa has changed his identity — and successfully so. Kiyokawa cannot and he is killed for it. The reason is that it is acceptable only to go down the social ladder.

The Marginality of Women

We now come to the problem of women's iconography in the period film. The truth of the matter is that the period film, for the most part, is not really about women. This is made very clear in the women's iconography, which consistently makes reference to the present, not the past.

Unlike men, women did not cut their hair in the Meiji period. Neither did their dress change significantly. The traditional hairstyles continued to develop and change, and actresses wore the latest versions in the period films. Women began cutting their hair in the twenties, but the trend did not peak until after World War II. There was a more serious attempt to make realistic wigs with historically accurate styles then, but not for the bulk of films, where Kabuki conventions prevailed. In the eighties, one often saw on television real hair arranged in the traditional styles with the latest techniques in hairdressing (no camellia oil) alongside Kabuki style wigs. However, since the war, the little tendrils hanging at the temples have disappeared and none but the littlest girls wear bangs.

This early studio portrait of Kurishima Sumiko (1902–1987) shows the influence of the West in the late teens and early twenties: her sash is bound very high on the chest, her lips painted in a cherub's bow, and the hair on the sides brought forward to frame the face. The only things to distinguish this contemporary fashion and the fashion of the period films are fabric patterns, the hair ornaments, and the set of fringes on each side of the temple. The anachronism of women's iconography is a constant reminder that period films are about the present.

Women continued to wear traditional clothing, and the latest styles were worn in the period films. In the twenties, the western vogue for the flat bosom was reflected in the style of wearing the robe with the sash particularly high and painfully tight; the actresses were correspondingly lightly built with narrow or sloping shoulders. These stylistic transgressions — anachronisms, if you will — date the films, just as they do in western period films. Except for the basics, the stylization of women in period films is determined less by conventions than by current fashions.

Of course, women's hairstyles and costumes indicate age, caste, rank, marital status, and even profession. However, women's iconography in films does not have the function, for instance, of identifying the insiders and outsiders. The reason for this is that a woman has no status, and therefore her status is flexible and lends itself to upward mobility denied a man. Her status depends on her father, brother, or the man she can attract or to whom she is married. A high-ranking courtesan who has her contract redeemed by a wealthy man will change her appearance from that of a *tayū* or *oiran* (high-ranking courtesan; the high clogs, huge sash tied in front for Edo or in back for Kyoto, gaudy, padded over-dress, and headdress with many pins radiating out of the forelock and a huge, flat bun split in the middle from the top) to that of a wealthy, young matron (blackened teeth, shaven eyebrows, plain hairstyle, plain dress with plain sash of good material in a pattern and color appropriate to her age). A merchant's daughter can become the mistress of a lord and mother of the heir: she will then wear the embroidered over-dress (*uchi-kake*) and long ponytail of her new rank. The dress is the easy part; the language is a much more difficult adaptation. For example, as seen in Mizoguchi's *Life of Oharu*, a lord's concubine is coldly reminded that she does not *bear* a son; she is *caused* (as a great condescension) to bear a son.

Period films are not about women. Therefore, the speech, costume, and dress of women in period films reflect less the political and psychological tensions of the present or the past than the progressive changes of life women go through: girlhood, marriage, motherhood, old age, widowhood. Except for the costume of high-ranking *bushi* women and high-ranking prostitutes, there is no clear line of demarcation between the pre-modern Japanese woman and the modern Japanese woman. The continuity of woman's traditional life, good or bad, like the continuity of traditional hairstyles and costume, blurs the demarcation line between past and present. The use of distinctive speech patterns has been much debased, especially in television, where the women try to speak in as "lady-like" a way as possible; the actresses seem to be very concerned with preserving their images as models for modern housewives. But, as I shall demonstrate later, this sort of anachronism is the essence of the period film, whose function is to discuss the present.

2

The Japanese Period Piece

A principal concern of the Tokugawa regime was to classify the population and to organize it into a hierarchy with the military caste on top (and the Tokugawa family atop them all). Just as sumptuary laws, which classified people, informed the social iconography, so social classification informed the production of narratives of the period.

However, there was so much borrowing back and forth of material that, in truth, any attempt rationally to classify narrative as "high" or "low" is pointless. There was, however, some attempt on the part of the government through censorship to effect a direct correspondence between caste of performer and narrative depending on who was lecturing to whom. Censorship laws promulgated in 1722 did forbid discussing the shogun, the warlords, and high-ranking samurai. These laws were rigorously applied to Kabuki, whose center was the capital, Edo. It does not appear that it was as rigorously applied to professionals lecturing in private to lords and high-ranking samurai or who were discussing the government in the proper context, or that they were arrested or prosecuted; however, those mocking members of the government in public performances were.[1] The result was (if only its extremes) a binary system of classification based on Kōdan (story-telling) and Kabuki/Bunraku (puppet theater) performance. This means that although high and low entertainment forms shared the same stories, the treatments were different. For example, in its treatment of the Daté household disturbance,[2] Kōdan might celebrate a noble woman who protected the interests of her charge, the rightful young lord, in a succession dispute. Kabuki/Bunraku, however, emphasizes the cost: she sacrifices her own young son.[3]

Kōdan and Kabuki (and Jōruri/Bunraku)

Kōdan, even though it had origins in Buddhist preaching and commentary on the texts, and as a narrative form of and for the upper class (especially the samurai), developed a strongly Confucian orientation. As educators rather than entertainers, Kōdan specialists functioned as the watchdogs of society and critics of government. Kōdan specialists performed in a variety of subgenres, whether reading directly from epics like the *Taiheiki* (*Chronicle of the Great Pacification*, fourteenth century) or *Taikōki* (*Chronicle of the Retired Prime Minister* [Toyotomi Hideyoshi], seventeenth century), lecturing on contemporary morals and government failures, or recalling the exemplary conduct of famous magistrates and worthy merchants. Their narratives stressed moral lessons (*kanzen chōaku*, or "reward the good, punish the wicked") and offered an ideal (if idealistic) view of the world — how things, especially social relations, ought to be.[4]

Kabuki and Bunraku (also called Jōruri[5]), on the other hand, as a narrative art form of and for the commoners, were principally Buddhist and Shintō in orientation. Derived as they were from religious functions (masters are traditionally addressed as *oshō-sama*, or "priest," not *sensei*, as are the Kōdan specialists[6]), Kabuki and Bunraku presented a realistic (Buddhist) view of the world, the suffering world as it was, and they also functioned in exorcising the resentment of the commoners by enshrining as heroes those who had been crushed by society or, specifically, by the government.[7]

Despite their different rhetorical orientation, the two basic narrative forms reflect a sense of social function shared by the performers. Kōdan, in the grand tradition of Confucian historiography, uses the actions and fates of real people to teach moral lessons. The heroes of the different narratives serve a didactic purpose in teaching people how to live — or how not to live. Kabuki actors, themselves, too, felt this to be their function.[8] They even demonstrated a great reverence for the values promoted by Kōdan even if Kabuki and Bunraku consistently emphasized the cost of those values in terms of human suffering. As a result, no matter what the narrative set in the past, Kabuki and Bunraku presented it in the dress, speech, and values of contemporary commoners.

The Classification Systems

Film was introduced into Japan in the late Meiji period; therefore, the narratives on which early cinema drew already had a long history of classification. The classification of Meiji-period Kōdan was based on the caste and class of the protagonists of the stories: the great military heroes of the past of battle pieces (*gunshō-mono*); the great nobles and samurai of the Tokugawa-household disturbance pieces (*oiesōdō-mono*); the middle- or lower-ranking warriors of the martial arts pieces (*bugei-mono*); the successful bosses of the champion-of-the-people pieces (*otokodate-mono*); the successful merchants and the lower-ranking warriors and commoners of contemporary scandals or true-life pieces (*sewa-mono*); the noble "white-wave" thieves of the *shiranami-mono*; the famous priests of religion pieces (*shūkyō-mono*). Meiji news Kōdan and political Kōdan, although they derive from similar traditions of the Tokugawa period, can not be classified this way, but, then, they are not set in the past of the Tokugawa period.[9]

The traditional program in a Kōdan performance consisted firstly of a battle piece, secondly of a household-disturbance piece, and thirdly of a true-life piece.[10] That is, narratives were classified according to the status of the main characters. The battle pieces were concerned mainly with the military exploits of the (nearly deified) warrior heroes of the past; they represent Kōdan's origins, the reading of epics and battle literature to illiterate soldiers, high and low. The household-disturbance pieces concerned the highest level of the contemporary military elite in the Tokugawa present; they reflect Kōdan's role in setting the moral standards of the ruling caste. The contemporary pieces were about the commoners and the lower ranks of *bushi* and even the Robin Hoods like Benten Kōzō who lived up to the ideals of the times.

The classification of Kabuki and puppet-theater narratives involves different types or levels of sub-classification. It is not based exclusively on the class or caste of the heroes, although, especially with contemporary-life pieces, there is a good deal of correspondence with Kōdan classification. Kabuki and puppet-theater classification could be said to be based on historical time because of its neat division into period piece and contemporary piece (*jidai-mono* and *sewa-mono*). But the truth is that time, historical time, is violated over and over in every conceivable way, including in speech, dress, and values. Another kind of sub-classification could be said to be based on the types of scandal because of the neat divisions of household-disturbance pieces (*oiesōdō-mono*), prostitute-buying (*keisei-gai*),[11] love-suicide (*shinjū-mono*),[12] murder (*satsujin-mono*),[13] and low-life pieces (*kizewa-mono*).[14] However, household-disturbance pieces are all period pieces while the rest, unless scenes in longer period plays, are contemporary-life pieces. Moreover, if we consider the two main groups of period pieces, court pieces (*ōchō-mono*, based on stories from up to the early twelfth century)[15] and the *jidai-mono* (based on stories from the twelfth to sixteenth centuries)[16] as classifications of deified heroes, political victims and battlefield victims, then we are forced to return to the religious function of theater, the exorcism of the resentment of the living and the dead, and classification as based on the different times of deification.

Recognizing that there is, indeed, no way to package things neatly, we can learn more from comparing Kōdan and Kabuki/puppet-theater than by trying to determine the rationalization for their classification systems independently. They must be considered together, like the two sides of a coin.

What we see here is a tension between that segment of society represented by Kōdan, the insider *bushi*, and that represented by Kabuki and the puppet theater, the outsider commoner. On the one side is the insider's demand for reform, represented by Kōdan's idealization of the present system and its Confucian values (filial piety, loyalty, duty, etc.). On the other is the outsider's ambivalence about the ruling elites' high-minded, rigid value system and, therefore, about the rulers themselves, represented in Kabuki's assertion of the values of the commoners through the consistent depiction of suffering caused families by acting in conformity with *bushi* and Confucian values.

The entertainment world was a no-man's land in an otherwise rigidly hierarchical society, and, as such, acted effectively as a social steam-valve. And there, *bushi* and commoner, Kōdan and Kabuki narratives, and different forms of protest against society mixed. In the end, the period film inherited from the Tokugawa period piece a combined tradition of criticizing the values of the *bushi*, of promoting the values of the common man, and of presenting and violating a precisely conceived historical past in order to refer to the present.

Kabuki and the Household-Disturbance Piece

The period piece was first established in Kabuki as a way to stage a "disturbance in a great house."[17] The idea of a scandal, such as a suicide, fight over the succession, or vendetta, in one of the great military or noble houses of Tokugawa Japan was fraught with significance: the samurai's right to rule and administration, acquired by naked power, was justified by the claim of higher standards of conduct and the role of model for the rest of society. A breakdown in the house, the unit of administration, was a breakdown in government, a political and moral failure on the part of the rulers of the country. The political system allowed only those having the traditional function of Confucian teacher to discuss, if to a limited degree, the failures and shortcomings of the government and those households making up the government.

Mitate and *Sekai*

Censorship prohibited Kabuki from presenting these incidents as contemporary plays. So, the incidents were simply set back a hundred years or more. Such plays comprise the third sub-division of Kabuki and Jōruri plays set in the past, the *oie-mono* (great-house piece), also called *oiesōdō-mono* (great-house disturbance piece) and *oie-kyōgen* (great-house play).[18]

Setting contemporary scandals in the past was accomplished by manipulating the distinct worlds surrounding well-known individuals or events, *sekai*, through a process of matching of past and present, *mitate*.[19] A *sekai* is composed of a group of characters and events taken from an established narrative source. In the case of the period piece, the source was usually a well-known historical work or epic like the *Heike monogatari* (*Tales of the Taira House*) and *Taiheiki* (*Chronicle of the Great Pacification*).[20] *Mitate* consists of matching present and past, taking an incident and setting it safely in the historical past.[21] There were more than twenty different incidents which were dramatized in several different versions. The first and most famous incident to be treated this way was the Akō ronin incident of 1701–1703.

The Akō Ronin Incident and Chūshingura

On January 30, 1703,[22] forty-seven former vassals of Asano Naganori (1665–1701) of Akō (in what is now Hiroshima Prefecture) broke into the residence of Kira Yoshinaka (1641–1703), master of ceremonies to the shogunal house, and took his head to avenge the sentence of ritual suicide imposed on their lord and carried out some twenty months before. Forty-six committed suicide on March 20, 1703.[23]

Two weeks after they were buried, their story was staged in Edo as the twelfth-century revenge of the Soga brothers; it was closed after only three performances.[24] Three years later, the famed playwright Chikamatsu Monzaemon (1653–1725) wrote *Goban Taiheiki* (*A Chronicle of Great Peace Played on a Chess Board*).

Goban Taiheiki is the story of the revenge of the Akō vassals disguised as the revenge of the vassals of Enya Hangan Takasada (d. 1338), assassinated by Kō no Moronao (d. 1351). The incident and characters make up a well-known world from the fourteenth-century epic, the *Taiheiki*. All subsequent Kabuki versions of the incident, including the definitive version, the 1748 *Kanadehon chūshingura* (*Treasury of Loyal Retainers*), were set in the *Taiheiki* world; Kira Yoshinaka was represented by Kō no Moronao, Asano Naganori by Enya Hangan, and Naganori's vassal Ōichi Kuranosuke by Ōboshi Yuranosuke.[25]

Mixing Contemporary and Period Pieces

There were two other ways to comment on the present in terms of the past. One was to mix in a single play contemporary and historical worlds, the main characters of a Tokugawa incident with the main characters of an earlier historical incident. This was accomplished through the device of the "hero in disguise." In *Sukeroku*,[26] the young dandy dallying in the eighteenth-century pleasure quarters reveals himself as *really* (*jitsu wa*) the twelfth century hero Soga Jurō, in hiding while searching for a stolen family treasure.[27]

Another was the anachronistic use of Tokugawa-period themes in plays set in a much earlier period. A standard theme is the conflict between duty (*giri*) and human feelings (*ninjō*). In contemporary true-life plays (*sewa-mono*), couples in love with no way to stay together, out of a sense of duty both to themselves and their obligations to indigent parents and helpless children, run away and die together. In the parallel domestic tragedy of the period piece (*jidai-mono*), parents kill their own children, for example, to save the child of their lord.[28]

The implied object of criticism is the Tokugawa-period Confucian standard of morality, which placed duty over love, whether between parent and child or between lovers. In Japan, the relationship of lord and vassal, lasting three lives, was given priority over that of parent and child, lasting but one; this was unnatural[29] and certainly not the prevailing Chinese Confucian model (Ming-period law, for example, prevented a son from testifying against his father). The assertion of commoners' values over those of the samurai would be a recurring theme throughout the development of the period piece.[30]

In the above analysis of the distinction between the period and contemporary plays of the Tokugawa period, there is one important principle to be noted. Classification becomes all the more necessary as violation becomes important. The contradiction between what the narrative was supposed to be and what was presented on stage worked itself into a game between performer and audience. Forbidden subjects — forbidden feelings — might be set in the past, and yet there was nothing in the presentation — neither in costume, language, or thinly disguised plot — to suggest that anything but the present was under discussion.

The Period Piece After the Meiji Restoration

After the Meiji Restoration of 1868, the period piece was lost to Kabuki. The matching of contemporary scandals with historical figures, *mitate* and *sekai*, disappeared from the new plays written for Kabuki: in February 1872, the three top figures in the Kabuki world (Morita Kanya, Kawatake Shinshichi Moku'ami, and Sakurada Jisuke) were summoned to the Tokyo Prefectural Office and there informed that Kabuki would be visited by aristocracy and foreigners and that nothing unfit should be presented; Kabuki was to become part of the government propaganda machinery.[31] And, then, in April, Kabuki was notified that real names were henceforth to be used in historical plays.[32] In the place of the Kabuki period piece came the historical novel. Not until 1913, however, after a long process of development involving the politicization, first, by the Liberal Party and, later, by socialists, labor unionists, and pacifists of newspapers, Kōdan, and western literature, including the historical novel, was the Japanese historical novel to take up the form and function of the period piece as conceptualized in the Kabuki household-disturbance piece.[33]

Nakazato Kaizan (1885–1944) and the *Bakumatsu-mono*

The first period novel was *Daibosatsu tōge* (*The Great Bodhisattva Pass*), begun in 1913 by Nakazato (Yanosuke) Kaizan, considered the founder of Japanese popular literature.[34] A Liberal Party supporter[35] and a follower of Tolstoy and the Christian pacifist Uchimura Kanzō (1861–1930), he was one of Japan's most famous pacifist poets and novelists.[36] He had been writing populist, historical novels[37] in the fashion of the time for a newspaper, the *Miyako shinbun*, since 1906 when, in 1911, his former associate Kōtoku Shūsui (b. 1871), co-founder of the socialist paper *Heimin shinbun*, was executed for his alleged role in the planning of an assassination attempt on the Meiji emperor; things got very hard for many of Nakazato's socialist and anarchist friends and acquaintances. Under these circumstances, a period of extreme political and police repression through 1912, Nakazato began planning *The Great Bodhisattva Pass*. Serialization in the *Miyako shinbun* began in 1913. Nakazato never finished it: he refused to join the government wartime writers' union (Nihon Bungaku Hōkokkai) and died in 1944.[38]

The Great Bodhisattva Pass: 1913–1941

The Great Bodhisattva Pass lies somewhere between Dostoevsky's *Crime and Punishment* and the very Buddhist epic *Heike monogatari* (*Tales of the Taira House*). Almost unknown in the West,[39] it was much admired by literary notables, who brought it into general circulation and even had it published as a book in 1925.[40]

The book looks to be a simple revenge story (*adauchi-mono*): the hero is a thief, Danshichi, who rescues a little girl; the villain is a fencing teacher's son, Tsukue Ryūnosuke, who has killed the girl's grandfather for practice on the road (*tsujigiri*). The book moves very rapidly to concentrate on Ryūnosuke, the first nihilist in Japanese literature. Just who the model was is unclear: the nihilists of the late Meiji period, many of whom were connected to Nakazato through publications and journals; or Raskolnikov, the anti-hero of Dostoevsky's *Crime and Punishment*.[41]

Through the medium of Ryūnosuke, Nakazato made a direct analogy with his times and a period in the past, a deliberate anachronism. He created a new world or *sekai* in what was to be called the *bakumatsu-mono*, or story set in the last years of the Tokugawa shogunate, the years between the arrival

Daibosatsu tōge **(*The Great Bodhisattva Pass*, 1935), directed by Inagaki Hiroshi. Tsukue Ryūnosuke (Ōkōchi Denjirō) is thoroughly evil: he kills an old man for practice; he brutally takes Ohama (Irie Takako) and then kills her husband in a fencing match. Nakazato Kaizan's original, unfinished newspaper serial, *Daibosatsu tōge* begun in 1913, established the nihilistic wing of the Japanese period piece. Drawing on Russian literature, Buddhism, and folk religion, Nakazato created the rhetorical system for discussing Japanese militarism, the *bakumatsumono* (story set in the last years of the Tokugawa period). Sawada Shōjirō, founder of the Shinkokugeki (New National Theater), was the first stage Tsukue; Ōkōchi, a student in his theater school, was the first film Tsukue. Inagaki, however, more usually worked in the humanistic wing of the period piece, established by Hasegawa Shin (photograph courtesy of Matsuda Film Productions).**

of Commodore Matthew Perry in 1853 and the establishment of a new regime in 1868. Nakazato paralleled the signs of resistance in the Meiji period — certainly the revolts of the 1870s and 1880s but more specifically the resistance of the Socialists and Christians against the government on behalf the people suffering from the side-effects of the quick military build-up and industrialization of the Meiji period — with the revolution of the Tokugawa period. But his judgment was that the restoration was nothing different from the shogunate, that both the shogunate and imperial rule represented hopeless betrayal and oppression of the common people. That is the lesson of the compulsive killer Tsukue Ryūnosuke: no matter what side he fights on, there is no benefit to his psychological condition, a darkness which reflects that of the years of repression following the execution of Kōtoku and the others. This nihilism is quite different from Russian nihilism, the sacrifice of any future in the new order through crime or sin committed for the sake of establishing the new order.[42] This Japanese nihilism, Nakazato's nihilism, is based on Buddhism,[43] on the idea of a world with no Buddha and no salvation, on a political context which gives no hope for a new order.

Bakumatsu-mono became very popular following the Tokyo earthquake of September 1, 1923. The *bakumatsu-mono* and the nihilist swordsmen modeled after Ryūnosuke were strongly associated with an anti-government stance. However, by the time of the Manchurian Incident (1931) and the outbreak of the war in China (July 1937), the rise of militarist feeling (not to mention censorship control) had exerted pressure on the *bakumatsu-mono* to change dramatically toward a pro-government, pro-imperialist stance (such films are probably better called Restoration pieces or *isshin-mono*). As a result, the role of the *bakumatsu-mono* as established by Nakazato and long-time associates in the socialist and proletarian movements of the 1910s and 1920s was taken over by a new genre, the *matatabi-mono* established by Hasegawa Shin.[44]

Hasegawa Shin (1884–1963) and the *Matatabi-mono*

Hasegawa Shinjirō was born in Yokohama to a poor carpentry workman, an itinerant craftsman whom Hasegawa followed about. His mother left when he was three. This proletarian background was to prove to be the foundation of Hasegawa's later success. He learned to read Chinese characters only after becoming a reporter.[45] In 1911, through the good offices of Ihara Seiseien (1870–1941; later famed for his scholarship on classical theater), he got a job at the *Miyako shinbun* where he worked and did his apprenticeship as a writer. In March 1914, his first novel was serialized. In 1924, he met Kikuchi Kan, who helped him get published using his real name for the first time. In 1925, he left the *Miyako* and became a founding member of the famous Twenty-first of the Month Club (Nichijūichinichikai) with other prominent popular-literature writers, including Edogawa Rampō (1894–1965) and Naoki Sanjūgo (1891–1934; in whose memory Kikuchi Kan established in 1935 the Naoki Prize for literature). He went on to a long and successful career as writer and journalist; in 1956 he was awarded the Kikuchi Kan Prize for *Nihon horyo-shi*, a study of prisoners of war, including those in Japanese POW camps during World War II.[46]

The *Matatabi-mono*

Hasegawa's first play, the 1928 *Suki no ie* (*Pickpocket House*)[47] was based on his own experiences: it is about Hasegawa's own circle of laborers and petty thieves — the urban poor. Reflecting Hasegawa's interest in traditional Kabuki plays about low life (*kizewa-mono*) and ordinary people (*sewa-mono*) and Rakugo stories about the urban poor (*nagaya-mono*), it established the world of the outsider and outcaste as Hasegawa's main focus of interest.

The same year he wrote his first big success, a period piece, *Kutsukake Tokijirō* (*Tokijirō from Kutsukake*).[48] Here, again, were the working class motifs, social structure, and language of *Pickpocket House*, a contemporary play. But *Tokijirō from Kutsukake* set the plight of the itinerant poor of the Meiji-Taishō period in the criminal (*yakuza*) or gambler (*toseinin*) world of the late–

Kutsukake Tokijirō **(1929), directed by Tsuji Kichirō. This is the first of several adaptations of the play by Hasegawa Shin, who established the *matatabi-mono*. Tokijirō (Ōkōchi Denjirō) escapes the gang life when he refuses to kill a woman (Sakai Yoneko — note the fringe just visible on the left temple) and her child (Onoe Sukesaburō [Kataoka Eijirō]) and, instead, runs off with them. The *matatabi mono*, stories about gamblers set in the last years of the Tokugawa shogunate, developed out of the anti-war movement initiated by the Russo-Japanese War (1904–1905): men trapped in a life of killing are offered the chance to escape, physically or psychologically, by creating — or recreating — ties with women and children (photograph courtesy of Matsuda Film Productions).**

Tokugawa or *bakumatsu* period to create the *matatabi-mono*, or story of a gambler's wanderings.[49]

The heroes of Hasegawa's wandering pieces are on the road, and for that they despise themselves. Under the Tokugawa, wanderers, traveling entertainers, and beggars had been classed as "non-human" (*hinin*), below the pariah class. Anyone reduced to the traveling life would feel stripped of caste, reduced to the lowest of the low. Many peasants were forced onto the road during the Meiji period; the rural areas bore the brunt of the cost of modernization, thousands were indebted and ruined — like Nakazato's father — demonstrations and armed resistance broke out up and down the country during the eighties, and the Liberal Party hounded the government on behalf of the small landowner. Many found work in the factories that had sprung up in the drive to modernize, militarize, and industrialize in the period between the war with China in 1894 and World War I. But the depression hit Japan long before it hit Europe: the country was rocked by rice riots in 1918. And, finally, it seemed that the entire effort to modernize had collapsed in the 1923 Great Earthquake because of the destruction of Tokyo, the showpiece of Japan's modernity.[50]

For the ordinary man, the depression was represented by this ultimate degradation: to become a wanderer, an outsider, casteless. There was a corresponding rise in the popularity of Kōdan and Naniwa-bushi (Naniwa melody, referring to the style of chanting) narratives about the plight of the late–Tokugawa period farmer who had had to quit and become an outsider (like the boss Kunisada Chūji) and about his drive to recreate a family and human attachments (as in the stories about Shimizu Jirōchō [1820–1893], the boss as father and fellow workers and their women as brothers and sisters[51]). Even the New Theater (Shingeki) film movement took on the itinerant poor in Murata Minoru's 1921 *Rōjō no reikon* (*Souls on the Road*).

Hasegawa combined his contemporary stories about day laborers and pickpockets with the world of the late–Tokugawa gang bosses celebrated in Kōdan and Naniwa-bushi. The result, the wandering-gambler piece or *matatabi-mono*, parallels the plight of the wandering gambler without human attachments with that of the thousands forced onto the road or into the cities to look for work. Hasegawa, who had experienced this life himself, offered a way for such people to regain dignity and respect as human beings, whether through a simple act of kindness or an extraordinary act of bravery. Thus, Hasegawa established the humanist tradition in the period piece, just as Nakazato had the nihilist tradition.

In the wandering-gambler piece, degradation is represented by the plight of the wandering gambler forced to pay for his one-night's board and lodging (*isshuku-ippan*) with a gang boss by killing a stranger. This plight has been likened by film critic Satō Tadao to that of the drafted soldier given his room and board (a considerable boon for many impoverished farmers' sons) and thereby indebted to the emperor (as the great *oya*, or "father") to kill men like himself, strangers on the battlefield.[52] The hero of the eponymous *Tokijirō from Kutsukake* regains his dignity and self-respect through a single act of mercy: Tokijirō kills a gambler like himself, but refuses to kill his wife and child, saves them, and finds himself saved. He leaves the gambler's world. When the woman dies, he goes on with her son.

Satō has noted that there are prototypes of the gangster as hero in Kabuki, Kawatake Moku'ami's white-wave pieces (*shiranami-mono*) about thieves and other bad men; however, the direct model for Kutsukake Tokijirō as "good-bad man" was William S. Hart (1864–1946), hero of many American silent films, mostly Westerns. His role was almost consistently that of a man with a past and connections to the wrong side of the law, who, for love of a pure woman, does the right thing and leaves.[53] This may very well be another example of a fictional character from western culture, in this case American film, being grafted onto a Japanese genre character, much the same way that Raskolnikov was Japanized to become Ryūnosuke. And, in much the same way, William S. Hart's Japanization into Kutsukake Tokijirō represents another aspect of matching (*mitate*), a violation of the historical characteristics of a narrative world (*sekai*) meant to make a direct correspondence between past and present.

The Period Film

This dependence on foreign models was accelerated in the development of film, as amply demonstrated by Yamamoto Kikuo.[54] Film, both as technology and as art, was thought of as exclusively western, and a long period of dedicated study and practice went into making film a Japanese narrative art form. In a sense, all Japanese film narrative is a reworking of foreign film narrative. In the period film, the combination of foreign film narrative (thus, a foreign world or *sekai*) and a Japanese historical setting to produce social and political commentary, or just an anti-authoritarian attitude, effected *mitate* and thus the Japanese period film.

The period film was established in the period between 1923 and 1939, a time whose increasingly difficult economic and political situation created a specific need for the period piece in film. The first half began with the Tokyo Earthquake and the murder of the anarchist Ōsugi Sakae (1885–1923), continued with the suppression of the labor unions, and ended with the annexation of Manchuria (1931). Censorship of films produced up to 1931 not only mutilated some of them but even left them unintelligible. Period films produced during these years are characterized by desperate rebellion and outrageously horrifying mass-fighting scenes.

The second half of this period began with the annexation of Manchuria in 1931 and moved on to the outbreak of war with China in 1937. The military began to dictate content and treatment to the film industry. Censorship killed the rebellion films: in 1939 the Motion Picture Law was passed and, in 1940, censorship was tightened to eliminate from the screen and from the consciousness of the Japanese people love, the bourgeoisie, the wealthy, foreign education, modern women, and any reference to a private life.[55]

These years produced two kinds of period film. The first was the tendency film (*keikō eiga*): rebellious, anti-authoritarian, "leftist." The second was the liberalism period film (*jiyū-shugi jidai-geki*), which promoted an alternative vision of hope and happiness for the people opposed to the sacrifice and suffering offered by militarism and fascism.

The Rise of the Tendency Film

"Tendency film (*keikō eiga*)" was the term for films, both contemporary and period, whose content was clearly leftist, progressive, anti-authoritarian, and critical — but tainted by the fact that they were produced at bourgeois-capitalist studios rather than being produced independently and thus disqualified from being recognized as truly "proletarian." They did, however, have a "tendency" to the left.[56]

The beginnings of tendency period films are traced back to a group of Taikatsu (Taishō Katsuei) studio personnel who came to Makino Educational Motion Picture Studios and became the nucleus of the "outlaw school" or "rough bunch (*burai ha*)" there: Uchida Tomu (1898–1970), Inoue Kintarō (1901–1954), Futagawa Buntarō (1899–1966), and others. Ahead of them had come an associate, Furumi Takuji (1894–1961),[57] who is credited with initiating the movement. However, he left after about a year and the leadership of the tendency period film movement devolved by default upon Makino actor Bandō Tsumasaburō (1901–1953) and scenarist Susukita Rokuhei (1899–1960). After Bandō and other stars left Makino, the movement at Makino was carried on by Makino Masahiro (1908–1993), son of the head of the studios and a member of the *burai-ha*. His greatest rival in the field was Itō Daisuke (1898–1981), then at Nikkatsu Studio.

What distinguishes the tendency period film movement is the connections of the directors to the left wing. Furumi was an anarchist, writer of anarchist reviews, associate of anarchists, and, on his return from Russia in 1929, a Communist.[58] Itō had been a union activist and a follower of Christian Uchimura Kanzō.[59] Makino had been in the same class as a future Communist

Party leader and had hung out with anarchists, not to mention the *burai-ha* at his father's studio.[60] Bandō and Susukita, however, were not political: perhaps that is why Bandō's films failed to maintain his position as leader of the movement.

The Rebellion Film

The tendency film has its immediate antecedents in the new period films exemplified by the early films produced by the team of Susukita, Bandō, and Futagawa. They, however, eschewed class-warfare rhetoric for a more popular and current rhetorical form modeled on American films: a young, romantic hero, unfairly treated by a cold, cruel world, finally turns on his enemies with a burst of passion, only to be drained, defeated, and dragged off by the authorities or, as often as not, killed in the end. Typical was Futagawa's *Gyakuryū* (*Retaliation*),[61] starring Bandō. The hero is a ronin whose life is

Orochi **(*Serpent*, 1925), directed by Futagawa Buntarō. Starring and produced by Bandō Tsumasaburō (center), *Orochi* set the standard for staged combat in the harrowing fight scene that ends the film. The blood is real: Bandō was covered with cuts and bruises received during the filming. The violence in the film is not gratuitous; it follows a long tradition in Buddhist preaching of depicting a world that must be rejected because of the suffering it causes (photograph courtesy of Matsuda Film Productions).**

ruined by the son of a chief councilor who kills his mother by running over her with his horse, seduces and abandons his sister (who commits suicide), and marries the girl our hero loves. When he interrupts the wedding to protest, he is thrown out of the fief. After some time of rough living, he sees the happy couple on the beach and, in a drunken rage, cuts down the entire party.

The Futagawa-Susukita-Bandō team made its mark with the second film of the independent Bantsuma Productions, the 1925 *Serpent*[62]; it made a leap from the rather juvenile and simplistic world-view of *Retaliation* (the cruel upper class takes advantage of the lower) to a more sophisticated analysis of society. Although compared with the 1922 American ex-con film. *Kick In* (directed by George Fitzmaurice [1885–1940]),[63] this film comes as close as anything to Russian nihilism.

The world of *Serpent* is bad: as in Russian nihilism, the moral order fails to coincide with the social order; there is a difference between a good man and a good reputation, a most important thing in Japanese society. Our hero, Heisaburō, learns the difference and is caught between them. The cost of doing the right thing is giving up one's place in society,[64] one's sanctity in Japan. And this *Serpent*'s hero does twice: he is expelled from his domain; later, he is expelled from his gang.

Serpent's hero throws away his second and last chance for a place in society. In the sense that he throws away his last hope, he is a Japanese nihilist hero. In that he does so for the sake of another, he is a Russian nihilist hero. Later, Japanese nihilism would turn into an expression of bored, cynical amorality. But, in *Serpent*, one can still see it in its original sense as an expression of religious, political, and social morality.

The Tendency Film

While *Serpent* is the best surviving example of the early period films infused with nihilism and anarchy, the real tendency film was characterized by communist class-warfare rhetoric. This feature was exemplified in the films of Furumi Takuji.[65]

In 1929, Furumi went to Russia, where his work was in fact known. Back at Ichikawa Utaemon's independent studio, he slipped easily into the tendency film movement with the 1929 *Nikkō no Enzō* (*Enzō from Nikkō*),[66] a film that was cut, cut, cut. Some of the lines contained the most blatant examples of class-warfare rhetoric:

> I'm a good example; unable to look with indifference on the oppression by the ruling classes and the miserable lives of the peasants, I abandoned the privileges I had as a samurai and stand at the fore in the liberation of the farmers...

> ... if you have the money, if the wickedness of a member of the ruling class is permitted, the rights of a poor man, what are they without the force of a group?
>
> ... It isn't just a question of Nikkō alone, but for the sake of all farmers, all property-less people [the proletariat] — isn't there any man ready to join me?...
>
> ... Quiet! I'm not speaking to you [the village headman], I'm speaking to all my brothers!...[67]

No wonder that the police were shivering in their boots! Nevertheless, it was not simply the class-warfare language that disturbed the authorities; it was the connection with the nightmare of the promotion of a farmers' revolt. It had been a frequent feature of the latter half of the Tokugawa government; moreover, revolts had rocked the country from 1881 to 1886 and they were still fresh in the minds of the police, especially the rice riots of 1918. One hundred and twenty-six meters of scenes of a farmers' revolt were cut from the 1930 *Sensengai* (*Front Line Street*): scenes of farmers sharpening their scythes within the temple precincts, scenes of farmers advancing in the fever of revolt, brandishing their bamboo spears — close-ups of weapons, and all corresponding titles.[68]

In 1930, enraged by the cuts to *Front Line Street* and *Ken* (*Sword*) made under police pressure because they were "agitation proletarian films" (*agit puro eiga*), Furumi attacked a censorship official and beat him up in his chair. He was detained and released as crazy rather than political.

Itō Daisuke and Makino Masahiro: Betrayal and Resistance

Itō Daisuke (1898–1981) and Makino Masahiro (1908–1993) have survived with the best reputations for the period films of the time, so perhaps a word or two should be said about their work.

Itō, the scenarist for those first period films made under the auspices of the Shingeki at Shochiku, including the first advertised as "new period play" or *shin jidai-geki*, was principally a writer of contemporary films. After moving about and establishing his own company, he moved to Nikkatsu in 1926. In 1927–28, he made the three-part *Chūji tabi nikki* (*A Journal of Chūji's Travels*), a version of the story of gambler-outlaw Kunisada Chūji (1810–1850). A deeply pessimistic story of resistance and betrayal, it established Itō as a leader of the tendency period film. His 1927 *Gero* (*Servant*) was a tale of

Opposite: *Nikkō no Enzō* (*Enzō from Nikkō*, 1929), directed by Furumi Takuji. The story of Enzō (Ichikawa Utaemon) is one more spin-off of the Kunisada Chūji cycle. Not only samurai could sling a sword; commoners, too, could wield the instrument of violence supposedly monopolized by the military class (photograph courtesy of Matsuda Film Productions).

vicious betrayal. A servant accompanying his master in the search for his father's murderer accidentally kills the man himself; when the murderer's family and associates demand the servant, his young master, too ill to have killed the man himself, sends the unwitting man, who is illiterate, to them with a note saying that he is the man to be killed. *Zanjin zanba ken* (*Man-killing, Horse-slashing Sword*, 1930) was about a Tsukue Ryūnosuke–type ronin who takes the lead in a farmers' rebellion against a local lord who, conveniently, is the object of his revenge of his father's death.

Itō's star, Ōkōchi Denjirō (1898–1962),[69] took over the cult of the bad man initiated by *The Great Bodhisattva Pass*. For Itō and Ōkōchi, the psychological darkness of Tsukue Ryūnosuke's blindness was expressed in other physical mutilations: Ōkōchi was Tange Sazen, the one-eyed, one-armed ronin betrayed by his lord, cut to pieces, and abandoned in the 1928 three-film series, *Shinpan Ōoka seidan* (*A New Edition of Tales of Ōoka's Administration*). Only bits and pieces of the film are extant, but one can see the dependence on the theme of betrayal by the upper class of the lower-ranking samurai, and the nihilism defined as contempt for the social order.

Makino Masahiro was twenty when, in 1928, all the stars in his father's studio having gone independent, he was left to direct unknowns. With cameraman Miki Jin, twenty-five, and scenarist Yamagami Itarō, twenty-three, Makino produced *Rōningai* (*Street of Masterless Samurai*[70]), a dark and uncompromising film (probably the reason it was screened in Russia). It is difficult to characterize Makino's early work, so little of it is left (only *Street of Masterless Samurai* I[71] and the final, horrendous fight at the end of III), although he remade many of his silent films after the war. He did not have a single star or signature motif. Perhaps, as with *Street of Masterless Samurai*, his success was in his contrast of impoverished ronin in the most degrading circumstances (one is living off a female professional thief) and their ability to come to each other's aid in one last fight for self-respect and dignity. It is clear, however, that he hit a nerve with his first films: *Street of Masterless Samurai* I was number one in the Best Ten list for 1928, his *Sōzenji-baba* (*Riding Grounds at Sōzen Temple*), based on a 1715 revenge gone wrong, was number four, and yet another was number seven. In 1929, *Kubi no za* (*Beheading Place*) was number one and *Street of Masterless Samurai* III was number three.

The Liberalism Film

Nihilism characterized the period literature and films of the Taishō period (1912–1925). Anarchistic nihilism did nothing but alienate intellectuals from society, but it is difficult to determine whether this had any effect of the popularity with the mass audience of the anarchistic, nihilistic film hero. The intellectuals of the period failed the people because they refused to address society and its problems, interested as they were with transcending it or destroying it. Perhaps this is another reason that the cult of the bad man was abandoned by the filmmakers who emerged in the first years of the Shōwa period (1926–1989), even before the tendency period films were suppressed by the police. A new group of directors came to the fore armed with parody, satire, and laughter — and a new kind of handsome, romantic, irreverent hero.

The vehicle for transition to the new movement in period films was the *matatabi-mono*, story of the gambler's wandering life. The works of Hasegawa Shin and Shimozawa Kan (1892–1968), who created the character of Zatoichi, were adapted for the screen, and the world they created became the basis for a new kind of period film, one in which the meaning of the wandering life was changed from "degradation" to "freedom," and the journey was given symbolic meaning as the journey of life.[72] Probably the single most important figure in this process was Inagaki Hiroshi (1905–1980),[73] the most highly acclaimed interpreter of *matatabi-mono*.

Inagaki should be credited with the creation of the "liberalism" (*jiyūshugi*) film, which goes back to the early works Inagaki made with Itami Mansaku (1900–1946), who also directed, but was often so ill that Inagaki took over. Their first, the 1928 *Tenka Taiheiki* (*Peace on Earth*[74]) was the first of actor-producer Kataoka Chiezō's (1903–1983) homages to Douglas Fairbanks, as was the 1921 *The Three Musketeers*. Itami's 1936 *Kimagure kanja* (*Capricious Young Man*) is a classic of the genre. A young man and his two pals (the three musketeers) decide to make their way in the world (and win fair maid) by bringing the neighboring domain to terms: they spread a rumor about a hen that lays golden eggs and create a rush on chickens. In the end, when our hero asks his lord for a reward, the lord enquires of his chief councilor as to whether a fief is available; upon learning there is not, he asks the councilor to find someone to commit suicide to free up a fief to bestow upon our hero.

Satō Tadao[75] has discussed two Inagaki films scripted by Mimura Shintarō, the 1936 *Matatabi sen'ichiya* (*Journey of a Thousand and One Nights*) and the 1941 *Umi o wataru sairei* (*Festival across the Sea*), as the most typical of the liberalism films. The light touch and the focus on ordinary people were based on Inagaki's study of American and European films and the Japanese versions of them current at the time as *shomin-geki* (plays about ordinary people). The violence directed against the people and the interference in their happiness by thugs, suggests Satō, reflect the threat to the ordinary people of Japan of the militarists in power.

Inagaki is especially regarded for his concept of the period film as "contemporary plays with topknots" (*chonmage o tsuketa gendai-geki*), the idea that period films should be indistinguishable from contemporary films or

films about common people (*shomin-geki*) except for setting and costumes. What could be closer to the Kabuki tradition of *mitate*? Inagaki was the first to use modern colloquial speech in his films: Tokyo dialect spoken in the government and business district of Marunouchi for the samurai and the working-class dialect spoken in Tokyo districts like Tsukiji and Asakusa for the commoners.[76] This produced a linguistic realism, even if an artificial one, in the tradition of Rakugo and Kōdan, that effected the technique of *mitate* that would be the dominant feature of the period films during the thirties.

The development of modern language in the period film was a principal project of the film study group Inagaki formed in 1934,[77] the Narutaki-gumi (Narutaki group), made up of scenarists and directors who studied Capra, Riskin, Mamoulian, and Duvivier and wrote under the name of Kajiwara Kinpachi.[78] Their most famous joint effort, Takizawa Eisuke's 1937 *Sengoku guntōden* (*Story of a Bandit Band in the Country at War*, Part One: *Tiger and Wolf*; Part Two: *Advance at Dawn*),[79] was based on Schiller's 1781 play *Die Räuber* (*The Robbers*) and, as a good representative of the liberalism film, told the story of a castle lord who finds refuge with a freewheeling band of freedom-loving "bush ronin" (*nobushi*).

A member of the study group was Yamanaka Sadao (1909–1939), considered the greatest of the pre-war period film directors. In 1935, Yamanaka began his focus on Ozu Yasujirō (1903–1963) and Shimizu Hiroshi (1903–1966) to create the tenement story (*nagaya-mono*, a Rakugo genre), or stories about common people in the period film (*jidai eiga no shoshimin-geki*). In this he literally reproduced Ozu's world in the period film. He abandoned the romanticism and moving camera of Itō for the realism and quiet camera of Ozu.[80] Where Inagaki effected *mitate* by using modern language and American and European film models in period genres like the *matatabi-mono*, Yamanaka did so by taking a genre recognized as a contemporary one, the *shoshimin-geki*, and transferring the film and narrative techniques to the period film.[81]

Yamanaka based his films (plot and shot) on foreign films and Ozu adaptations of the same. For example, his 1935 *Tange Sazen yowa: Hyakuman ryō no tsubo* (*Sazen Tange and the Pot Worth a Million Ryo*) was based on Stephen

Opposite: *Sengoku kitan: Kimagure Kanja* (*Capricious Young Man*, 1935), directed by Itami Mansaku. Three adventurers, Kimagure Kanja (Kataoka Chiezō) and his pals Kisozaru (Onoe Kajō, left) and Seki Nizaemon (Segawa Michisaburō, right), try to bring down a domain by floating a rumor about golden eggs and creating a run on chickens. Kataoka worked with Itami Mansaku and Inagaki Hiroshi to create nonsense comedies set in the past, precursors of the *jiyūshugi jidai-geki* (liberalism period film) (photograph courtesy of the Kawakita Memorial Film Institute).

Roberts's 1932 *Lady and Gent*, about a boxer and a barmaid who bring up an orphan.[82] In Yamanaka's period-film *shomin-geki* version, one-eyed, one-armed nihilistic swordsman Tange Sazen squabbles with (and usually loses to) his waspish mistress over whether to raise a waif and how.

Yamanaka's 1936 *Kōchiyama Sōshun* takes its plot from Ōzu's 1933 gang film *Hijōsen no onna* (*Dragnet Girl*), based on an American original, rather than from the low-life Kabuki play by Kawatake Moku'ami, one of whose low-lifes, a fallen Buddhist priest, provides the film's title.[83] In Yamanaka's film, Sōshun and his pal Kaneko Ichinojō, like *matatabi-mono* heroes, transcend the degraded circumstances of their lives by doing a great thing just once: they put on a grand charade to trick a lord out of his money (probably the only scene from the original play), give it to a young punk and his sweet sister, and die in the sewers (probably suggested by Victor Hugo's *Les Misérables*) to cover their escape.

Yamanaka's last film, the 1937 *Ninjō kamifusen* (*Humanity and Paper Bal-*

Ninjō kamifusen **(*Humanity and Paper Balloons*, 1937), directed by Yamanaka Sadao. The tenement landlord Chōbei (Sukedakaya Sukezō, left), ronin Unno Matajūrō (Kawarazaki Chōjūrō, center), and barber Shinza (Nakamura Kan'emon) share a drink. This film, starring the Progressive Troupe (Zenshinza), was Yamanaka's last. A "story of tenement life" (*nagaya-mono*) combined with the style of Ozu Yasujirō, it represents Yamanaka's perfect realization of Inagaki's concept of stories of ordinary people set in the past (photograph courtesy of Matsuda Film Productions).**

loons), is a free adaptation of Moku'ami's play *Tsuyu kosode mukashi hachijō* (1873), better known as *Kamiyui Shinza* (*Shinza the Barber*).[84] Like the original, *Humanity and Paper Balloons* is about a kidnapping; however, the kidnapper, Shinza (Nakamura Kan'emon), is the hero, not the villain. By this time, Yamanaka had come under the influence of the French dead-end films: the balloons of the title are taken from the end of Jaques Feyder's 1935 *Pension Mimosas*: the poor ronin's wife makes and sells toy balloons to feed them.[85]

Yamanaka, like Inagaki, was a serious student of films, French, American, Ozu's. His films, extremely calculated deconstructions of western narrative techniques used to interpret Japanese classics as a basis for *mitate*, are models for filmmakers (and greatly informed Kurosawa's early work). His was, perhaps, the most sophisticated grasp of cinematic structure and the use of traditional *mitate* and *sekai* as a rhetorical system with which to attack the present.

3

The Japanese Hero

Introduction

The characteristics of the traditional hero, or one modeled on him, make him eminently suitable for the purpose of the period film, to offer a critique of the present in terms of the past, through an analogy with the past. The Japanese hero is distinguished by three characteristics. First, the hero is a real, historical character. Until the Restoration of 1868, there was, technically, no such thing as a fictional hero. There was no fiction to speak of. In both Confucianism and Buddhism, fiction was equated with "false speech," and even Lady Murasaki was thought to be burning in hell for writing *The Tale of Genji*, a fictional account of palace life. That does not mean that the traditional accounts of the lives of heroes have come down to us in pristine historiographical purity. Heroes tend, in fact, to acquire a large entourage of supporting characters, including lovers and henchmen. Thus, any sort of reinterpretation of the hero's life is acceptable as long as his name and the salient points of his career are preserved intact. This concept of the historical reality of the hero has carried over to modern Japanese period pieces in the sense that, even if their heroes are fictional, their situations are perceived to be very real indeed. In addition, fictional accounts will often assume the rhetorical devices of historical accounts. For example, we often see the convention of prefacing the narrative with a date, as in Kurosawa Akira's 1954 *Shichinin no samurai* (*Seven Samurai*) and Shinoda Masahiro's 1986 adaptation of a play by Chikamatsu Monzaemon, *Yari no Gonza* (*Gonza the Spearman*). Both Okamoto Kihachi's 1965 *Samurai* (*Samurai Assassin*) and Kobayashi's Masaki's 1962 *Harakiri* take the convention a step further by invoking the voice-over of a scribe writing the official record of the event. Sometimes, merely naming the local lord "Matsudaira" (the original Tokugawa family name) is enough to set the proper, historical tone, as in Mizoguchi Kenji's 1946 *Utamaro o meguru gonin no onna* (*Five Women Around Utamaro*), in which Matsudaira is the name of the lord who has his ladies-in-waiting strip to go fishing.

Second, there is, traditionally, little in the way of a local hero; Japanese heroes are overwhelmingly connected with the political centers — Kyoto, Kamakura, Edo.[1] The older the hero, the more this is true. For example, Sugawara Michizane (845–903), worshiped by every university applicant as Tenjin, was a Kyoto court official who died in exile. Minamoto Yoshitsune (1159–1189), known to every Japanese child by his childhood name Ushiwaka, was the younger brother of the first Kamakura shogun — and was killed by him. Oda Nobunaga (1534–1582), Toyotomi Hideyoshi (1536–1598), and Tokugawa Ieyasu (1543–1616) unified Japan after a long period of political fragmentation. The forty-seven Akō ronin (d. 1703) avenged their late lord by killing the master of ceremonies of the Tokugawa shogunal house in Edo. Local heroes were eventually made national heroes, especially successful provincial warlords who had established domains of their own, such as Daté Masamune (1566–1636) in the far north and Mōri Motonari (1497–1571) in the far west. The nineteen boys of the White Tiger Brigade (committed suicide 1868 during the battle against imperial troops) moved from their position as local heroes of Aizu-Wakamatsu (a northern domain whose lord bore the Tokugawa family name Matsudaira) to national heroes as representatives of all the boys of pro-Tokugawa provinces — and later, of course, of Japan as a whole — who had died for their country.[2]

Third, the Japanese hero is overwhelmingly a tragic hero. This is not to deny or to diminish the importance of the hero as winner, the victorious *bushi* or the revered administrator. However, the heroes accessible to and worshiped by the Japanese at large are overwhelmingly tragic heroes, such as Soga Gorō Tokimune (1174–1193), who was sentenced to die a slow death (by an inadequate sword) for successfully carrying out his revenge in the shogun's hunting camp. In addition, because he had submitted a petition over the head of his lord to the shogun, Sakura Sōgo saw his children decapitated before he and his wife were crucified in 1653.

These three characteristics of the traditional Japanese hero make him particularly suitable as the subject of the period film, whose function is criticism of society. Because of his universality, he stands as a representative of the plight of all Japanese; because of his historicity, he stands as a valid proof of the argument; because of his political associations, his situation refers directly to political and social problems criticized in the film.

The Three Kinds of Hero

The Tragic Hero

Broadly speaking, we can recognize three basic types of protagonists in the Japanese period film. The first is the tragic hero. Victimized by political slander, defeated and slain on the battlefield, or sentenced to death for carrying out an illegal revenge, the Japanese hero falls, loses all there is to lose in life, and dies in great resentment and suffering. The tragic hero is portrayed as conventionally noble and done in by villains, traitors, or fate. However, except for the Tokugawa martyrs (*gimin*, leaders of farmers' riots who risked and received the punishment), rarely has a hero fallen for having done something particularly good and noble, but strictly for having failed and died a dog's death. The reason is that the Japanese have a fear of the lingering resentment of those who have died unhappily and before their time. Rites and ceremonies of pacification — Shintō, Buddhist, and Yin-yang magic — have been the rule at all levels of society since the ninth century.[3]

The best-known examples in history and in film are, of course, the forty-seven Akō ronin, who did what they thought was right and died for it. Others include the love suicides on whom Chikamatsu Monzaemon based his plays, several of which were adapted for film, such as Mizoguchi's *A Story from Chikamatsu*[4] and Shinoda Masahiro's 1969 *Double Suicide*. Women generally fall under this category: Ohama, forced to commit suicide for adultery in Imai Tadashi's 1958 adaptation of another Chikamatsu masterpiece, *Yoru no tsuzumi* (*Night Drum*)[5]; Oiwa, whose husband poisons, mutilates, and murders her to marry into money in Toyoda Shirō's 1965 *Yotsuya kaidan* (*Illusion of Blood*)[6]; and Kesa, who commits suicide as the only way to escape a fatal attraction in Kinugasa Teinosuke's 1953 *Jigokumon* (*Gate of Hell*).[7]

Immortalized in the great epics like the fourteenth century *Heike monogatari* (*Tales of the Heike*)[8] and *Taiheiki*[9] or in biographies like the fifteenth century *Gikeiki* (Record of Yoshitsune)[10] or the *Soga monogatari* (*The Tale of the Soga Brothers*),[11] the hero is victim to a nebulous complex of historical, social, and personality factors commonly referred to as "fate" (karma/*innen*). The concept of the tragic hero was fixed by the early fourteenth century and the most famous of the tragic heroes date from the middle ages. Film adaptations of their stories are not totally unknown in the West: Shima Kōji's 1956 *Shin Heike monogatari: Shizuka to Yoshitsune* (*The Warrior and the Dancer*) tells of the great love story of the twelfth century hero Minamoto Yoshitsune; the story of Enya Takasada (d. 1338), hunted down and killed by the man who wanted his wife, has been filmed by Shindō Kaneto (*Akutō* [*Scoundrel*], 1965)[12]; the story of the concubine of warlord Takeda Shingen (1521–1573) is told as that of the pawn of Shingen's general Yamamoto Kansuke (1501–1561) and of Kansuke, pawn of his own ambition, in Inagaki Hiroshi's 1969 *Furin kazan* (*Under the Banner of the Samurai*).[13] More familiar to western audiences is the tragic hero who plays a secondary character whom the hero avenges: Lord Asano, for example, who is avenged by his forty-seven vassals. The model is frequently taken up in fiction as with Chijiwa, the son-in-law avenged by Tsugumo Hanshirō in *Harakiri*.

The Anti-Hero

The second type of Japanese period film hero is the nihilist type, the anti-hero. These protagonists are dropouts, outcastes, and criminals. They tend to be youngish, scruffy (either scratching their beards or their fleas, a favorite motif of actor Mifune Toshirō), and so totally contemptuous of society as to commit the most heinous of crimes, despite the fact that they are, more often than not, members of the *bushi* caste. Whether through mental illness (Tsukue Ryūnosuke in *The Great Bodhisattva Pass*), desperation (Iuemon, the uxoricide protagonist of *Illusion of Blood*), betrayal (Tange Sazen, the one-eyed, one-armed pop-lit hero of the eponymous films), or disenfranchisement (the illegitimate son, Niino Tsuruchiyo, turned patricide in *Samurai*), they have become totally alienated from society and its values.

The anti-hero is rightly traced back to the Russian nihilist hero adapted by Nakazato Kaizan in *The Great Bodhisattva Pass* as well as to the thieves, pimps, and renegade priests of Kawatake Moku'ami's (1816–1893) Kabuki adaptations of white-wave Kōdan. However, important aspects of the anti-hero can also be traced back to the devils, demons, and angry spirits of the dead which randomly attack both innocent and guilty in their search for vengeance, redress, and purification and which are appeased in the rituals performed before planting (New Year) and especially before harvest (All Souls'/*obon*).[14]

The Social Hero

The third kind of hero is what I call the "perfect merchant, perfect magistrate" type, the social hero, who is usually based on an historical figure: lords and magistrates of the upper-samurai rank (Mito Kōmon,[15] Tōyama Kinjirō,[16] Ōoka Bizen no kami[17]), prominent merchants (Shiobara Tasuke[18]), and even gang bosses (Banzuiin Chōbei,[19] Shimizu Jirōchō,[20] never into anything worse than gambling). In the films, as establishment figures, they tend to be middle-aged or aged (a blessing for stars growing out of their lean and mean looks), impeccably dressed and groomed, benevolent, kind to children, and surrounded by younger, adoring disciples who help them solve people's personal problems as well as murder mysteries.

The social hero is the point of intersection for several, specifically three, models of benevolence. Take for example the case of the period film hero, Mito Kōmon, retired head of the Tokugawa house of Mito. First, with his little white beard and cheeks wrinkled up by a smile nearly obliterating his bright little eyes, he is the living mask of the *okina*, the old man, with which all Nō performances begin. This is the representation of the ancestral spirit (in purified form), bringer of all blessings, signifier of all things auspicious.

***Mito Kōmon manyūki: Nihonbare no maki* (*Mito Kōmon's Pleasure Trip: The Clear and Cloudless Sky Volume*), directed by Saitō Torajirō. Head of a cadet house of the Tokugawa, Mito Kōmon Mitsukuni (Tokugawa Musei, center), with his companions Sasaki Sukesaburō or "Suke" (Fukumi Taizō) and Atsumi Kakunoshin or "Kaku" (Ōsaki Tokiichirō), travels incognito and dispenses justice and mercy to the oppressed. This story first emerged in the late–Tokugawa period and demonstrates Kōdan's dual origins in Buddhist and Confucian preaching: the saving grace of the bodhisattva and the justice of the Sage King (photograph courtesy of Matsuda Film Productions).**

Second, as the retired lord traveling incognito and rescuing poor commoners and honest samurai from dishonest tax collectors or gang bosses, he is any one of a throng of buddhas and bodhisattvas who have taken human disguise in this world to act as saviors. And third, as the lord who goes out of his way to inspect the true conditions of the people under his care, he is both the perfect Confucian administrator, the Sage or deified cult object of those who have benefited from his attention (or those who wish they could), and the perfect Kōdan hero, the gold standard of conduct and rule, and, implicitly, a reproach to those who do not meet this standard in carrying out their duties.

The Hero as God

What is a hero, really? A hero is a human being who has been deified, that is, made a god. The story of the hero falls into three parts. The first is the story of how the hero became a hero, the biography (or autobiography) of the man. The second part concerns the circumstances and process of deification. The third part tells how the hero, now a god (little "g") functions in bringing aid and assistance to others in this world. In each part of the story, the hero has a different face.

Like the jewels in Indra's net, the three faces of the hero reflect each other. These three parts of the story and the three different faces of the hero are used by the period film as three different ways of evaluating the present through an analogy with the past. The tragic hero suffers and dies as a result of the problem. The anti-hero turns on the world and demands redress. The social hero works to ensure the happiness and well being of society.

What is not realized is that by focusing only on one face at a time, the single period film cannot include the entire story of the hero: except in adaptations of famous ghost stories, nothing is said of how the angry spirit of the tragic hero manifested itself by bringing misery and grief to friend, foe, and stranger alike or of how it became a proper benevolent patron god upon enshrinement, bestowal of posthumous honors, and constant propitiation (as with Sugawara Michizane, god of thunder, patron of calligraphy and university applicants). The years hammered out the religious content, if not the structure, of the stories of the origins of the hero/god. The religious content, the negative image of the unpurified hero/god was reintroduced to popular narrative as the nihilist anti-hero by Nakazato Kaizan. In doing so, Nakazato played upon the deep layers of pre-modern Japanese religious feeling and imagery of transgressive sacrality. The period film combines these three faces in limited and very specific ways. The tragic hero may turn briefly into the anti-hero: his ultimate defeat is a horrific battle in which he fights desperately, compulsively, until killed or captured. This combination was the specialty of Bandō Tsumasaburō in the twenties in films such as *Serpent*. The social hero may be replaced briefly by the anti-hero in battle against evil: a particularly hair-raising example of this is the good doctor's bone-snapping judo match with thugs in Kurosawa Akira's 1965 *Akahige* (*Red Beard*). However, the most typical combination is not in a single film, but in the career transition of the young actor specializing in tragic hero and anti-hero roles to social hero roles in late middle age.

The three specific types of Japanese hero represent the three specific stages of the story of the deified loser: having suffered a tragic death, the victim returns as a vengeful spirit, which through enshrinement and propitiation is gradually transformed into a benevolent patron deity. If it is possible to identify our film protagonists as gods, heroes, or deified humans, what is the narrative of the hero supposed to be telling us?

The Anti-hero: Resentment

Again, the image of the anti-hero represents the angry spirit of the defeated and slain hero which attacks its enemies and even innocent people in its search for redress and thus makes known its identity and will . The basis for the anti-hero is to be found far back in the religious pre-history of the Japanese, in the fear of the curses of the dead, of retaliation from the grave. A corollary to this is the fear of the spirits of those who have died without leaving a family to perform memorial rites, a differentiation of the fear of being cast out of society.

Early in Japan's religious history, only the spirits of the high-born could be powerful enough to return for retaliation and enshrinement.[21] However, Buddhism introduced the notion that everyone had Buddha-nature and, thus, access to salvation: this concept was extended to the idea that deification, too, was available to everyone.[22] The rise of tragedy on the stage of the seventeenth century attests to the belief in the capacity of every human being, even petty shop clerks and prostitutes, to return after death to demand redress and the need to propitiate such angry spirits.[23] Even the spirits of crucified criminals were worshiped in the execution grounds until the Tokugawa government stopped it.[24]

The process of deification involves the hero's suffering, destruction, and, especially, his revenge. From the twelfth century, the defeated *bushi* killed in battle has been the primary representative of the heroic model and his angry spirit has been the one most feared, for such an angry spirit will blight the rice crops by attacking the cherry trees: if the cherry blossom falls early, so will the blossom of the rice flower, resulting in famine and pestilence.[25] This fear is in fact the origin of the almost trite saying, "Among flowers it is the cherry, among men it is the samurai."[26] Thus, horror is the response evoked by the film anti-heroes, the lineal descendants of the angry spirit of the defeated *bushi*: how else could one respond to Bandō Tsumasaburō as the assassinated, early pro-Restorationist in the eponymous *Sakamoto Ryōma* (dir. Edamasa Yoshirō, 1928), with his crossed eyes, and bloody hair, face, and hands, crawling across the floor?

Retaliation

The anti-hero evokes horror because, in suffering, he inflicts terrible suffering on the community of the living. The ghosts of the Soga brothers drive passers-by mad and even kill them.[27] To avenge herself on her much younger lover, Lady Rokujō's spirit must kill her unknowing rival in love, Lady Aoi, in the Nō adaptation of her story in *Genji monogatari*, *Aoi no ue*

Sakamoto Ryōma **(1928), directed by Edamasa Yoshirō. The restorationist hero Sakamoto Ryōma (Bandō Tsumasaburō) is assassinated. Bandō's bloodied face and hands signify not the victim but the enraged spirit of the dead. Those who come to unhappy ends must be pacified, and, in the end, Sakamoto was, through his enshrinement with other war dead at the Shrine for the Protection of the Nation (Gokoku Jinja) in Kyoto. The film, then, conflates two stages in the story of the deification of the hero, that of the appearance of the powerful, angry spirit with that of the sympathetic story of the victim, which, apparently, Ryōma deserved: he envisioned the creation of a modern Japan united under the emperor and engineered the government transition known as the Meiji Restoration (photograph courtesy of Matsuda Film Productions).**

(*Lady Aoi*). In *Illusion of Blood*, Toyoda's version of the Yotsuya ghost story, the spirit of the murdered wife Oiwa haunts her husband and causes him to murder his new wife and members of the wedding party.

Since the twenties, the thrashing, slashing swordsman has been the popular image of the vengeful, infuriated spirit of the defeated tragic hero. Thus, we have the frantic, bleeding hero, driven by rage and resentment, fighting to the death. For example, in *Serpent*, Heisaburō's every attempt to be reintegrated into society is frustrated by society's misunderstanding of his sense of justice. In the end, in saving his former sweetheart and her new husband from his gang boss, he is attacked by the combined forces of his own gang and the police: in the rage of the turned worm, he fights off swords, lances, ropes, and even tiles thrown from a roof. Like a madman, he cuts, cuts, cuts, and is himself jabbed and sliced innumerable times, until, torn and bleeding and horrified by the number of men he has killed or wounded, he himself makes the decision to submit; he cannot drop his sword, but must peel his fingers off the hilt one by one.

Resentment

The hero's transition from victim to perpetrator of suffering is catalyzed by his reaction to the suffering endured, his resentment or *iji*. Thus, in *Harakiri*, Kobayashi confronts the anti-hero Tsugumo Hanshirō with the fact that the Ii house acted cruelly but correctly in their handling of his son-in-law. Nevertheless, Hanshirō satisfies himself— and us — with his power — his skill with the sword learned on the battlefield — to support his side of the story and to take revenge. Therefore, Hanshirō is the hero not because he is victimized by a sadistic version of the way of the *bushi, bushidō,* but because he exposes dishonor in the Ii house — samurai who have lost their topknots to him without taking their own lives — just as they had exposed his son-in-law's attempted extortion. Above all, the ultimate source of authority and recognition is the strength of will of the individual translated into power, usually superhuman power with the sword.

Iji and Mental Disturbance

The *iji* of the anti-hero is identified as madness. The modern characterization of the anti-hero as mentally disturbed was introduced by Nakazato's *The Great Bodhisattva Pass*: Tsukue Ryūnosuke is obviously not sane. *Serpent*'s hero, Heisaburō, is, frankly, a crisis addict who responds compulsively to each situation by swinging his fists or his sword. Others commit crimes against humanity or society in desperate, misguided responses to their situations. Iuemon, driven by desperate poverty, kills wife and masseur in a scheme to marry the daughter of a wealthy man. *Samurai*'s Tsuruchiyo joins the plot to kill the chief minister of the Tokugawa shogunate, not knowing he is his father, in his general resentment against a social order which prevented him from marrying the highborn woman with whom he had fallen in love. Hanshirō attacks the Ii house, in effect, to redress the wrongs he himself is responsible for.

In the period film, the retaliation of the angry spirit of the dead is translated into a wholesale attack by the anti-hero on human values and human society: crime, especially killing. Some films present the hero as victim of an incorrigibly corrupt world and thus justify the hero's violent response, whether the hero is totally opposed to society's values, as in *Serpent*, or totally incorporated and only liberated (enlightened) through suffering, as in *Harakiri*. Some films, like *The Great Bodhisattva Pass*, present the corrupt world as an extension of the anti-hero's mind, the product of a collusion between his sickness and that of the others who want to hire him. And still others, like the wandering gambler stories or *matatabi-mono*, present an alienated insider of a world he hopes physically or ethically to escape. No matter how attractive, none of these anti-heroes can be said to be mentally balanced. They are looking for the wrong thing and in the wrong place, and in doing so they end up criminals and outside society. Anyone who stays in that world finds his expectations violated, himself at best disappointed, at worst, destroyed.

Nakazato's characterization of the nihilist hero as mentally disturbed is profoundly Buddhist. Buddhism identifies suffering as attachment, attachment as any compulsive response to a situation based on fear, anger, or delusion, and, therefore, suffering as addiction. Thus, in Uchida Tomu's 1955 *Chiyari Fuji* (*Bloody Spear at Mount Fuji*), a middle-aged spear-carrier's beloved young samurai master is killed in a mockery of a duel. Insane with grief and rage, this stumbling old family servant takes his master's spear, goes after his superiors, trained samurai, and butchers them one by one. We are totally with him, and his revenge is vindicated, too, by the domain of those he killed. But all that serves only to indicate the insanity shared (if temporarily) by the servant, shown to be a kindly man, his society, and the audience.

In the period film, this compulsive attachment is to the code of the *bushi*. Chijiwa's use of the bamboo swords on himself indicates his madness, his internalization of a foreign spirit, *bushidō*. Of all the forms of suffering, suffering by the sword is the most horrible.

The anti-*bushidō* films of the twenties and sixties were based on the rhetorical motif of the *bakumatsu-mono* and the *matatabi-mono*, the journey through hell. In *The Great Bodhisattva Pass*, Tsukue Ryūnosuke walks through the physical extension of his own mind, the darkness of the battlefield, the *shuraba*, of the civil war ending in the Restoration. Those he kills escape; he himself does not. He is a salvation to others (whom he dispatches to the Pure Land), but he cannot save himself, because his compulsion to kill and his superior abilities to do so keep him in this world of suffering. In the *matatabi-mono* of Hasegawa Shin, the hero tries to rescue himself— or his self-esteem — from a militarist world of travelers bound to kill in exchange for a meal and a night's lodging. Several series from the sixties and seventies (*Nemuri Kyōshirō* [*Sleepy Eyes of Death*], *Kozure Ookami* [*Lone Wolf and Cub* or *Sword of Vengeance*], *Zatoichi*) work along the same theme of the super-human swordsman on his journey through hell. The world of the nihilist hero, the *shuraba*, is a sick world. The *shuraba* is the world of madmen. War is madness and militarists madmen. Suffering makes a human a god. Suffering is and causes madness. The sword is the symbol of madness.

Madness as Possession

The sword, like anything held in the hand, signifies madness because it indicates invitation to possession. In Nō plays, a willow branch is conventionally carried by one driven insane: it indicates that a spirit from the outside has taken over the body and mind of the victim.

The sword as motif of power is an ancient, religious one that precedes the development of swordsmanship in Japan (sixteenth century): when inviting the presence of a god or divinity, it is a thing held in the hand (*torimono*) — like a fan, bucket, tray, or bell — which attracts the god and by which it attaches itself to a human.[28] Power, then, comes from the outside, outside the body, outside the community. The source of the power, the angry spirit, the anti-hero, is an outsider.[29]

The Outsider: Trying to Get Back In

There are, of course, two kinds of outsider. The first is the stranger, the traveler, the stranger to the village or community. Hasegawa Shin's *matatabimono* are about traveling gamblers who, as sword bearers and killers and potentially dangerous to the community of men, come to the aid of men, women, and children in need of defense from their fellow gamblers. Like Kutsukake Tokijirō, they are enabled to leave the death world of the gamblers by acting as savior, or, like Yatappe (*Seki no Yatappe* [*Yatappe from Seki*, seven versions 1930–1963]), they save their sense of dignity or self-esteem by saving, for example, a child, while remaining outsiders. They are capable of being reintegrated into society whether they are or not.

The psychological outsider does not share the community's values, although he desperately wants a place in it. In *Assassination*, Kiyokawa Hachirō is dangerous to the very community of rulers he wishes to join because his desire to rise in society challenges the very basis of the system. In *Samurai Assassin*, Niino Tsuruchiyo is distrusted by the very group of men he has joined to assassinate the chief councilor of the shogun because his reasons are different from theirs: they want to keep foreigners out of the country; he simply hopes to be rewarded and recognized with a position.

The Ambivalence toward Power

While the outsider may demonstrate a yearning to be reintegrated into the society of men, the community itself does not demonstrate a reciprocating opening of home and heart to the outsider. The farmers of Kurosawa's *Seven Samurai* display a typical ambivalence to the outsider. They have gone out of the village to recruit seven masterless samurai to protect them against bandit masterless samurai (*nobushi*). That is, following the advice of the old man, himself an outsider, they look to the outside for help. However, they are afraid of the men they have hired: they hide their food, wine, weapons, and women. They do not really trust these seven any more than they do their equivalents, the bandits. The tension comes to a head when the hired men find out that their employers have in fact killed defeated *bushi* like themselves: they are prevented from killing the villagers only by the peasant Kikuchiyo (played by Mifune Toshirō), who points out that the villagers have been molested constantly by samurai and are therefore none too discriminating when it comes to paying them back. Strictly speaking, there is no difference between the bandit samurai and the hired samurai Kanbei, who in Confucian benevolence cuts off his top-knot and disguises himself as a priest to rescue a baby from an hysterical kidnapper,[30] or Katsushirō, who in Buddhist mercy throws money to the peasants Rikichi and Yōhei to buy rice when theirs is stolen. Only constant watchfulness, propitiation, and feeding will keep the seven, like the gods, on the side of the villagers. Hospitality is an expression of fear, a bribe. In the end, the surviving samurai must leave the village, even the youngest, who has fallen in love with a village girl: she ignores him at the planting; he is a traveler, an outsider, and he has no place in the village after his work is done. The god is summoned, performs his task, and is returned again. The god is an outsider.

Instinctively, the Japanese fear the swordsman as madman, and the madman as power directed potentially against them. Warfare is not human. The swordsman is not human. Therefore, he must be a god. Madness is not human. It must be the manifestation of the god. This model of divinity based on the concept of transgressive sacrality is the oldest, most dominant concept of divine power in Japan. Only constant propitiation and purification will turn that power to good. It is not without justification that in Kurosawa Akira's 1962 *Tsubaki Sanjūrō* (*Sanjuro*) the councilor's wife tells Sanjūrō, who has been killing just too, too many people, that really good swords are kept in their scabbards.

The Tragic Hero and His Story

The concept of the Japanese hero emerged in conjunction with the development of religious rituals for dealing with evil and harmful spirits. The tragic hero represents the pacification of the angry spirit of the dead. Once the resentment of the angry spirit has manifested itself, the victims of the spirit's attack attempt to identify the source of their misfortunes. Typically, this involves recruiting a team of religious specialists, a male exorcist and a female medium. The exorcist subjects his partner to a trance; the spirit takes possession of the medium and speaks through her; and, finally, the exorcist prescribes the rituals or other actions necessary to appease the spirit.[31] Such a possession ritual is rendered in Kurosawa Akira's 1950 *Rashōmon*, in which the court hears the testimony of the murdered samurai through a medium.

Although there are several kinds of exorcist and several kinds of procedures for pacifying the angry spirit, typically the spirit is pacified through dialogue or *mondō* with a religious specialist.[32] Ultimately, the purpose of the dialogue is to persuade the spirit that what happened to it was not the fault of the community it is attacking or perhaps, in addition, to negotiate a contract to provide (religious) services in exchange for a cessation of its predations. In this pacification procedure can be identified the cognate of the tragic hero, who is absolved of responsibility for his condition and, at the same time, held up as an example and warning to others.

Complaint in the First Person: *Monogatari*

First, the angry spirit gives its version of the story, its autobiography.[33] The purpose of what is essentially an oracle is to demand redress. Therefore, we must expect a one-sided, totally subjective version of the story. Of all period films, those scripted by Hashimoto Shinobu (b. 1918) most closely resemble the structure of oracle: they focus on the first-person, "my side" of the story, a point of view strengthened by the use of flashbacks as film narrative structure.

Hashimoto's first scenario was for *Rashōmon*. Based on two stories by Akutagawa Ryūnosuke (1892–1927), the film is a series of first-person narratives describing a rape and murder. No one tells the same story and no one is telling the whole truth, not even the ghost of the man murdered. Each tells the story strictly in terms of the way he perceives himself: brave robber, deceived husband, pitiful, weak woman, poor but honest woodcutter.

In *Rashōmon*, Hashimoto confirmed the tradition of *monogatari* as first-person narration in religious ritual and theater. In period films without the flashback construction, too, the version of events can be expected to be totally one-sided. Even in very complex stories, where the protagonist takes some responsibility, a rational evaluation of the situation will be side-stepped and all sympathy be given the protagonist, even the anti-hero. The protagonist is a victim.

Consider Imai Tadashi's version of the play by Chikamatsu Monzaemon (1653–1725), the 1958 *Night Drum*, also scripted by Hashimoto, which reinforces the plight of the adulteress Ohama as victim of family and society. Her sister is paralyzed by embarrassment and cannot prevent the unwanted suitor from threatening her. Ohama is left to her own devices, and her promises to come to him later are overheard by the drum-teacher. To keep the drum-teacher quiet, Ohama makes him an accomplice by seducing him. The family council is hot to punish her to save themselves from confiscation and expulsion for the crime of failure to maintain order in the house. What is more, her sister-in-law runs in as righteousness incarnate (rather than, as in the play, as the wife expelled from her family because of her sister-in-law's shame) demanding punishment. This is not Chikamatsu's analysis of the sources and effects of Ohama's alcoholism or of family ambition.[34] However, the reduction of the protagonist to blameless victim is consistent with the tradition of the tragic hero's version of the story.

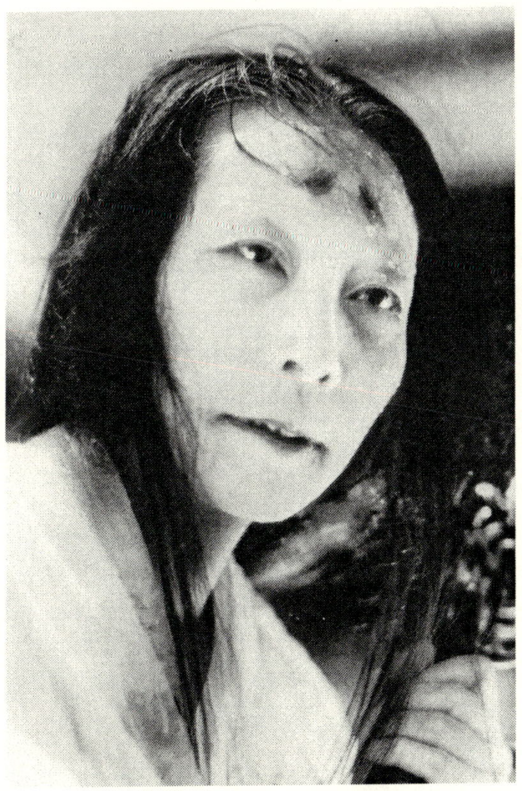

Rashōmon **(1950), directed by Kurosawa Akira. A medium (Honma Fumiko) is summoned so that a murdered man can be interrogated by the court. In Japan, the tradition was for a woman to become a medium either through training (especially if blind) or through possession by a spirit. Either way, the function of such mediums was to speak for the dead or for a spirit that had taken possession of a man or woman. Through the medium, the will of the spirit was made known; a religious specialist, usually the partner of the medium, would prescribe the rituals needed to put the spirit to rest, send it to the Pure Land, or convert it into a protective deity of the community (photograph courtesy of the Kawakita Memorial Film Institute).**

The Interpretation: The Sermon on Suffering

If in *Rashōmon* Hashimoto confirmed the tradition of *monogatari,* he also exposed its limitations by questioning the validity of the *monogatari* or testimony of each protagonist. Who, in the end, *did* kill the husband? What *did* happen to the murder weapon? This wariness has emerged in different ways in Hashimoto's films, including Kobayashi's *Harakiri* and 1967 *Jōiuchi* (*Samurai Rebellion*) as well as Okamoto Kihachi's 1965 *Samurai Assassin.* In *Harakiri*, as noted above, Hanshirō is forced to admit his complicity in the gruesome end of his son-in-law: his pride in his *bushi* status had precluded even the idea of selling his own swords to pay for medicine or a doctor for his daughter and grandson; his son-in-law, in contrast, had been willing to resort even to attempted extortion.

Thus, within the tradition of the tragic hero is a challenge to it. This is analogous to the response of the religious specialist. The purpose of the ritual is to pacify the angry spirit of the dead and to persuade it to desist from its depredations. Under the influence of Buddhism, the function of the response was less a negotiation for an exchange of services (protection in exchange for propitiation) than an offer of consolation. Stories about the dead are believed to console them: some of Chikamatsu's domestic tragedies were written to commemorate the death anniversaries of the protagonists.[35] And in Kobayashi's 1964 *Kaidan* (*Kwaidan*), Hōichi the blind lute player (traditionally exorcists),[36] is dragged off by the ghost of a *bushi* to chant to the ghosts of the Taira the tale of their fall and destruction.

The consolation, the story that contains an explanation of the causes of the spirit's fate, functions in effect as a sermon, specifically a Buddhist sermon. Here, the Buddhist priest or monk functions as a therapist. His job is to teach the angry spirit the cause and meaning of its suffering.[37]

The Meaning of Suffering

Suffering is important to the self-image of the Japanese people. Suffering is the experience needed to make a complete human being, a perfected spirit. Well, one understands that: a musician will not break through until the teacher gashes his hand with a pick; a fencer will not break through the barrier until he goes through one of those crushing make 'em-or-break 'em, week-long fencing matches; soldiers get slapped around; so do apprentices; new entrants to corporations have to go through a pretty grueling training period. For their own good.

The nature of suffering in a period film, however, has little or nothing to do with mothers-in-law, but with the idea that nothing is accomplished without effort. Suffering is the means by which one becomes the hero, the god, the truly accomplished and finished human being.[38] As a friend once observed of a film heroine, "You can tell she's really happy now. She's finally suffering."

However, the issue of suffering was complicated by the introduction of

Buddhism. According to Buddhist doctrine, suffering characterizes the human condition, and the many examples of suffering exemplified in the traditions of the tragic hero function as conclusive evidence of the infallibility of the Buddhist diagnosis. Suffering is inescapable.

Suffering is the single unifying characteristic of the six stages, or Six Realms (*rokudō*), of existence in this world into which a sentient being might be reborn: those of gods, men, fighting titans, animals, hungry ghosts, and of hell.[39] And of these, the plight of the titans, the *shura*, condemned to eternal battle, came to typify the human condition during the battle-weary years of the Middle Ages.[40] The place of the *shura*, the *shuraba* or battlefield, was feared as a place where one could be seized by the spirits of dead *bushi* and killed — or driven insane.

In the period film,[41] the *shuraba* is the world of the code of the *bushi* (*bushidō*) and it has been used to attack a perverted *bushidō* and its extension, modern militarism. The fate of men to live as fighting demons, that is, to experience the horrors of the sword and the battlefield, is the basis of the *matatabi-mono* as it is of the *bakumatsu-mono*. The code of a meal and a night's lodging (*isshuku ippan*) in exchange for a killing, *shuraba*, as the world of the soldier and murder, represents modern militarism in the *matatabi-mono* as it does in the *bakumatsu-mono*. Kutsukake Tokijirō saves himself when he acts as a man (as ersatz husband and father) to a woman and her son; by saving others from and by leaving the world of the *shuraba* he himself is saved.

Thus, a constant theme running through the narrative of the Japanese period film is a Buddhist one: that suffering is to be found in self. If there is blame, the blame lies in the false attachments and internalized values of a false world. Often, the hero, such as *Harakiri*'s Hanshirō, cannot destroy the evil without destroying himself.

What the sermon does, of course, is to explain to the angry spirit that what happened to it was certainly not the fault of the community it is attacking, not even the fault of those who did it in, not a false and cruel world which drives a man to the breaking point. The roles of victim and victimizer have been determined by fate. Full acknowledgment of its suffering will be expressed, but it will be pointed out that for those born in the Six Realms, suffering cannot be avoided.

More *Monogatari*, More Sermons

The proper response to the realization of the inescapable suffering of the human condition is not indicated by the tragic hero, any more than by the anti-hero. This function is generally relegated to any one or more of the substantial cast of secondary characters in the story. Whenever a hero dies, someone is left to mourn him: a mother, a lover, a servant. Without fail, they become nuns or ascetics and dedicate themselves to praying for the souls of their dead.

Stories about such members of the family or of the house are called stories about taking the tonsure (*shukke-mono*, or "leaving-home stories," after the Buddhist expression for entering religious life). In a world characterized by suffering, grief and the trauma of loss, the only appropriate response is to leave the world, physically, emotionally, ethically, for the liberation or salvation offered by Buddhism.[42]

It is up to the living, usually family, to secure the peace of the spirit either by avenging it or by working for its salvation and enlightenment. Avenging the dead is common enough: we have only to think of the bulk of Japanese period films, including *Harakiri* and the numberless versions of *Chūshingura*. However, because the period film is not about women, and women's principal role in the tradition of the tragic hero is that of mourner, the function of securing the peace of the angry spirit through religious means is very rarely represented in the period film. There is, of course, the scene of Lady Asano cutting her hair after the death of her husband in Mizoguchi Kenji's 1941–2 *Genroku chūshingura* (*The 47 Ronin*). Or, again, Princess Sen becomes a nun and vows to pray for the man who died for her in Misumi Kenji's 1960 *Sen-hime goten* (*Princess Sen in Edo*; she was the daughter of the second Tokugawa shogun). Perhaps we can also look to the many depictions of women suffering at the hands of unenlightened men as a residue in reverse of this tradition: the daughter, whose socially progressive father refuses her an education in Tokyo after the Restoration in Yoshimura Kōzaburō's 1953 version of *Yoake mae* (*Before [the] Dawn*); or the wife and mother of a peasant household who cannot keep her husband or children out of the Takeda family's ambitions for conquest in Kinoshita Keisuke's 1960 version of *Fuefukigawa* (*The River Fuefuki*). In these examples, the heroine fails in her function toward the hero. It is the women who play the major role in imbuing the tradition of the hero with the tragedy which characterizes it; for the hero may die, but it is his loved ones who are left to deal with the trauma and grief. It is through their stories that the pathos of life in the world of suffering is expressed, and it is they who achieve the enlightenment denied the hero.

Also rarely represented in film is the hero's slayer who, like the hero's survivors, suffers through his death and takes responsibility for his afterlife. In the original Buddhist version of the story of Taira Atsumori (1169–1184), the real hero is not Atsumori; it is the grizzled eastern *bushi*, Kumagai Naozane (1141–1208): killing Atsumori at Ichinotani is said to have been the catalyst to Naozane's abandoning the world to become the famous Pure Land priest,

Rensei.[43] Stories of *bushi* shocked into religious awakening by the horrors of the battlefield are in fact called religious awakening stories, *hosshin-mono.* There is a trace representation of them in the period film. In *Harakiri,* Tsugumo Hanshirō's young son-in-law is forced to commit suicide with bamboo blades; however, it is Hanshirō who is transformed by the experience. Not only does he abandon *bushidō,* a this-worldly value system, but he acquires such power and intent of purpose as to disgrace three men and to desecrate the cult object of the Ii house. A tragic fate destroys the young hero, but enlightenment destroys the witness as the false person he was.

Naozane kills Atsumori after promising to take responsibility for prayers for his soul. One way of expiating sins is to confess them, for oneself or for another.[44] The transition from confession to narrative tradition takes little time. The original story of Sanshō Dayū (as in Mizoguchi Kenji's 1954 film *Sansho the Bailiff*) has been identified as originally a confession of evils told to expiate sins — the worse the sins, the better the expiation. Thus, the whippings and burnings receive so much emphasis: the worse the villainy of the villains, the more effective the expiation of their sins.

Narrative Structure as Reaction Rather Than Action

The traditional narrative of the tragic hero is made up of so many episodes involving different people that one might well ask, "Whose story is this?" Although the film is called *Sanshō the Bailiff,*[45] the plot focuses on the vicissitudes of a noblewoman and her two children, especially the boy. The tragic hero of Inagaki's *Chūshingura* is obviously Lord Asano — he is the one forced to commit suicide; and yet, the focus of the tale is the leader Ōishi Kuranosuke, and even more, the stories of his comrades are obviously equally familiar to the Japanese. First-time American viewers squirm. So, whose lance is that given a quick close-up in the attack scene? Whose bodies are those in the alley? If this series is named after Shimizu Jirōchō, why don't we see much of him after the first film? Consider *Rashōmon.* It is aggravating, is it not, not to know what *really* happened, and we do not know what really happened because we get so many different versions of the samurai's death.

Believe it or not, the presence of multiple heroes in a narrative has nothing to do with Japanese group psychology, but with the principle(s) of narrative composition. For the narrative of the tragic hero (or of a tragic event, such as a battle or series of battles), material is collected from every possible witness to the hero's life (or composed concerning every possible witness): mother, nurse, sweetheart, servant, and even killer. The tradition of the tragic hero is not only the story of (his life and) death, but the stories of the reactions to his death.

Thus, the tradition of the tragic hero presents a chain reaction of suffering beginning with the dead hero and extending to the members of his family and house and even to his slayer, and ultimately to any who hear the story. The fate of the tragic hero proves that suffering characterizes existence in this world. The fates of the mourners, those who assume responsibility for the afterlife of the hero, bear witnesses to the truth of suffering and give models of the proper response to it. Even though the tragic hero's narrative is fragmented by its multiple voices or points of view, consistency is maintained throughout by the common theme of all the stories.

The Medium

Although period films are, in the main, not about women, women do have important roles in period films, roles that equal the men's in function. Women do play the social hero: the mistress of the Teradaya Inn (Awashima Chikage) in Gosho Heinosuke's 1958 *Hotarubi* (*Firefly Light*). Sometimes women play the anti-hero: Fushimi Naoe pioneered the anti-heroine in roles such as Tange Sazen's vamp girlfriend, complete with pistol, the convicted thief's bands tattooed on the arm, and dress falling over her slatternly shoulders in Itō Daisuke's *A New Edition of Tales of Ōoka's Administration*. More often women play the role of the tragic heroine: Kyō Machiko as the unwilling object of a determined *bushi*'s affection in Kinugasa Teinosuke's 1953 *Gate of Hell* or Kagawa Kyōko as the unhappy wife of the emperor's calendar maker in Mizoguchi's *A Story from Chikamatsu*.

The archetypal woman's role is that of victim. In this, she is usually paired with the tragic hero, usually a victim of politics, and her status as tragic heroine comes through him. One of the earliest examples is that of Shizuka, mistress of Minamoto Yoshitsune (1159–1189), whose child by him was exposed on a beach to die. Concomitantly, the archetypal heroine is a prostitute, courtesan, or entertainer of some sort. Shizuka was, as was Tora, beloved of Soga Jūrō Sukenari (1172–1193), and Terute-hime, beloved of Oguri Hangan — all famous Japanese heroines.[46]

The role of victim is based on the woman's function as medium or shamaness in the ritual to appease the angry spirit of the dead. Just as the shamaness indicates to the exorcist the source of the evil attacking the community by being subjected to possession by the angry spirit of the dead so that it can use her voice to communicate its identity and will, so the period film narrative operates as a shamanic ritual in which a woman indicates to the hero the source of social or personal evil by becoming the victim of it.

There are two reasons given to explain why the prostitute, courtesan, or entertainer is associated with the function of shamaness. Firstly, in terms of historical development, it is suggested that when shamanic women were forced out of shrines in the mid–ninth century, their religious functions were differentiated into a variety of entertainments such as singing, dancing, and story telling.[47] And secondly, in terms of function, it is suggested that the shamanesses who carried on their original function also carried the tradition of the tragic hero: in telling his story, in identifying his angry spirit as the source of a community's troubles, they often identified themselves as principal characters in his story, most often as the lovers of the spirits they served.[48]

This origin in religious functions, the identity as victim of politics and lover/high priestess of the tragic hero, gave the prostitute-entertainer a particular role to play in developing the period piece as a form of protest against a social or political evil. In medieval times and later, the relationship to the tragic hero she claimed gave her access to the power of his angry spirit. In the Tokugawa and especially Meiji periods, when erotic love and passion were not considered decent for respectable women, *geisha* and courtesans were considered more suitable for representing such emotions in novels and plays. And in the post-war period, the institution of prostitution was used to represent the evil feudalism of the past.

Thus, in short, from medieval times to modern, the prostitute-entertainer has been the principal image of female victimization. Indeed, it is the role of prostitute or entertainer that maintains the continuity between Shinpa and the post-war period films.

Women and Shinpa

Women were allowed on the stage for the first time in over two hundred years with the development of modern theater, the "new school" or Shinpa, in the 1880s. Shinpa is about women trapped functionally in the kind of feudalism ostensibly escaped by men in the modern period: unhappy wives in marriages forced on them or *geisha* whose lives are bound by contracts and obligations like those of Tokugawa courtesans. These women die beautifully. They give up their children to their lovers' childless wives. They are betrayed by the very men they look to for help. Indeed, they limit their search for or expression of freedom to the choice of the men by whom they will suffer.

During the war years and the following American occupation (1945–52), censorship forced an increasing number of period-film specialists to begin to turn to Shinpa plays and the Meiji period in general. In 1942, Makino Masahiro released his version of the Shinpa play based on a novel by Izumi Kyōka, *Onna keizu* (*Genealogy of Women*), the story of a woman in love with a poor student who must marry the daughter of his professor patron and who, under the law, must give up her daughter by him to his childless wife. In 1948,

***Onna keizu* (*Genealogy of Women*, 1942), directed by Makino Masahiro. A *geisha*, Otsuta (Yamada Isuzu), falls in love with a student, bears a daughter, Taeko (Takamine Hideko), and is forced to give her up to the student and his childless wife. Nevertheless, she meets her daughter again, although she cannot reveal their relationship. Her friend, Tsunaji (Yamane Hisako), looks on sympathetically. During the war, Makino and other directors made Shinpa films, which could be seen as extremely inappropriate for wartime except for their themes of personal sacrifice and suffering (photograph courtesy of the Kawakita Memorial Film Institute).**

Itō Daisuke's *Ōshō* (*Go Champion*) was released: an impoverished go addict finally wins the championship after his desperate wife finally decides to support him instead of fighting him. Inagaki Hiroshi won best film of 1943 with *Muhōmatsu no isshō* (*The Life of Matsu the Untamed*), the story of a rough rickshawman and his life-long devotion to the widow and son of an army officer.[49] The Shinpa style, exemplified in the films starring the team of Hasegawa Kazuo (1908–1984) and Yamada Isuzu (b. 1917), was characterized by long shots, long takes, and especially crane shots, not identified with the period film.

The Shinpa films are the basis of the feminist period films of the postwar years, which were exemplified, of course, by the films of Mizoguchi Kenji, such as the 1952 *The Life of Oharu* and *A Story from Chikamatsu*. However, other directors made films about women and life under Tokugawa feudalism.

Gosho Heinosuke described the plight of the bride in the 1958 *Firefly Light*. Imai Tadashi adapted a Chikamatsu play about the situation of samurai wives left to manage alone when their husbands are called away to year-long service in the capital in the 1958 *Yoru no tsutsumi* (*Night Drum*).

Yoda Yoshikata (1909–1991) and the Shinpa-Style Period Film

Where most directors and scenarists are willing merely to describe the plight of women, only Yoda Yoshikata has tried to explain it as something more than Buddhist "fate," the "evil of having been born a woman," or even "the system." In Yoda's hands, the world of women, that of the puppet-play courtesan torn by her obligations and the Shinpa tradition of the *geisha* used and abused by men as a microcosm of so-called "feudal" society, became the rhetorical basis for a description of the relationship of the individual to his society. Yoda is, of course, best known for his scripts for Mizoguchi Kenji which feature the ugly — because normal — situation of the individual assimilated by "feudal" society.

The point of assimilation of the individual by a repressive social system is the moment when he takes advantage of the privileges afforded by the system — usually the abuse of someone else. Take, for example, Mizoguchi's 1946 *Five Women around Utamaro*, which was made in compliance with SCAP[50] directives. Utamaro, the wood-block print artist, is portrayed as anti-feudal, a democrat who is identified as such by his choice of an art style not patronized by the government as well as by the life he leads in the licensed quarters. Hedonism is one way of protesting a repressive regime; but, then, women are victimized by this kind of protest.

Among the five women of the film is Oran, daughter of a wealthy merchant and in service to Lord Matsudaira. Oran is the most beautiful of the young women who go fishing in their underwear for Lord Matusdaira's rather curious, even innocent, form of voyeurism. However, her function for Utamaro is no less susceptible to criticism than that for Matsudaira. Matsudaira, at least, is more honest: he sends her fishing in order to get a good look at her body. Utamaro has her strip in order to pose for him. Yet Matsudaira stands convicted by his name alone: he is berated as "a very loose man ... using his great wealth to amass beauties." Utamaro's friends plead with Oran to pose half-dressed for him, "[f]or the sake of *ukiyo-e*."[51] The girl does so, never realizing (any more than the director or the audience) that for one reason or another, for Matsudaira's pleasure or for Utamaro's, she is being exploited. Although Yoda tries to incorporate the rhetoric of anti-feudalism (anti-samurai) for the sake of SCAP, Utamaro's status is solidly based on the sexual exploitation of women. Oran's situation is a close parallel with that of the women of the licensed quarters, Tagasode, Okita, and the ugly courtesan who lives to finish her contract and marry Utamaro's servant (and, as a sensible and successful woman, is of no interest to Mizoguchi).

The women function as the object of evil perpetrated by a state which not only tolerates but officiates in the institutionalization of the indenture of women to prostitution. As a highly supervised social steam valve, sex was used as the opiate of rich commoners (who had no place to spend their money except in the licensed quarters) and samurai posted to major cities without their wives and family. Oran's service to Lord Matsudaira is tolerated in a highly moral society because it keeps him out of trouble. Utamaro, as patron of the quarters and in the way he uses women as objects to draw, participates in the process and thereby becomes famous.

Yoda's principal contribution to the rhetoric of the post-war period film was to entrench the shamanic role of women in identifying the source of social, political, and personal hardships — and sometimes that source is the hero. Yoda frequently questions the role of the carriers of the tradition of the cultural hero, cultural heroes themselves such as Utamaro and Mizoguchi, who ostensibly enshrine women as heroines or victims of society and yet who participate in the abuse of women by the very fact that their careers were wholly dependent on exploiting them.

Love, Loyalty, and Obsession

The real nature of the society under analysis is revealed through the fate of those living up to certain ideals. Period films teach us, for example, that the ideal of absolute loyalty is impossible to realize without self-destruction, because absolute loyalty is given long after the evidence has demonstrated that the basis for such loyalty has long disappeared — Tsugumo Hanshirō's to his sword, that of the forty-seven Akō ronin to their lord. Shinpa-influenced period films about women teach us that in this world love is not possible and anyone who looks for it is in for trouble. The love that is presented in plays and film is totally normal — statistically speaking — but it is no more healthy than the resentment of the anti-hero.

Take, for example, Okita in *Five Women around Utamaro.* She's a "bad woman," a passionate creature given to drinking and intent on finding true love with one man, even though the object (baby-faced, long-lashed Shōzaburō) on whom she has projected her ideals is hardly worthy of such emotional effort. When her rival runs off with him for the second time, Okita follows with a knife. While the two women push poor Shōzaburō for a decision, he innocently declares, "I like and belong to you both." Frustrated beyond endurance, Okita kills them both.

"I wanted to be true to myself ... I felt I have known the path for a woman to follow," she tells Utamaro. Sincerity is as much the ideal for a teahouse maid as it is for a revolutionary. But, come now, is a man who visits the prostitute quarters looking for sincerity? Okita has as much hope of making Shōzaburō the justification of her life as the hotheaded *bushi* Moritō has of winning the faithful and loving wife of another, Kesa, in *Gate of Hell.*

A film heroine does not simply wash her hands of a bad situation, chalk it up to experience, and go on to find revenge in living well. Like Otsu in Inagaki's 1955–56 *Samurai* trilogy, she waits and wilts forever. Yuki, too, in *Utamaro*, will spend her existence in selfless sacrifice and devotion with only the faintest hope of achieving her goal of marriage to Koide, Utamaro's disciple, who used to be her father's. This is called being true to yourself. Actually, it is the highest form of egoism, the refusal to accept the will and inclination of another, and is the secret hope of shaming the man into changing his mind — a nice girl's expression of "fatal attraction."

In Buddhist terms, this is the adherence to the delusion of happiness. As the period films demonstrate, men believe that they will find meaning in life by their adherence to the sword and women believe they will find life's meaning in true love. But the religious function of the films is supposed indicate that these are delusions, the internalization of the values of a repressive society, and that only bitter disappointment or death can be the result.

Films for Women: A Separate Reality

In Shima Kōji's 1956 *The Warrior and the Dancer*, the first shogun Yoritomo's wife, the famous Masako, reveals great and totally atypical sympathy for Shizuka, forced to dance before her lover's brother and enemy and using the opportunity to declare her love for and loyalty to Yoshitsune. I call this sympathy atypical for two reasons: Masako herself was known for her hard-headed, political practicality, and, as traditionally presented, women, in general, really and truly belong to their groups, their families, and have little sense of solidarity with other women.

However, a new rhetoric has been coming out of Japanese TV period dramas by way of the morning soap opera, where women sit around a table and complain about their men. This seems due to the overwhelming influence of Hashida Sugako (b. 1925) and her work in television. In her *Onna Taikōki* (*Women's Taikōki*), the 1981 NHK Taiga Drama, a year-long version of the life of the sixteenth century peasant-turned-national-hegemon Toyotomi Hideyoshi (Nishida Tomoyuki) and his wife Oné (Sakuma Yoshiko), the theme running throughout is the opposition of the values of men and women. Oné (called by Hideyoshi "Okaka," an obsolete term of address for wives) and other women are not presented as they historically were, fighting tooth and nail for their families' interests, but as enlightened outsiders hurt and discouraged by the unhappiness caused them and others by the ambition of their menfolk. Similarly, her *Onnatachi no Chūshingura — inochi moyuru made* (*Women's Chūshingura: Until Death*), a series aired in 1979, takes a hard look at the famous incident from the point of view of a few of the wives and daughters of the magnificent forty-seven: the picture is not pretty. As one daughter (played by Matsubara Chieko), sold into a high-class brothel, observes scornfully to a rich merchant customer who thinks the revenge is the most wonderful thing he has ever heard of, people like him will never know what it cost, and she walks out on him.

Television, like the Shinpa stage, is the domain of women. And television period dramas, like the regular morning soaps (so many of them written by Hashida), reflect women's attitudes about men's values, sacrifice and loyalty to the company and all that: loyalty is due strictly to the family. As the July 1989 elections in Japan demonstrated, women have considerably different expectations, the ones promoted in social hero narratives, than men and they are willing to use their vote (as they have used boycotts) to prove their point. And since Hashida Sugako's enormously successful productions for television, like *Women's Chūshingura* and *Women's Taikōki*, promote these values, these *modern* family and community-oriented values, they too are true period pieces.

The Social Hero: Benevolence and Paternalism

Whom the spirit attacks must become responsible for meeting its demands, if only to prevent further attacks. Strictly speaking, it is improper for those other than the family of the deceased to assume responsibility for funerals or memorial rites. Therefore, when a spirit attacks a community in order to make its identity and needs known, the only way the community can assume religious responsibility permanently is, in effect, to enter into a fictive familial relationship. Eventually, the spirit thus enshrined becomes the tutelary deity (*ujigami*, "clan god") and the members of the community, as worshipers, become its "children" or *ujiko*. Thus, in Japan the community is defined as a family and its head, the father. Lord Takeda Shingen, for example, is always addressed by his vassals as "sire" (*oyakata*) and gang-boss Shimizu Jirōchō is always addressed as, well, "godfather" (*oyabun*).

The benefits to the community of successfully meeting the demands of the angry sprit of the dead are demonstrated in festival skits, the prototypes of comedy, which, in period films, are represented by the festival (*matsuri*) scenes. In some skits, happiness and prosperity are symbolized by husband

and wife pounding rice for ritual rice cakes (*mochi*) at New Year,[52] just as in the last scene of Inagaki Hiroshi's 1930 *Isshin Tasuke* (*Single-minded Tasuke*). In Makino Masahiro's ten-part 1952–1954 series *Jirōchō and the Record of the Three Kingdoms*,[53] the festival is a time when master and servant eat and drink together, lovers have a chance to be together, and the whole community dances in the street. The comedy skit and the festival itself express the harmony of a society under the protection of its tutelary deity, the purified ancestor — or the formerly angry spirit. Indeed the festival, the celebration or worship of the enshrined spirit, has in the period film become the principal image of the community, of society itself.

The identity of the threat to the community is made by means of opposition to or comparison with the festival. Banzuiin Chōbei dies to protect the festival from the violence of totally misguided rival frats of protectors of the people, commoner and samurai alike, in Itō Daisuke's 1951 *Oedo gonin otoko* (*Five Men of Edo*). In Inagaki's 1941 *Festival across the Sea*, bullies threatening the enjoyment of the festival represent the militarism threatening the ordinary people of Japan during the war.[54] In the 1954 *Jirōchō sangokushi dai hachi bu: Kaidō ichi no abarenbō* (*Last of the Wild One*), festival and festival music are contraposed to the horror of combat and murder scenes in Makino Masahiro's description of the death of Mori no Ishimatsu during a festival, "when not even an insect should be killed." Finally, in Imai Tadashi's 1958 *Night Drum*, a samurai family avenge themselves on the drum teacher who seduced the wife: the frantic running, thrashing, and slashing are given counterpoint by the flute music of the Gion Festival, a festival for the pacification of angry spirits. In all cases, the absurdity and pathos of those who live by the sword are underlined by the reminder of common, human values represented by the festival. Even in Kurosawa's 1957 *Seven Samurai*, the outsider status of the surviving samurai is made clear by the fact that they do not, can not, take part in the festival — the music, singing, and work — of the rice-planting that defines the community of men.

Paternalism

It is no accident that the concept of the benevolent and protective ancestral spirits represented by the "old man" (*okina*) of folk religious plays and Nō intersects (or interfaces) with the benevolent lord, master, and magistrate. One should not be surprised, then, to see the social hero portrayed as that virtue incarnate, paternalism (*onjō shugi*), or paternalism itself advanced as the cardinal virtue and highest ideal of Japanese society, past and present.

Paternalism, the idea of providing conditions for the happiness and prosperity of people as for one's children, has both religious and political value which only since the end of the war finds expression as a common expectation of total care and protection in exchange for loyalty and service. During and after the 1950s, the social hero remained popular, no doubt because he affirmed the values of paternalism and family in post-war Japan, coded as "my home-ism," which were meant to displace militarism and imperialism.

Kōdan and Good Government — the Comedic Model

The image of the enshrined god merged with the Confucian models of conduct depicted in Kōdan. Kōdan heroes were celebrated for their diligence in providing good administration as official representatives of the government, the primary expression of humanity (*jin*), according to Confucianists. Often, men famed for economical and political administration were enshrined and worshiped after the Chinese model of deifying culture heroes known as the Sages,[55] the first rulers, who invented human institutions. Sometime around 1900, these paragons of Confucian virtue were incorporated into the new genre of detective novel. Thus, period films feature the social hero as magistrate, detective sergeant, public prosecutor, judge, and jury all rolled into one. Being a samurai, of course, he cannot also be executioner.

Some of these heroes have already been mentioned. The famous judge and magistrate Ōoka Tadasuke (1677–1751) had been canonized in the Kōdan *Ōoka seidan* in the Meiji period long before he became a staple of the period film. For example, beginning in 1928 with *A New Version of the Tales of Ōoka's Administration*, Itō Daisuke made a series of three films based on this popular hero.

Mito Kōmon, Tokugawa Mitsukuni (1628–1700), grandson of Ieyasu, responsible for the historical work *Dainihonshi* (*History of Great Japan*) and for the suppression of committing suicide to follow one's lord (*junshi*), is the star of oodles and oodles of films and tv series. Flip through the tv channels till you find a group of people in tense confrontation on a country road; a traveler will whip out a tobacco case displaying the Tokugawa crest, and everyone will drop to the dust with the appropriate cry, "Ah-haaaah!" A little old man with a white beard will nod and smile benevolently on those he has saved — that's him. (In the old days, he used to whip out the tobacco case himself, just in the nick of time.) He is always on the road, incognito, and, although retired, on inspection to root out injustices (originally, those involving disturbances in great houses).

And, of course, there is Tōyama no Kin-san (Kinshirō), known more formally as Tōyama Saemonnojō Kagemoto (1793–1855), also a city magistrate in Edo. Although he was famous for such mundane administrative achievements as putting in a decent drainage system, he is depicted in popular film as having a flashy tattoo that permits him to travel incognito in the underworld.

Pervasion of Ideals Throughout Society

All samurai were considered to be part of the government, even if they did not have administrative positions, so one should not be surprised to find someone like the idle vassal to the shogun (*hatamoto taikutsu otoko*), Saotome Mondonosuke, who, in an unofficial capacity (he never wears over-trousers, or *hakama*) does what the others do: defend the commoner from evil. The creation of pop-lit writer Sasaki Mizumi, Mondonosuke was played for nearly thirty years by Ichikawa Utaemon (1904–1999), the ideal lord (*tonosama*). He was distinguished by a scar on his forehead, a crazy laugh, and terribly beautiful *kimono* (Utaemon used to walk the ladies' sections of the main department stores looking for materials).[56] This vassal has an income and nothing to do, and so, like Mito Kōmon, he wanders town and country and gets involved in similar situations, protecting the weak and the like.

Additionally, in his most popular role as Kurama Tengu, Arashi Kanjūrō (1903–1980) is the perfect *bushi*: not only does he fight for the restoration of imperial rule, but he picks up stray boys and puts them to work learning to write their letters of the syllabary. Kanjūrō functions something like a model of deportment of the proper Confucian: he may wear paper garments, but his hovel is filled with books. The very way he sits bespeaks the traditional Confucian discipline and courtesy of the ideal samurai.

Samurai have their imitators in the lower classes, members of which see their duty as social justice if not the law. At the bottom of the ladder are the ever-popular low-life thieves Nezumi Kōzō and Benten Kōzō, presented as Robin Hoods of Edo: versions of their stories are countless.

Ordinary respectable commoners are also recognized as sharing the same social ethics. Shiobara Isshin Tasuke (1743–1816), the poor peasant with a horse who became a rich merchant, was made famous nation-wide with the publication of his story by Sanyūtei Enchō in 1885. In film, he has been teamed at least since 1936 with Ōkubo Hikozaemon Tadanori (1560–1639), councilor to the second and third shoguns[57]; as portrayed by Nakamura Kinnosuke,[58] he is a fishmonger with the soul of a samurai (not to be expected of a man of his class, as Livy might have said) and Ōkubo's agent in solving crimes and in solving people's personal problems. Inagaki's 1931 version is much more the common man's version: Tasuke quarrels with his best friend and still tries to help him when he gets into difficulties, despite the fact that his friend will not speak to him. Here Tasuke exemplifies the common man's social values of trust. In this character we see most poignantly the idea that whatever rigid social caste system there might be due to the vagaries of history and custom, a man is a man and is recognized as such even by social superiors if he exemplifies the ideals of his society: he is a loyal retainer, a considerate husband, a responsible boss, and a concerned friend and neighbor.

There was in Tokugawa society a strong concept that historical accident and political necessity demanded a strict hierarchy based on rigid caste distinctions but that all shared a fundamental humanity. Fate might decree one's lot in life, but all shared a basic function in providing good government to society and good regulation of the family, which provided for the welfare and happiness of those for whom one was responsible.[59] Rewards came in the form of worldly benefits, mostly good relations with others, respect, and reputation.

The fact that many of these social heroes are commoners reinforces the sense that status is based on function, that the underlying quality of being human, exhibiting humanity, is expressed by functioning as an active member of society.[60] This humanity as a value acts as a basis for identity and self-esteem. For if a man cannot be a lord or magistrate, he can be a good master, a good father and husband, and a good friend. The ability to shine in the areas of relative status compensates for the lack of absolute status or caste. This is the commoner's code, the way of a man, *otoko no michi*.

Benevolence and Society

All these social heroes defending the general populace against evildoers make the system work because they secure the safety and prosperity — and sometimes the personal happiness — of the people. They are ideals. They represent the best of a society that takes care even of its individuals. They also represent the idea that society is basically good and that evil is an aberration. Such ideals are an implicit criticism of those in power who fall short. Such is the purpose of traditional Japanese narratives supposed to reward the good and punish the wicked.

Whether samurai or commoner, the cardinal virtue to display is the old Confucian virtue of humanity or benevolence (*ren* or, in Japanese, *jin*), necessary to secure the happiness of other people. Who best exemplifies humanity is the best example of a human being. Moreover, it is the recognition of this value that brings people of all castes and classes together; it is what makes Ōkubo Bizen no kami appreciate Isshin Tasuke and what makes Saotome Mondonosuke prefer his commoner friends.

The Breakdown of Barriers between the Castes

The hero as exemplary humanist, as exemplary member of society, as both samurai and commoner, is expressed in a variety of ways in period films.

One is the breakdown of caste differences in terms of association. Saotome Mondonosuke associate with commoners. On TV, samurai and commoner work together to solve crimes. One notices, too, a genial indulgence of what is really freshness or forwardness, as when a very young waitress pouts like a five-year-old at our vassal to the shogun; this intimacy suggests their equal status in their common function in "rewarding good and punishing the evil."

Other ways of minimizing caste or class differences are seen, for instance, in the tendency to over-produce, which is very obvious in color films. Only the basic iconography distinguishes commoner from samurai, for everyone has richly abundant black hair, is perfectly groomed, and lives and works in well-lit, roomy surroundings. In addition, when the samurai, like Ōkubo no kami, is elderly and the commoner, like Tasuke, young, then the suggested rule ordering their relationship is that of parent and child: respect for the aged — or seniority — or that of teacher and student rather than that of lord and vassal.

In the thirties Liberalism films, especially those made by director Inagaki Hiroshi, scenarist Mimura Shintarō, and the actors of the Zenshinza, little enough awe is shown the samurai. In *Journey of a Thousand and One Nights*, the gambler turned day-laborer runs off with a young lord's horse — and, what is more, calls him "leaky drawers."[61] For the most part, there is no interest in climbing up the social ladder — the lord may even leave his castle to live with robbers (as in Takizawa Eisuke's 1937 *Sengoku guntō-den* (*Story of a Bandit Band in the Country at War*, Part One: *Tiger and Wolf*; Part Two: *Advance at Dawn*) — and the focus is on the lives of ordinary people.

Humanism as Heaven

The culmination of the development of the social hero came essentially in the Tokugawa period, when Confucian values were first disseminated throughout Japanese society. They do have precursors in the miracle stories of the saving grace of buddhas and bodhisattvas, who bring help and relief to those suffering in this world. But they are heroes created by the Tokugawa period and its orientation of Confucian, humanist, social values and are Chinese rather than Japanese in origin. But such heroes are a constant assertion of the values and goals of ordinary men and women: law, justice, a decent community to bring up one's children in, friends, family, children, enough to eat, a nice house, some education, and time off and something nice to wear for festivals — people of all classes working together to achieve the same goals. Life is given by reciprocation between the living and the dead, the ancestors and the descendants, parents and children, masters and servants, husbands and wives, the elder and the younger, friends and friends. Period films in this comedy (a play depicting happiness) tradition are not well represented in the West. It is important to realize that the films in this line are very important to the Japanese: if the world of the anti-hero and the tragic hero is hell, then the world of the social hero is heaven.

Tragedy: Sin, Suffering, and Society

In the tragedies of the Tokugawa stage, the hero commits a transgression against society, falls, suffers, and dies; through the story of his suffering, the audience achieves insight into the nature of the world. In this way the play functions as a form of Buddhist sermon analyzing the social and political forces which contributed to or caused the hero's death. The Japanese stage is still a ritual site to which the angry spirit is invited to state its grievances; however, the ritual is meant to demonstrate that the spirit's sufferings were self-induced and that they had catalyzed a chain reaction of suffering to others, especially those near and dear to it. Yes, the world is cruel, but the hero had taken active part in it. That is why the hero had suffered. The Tokugawa stage offers a Buddhist critique of Confucian society, indeed of Confucianism itself: if Confucianism teaches that one can be a full human being only through full participation in society, then Buddhism counters that all human experience is characterized by suffering and that, therefore, participation in human society, Confucian society, can only lead to suffering.

On the other hand, in Tokugawa Japan another response to suffering — real political or social protest — came from Confucianism: a society which does not provide for the happiness of the people is a badly run society and its rulers deserving of an indictment.[62] Even so, the failure of individuals within society was not necessarily the fault of society. The lesson of tragedy, then, is very complex. A close look at Japan's most prominent heroes will make clearer the interplay of religious and philosophical concepts contributing to the idea of Japanese tragedy.

The Akō Ronin[63]

The story of the forty-seven ronin from Akō (now in Hiroshima Prefecture), Japan's most celebrated heroes, is memorialized every December with religious ceremonies, parades, and a spate of television and theater performances. The incident is one of the three great vendettas of Japanese history: on a snowy night in 1703, forty-seven vassals of the late Asano Naganori burst into the mansion of Kira Yoshinaka, master of ceremonies to the Tokugawa house, and took his head to avenge the death of their lord the previous year: Naganori had unsheathed his sword in the palace of the shogun, a crime punishable by death, and had cut Yoshinaka on the forehead. The Asano vassals presented Kira's head to their lord's grave at Sengakuji and then turned themselves in to the government. They were sentenced to commit suicide honorably by disembowelment (*seppuku*).

Within weeks, the vendetta had been staged (and the staging shut down). Later, new versions of the play appeared. The stories of each and every one of the participants were collected and used in lectures by *kōshakushi* (the term at the time for Kōdan lecturers). Scholars argued the incident for a century and a half. The vendetta was raised to new heights of glory in the Meiji period and has since remained a staple narrative in all the oral and stage arts. It is best known in the West through Inagaki Hiroshi's 1962 version, *Chūshingura.*

The Meaning of the Incident

The Akō ronin have come to be regarded as paragons of the virtue, loyalty with a capital "L"; they gave up homes, families, and their own lives to avenge their lord. During and after the Meiji period, this theme of sacrifice, of course, dovetailed nicely with the new all-loyalty-and-filial-piety-belong-to-the-emperor centered nationalism of the modern period in Japan. Yet, it might help to put the story back into its original historical context. It is best considered in the context of the great change in the samurai class that gradually emerged after the establishment of national peace in the early seventeenth century. What was a samurai? The sixteenth century, freelance, professional soldier with blood-smeared sword who fought tooth and nail for land and reputation? Or the eighteenth century, underpaid, nine-to-five bureaucrat loyally and gratefully wielding pen dipped in ink in the service of his lord?

Popular analyses, like Mizoguchi Kenji's 1941 *The 47 Ronin*, see the incident as pitting honesty against corruption, courage against calculation, and loyalty to lord against self-interest. The Tokugawa government is portrayed as, at best, controlling the great lords, and, at worst, hiding personal interest under the cover of punctilious application of the law. The Akō men are represented as typifying the samurai value of loyalty to lord resulting from generations of service on the battlefield. Absolute loyalty to lord, however, developed out of the increasing dependence of samurai on their lords for their stipends and the concomitant sense of gratitude to their lords for their positions. The scene in *Seven Samurai* of Kanbei bowing to the peasants in gratitude for the rice offered him does not exactly represent the medieval samurai who owned his own estate and served his master as it suited him and for as long as it suited him. For an example of this old-fashioned independence, consider Kumagai Hisatora's 1938 *The Abe Clan*, based on a true story: a samurai family revolt against their lord as a result of a series of slights to the family.[64] However, what is really at issue is the tension between two competing definitions of a samurai, both Confucian.

Representing the first position would be Yamaga Sokō (1622–1685), strategist, teacher, and codifier of the modern way of the samurai, later called *bushidō*.[65] Yamaga was the strategy instructor of the lord of Akō from 1652 to 1666, when he was exiled for ten years to Akō on the orders of the shogunate. His offense was attacking the orthodox Neo-Confucian doctrines of Zhu Xi/Chu Hsi (Jp. Shushi, 1130–1200).

Sokō taught that the only full and complete expression of humanity was a *bushi*. Everyone, including farmers and merchants, shared in fundamental moral obligations, those between parent and child (love), elder and younger (seniority), husband and wife (separation of spheres), and friend and friend (trust); however, only the *bushi* was able to exemplify righteousness or duty (*gi*), on which the relationship between lord and vassal was based.[66]

As duty (*gi*) was the distinguishing characteristic of the *bushi*, and as it was expressed in the relationship between lord and vassal, Sokō emphasized its priority in the value system of the period. Therefore, for the Akō ronin (none of whom is known ever to have met Sokō or personally heard his lectures) nothing in the world could be as important as their relationship to their lord, their duty, their status as samurai, which identified them as the only full representatives of humanity in Japanese society, and whose social role justified their existence on this earth. But this interpretation of the five social relationships (the Way) and the resulting sense of priorities was a direct challenge to the Tokugawa government and the rule of law.

The representative of the second definition of a samurai is the man who is supposed to have advised the government as to what to do with the Akō ronin, Ogyū Sorai (1666–1728). In the service of the shogunate, Ogyū defined full humanity as providing government, providing conditions which benefited the people. The fullest expression of humanity, the function of the samurai, was strictly to educate and train oneself for government service, not one's relationship to one's lord. The Way as government was public; the Way as the relationship between lord and vassal was personal. Law had priority over personal relationships.[67]

For the Tokugawa regime, humanity was not defined in terms of personal relationships, but in terms of law. The Akō ronin broke the law to affirm a personal relationship. Therefore, they put themselves outside human society, even against human society. The Akō ronin were permitted the privilege of taking their own lives: society might condole, but it does not necessarily condone.

Commoners and Their "Duty": *Double Suicide*

Tokugawa theater also staged the offences against society of commoners. Let us look at the story about commoners staged by Chikamatsu and filmed by Shinoda Masahiro (b. 1931), the 1969 *Double Suicide.* A shopkeeper, Jihei, loses wife Osan, children, and shop because of his attentions to a prostitute, Koharu. She is going to be redeemed by his hated rival. Jihei's wife and brother have tried, in their own ways, to help. But he can neither keep his business going nor afford Koharu, and she could not effectively withdraw her affections so that he would pay attention to family and business. Unable to stay together, unable to part, they decide to commit suicide together.

Jihei has failed his family (society) and the Koharu hers (she has an elderly mother to support and she is under contract to serve out a term of service in the house of prostitution). Their passion and determination not to allow Koharu's contract to be bought out by the hated rival lead them to reject obligations and to die together. In effect, they put themselves outside society.

The relationship between lovers, as opposed to that of man and wife, was not recognized as one of the five relationships of Confucian society and was thus considered immoral. In the Neo-Confucian system, passion was thought to be the result of being loaded down with *chi,* the material; failure to scrub away this evil through meditation and education meant failure to achieve the Neo-Confucian definition of "humanity." This failure was tantamount to tragedy in rational society and it raised Jihei and Koharu to the level of the powerful spirits of the dead. Like the Akō ronin, they acted against society to affirm a personal relationship; they put themselves outside human society, even against human society.

The Non-human Nature of Feelings

The modern and western audience tend to view the Akō ronin incident and *Double Suicide* as representing a great, popular foment over the questions of the value of the personal over and against the public, the identification of self in terms of personal relationships rather than in terms of public functions, and the right to a private life free from the judgment of public morality. The Akō ronin and the love suicides identified for themselves and others a personal relationship as duty and justified it with their deaths. They established loyalty to lord and lover as the ultimate expression of humanity and an ultimate reality worth dying for. In doing so, they defined society as a world that could not accept the personal or the best. Seen in this light, stagings of the incidents can be seen as protests against society.

Society, on the other hand, well recognized that such strong feelings as passion (*jōnetsu*) and resentment (*iji*) were not "normal," not "human," and, furthermore, dangerous to human society because of the suffering they caused. Indeed, it must be understood that the Tokugawa plays emphasize the suffering caused by the tragic heroes and heroines. Tokugawa society and stage defined the Akō ronin and the love suicides as against society, as outside — and therefore above — the human world. Their values, their deeds — so noble, so lofty, so loyal — defined them in terms of transgressive sacrality, power demonstrated against the community of humans. Breaking the law of the land and breaking up families defined them as anti-society, anti-human. Their persistence in the face of such odds, flying in the face of the shogun himself, flying in the face of loyal, helpful brother and wife, the terrible suffering inflicted on their families and themselves defined them as non-human, divine. And for this reason, they strike such awe and their spirits receive continuous consolation (purification) in the religious observances performed on their behalf and in the sympathetic telling and retelling of their stories.

In Japanese tragedies, families are broken up, daughters and wives sold into prostitution, and children orphaned because of the heroes and heroines of the stories. There is a lesson to be learned. The tragedy can be expressed as a syllogism. If, according to Confucian doctrine, full humanity is to be achieved only through social relationships; and if, according to Buddhist doctrine, humanity is characterized by suffering; then, social relationships, that is, society, are characterized by suffering — are indeed the source of suffering. Certainly, the more one tries to realize the values of one's society, the more likely one is to suffer and cause suffering. This confrontation between Buddhism and Confucianism is the basis for the Japanese concept of tragedy.

Japanese tragedy offers another, parallel syllologism. If, according to Confucianism, human feelings (passions) are anti-social and, if, according to Buddhism and Shintō, human feelings (passions) are divine, then anti-social behavior is the expression of the divine. Here, we see both Confucianism's and Buddhism's view of the angry spirit's position — and it is its side of the story — that its situation was caused by an immoderate level of feeling, whether physical passion or sense of gratitude and loyalty to one's lord.

The problem reflected in Tokugawa stage narratives can be reduced to a discussion of the definitions of what is human and what non-human. "Human" is what contributes to the prosperity and well being of the community of human beings, society. Anything that threatens the community is not "human," is more than or less than human. The period film, in criticizing the present through the analogy with the past, still functions basically as the investigation of the precarious relationship between "human" and "other-than-human," which are represented in terms of human feelings or passions.

Over and over again, the same model prevails for the tragic protagonist. Participation in the divine is defined in terms of strong feelings — passion and resentment. These feelings are neither human, for they result in terrible suffering, nor social, for they pit the protagonists against friends and family, the community. The tragic hero is worshiped as a god not because he does good, but because he is capable of doing such evil. The tragic hero is a reverse image of society's values. Beware of passion in women and resentment in men!

4

Sixteenth Century Japan in Film

Japanese drama follows a long tradition of criticizing the past. One has only to look at fourteenth and fifteenth century Nō plays about *bushi*: in the second half, the ghost of the deceased *bushi* in his true form appears to tell of his resentment at his sad end. In the late seventeenth and eighteenth centuries, plays were put on to memorialize and pacify the dead; to the modern eye, such plays seem merely to capitalize on contemporary scandals. And yet the theater itself preserves vestiges of the religious site to which a spirit was summoned and pacified: the *hanamichi*, or runways leading from a greenroom at the back of the theater to the stage (the route to the ritual site) and the *yagura*, the tower through which the spirits enter the theater or even their seat in the theater. In the early eighteenth century, a twist was added: under the pressure of censorship, the popular theater began setting in the past contemporary scandals in the houses of the upper ranks of the military and nobility. In the modern period, the popular rights movement of the 1880s, under the influence of Victor Hugo (1802–1885),[1] began to promote its stance in period novels. In response to the 1904–1905 Russo-Japanese War, writers like Nakazato Kaizan (1885–1944) began attacking militarism in period novels and plays. By the 1920s, adaptations were being filmed.

In setting a contemporary issue in the past, the problem is to find a suitable parallel. In the Tokugawa period, the eighteenth and nineteenth centuries, the sixteenth century and the circumstances of the founding of the Tokugawa shogunate were still considered sensitive issues. Therefore, parallels were sought in earlier periods: medieval epics like the *Heike monogatari* (*Tale of the Heike*) and the *Taiheiki* (*Chronicle of the Great Peace*), which recount the civil wars and chaos of the twelfth and fourteenth centuries, were scoured for their possibilities, some of which had to be stretched quite a bit. For example, consider the 1701–1703 forty-seven ronin incident: a great domainal lord sentenced to death for drawing his sword in the shogun's palace was avenged by his vassals, who took the head of the man he had attacked but failed to kill. On stage, this scandal was set in the fourteenth century and matched with the tale of Enya (Sasaki) Takasada Hangan, pursued to his death in 1341 by Kō no Moronao (killed in 1353) because he wanted Takasada's wife; in the *jidai-mono* (period piece) *Kanahedon chūshingura* (*The Treasury of Loyal Retainers*),[2] Enya, of course, has to be avenged by his own vassals. As a rule, great liberties were taken with historical details; otherwise, the point of matching the two incidents would have been lost.

On the other hand, the Tokugawa period itself (1603–1868), especially the ten years of instability before the end of the shogunate or *bakumatsu*, was considered a gold mine for the writers of the twentieth century. Indeed, the two most important anti-militarist writers, Nakazato Kaizan and Hasegawa Shin, set their work in the period of the end of the shogunate, or *bakumatsu*. The Tokugawa period worked for the anti-militarists because of the theme of loyalty to lord, the essence of the Japanese military man. The sixteenth century was for the most part ignored.[3]

Japan's sixteenth century marks a wide division between the medieval and early modern periods. It begins, depending on the historian, some time after the ten years of civil war known as the Ōnin War, which petered out in 1477. It ends, depending on the historian, with the reunification of the country and establishment of the military dictatorship, or shogunate, by the Tokugawa family. The official commission from the emperor came in 1603; however, consolidation was not achieved until the defeat of the main rivals of the Tokugawa after two major campaigns in 1615 and the suppression of a major rebellion in 1638. During this period, Japan devolved into some two hundred and fifty smaller and larger independent domains which gradually, in their attempts to increase in size at their neighbors' expense, carried out a large number of experiments in organization and administration as they turned themselves into the most efficient war machines possible. Competition pitted warlord not only against warlord, but also against the armies of the old temple complexes (the remaining vestiges of imperial power), new Buddhist sects, and alliances of local military families and peasants. The sixteenth century is also the so-called "Christian century," because the Portuguese arrived in the 1540s bringing not only the musket but also St. Francis Xavier (1506–1552); he was followed by missionaries of the Jesuit, Franciscan, and Dominican orders.

Considering the narrative possibilities of so many social, religious, and other developments, one would think that the sixteenth century had been well exploited by popular media, especially by film. Nevertheless, only a very few films have ever been set in the sixteenth century, despite what is suggested by their over-representation in the works of Kurosawa Akira. Indeed, the reason may be seen in Kurosawa's period films themselves: they are mainly fictional narratives and two of them were adapted from western works. This suggests that the sixteenth century is not characterized by a single, coherent body of meaning or set of narrative assumptions like those provided by the Tokugawa period — such as the suppression of the individual by a class segregation enforced by violence or dedication to values that are used against the individual. This is important, given the function of the period piece in Japanese dramaturgy, which is to criticize the present in terms of the past. There are no absolute one-to-one correspondences or parallels between the present and the sixteenth century. The sixteenth century, in terms of narrative, is an open system.

Japan has a long history of importing narratives, first from Korea and China and then, in the modern period, from the West. What facilitated importation and naturalization was the success in finding suitable parallels in existing Japanese narratives.[4] For example, one of the themes that cannot be supported by the Tokugawa period is revenge taken against one's own lord. Indeed, the theme that figured prominently in many early period films was that of the lord's betrayal of his own servant or vassal.[5] Yet, so strong was the resistance to the idea of vengeance on one's lord that films on the theme of betrayal by one's lord had to end with the death (real or social) of the victim.[6] The only place to feature revenge against or the killing of one's direct organizational superior was in the yakuza film set in the contemporary 1960s and seventies (see below). Therefore, when translating to a Japanese setting Shakespeare's *Macbeth*, a tale of regicide, murder and guilt in medieval Scotland, Kurosawa had to choose for his setting the first half of the sixteenth century. In this period Japanese historians had long identified a distinctive pattern of vassals overthrowing their overlords, *gekokujo*, or the low overthrowing the high. Thus, by setting *Macbeth* in the sixteenth century in *Kumonosujō* (*Throne of Blood*, 1950), Kurosawa was able to provide the appropriate historical and narratological context for this imported story, one that offers the life and death situations not generally available in the Tokugawa period narratives.

The sixteenth century provided a wide range of famous warlords suitable for the function of Chinese historiography, to provide examples of successful and of failed leadership: Oda Nobunaga, Toyotomi Hideyoshi, Mōri Terumoto, Daté Masamune, Uesugi Kenshin and others. Takeda Shingen (1521–1573) has been the subject of several films.[7] In Kurosawa's 1980 *Shadow Warrior*, for example, even in death he provides a model of leadership for his double, whose mantra becomes "Do not move!" On the other hand, an example of failed leadership is provided by Shingen's son Katsuyori (1546–1582), who does quite the opposite and leads the Takeda army to a disastrous defeat in 1575.

Stories about these same warlords can be used to exemplify Buddhist themes of history, which are most clearly represented in medieval epics.[8] Again, the fate of the Takeda family provides the perfect vehicle for Buddhist themes: the epic's narrative of the lord whose arrogance eventually leads to the destruction of his family, the suffering he himself endures, the suffering he causes others, and the realization of the suffering characterizing the human condition experienced by those who learn of the story. Inagaki Hiroshi's 1969 *Furin kazan* (*Under the Banner of the Samurai*)[9] offers two proud and arrogant men, Shingen and his strategist Yamamoto Kansuke, who sacrifice one and all to their ambitions. This sacrifice is represented by Shingen's concubine and mother of his son Katsuyori, the daughter (called Yū in the film) of Suwa Yorishige, by Shingen's general and Kansuke's friend Itagaki Nobukato, as well as by Kansuke's captain and his spearman Buhei. The film ends with the same scene with which it begins (not counting the prologue): an old farm woman working away at a stone grinder. All those great ambitions have come to naught; nothing has changed, except that Buhei's aged mother has been replaced by Buhei's aged widow.

The suffering caused such farm families lured or drafted into the Takeda project is the focus of Kinoshita Keisuke's 1960 *Fuefukigawa* (*The River Fuefuki*)[10]: one farm family serves the Takeda as foot soldiers for generations until the entire family is destroyed along with Katsuyori in the battle of Tenmokuzan. The last shot of this film, the Takeda banners floating down the river, itself a Buddhist symbol of transience, expresses the futility of the Takeda's goals; a shot of Takeda banners floating down the river also ends Kurosawa's Takeda film, *Shadow Warrior*.

The Japanese government sought to use the story of the sixteenth century warlord to glorify the imperialist project by analogy. Kinugasa Teinosuke's 1941 *Kawanakajima kassen*[11] (*Battle of Kawanakajima*) concerns the fourth of five battles fought at Kawanakajima (1553, 1555, 1557, 1561, and 1564) against his great rival Uesugi Kenshin (1530–1578), who ruled Echigo Province. Kinugasa presents the audience with exciting Eisensteinian shots of lines of horsemen criss-crossing each other and a host of characters willing to fight and die for the Takeda and Uesugi causes, including the peasant foot soldier (a really nice guy — he saves a traveling entertainer from rape at the hands of his own brothers in arms) and the widow of a samurai who begs and receives permission to fight. The nobility of death for the cause is, however, vitiated by the last shot: an overhead view of the carnage in the aftermath of the battle, a shot very much like that ending another epic, one pitting family against lord, Kumagai Hisatora's 1938 adaptation of Mori Ōgai's *Abe ichizoku* (*The Abe Clan*). Such scenes of the bloody aftermath of battle are *de rigueur* in the Japanese epic; they provide the Buddhist lesson of the terrible consequences of war.

The fragmentation and unification of Japan during the sixteenth century is usually thought of as an affair strictly of the military classes, warlords and their loyal vassals. Nevertheless, the competition for survival and power was fought among various social groups: soldiers, peasants, religious institutions, etc. Indeed, an interesting feature of films about the sixteenth century is that so many deal with the non-military classes as those who suffer in the process of the wars of unification and as those who actively resist the warlords responsible for that suffering. These warlords are usually represented by Oda Nobunaga (1534–1582), who unified one-third of Japan before being assassinated by a subordinate, a typical example of "the low overthrow the high." Less often, the villain is Oda's general, Toyotomi Hideyoshi (1536–1598), the peasant turned national hegemon who unified all Japan.

Peasants in the sixteenth century often armed themselves, formed alliances with other villages, and even traveled long distances to fight with co-religionists to defend territory against the depredations of warlords like Nobunaga. Inagaki's 1966 *Abare Goemon* (*Rise against the Sword*) pits peasants against a warlord and even toys with the idea of a romance doomed from the beginning by a very wide gulf in status. Such peasants are also the subject of Kurosawa's 1954 *Seven Samurai*. Kurosawa's own sympathies are clear: the peasants are presented as a selfish, whiny, cowardly — and, let us not forget, murderous — lot until whipped into shape by their officers, a motley crew of defeated and out-of-work soldiers hired to defend the village from bandits, who are defeated and out-of-work samurai much like themselves. (Truly, this is the movie that the wartime government should have made!) However, the words spoken at the end of the film by Kanbei, the grizzled old soldier who is their leader, contain the true lesson of the sixteenth century: the peasants were the winners, not the samurai. The peasantry emerged from the frays of the sixteenth century with village autonomy and various taxes commuted to a single tax in rice; the samurai found themselves removed from the land,[12] forced into samurai ghettoes in the castle towns, and totally dependent on their lords for a salary paid in rice, which steadily lost value throughout the Tokugawa period.[13]

Mizoguchi Kenji's 1953 *Ugetsu monogatari* (*Ugetsu*) is set in the historical context of the seemingly paradoxical increase in trade alongside the increase in violence in sixteenth century Japan. A farming family with a sideline in pottery find themselves both threatened by and profiting from the wars waged by Oda Nobunaga. Their village is attacked, the food confiscated, the men marched off, and the women raped. Even the heroine is killed by starving soldiers on the run. The hero, however, makes it to the big town that serves as the headquarters of one of Oda's generals, sells his pottery at surprisingly high prices, and even finds the woman of his dreams (yes, she is a ghost, an illusion).

***Ugetsu monogatari* (*Ugetsu*, 1953), directed by Mizoguchi Kenji. The peasant-potter Genjūrō (Mori Masayuki) first encounters the lady Wakasa (Kyō Machiko) and her old nurse Ukon (Mōri Kikue) in the market of a castle town. This film is set against the backdrop of sixteenth century Japan, which offered unimaginable opportunities both mercantile and military: Genjūrō makes a small fortune selling pottery; his brother-in-law Tōbei makes off with his share to buy the armor and weapon needed to join the army and seek his fortune. However, this historical setting is used to comment on the Japanese defeat in a much more recent war. Genjūrō marries Wakasa; however, his sojourn with the dead, an illusion of pleasure and happiness, comes at the price of his wife's death. Tōbei receives an unmerited commission as an officer and is rewarded, beyond his horse and helmet, by the sight of his wife dunning a "john" for her money. The lesson is that all who come in contact with war will suffer (photograph courtesy of the Kawakita Memorial Film Institute).**

His partner runs off with his share of the money to buy armor and undeservedly makes his name as a soldier, only to enter a brothel and find his own wife there. The lesson learned is that those who participate in or profit by war will only suffer in the end and lose everything of value. Again, the plot is possible only because the sixteenth century is characterized not only by military exploits and social advancement through meritorious performance in the field but also by rapid urbanization, great fortunes brought about by trade, and new developments in the arts.

An important example of these last three characteristics is Sen no Rikyū (1522–1591), a tea ceremony expert born into the merchant community of

Sakai. Sakai was a port town on the Inland Sea that gained in importance in the fifteenth century. Very much like Venice, Sakai was independent of the rule of any warlord or temple and was governed by a council of thirty-six (later ten) great merchants of the city (*egōshū*). Its wealth was based first on the trade with Ming China and later on its position as a leading supplier of armaments to warlords. Through Rikyū, and tea men like him, the tea ceremony passed from the wealthy merchants to the warlords: the tea ceremony had a double function of conferring cultural cachet and providing warlords with rare objects which could be conferred as rewards instead of land. Rikyū served both Oda Nobunaga and Toyotomi Hideyoshi as a political negotiator and a connection with the wealthy merchants of Sakai. In 1591, Hideyoshi demanded Rikyū commit suicide: the reason was not clear. The 1960 and 1978 film versions of *Ogin-sama* (*Love under the Crucifix* and *Love and Faith*),[14] and the two 1989 releases, *Sen no Rikyū* (*Death of a Tea Master*)[15] and *Rikyū*[16] repeat arguments previously made by historians: Hideyoshi was angry both at Rikyū's daughter's refusal to become his concubine (she was in love with a Christian warlord) and at Rikyū himself for opposing Hideyoshi's plan to invade Korea and China. Moreover, the Zen temple Daitokuji had in gratitude for a donation placed a statue of Rikyū in the second story of its entrance gate (under which Hideyoshi would have to pass). Other reasons given include the incompatibility of the tea styles of Rikyū and Hideyoshi (the rustic and refined as opposed to the rich and colorful) and the incompatibility of art and politics. All the reasons given make a hero of Rikyū and a villain of Hideyoshi. However, they have much more to do with modern concerns than with those of the period (which is why they are true period pieces): the real story is that Rikyū was apparently in the way of an ambitious vassal, Ishida Mitsunari, among other things strictly political in nature.[17]

One of the most interesting developments in films about the sixteenth century is the expression of resistance to the warlords' goal of unification, the ninja film. The ninja are commoners trained to serve as spies and assassins. Ninja are more properly called *shinobi no mono* (men who practice the hidden arts).[18] Prequels and sequels take us all the way from the time of Takeda Shingen to the Shimabara Rebellion of 1637–38 and beyond. From Yamamoto Satsuo's 1962 *Shinobi no mono* (*Band of Assassins*, popularly referred to as *Ninja I*) to Shinoda Masahiro's 1999 *Fukuro no shiro* (*Owls' Castle*), resistance to unification is represented by ninja who have dedicated themselves to fighting Oda Nobunaga or Toyotomi Hideyoshi in order to avenge the deaths of family and friends caused by them. With their plots and subplots, conflations of historical characters (the hero of *Band of Assassins* is Ishikawa Goemon, a thief boiled alive in Kyoto in 1594 after breaking into Hideyoshi's palace) and capricious handling of the details of history, these films, like their predecessors in popular theater and "comics" going back to the late eighteenth century, are more about entertainment than history. Nevertheless, their plots depend very much on a setting of violence, autocratic rule, and the possibility (but not the guarantee) of resistance provided by the sixteenth century.

In the 1960s, the ninja films prefigured the yakuza film in providing a way to destroy the lord and father, the focus of militarism, without destroying oneself. Consider a film set in the Tokugawa period, the 1962 *Harakiri* of Kobayashi Masaki: an impoverished old soldier comes to the headquarters of a close vassal of the Tokugawa to avenge the death of his son-in-law, whom they had forced to commit suicide with bamboo swords. In the end, however, he has to face the fact that his son-in-law would not have tried to extort money from the house had he himself not been so committed to the samurai code that he would not sell his own swords to buy medicine for his daughter and grandchild, both of whom subsequently died. The old soldier would have to destroy himself in order to destroy the system that had destroyed his family. The yakuza film, on the other hand, offers an alternative to a description of the cruelties and betrayals perpetrated by lords on their vassals: yakuza can fight back.[19] Probably the best example of this is that of the yakuza (played by Tsuruta Kōji) tricked into killing his best friend and his bloody vengeance on his boss in Yamashita Kōsoku's 1968 *Bakuchiuchi: sōchō tobaku* (*The Gambler: The Game to Be Chairman*).[20]

Films set in the grey zone overlapping the end of the Warring States period of the sixteenth century and the beginning of the Tokugawa period have been used to extol social mobility and success through dedication to a vocation, as does Inagaki Hiroshi's 1954–56 *Samurai* trilogy[21] on the life of the famed swordsman, Miyamoto Musashi (1584?–1645): he is presented as a peasant boy who makes good with the sword — with emphasis on the cost and the emptiness of success by killing. Like most of the films set (at least partially) in the sixteenth century, *Samurai* provides an exciting cavalry charge (with the obligatory scene of the carnage left in the aftermath); indeed, the film set in the sixteenth century gave directors the opportunity to use horses *en masse* and to shoot exciting charges and attack scenes of the American Civil War films and Westerns that had so excited the young Japanese directors of the 1920s.

5

The Yakuza[1] Film

Introduction and Overview

Japanese cinema in the 1960s saw the rise and disappearance of a new genre. In America it is popularly referred to as the yakuza film; yakuza, or "good-for-nothings" (eight-nine-three was a useless hand in cards), were in the past members of smaller and larger gangs that offered and controlled gambling (and other — legal — businesses)[2] in specific areas along major and minor highways; in the modern period they include members of organized crime syndicates involved in a range of activities from prostitution to squashing strikes. There are indeed yakuza films, but their protagonists are usually the punks, petty thieves, and professional criminals of the post-war period (in the tradition of the post-war gang film) and the bulk of these films were made in the 1970s and later.

However, the films I am speaking of are in Japan called more specifically chivalry films (*kyōkaku eiga, ninkyō eiga*). The protagonists of these films may indeed be professional gamblers or they may be ordinary workers, sometimes carpenters, sometimes members of the local volunteer fire brigade. Some of them go to jail for getting involved in killings in fights defending turf. The setting is the traditional working-class neighborhood in a big city; the time is the modern period, the Meiji, Taishō and early Shōwa periods. Modernization, with its rampant capitalism, militarism, and colonialism, is what the protagonists are up against.

The chivalry film has a complicated genealogy: the problem is how to get from the historical thief/outlaw/gangster/boss of the Tokugawa period (1603–1867) to the shady but romantic loners who epitomize the heroes of the chivalry film of the 1960s. Just as one has to follow the marriages, births (legal and illegitimate), adoptions, even the education and profession to understand the history of any one family, so we have to keep track of various factors in the development of the chivalry film: the historical character serving as the vehicle, the crucial point at which his story is made to take on the form that is now recognizable, and the principal performers of the story, whether writer, director or actor.

The end result shows up in the 1960s as three genres of film working independently to protest the betrayal and abuse of the ordinary people by their rulers. The story of the thief Ishikawa Goemon, boiled in oil for invading the palace of Toyotomi Hideyoshi, leads fairly directly to the *Shinobi no mono* (*Ninja*) series, which is set in the sixteenth and early seventeenth centuries, the period of unification. The story of Kunisada Chūji, a thug and gambling boss with a soft spot for the starving peasants of the 1830s and forties, became a premier vehicle of the tendency films (*keikō eiga*) of the 1930s, which reappeared as the 1960s period films about the cruelty of *bushidō*, the martial code (such as Imai Tadashi's 1963 *Cruel Tales of Bushido* and Kobayashi Masaki's 1962 *Harakiri* and 1967 *Samurai Rebellion*).

The most complicated line of development is presented by the stories connected with Shimizu no Jirōchō, who lived during both the Tokugawa and the Meiji periods. Although he controlled the gambling along the highway between the shogunal and imperial capitals, Edo and Miyako/Kyōto, and the dockworkers of the port of Shimizu as well, he was pardoned by the new government and became an honored city father. Although most of the stories about him are set in the Tokugawa period, the stories themselves promote the ideals which bind the modern nation state: martial masculinity (characteristic of a society with a conscript army) and obligation to one's "boss" and others from whom one receives favors (paternalism, epitomized by the father of the nation, and fraternity — the attractive presentation of military life). The ideology of militarism and obedience in the Jirōchō stories since the wars with China (1894–95) and Russia (1904–1905) was countered by Hasegawa Shin's *matatabi-mono*, which condemn militarism and the demand to kill in exchange for a meal and a place to stay; the genre was initiated using as its vehicle a gambler who figures briefly the Jirōchō cycle, Kutsukake no Tokijirō.

Jirōchō's position straddling two vastly different historical periods made it possible for stories of the chivalrous commoner to jump from the Tokugawa period to the modern period. The first and most popular example was provided by Ozaki Shirō's enormously successful and enormously long *Bildungsroman* begun in the 1930s, *Jinsei gekijō* (*Theater of Life*). The 1963 and 1964 versions of the story were as or even more successful; their two stars, Tsuruta Kōji (1924–1987) and Takakura Ken (b. 1931), brought the films' romanticism and appeal to the ideals of the past along with the grit of contemporary gang films to the chivalry film and became the genre's most famous, most popular, and most representative actors. They starred in the first chivalry film series to be launched, *Nihon kyōkaku den* (*Tales of Chivalry in Japan*;

eight films 1965–69), directed by Makino Masahiro, the master *non pareil* since the twenties of the massed fight scene. Makino, because it was he who made the transition from the most celebrated film adaptations of Jirōchō's story to the first of the chivalry films series, was the leader in the development of the chivalry film as a new genre and established its form. These chivalry films, like the 1968 *Bakuchi-uchi: sōchō tobaku* (*Gambling: The Game to be Chairman*),[3] and the ninja films were pitted against the "cruelty of *bushidō*" films because the hero, the commoner, was able to take revenge on his superiors (and live to tell the tale) whereas the samurai was not.

Ishikawa Goemon

The popular and peculiar fusion of criminality and virtue that makes up the hero of what the Japanese call the chivalry film (*ninkyō eiga, kyōkaku eiga*) goes back to the mid-Tokugawa period. We begin, however, in 1594, when ten thieves, along with one other, were boiled alive in the capital.[4] Not until 1642 is mention made of a name: the *Toyotomi Hideyoshi fu* (*Sequence [of events in the life] of Toyotomi Hideyoshi*) reports that Ishikawa Goemon, along with his mother and twenty-seven others, had been arrested for his crimes by Toyotomi Hideyoshi's chief magistrate (*shōshidai*) of Kyōto and killed at a site along the Kamo River at Sanjō Avenue.[5] In his commentary on an entry in the 1615 *Relacíon del reino del Nippon* by Bernardino de Avila Girón,[6] the Jesuit Pedro de Morejón (1562–1634?), vice-superior of the Japan mission, noted that the name of the chief of the thieves executed was "ixicava goyemon."[7] Bunraku and Kabuki plays abounded after about 1700. One of the earliest Kabuki plays about him, *Ishikawa Goemon*, was first staged in Osaka in 1698.[8] However, the more popular play, *Sanmon gosan no kiri* (*The Temple Gate and the Paulownia Crest*),[9] written by Namiki Gohei I, was first staged in 1778 in Osaka: Goemon is presented as the adoptive son of Takechi Mitsuhide, a cover for Akechi Mitsuhide (1526–1582), who assassinated Oda Nobunaga and was in turn killed by peasants after his defeat by Toyotomi Hideyoshi. The play, then, presents him as obliged to kill Mashiba (Hashiba was one of Hideyoshi's previous names), who had killed both his father and his adoptive father. Thus, he is presented as virtuous in his filial piety. This lead to the story that Goemon, who had trained as a ninja, sneaked into Hideyoshi's bedchamber in Fushimi Castle to assassinate him, woke Hideyoshi, and was caught and executed. This story comes from *Ehon Taikōki* (*The Picture Book of the Taikō*; 1797–1802) of Okuda Gyokuzan (1737–1812).

By the early twentieth century, Goemon's identity as a ninja was a given: in the first publication of the Tachikawa Bunko series, *Sarutobi Sasuke,*[10] written by Sekka Sanjin and published in 1913, the catalyst of the ninja boom and the first text to present the ninja as heroes, Goemon appears as the ninja rival to the completely fictional hero: Sarutobi Sasuke supports the Toyotomi side, a regional, Osaka theme carried by the Tachikawa series.[11]

Between 1912 and 1951, twelve films at least were made about Ishikawa Goemon. In 1962, *Shinobi no mono* (*Ninja 1*) gave new life to the character and kicked off a new ninja boom. Murayama Tomoyoshi (1901–1977), on whose novel in five volumes the first three of the eight films were based, had the best possible credentials from the leftist movements in art and theater going back to the 1920s. The director of the first, Yamamoto Satsuo (1910–1983) had leftist credentials equally impressive, although his concentrations were in film and theater. What came out of this film series, an exemplar of the use of *mitate*, matching past and (recent if not immediate) present, was a fine, leftist denunciation of the imperialist project, with the ninja representing the victims: the civilians and the low-level soldiers used, abused, and (considering the complicated plots) confused by their masters, represented by Oda Nobunaga (who massacres them), Toyotomi Hideyoshi, and Tokugawa Ieyasu, the "unifiers" of Japan. What makes the ninja film interesting compared with the period films of the same time is that ninja are compelled to take vengeance for personal reasons: for example, in *Ninja 2*,[12] Goemon kills Nobunaga to avenge his village and friends and tries to kill Hideyoshi for the deaths of his wife and contacts in the peasant alliance under the banner of the True Pure Land, the Ikkō-shū.[13] The *Shinobi no mono* series compares the losers of the unification process of the late sixteenth and early seventeenth centuries with those of the war against China of the 1930s and 1940s. Ninja films, as *shuraba*, with their focus on bloody killings, are pictures of the hell of the unification of Japan in the late sixteenth and early seventeenth centuries.

Kunisada Chūji

The second great outlaw of the Tokugawa period was Kunisada Chūji (1810–1850), whose real name was Nagaoka Chūjirō. Born into a farming family in what is now Gunma Prefecture, he left home and made a name for himself as a gambling boss, murderer, and all-round thug: he smashed the official barriers at several points in both Kōzuke and Nagano Provinces. Between 1842 and 1850 he dropped out of sight but was finally arrested and executed in 1850.[14]

Chūji's success coincided with the Tenpō era (1830–1844) and the general social breakdown resulting from the waning authority of the Tokugawa government and famine in the area. He got a reputation as a philanthropist and savior of the starving peasants when the local officials were doing nothing;

the Tokugawa supervisor or representative (*daikan*) of the area, Hagura Mochihisa[15] (1790–1862), wrote in his *Sekijōroku* (*Chronicle of Akagi*), "The locals say that there are bandits in the mountains. One of them, called Chūji, has formed a gang of some several tens; since last winter he has often given relief to the poor and orphans."[16] The reputation was strong enough for a Confucian scholar of the Isezaki domain, Arai Jakuri, to carve on his grave marker the characters for "a character from the Suikoden" (*Suikoden no jinbutsu*).[17]

The *Suikoden* is the fourteenth century *Shuihu Zhuan* (*The Water Margins*), the story of 108 outlaws of the Song period who band together to fight corrupt officials and save poor peasants. Part of it was edited to be read as Japanese and published in 1728; from 1757 to 1790 it was published in whole as *Tsūzoku chūgi suikoden* (*The Faithful and Just Men of the Water Margin for Everyman*)—with illustrations.[18] It created a boom of its own. The *Yamato kotoba suikoden* (*The Tales of the Water Margin in Japanese Words*) was staged in Osaka in 1776.[19] Stories about Japanese modeled on them began to appear in the titles of Kōdan and novels and illustration books about contemporary outlaws or dropouts of one sort or the other—especially toward the end of the Tokugawa period and into the Meiji period: *Tenpō suikoden* (1820–1834?) of 1844, *Kaiei suikoden* (1850–1854), *Shunketsu shintō suikoden* (1828–1882), *Keisei suikoden* (*The Beauties of the Water Margin*, by Kyokutei Bakin; 1825–1835), *Kinsei suikoden* (*Modern Tales of the Water Wargin*; 1861), and *Suikoden jigoku mawari* (*Tales of Wandering through the Hell of the Water Margin*; 1864).[20] However, it was a series of woodblock prints that fired the craze, Utagawa Kuniyoshi's c. 1827 illustrations of the original Japanese edition. Other illustration series included the *Tsūzoku suikoden goketsu hyakuhachinin no hitori—Rorihakucho Chōjun* (1820s) of Utagawa Kuniyoshi and the *Tosei suikoden* (1851) and *Kinsei suikoden* (1861) of Kunisada Toyokuni III.[21] Kunisada Chūji is featured in the *Kaei* (1850–1854) *suikoden* and the 1861 *Kinsei suikoden*.[22]

Chūji, too, by the 1860s, was being memorialized in illustrated prints, Kōdan, and *jitsuroku* ("true stories"). Ichikawa Danjūrō IX was portrayed by Utagawa Toyokuni III in his 1862 role as "Kumisada Jūji" (with a short description of the hero written by Kanagaki Robun),[23] and in 1884 Onoe Kikugorō played Chūji at the Ichimura Theater and a series of prints of him in the role was published.[24]

Kabuki and *Shiranami-mono*

In Kabuki, stories about outlaws came under the rubric of *kizewa-mono*. They were first developed by Tsuruya Nanboku IV (1755–1829), who wrote the famous *Tōkaidō Yotsuya Ghost Story*, first performed in 1825.[25]

The real exponent of the genre was Nanboku's disciple Kawatake Moku'ami (1816–1893), who wrote Kabuki plays called "white-wave" (*shiranami*) stories about thieves and other low-lifes, several of which were based on the works of Kōdan specialist Shōrin Hakuen II (1834–1905).[26] What is interesting about these stories is the rubric *shiranami*: this is another clue to the Tokugawa-period identification of contemporary thieves with Chinese bandits, this time heroes of the Latter Han dynasty of China (A.D. 206–220).

The term *shiranami* (*beibo/baibo*) first appears in one of the four great histories of China, the 445 *Houhanshu* (*History of the Latter Han Dynasty*) by Fan Ye. The word *shiranami* is the Japanese reading of the Chinese characters for "White Wave," the name of a mountain valley, where, according to the *History of the Latter Han Dynasty*,[27] "bandits" (this is, after all, a government-sponsored text) had established a base. The word *shiranami* entered the Japanese vocabulary as a name for robbers and thieves long before it became the name for a category of Kabuki plays and Kōdan stories.

Chūji in the Modern Period

In the Meiji era (1868–1912), print media were the dominant factor in the dissemination of Chūji's story, as they were with all Kōdan and Rakugo: with the invention of shorthand in 1881, publication of edited transcriptions of raconteurs' performances was initiated in 1884 with that of Sanyūtei Enchō's *Kaidan bōtan dōro* (*The Peony Lantern Ghost Story*), while serialization in newspapers began in 1886 with that of Enchō's *Matsu no misao bijin no ikiume* (*Buried Alive: The Chaste Beauty of the Pines*) in the *Yamato shinbun*.[28] Chūji continued to be a fixture of modern popular narrative, oral and printed.

He made it to the cinema, too. Between 1909 and 1927, of the 964 films made by the first Japanese movie star Onoe Matsunosuke, at least four were titled *Kunisada Chūji*.[29] Since 1911, according to the Japanese Movie Database, literally dozens of versions have been made. In 1919, the Shinkokugeki (New National Theater) first staged the perennial favorite by Yukitomo Rifu, *Kunisada Chūji*, and Makino Shōzō filmed it first in 1922 and again in 1925 with the company headed by Sawada Shōjirō himself.[30] An actor in Shōjirō's second company, who later filled in for him on stage when he died, Ōkōchi Denjirō starred in the stunning, three-part *A Diary of Chūji's Travels* that Itō Daisuke released in 1927 and earned him the first and fourth places on the Kinema Jumpō Best Ten list (and the eighth with yet another film).[31]

Not all the films made about Chūji end with his death; some manage to end on a hopeful if not a high note. Yamanaka Sadao's 1935 *Kunisada Chūji*, scripted by Mimura Shintarō, follows the characters staying at an inn where Chūji is also staying: Chūji kills a man who attacks him and secretly helps a farmer who has to sell his daughter into prostitution.[32] Again, in the 1960 *Kunisada Chūji* (*The Gambling Samurai* [sic])[33] ends with Chūji (Mifune Toshirō), with little Kantarō on his back, cutting his way down Mount Akagi and escaping the police.

Shimizu no Jirōchō (1820–1893)

Chūji was rivaled in fame only by Shimizu no Jirōchō (his real name was Yamamoto Chōgorō), who controlled the gambling along the Tōkaidō, the main highway between the shogunal capital of Edo, now Tokyo, and the imperial capital, now Kyoto. Unlike Chūji, however, Jirōchō survived the Restoration of 1868 to become an honest man and pillar of the community. In 1868, the imperial forces captured the *Kanrin Maru*, one of eight modern warships of the shogunate under way to northern Japan for a last-ditch stand against the imperial forces; damaged in a typhoon, she had put into Shimizu.[34] Although the burial of the enemies of the imperial court had been forbidden, Jirōchō had disobeyed, citing reasons of religion and hygiene.[35] This is when he first came to the notice of shogunal official Yamaoka Tesshū (1836–1888),[36] who later served as the local administrator. Jirōchō helped him in the development of the area. Not only did he establish the first English language school in Shimizu but also, because of his control of the docks, was entrusted with the behind-the-scenes management of the landing of President Ulysses S. Grant in 1877.

It was also Tesshū who persuaded Chūji to take in his twenty-five year old student, Amada Gorō (1854–1904), later the poet and Rinzai monk Guan.[37] It was this Gorō who shortly after, in 1879, wrote the first record of Jirōchō's life, *Tōkai yūkyō den* (*Tales of a Chivalrous Person of the Eastern Seaboard*), published in 1884. (Jirōchō could not read it; nevertheless, he did buy two hundred copies and gave them away to friends and visitors.)[38]

It was, however, eagerly read by the entertainment world, which had carried a variety of stories about Jirōchō, and became the basis of the Kōdan *Jirōchō den* (*Tales of Jirōchō*) of Kanda Hakuzan III (1872–1932)[39] and then of the Naniwa-*bushi* version of Hirosawa Torazō II (1899–1964). Although Hakuzan is given credit for the original stories of six silent films between 1912 and 1930,[40] it was Torazō who made the most of cinema. He performed the Naniwa-bushi voice-over narration for the 1936 *Chūji and Oman*,[41] and two others; in 1938 he began appearing in feature films. He appeared in thirty-eight through 1957.[42]

The fourth was a vehicle for Kataoka Chiezō, the 1939 *Shimizu minato* (*Harbor of Shimizu*), directed by Makino Masahiro.[43] The film was yet another contribution to the vast Shimizu Jirōchō cycle. Torazō, the most famous performer in any medium of the Shimizu Jirōchō cycle, portrayed a character called Torazō (different Chinese characters). No doubt he performed some Naniwa-*bushi* in his role (the film is no longer extant). However, the follow-up 1940 *Zoku Shimizu minato* (*Harbor of Shimizu Continued*) is a dream sequence in which Torazō plays a very interesting role: the character played by Kataoka Chiezō puts on a record of Torazō's version of the story of Mori no Ishimatsu's trip to the shrine of Konpira to dedicate Jirōchō's sword and then lies down on a couch to listen; he then suddenly wakes up in the character of Ishimatsu in that very story. Torazō (the record) continues to sing the voice-over narrative; he also appears as a character met on shipboard who chants to Ishimatsu a bit of his own story just before he goes off to his last fight. The ability to play with sound and time was made possible by the fact that the audience knew the characters and the actors so well that they could appreciate a very radical and entertaining fusion of past and present.

Torazō's next significant experience with Makino was a masterpiece, the 1952–1954 nine-part adaptation of Murakami Genzō's *Shimizu Jirōchō sangokushi* (*Shimizu Jirōchō and the Record of the Three Kingdoms*). He appeared in the first four parts. Hisaya Morishige, in his role as Mori no Ishimatsu in parts two through eight, favored the audience with a little of his own style of Naniwa-*bushi*, Morishige-*bushi*, in the eighth, the 1954 *Kaidō ichi no abarenbō* (*Last of the Wild One*).

Jinsei Gekijō

Jinsei gekijō (*Theater of Life*), written by Ozaki Shirō (1898–1964) and serialized from 1934 in the *Miyako shinbun* and other newspapers, was an enormously successful best-seller. The plot (and subplots) revolve around a young man, son of an upstanding boss who fails and eventually commits suicide; the son goes to university to prepare for a legitimate career as a writer. His father's former follower, Kiratsune, who has been as far afield as Shanghai, returns to watch over the boy; he takes in a fellow traveler, Hishakaku, who has killed a higher-up in a fight and is on the lam. Hishakaku goes to prison, his girlfriend falls in love with another man (...but I shall not reveal the resolution!).

The first film version of the novel, directed by Uchida Tomu in 1936 (he did not direct the second part, *Zankyaku hen* (*The Volume on the Last of Chivalry*; 1938), was produced by Nikkatsu; the first film Hishakaku was Kataoka Chiezō (with Yamamoto Reizaburō as Kiratsune). Chiezō was also the second (Tsukigata Ryūnosuke was Kiratsune) in Tōei's 1952–53 two-part version directed by (and starring) Saburi Shin.[44] A 1958 version from Tōhō featured Morishige Hisaya (with "Jirōchō" credentials) as Kiratsune and

Jinsei gekijō: Zankyaku hen (*Theater of Life: The Last of Chivalry*, 1938), directed by Chiba Yasuki. Hishakaku (Kataoka Chiezō) is right and Kiratsune (Yamamoto Reizaburō, fully dressed) is second from the left. Ozaki Shirō's blockbuster novel (part one, directed by Uchida Tomu) came to the screen first in 1936. This second part focuses on the story of Hishakaku, in trouble with the law, who is advised by his protector Kiratsune to give himself in. While he is in prison, his girlfriend, Otoyo (Hanayagi Kogiku), falls in love with another man. This story, only part of the book, was about the intricate relations and obligations obtaining among contemporary gangs. Remakes, especially those with Tsuruta Kōji and Takakura Ken, composed the core of the *ninkyō eiga* (chivalry films) of the 1960s (photograph courtesy of Matsuda Film Productions).

Mifune Toshirō, who had played gangsters for Kurosawa Akira, as Hishakaku.[45] Tōei's next version (nobody you know) was released in 1961.

Tōei's next foray in 1963 touched off the chivalry film boom in conjunction with a series of *matatabi-mono* films starring young screen idols Ichikawa Raizō and Nakamura Kinnosuke and the success of a range of gang films featuring Tsuruta Kōji and Takakura Ken. The team of Tsuruta and Takakura, playing Hishakaku and his rival in love Miyagawa respectively (with Tsukigata Ryūnosuke reprising his role as Kiratsune), starred in four films which focused on Hishakaku's story: *Jinsei gekijō: Hishakaku* and *Jinsei gekijō: Zoku Hishakaku* in 1963, in 1964 *Jinsei gekijō: Shin Hishakaku* (with Shimura Takashi as Kiratsune) and in 1968 *Jinsei gekijō: Hishakaku to Kiratsune* (Tatsumi Ryūtarō in the role).

Other studios produced versions of *Jinsei gekijō* and chivalry films. Nevertheless, *Jinsei gekijō*, Tsuruta and Takakura — indeed the chivalry film genre — were inextricably linked with Tōei Studios.

Makino Masahiro

Tōei Studios were established in 1951 by Kataoka, along with Ichikawa Utaemon (famed as the shogun's idle vassal). One of their most important recruits was Makino Masahiro, who moved there in 1957. Throughout the late fifties and sixties, Makino worked at remakes of old favorites (including his own and spin-off "Jirōchō" films); the master was entrusted with breaking in a new generation of stars (Nakamura [Yorozuya] Kinnosuke, Ōgawa Higashi, Azuma Chiyonosuke, Ōtomo Ryūnosuke, Kitaōji Kinya [son of Ichikawa Utaemon], Takakura Ken, Tsuruta Kōji, and Fuji Junko), who were sometimes backed up by older stars. Although never a specialist in the *matatabimono* (he had, however, made a few), he came to specialize in this world of those who are forced to do evil in order to protect good. In addition to several independent "Jirōchō" films was a 1960–1962 three-part *Wakaki hi no Jirōchō* (*The Early Days of Jirōchō*), starring Kinnosuke, and in 1963–65 a four-part remake of *Jirōchō sangoku shi*, starring Tsuruta Kōji. Because of the success of his 1964 *Nihon kyōkaku den* (*Tales of Chivalry in Japan*), Tōei put him together with Tsuruta Kōji (instead of Kinnosuke) and Takakura Ken, who had made a hit with their two remakes of *Jinsei gekijō* in 1963 and 1964, for a series of more gang films: between 1964 and 1969 he directed eight more *Tales of Chivalry in Japan*, among many other films in *ninkyō* series. Makino was kept busy in this genre throughout the sixties because of his great experience and specialization in staging mass fight scenes, needed in stories about bosses such as Shimizu Jirōchō, who, with their many loyal followers, are compelled — depending on the situation — either to defend territory or to avenge wrongs. Such stories offered many roles for both old stars and new actors and kept multi-generational audiences in the theaters.

Thus, Makino, whose career went back to the earliest days of Japanese cinema, moved the ethical outsiders of *Street of Masterless Samurai* out of the Tokugawa period and into the era of Japan's surge toward militarism, capitalism, and colonialism, whose representatives and henchmen are resisted by traditional, local communities defended by the traditional, local organizations of craftsmen (carpenters or construction workers) and volunteer firemen. Makino was a pivotal agent in the development of the yakuza film as a complement to the period film as a vehicle for political and social protest.

Caught in the Net of Obligations

The place is Tokyo; the time, the 1920s and early 1930s.[46] The world of the gambler is divided into two camps: that of the good, represented by gamblers who restrict themselves to gambling, and the bad, who are involved in a myriad of crimes and sometimes linked to big business (polluting factories),[47] corrupt politicians, and colonialism. Good guys wear Japanese clothes; bad guys, western. In a series like *Nihon kyōkaku den* (*Tales of Chivalry in Japan*) or *Jinsei gekijō*, the hero is firmly in the good camp, trying to uphold the traditional commoner's values of *jingi* (humanity and righteousness)[48] and, like the (fictional) *kyōkaku* of the past, protect the helpless against the bully. After patient and ultimately futile attempts at negotiation and pacification with the bad gang, for love, honor, and community, the hero and one or more colleagues go off to fight the villains.

In other films, the line between the good and the bad is not so clear; the hero is pitted against his own gang. In Yamashita Kōsaku's 1968 *Bakuchi-uchi: sōchō tobaku* (*Gambling: The Game to Be Chairman*), for example, a loyal gang member, and true to the code, finds in the end that he has been lied to, betrayed, and tricked into killing even his friend. He finally goes after his boss and kills him in a gruesome and soul-satisfying slice 'em up; in response to the man's pleas for mercy he has nothing to say but, "What do I know about taking the high road [*ninkyō-dō*, the way of chivalry]? I'm just a common butcher!"

These films of the sixties are distinguished by their rhetorical form and function: they are in the tradition of the *matatabi-mono* of Hasegawa Shin. The heroes of the *matatabi-mono* are saved, one way or another, by their choice of human values — hearth and home, women and children — over those of the itinerant and fascist fraternity of the gambler. Kutsukake no Tokijirō is given the opportunity to escape the obligation to murder for the sake of a meal and night's lodging when he saves and runs off with the pregnant woman and child he has been ordered to kill. Gambler Seki no Yatappe comes to the rescue of a little girl whose grandfather dies on the road and goes out of his way to take her to her home; this one act of kindness so redeems him in his own eyes — defines him as a proper man despite his membership in a confraternity of thugs and other social outsiders — that he continues for years to keep an eye on her. In the end, to save her from a man who will ruin her life, he kills a friend, a fellow traveler, who plans to run off with her.

The need to preserve familial relationships, or more precisely pseudo-familial relationships, in order to maintain one's identity and dignity as a human being, is crucial to the rhetoric of the *matatabi-mono*. As noted in a previous chapter, Hasegawa created the *matatabi-mono* as a new genre, the humanist tradition of anti-militarism created in the wake of the Russo-Japanese War of 1904–1905. The world of the Tokugawa-period gambler, his obligation to his godfather (*oyabun*) and loyalty to the society of gamblers, enforced by threat of violence, represent the plight of the modern common soldier, more likely than not an impoverished peasant, conscripted to kill at the order of his ultimate patron and father figure, the emperor. The act of killing both identifies the group and binds him irrevocably to it. No matter how noble or tragic the hero, played by the stoic Takakura Ken or the romantic Tsuruta Kōji, the lesson is the same: killing, for whatever the reason, places one outside the society of human beings; imprisonment and death are the only possible results. The gambler, as a traditional tragic hero, is a sympathetic figure; the *matatabi-mono* and *ninkyō eiga* are traditional Buddhist pictures of hell, of the *shuraba*. His plight evokes the sympathy of the audience, but, hopefully, not the desire to emulate him — his story is a lesson on the evils of life. What differentiates the fictional world of the gambler from the real world of the soldier is that in the *matatabi-mono* the act of killing itself is defined in as transgressive, unequivocally evil.

The theme of the *matatabi-mono* was taken up by the *ninkyō eiga*, which equates Japan's modern militarism with modern criminal life and organizations. This is nowhere so clearly foregrounded as in the career of Tsuruta Kōji, whose films epitomized the *ninkyō* films: he had been a pilot in the Japanese navy and a *kamikaze*, although he never received orders to fly. As late as 1976–1982, he was playing himself in an NHK thirteen-part series, *The Journey*, as a former *kamikaze* pilot crippled by his past and isolated from the generation that knew nothing about the war.[49] In an interview in 1981, he stressed the relationship between his military experience and the films in which he had acted.[50] And, indeed, it is his films which best exemplify the *ninkyō* films and their continuity with *matatabi-mono*: by stoically adhering to the code, the gambler's code, which is the soldier's code, he loses the relationships that define him as a human being, those with a woman and a good friend.[51] No longer human, like his counterpart the samurai, he vents his rage against a perverted system of loyalty in a bloody orgy of violence that rips apart the net of obligations in which he was trapped.

Part Two

Realism in the Narrative

6

The Shinkokugeki and the Zenshinza: Western Representational Realism and the Japanese Period Film

The function of a Japanese period piece, in print, on stage, or in film, is to discuss politically sensitive material and, at the same time, to evade government censorship. This is done, as James Brandon has demonstrated, by a matching of past and present which places the current issue safely in the past.[1] Between 1913 and 1939, the period piece perfected a rhetorical system matching historical periods and current expressions of anti-feudal and anti-militarist sentiments derived from foreign sources. In literature, theater, and film, the modern period piece increased its reliance on modern language and foreign models of narrative and characterization, on what we can loosely call western representational realism.

Perhaps I should start out by explaining what *I* mean by western representational realism: the style of theater as performed in the capitals of Europe in the late nineteenth and early twentieth centuries, especially the theater of Ibsen and Chekhov. It is characterized by depth of field and the physical simulation of real space and real time. Characterization depends on naturalism, modern colloquial language, and careful reproduction of appropriate costumes and mannerisms. The net effect is that of looking through a window into a kitchen or parlor and watching, unobserved and disengaged, the inhabitants going through their daily rituals or personal crises. This theater was the model for modernizing the Japanese stage, the Kabuki stage, in the 1910s.

In the process of assimilating western theater, the Japanese included in their definition of western representational realism the western narratives themselves (the plays or adaptations of western literary works) and western characters, their situations and psychologies, which represented and expressed foreign ideas and sentiments. This inclusive concept of western representational realism dominated the development of the Japanese period piece. In addition, the western representational realism of the stage was reinforced by a film realism which replicated the effect of the stage and was characterized by deep focus, minimal camera movement, and simple, straight cuts.

Critical to the assimilation of western representational realism by the Kabuki stage in the 1910s and its transfer to the period film in the 1920s was the New National Theater or Shinkokugeki.[2] Its founder, Sawada Shōjirō (1892–1929),[3] was a graduate in English of Waseda University and of Waseda's training program for actors. The program had been established in 1913 by the scholar, author, and writer of historical plays for Kabuki, Tsubouchi Shōyō (1859–1935),[4] who, taking seriously the emulation of western theater and its performance techniques, was determined to make actors of educated men. Out of this training center came the Geijutsuza or Art Theater (1913–1917), led by director Shimamura Shōgetsu (1871–1918) and main actress Matsui Sumako (1886–1919), considered the first modern theater or Shingeki troupe, which staged mostly western works — Ibsen, Chekhov, and Tolstoy.

Sawada was a leading actor of the Arts Theater, but he left in 1917 to found the Shinkokugeki or New National Theater.[5] He was deeply dissatisfied with Shingeki itself and was determined to establish a theater for the people rather than for intellectuals.

The New National Theater specialized in using western acting and staging techniques in productions of familiar and new Japanese historical narratives. Sawada tied in with the new period piece, the *bakumatsu-mono* and brought this new period genre to the stage. Sawada was Kunisada Chūji, the first Tsukigata Hanpeita, indeed, the first Tsukue Ryūnosuke. It was Sawada's characterization of Tsukue Ryūnosuke that changed the face of popular culture. His intensity on the stage sent shivers up the spines of the audience and frightened even his fellow actors: at least one has confessed that he believed that Sawada really would kill him on stage. And his interpretations are still the standard against which period film roles are played.[6]

Sawada's influence on the period piece extended also to staged combat. Staged combat in Kabuki is more like ballet than fighting. Sawada popularized a new form of staged combat which effected greater realism through new forms and great speed.[7] The new staged combat became the core expression of nihilism as a fight in which the trapped hero fights desperately, even wildly, against a throng of opponents. Through the New National Theater, the new style of narrative, of presentation, and of staged combat, all associated with western representational realism, spread to the period film.

Sawada himself made only five films before he died at thirty-eight after ear surgery.[8] The most perfect example of the style of period film made under

***Onshū no kanata ni* (*Beyond Love and Hate*, 1925), directed by Makino Shōzō. Ichikurō (Sawada Shōjirō) and Oyumi (Hisamatsu Kiyoko), whose husband he has murdered, have ended up working together as thieves. Kikuchi Kan's version of the story of the penitent Zenkai, credited with digging a tunnel in northern Kyushu, was filmed by the avant garde of the use of traditional narrative in theater, film, and popular literature: the Shinkokugeki (New National Theater) with Makino as director and Kikuchi's friend, the novelist Naoki Sanjūsan, as scriptwriter. Sawada's work on stage (as one of the very first Japanese actors trained in western theater) and three films at Makino's studio set the standard for realism in the genre and inspired the next generation of Makino's film makers (photograph courtesy of the Kawakita Memorial Film Institute).**

Sawada's influence is the 1925 *Serpent.* The director Futagawa Buntarō had been assistant director for Makino Shōzō on two of Sawada's films. However, the real beneficiary of Sawada's legacy was Itō Daisuke (1898–1981).[9] Itō had been trained as a scenarist of contemporary films at the Shōchiku studios research institute by Osanai Kaoru, a leader in the Shingeki movement (to be discussed below). Indeed, Itō had scripted the first film designated a "new period film." In 1926, he and his cameraman Karasawa Hiromitsu (1900–1980) started to work on *Chōkon* (*Long-standing Hatred*) with a disciple of Sawada, Ōkōchi Denjiro (1898–1962),[10] and first began to exploit the camera fully. Itō showed off Ōkōchi's abilities in rehearsals of a long scene shot with panning and tracking shots of Ōkōchi moving and talking at the same time, an arduous task not previously attempted: traditionally, in Japan, people speak only when "seated." On the one hand, Itō made Ōkōchi's reputation as an actor; on the other, only an actor with Ōkōchi's training could have made Itō's use of the moving camera possible. Indeed, Itō's moving camera earned him the name Idō Daisuki ("I love moving") and unheard-of full billing with the stars.[11]

Ōkōchi was Sawada's film heir (Sawada's stage company was continued by two other disciples). He was said to have been exactly like Sawada on stage. Ōkōchi played Sawada's roles in film: Kunisada Chūji, Kutsukake Tokijirō, Tsukigata Hanpeita, and even Tsukue Ryūnosuke. Not only did he carry on Sawada's tradition, but with Itō he also played other nihilist characters such as Tange Sazen, the one-eyed, one-armed ronin betrayed and left for dead by his lord (*Shinpan Ōoka seidan*, 3 parts, 1928) and Niino Tsuruchiyo, the angry and hopeless bastard who assassinates the man he does not know is his father (*Samurai Nippon*, 2 parts, 1931).

While the New National Theater was crucial in the process of introducing western representational realism (western-style narratives, characterizations, and staged combat) to the period film of the twenties, the Progressive Troupe or Zenshinza took over leadership during the thirties.

The Progressive Troupe was the culmination of the movement to retrain Kabuki actors in modern, western stage techniques initiated by those actors outside the world of Grand Kabuki, led by a small clique and patronized by the government.[12] Among these outsiders was Ichikawa Sadanji II (1880–1940),[13] the first Kabuki actor to go to Europe (in 1906) and see for himself what western theater was like.

When Sadanji got back from Europe in 1909, he established the Free Theater or Jiyūgekijō (1909–1919),[14] named after the French theater of the same name, and thus became a co-founder of modern theater, Shingeki, in Japan. The theater's purpose was to reeducate and to train his troupe's Kabuki actors and to act as a research center for French and English theater.[15]

The co-founder was his boyhood friend, Osanai Kaoru (1881–1928),[16] the man who later brought western stage and film techniques and a training center to Shōchiku Studio. From December 1912 to August 1913, Osanai was in Europe himself; he studied Reinhardt and Stanislavski and brought back a compilation of notes called "the Bible."[17]

Osanai was a member of the Ibsen Group and brought in others as dues-paying members: on the suggestion of author Shimazaki Tōson (1872–1943), the decision was made to produce as their first play *John Gabriel Borkman* (November 1909), and they went on to produce *A Doll's House* and *Enemy of the People*.[18]

In 1918, Sadanji was joined by sixteen-year-old Kawarazaki Chōjūrō

(1902–1981), future co-founder of the Progressive Troupe. Kawarazaki was to become the exemplary model of the Kabuki-Shingeki actor. He too received direct experience in Europe. In 1928, Kawarazaki went with Sadanji on his famous tour to Russia (where he was seen by Sergei Eisenstein). He went by himself to Germany and to France.[19]

In 1930, Kawarazaki, another Kabuki outsider, left Kabuki.[20] In 1931, he joined the troupe of another Kabuki maverick, Ichikawa Ennosuke II (1888–1963), the first Grand Kabuki actor to appear in a commercial film.[21] Kawarazaki appeared in Ennosuke's landmark Shingeki production, *Wind of Asia* (Sergei Mikhailovich Tretyakhov's [1892–1939] 1926 *Roar, China*).

In May 1931, Kawarazaki formed the Progressive Troupe with a colleague from Ennosuke's troupe, the *enfant terrible* of the Kabuki world, Nakamura Kan'emon (1901–1982).[22] The Progressive Troupe revived many old Kabuki plays no longer performed, updated the language, and established a populist Kabuki theater[23] which performed classical Kabuki, adapted Kabuki, standard Shingeki, and Shingeki period pieces in the tradition of the New National Theater.

The first years were rough, but they had help from popular playwright Hasegawa Shin (1884–1963),[24] who greatly admired Kan'emon as an actor.[25] They produced several of his plays, mostly period pieces; they were the first to produce the *matatabi-mono Kutsukake no Tokijirō* (*Tokijirō from Kutsukake*), in 1928.[26]

The foremost film interpreter of "stories of gamblers' wanderings" was Inagaki Hiroshi (1905–1980),[27] who told me in 1978 over lunch that Nakamura Kan'emon was his favorite actor. In 1933, he wrote the script for the Progressive Troupe's first film, an adaptation of their stage production of a Hasegawa play (*Shigure no Danshichi*)[28] and helped direct the second, the 1935 *Shimizu Jirōchō*.[29] Inagaki is especially highly regarded for his concept of the period film as "contemporary plays with topknots attached," the idea that period films should be indistinguishable from contemporary films or films about common people except for setting and costumes. Inagaki, the first to use modern colloquial speech in his films,[30] worked with scenarist Mimura Shintarō (1895–1970) to establish the rules: *bushi* were to speak like office workers in the prestigious Marunouchi district of Tokyo; travelers, gamblers, and gangsters were to use the Tokyo blue-collar idiom.[31] The acknowledged stage experts in modern language in period settings were the Progressive Troupe,[32] and they starred in Inagaki and Mimura's 1936 *Matagami sen'ichiya* (*Journey of a Thousand and One Nights*).[33] The use of modern language effected a real sense of the matching past and present that was the dominant feature of the period film during the thirties.

Inagaki recommended[34] Yamanaka Sadao to direct and script the Progressive Troupe's third film, another Hasegawa period play that had been in their repertoire since 1932, the 1935 *Machi no irezumimono* (*The Village Tattooed Man* [Neighborhood Ex-con]). A tragic period film about a gangster who comes out of prison and finds it hard to find a place again in society, it won second place in the ranks of the film magazine *Kinema Junpō*'s Best Ten that year.[35] They went on to make two more films together: the 1936 *Kōchiyama Sōshun* and Yamanaka's last, the 1938 *Ninjō kamifusen* (*Humanity and Paper Balloons*).

These films represent the culmination of the development of the period piece on stage and in film that focused on modern language, ordinary people,

Kōchiyama Sōshun **(1936), directed by Yamanaka Sadao. Sōshun (Kawarazaki Chōjūrō, left) and his pal Kaneko Ichinojō (Nakamura Kan'emon) share a drink. The fallen priest and the toothpick-chomping ronin will die fending off a gang so that a young punk and his sister can get away. This was the Zenshinza's (Progressive Troupe) fourth film, the first of three with scenarist Mimura Shintarō and second of four with Yamanaka. Among the first Kabuki actors with experience in western and modern plays (Kawarazaki had spent a year in Europe in his teens), they were the ideal troupe for Yamanaka's exploration of the *jidai-geki* (period film) as *shomin-geki* (film about ordinary people), which required a mastery of the naturalistic style of acting and ease with modern language. As such, they expanded on the work of Sawada Shōjirō and the Shinkokugeki (New National Theater) (photograph courtesy of the Kawakita Memorial Film Institute).**

and foreign adaptations. But little credit has been given the Progressive Troupe, which made them possible. They brought in realistic acting techniques from the modern stage: they introduced the ensemble acting characterizing Kurosawa's films and, in the Kumagai Hisatora's 1938 *The Abe Clan*, the naturalistic scratching and pimple-picking that would so distinguish Mifune Toshirō's acting. They made it possible for Shingeki actors to play period roles, and therefore character actors, whether old, fat, or homely, to play leading roles, as in *Seven Samurai*. They even brought in realistic wigs, historical costumes — a sense of authenticity — and an ability to make history truly contemporary, as they did in *Abe ichizoku* as well as the 1941–42 version of their successful stage production *Genroku Chūshingura*, which Mizoguchi Kenji directed.

The role of actors in the development of Japanese cinema is rarely considered, and certainly not here in the West. But it is only through a study of the actors in the films of Japanese directors we regard so highly that any real sense can be made of the process of the development of Japanese cinema. The Progressive Troupe, for example, starred in most of the films produced by the eight-man (including Inagaki Hiroshi and Yamanaka Sadao) Narutaki film study group.[36] In the Progressive Troupe, with Kawarazaki's modern theater techniques and Nakamura's ideological bent, the nucleus of a true political theater was formed in which "matching of present and past" had a particular place: the ability to combine Tokugawa-period iconography with a purely modern use of narrative and language was the very essence of the Japanese period film of the thirties. This was very much in the hands of the actors rather than of the director. An observer on the set of *Kōchiyama Sōshun* noted that everyone was on the set at nine a.m. for the beginning of shooting: it was not Yamanaka, but Kawarazaki, following Osanai's methods, who led the rehearsals for the scenes to be shot that day.[37]

7

Historical Realism

Introduction

During the Tokugawa period, censorship forbade Kabuki and puppet theater to stage events concerning the upper ranks of the *bushi* and the nobility. Kabuki responded by developing a rhetorical device to evade censorship control, the matching of past and present (*mitate*), whereby contemporary events were carefully hidden in well-known historical events of the past. In these plays, historical events were notoriously unhistorical: the names were faked, the language was modern, the costumes and wigs were modern, and the themes were modern.

On the other hand, some Confucian lecturers and their collaterals, performers of popular didactic stories based on Confucian themes, *kōdanshi* or *kōshakushi,* were of high status: many of them were descended from *bushi* and or were the younger sons of *bushi.* As such, they were patronized by *bushi* and nobles, who had them lecture privately. To them alone was allowed the privilege of discussing events in the great *bushi* houses which made up the government of the country. The purpose of Confucian history was to teach by examples of the good and of the bad the proper way to govern; the purpose of the critique of contemporary society was, through good examples and by bad, to teach people how to live. Some Kōdan specialists were allowed, within limits, something akin to historical accuracy[1] and accuracy in reporting. A few who went too far were imprisoned and one even executed. Their special status in society is seen in the fact that, even today, Kōdan specialists are addressed as "teacher" (*sensei*), while Rakugo specialists are addressed as "reverend" (*oshō*).[2]

During the Meiji period (1868–1912), Kabuki, under the patronage of the new government, obtained the high status previously granted only certain Kōdan performers because of its reforms of the theater. In essence, what was accomplished was a new combination of the naturalism of the contemporary play with the educational function of Kōdan to create a new and native representational theater. Almost every presentational aspect of Kabuki was stripped out of Meiji theater and historical pieces in particular: wooden clappers, samisen accompaniment, previews of the play outside the theater, personal escorts to seats, walking across the stage to get to and fro, the stage thrust into the audience, actors walking the corridors to get to the stage entrances to the sides of the theater, peddling food in the auditorium, displays of presents to the actors, and even familiar props. Ordinary people were priced out and replaced by the elite of the new regime and their foreign guests and dignitaries.[3]

Kabuki and the Loss of *Mitate*

While denied the privilege of discussing history or history in the making — which was the purview of individuals superior to them in rank and position — Kabuki actors tried to transcend social caste through participation in an ethical sphere identified with their social superiors: they did appropriate the didactic function of Confucianism and Confucian narrative, to teach people how to behave according to status and function.[4]

However, Kabuki actors desired more. This desire was most pronounced in the Ichikawa family and fulfilled by Ichikawa Danjūrō IX (1838–1903). When he was growing up, he was a member of a despised group, the actors, who had barely escaped being relegated to the same pariah caste as brothel owners and wandering street entertainers.[5] His father, Danjūrō VII (1791–1859), had been punished for using real armor on stage in 1842[6] and, in order to stage *Kanjinchō* (*The Subscription List*, based on the Nō play *Ataka*), had had to get down on his knees and beg costumes from the Nō wardrobe masters, the Sekioka.[7] Nō was the drama patronized by and identified with the military class; from 1656, once in his life, the head of the Kanze school was permitted to perform in public.[8] Kabuki actors could not watch Nō: Danjūrō VII had himself smuggled into the Kanze school theater so that he could study *Ataka*.[9]

After the Meiji Restoration, the new government decided not only to control theater (through a licensing system) but to use it. In 1872, all entertainers came under the purview of the Ministry of Religious Affairs (*kyōbushō*), which intended to use them to educate the people "'to comply with the principles of piety and patriotism ... to clarify the principles of heaven and the way fit for men,' and 'to bring about reverence for the Emperor and observance of the Imperial will.'"[10] Thus, Kabuki came under the patronage of the ruling elite beginning with a group surrounding top politician and Japan's first modern prime minister, Itō Harubumi (1841–1909). The crowning glory of the transition of the Kabuki world was the opportunity for Danjūrō, along with top actors Onoe Kikugorō V (1844–1903) and Ichikawa Sadanji I (1842–

1904), to give the first Kabuki performance before the emperor in April 1887 at the home of Inoue Kaoru (1835–1915; successively foreign minister, minister of the interior, and minister of finance). Kabuki became identified with the new aristocracy, the ultimate transcendence of their former despised status under the Tokugawa.

The first thing that the new government demanded from Kabuki was historical accuracy: dismissing out of hand the function of "matching past and present" and the changing of names in period pieces, they demanded a correction of this corruption and that Kabuki use the real names — children might be confused! After all, Kabuki was supposed to be instructive, that is, an arm of the government propaganda system. In 1872, Morita Kanya (1846–1897, owner of the theater Morita-za) as well as the playwrights for his theater, Kawatake Mokuami (1816–1893) and Sakurada Jisuke (1802–1877), were summoned to the ward office and the law was laid down. The real possibilities of Kabuki were soon recognized by highly placed people in 1878. Morita's production of a play based on the Satsuma Rebellion of the year before, *Okige no kumo harau asagochi* (*East Wind Clearing the Clouds of the Southwest*), featured such novelties as real names and fireworks for the exploding shells. It made an impression: the next month, on April 28, 1878, Morita and the top Kabuki stars who had appeared in the play were invited to the home of the chief secretary of the Ministry of Home Affairs, Matsuda Michiyuki,[11] to discuss the play with important statesmen such as Itō Hirobumi and the scholar of classical Chinese studies Yoda Gakkai (1833–1909); other topics included the superiority of western theater and the need for historical accuracy in plays.[12] By October, Morita, Danjūrō, and Mokuami had so changed Kabuki period pieces (*jidai-mono*) into realistic recreations of historical events that the satirist Kanagaki Robun (1829–1894), writing for the paper, the *Kanayomi shimbun*, October 20, 1878, dubbed them "living history" (*katsurekishi*)— not entirely as a compliment. He noted the apparent influence of the "antiquarians (*kojitsusha*)," the "soberness (*shibui*)" of the acting style, and the authentic costumes exact "to the period."[13] Danjūrō would create "living history" for about twenty years.

Luckily, the government's ambitions coincided with Danjūrō's: Danjūrō's personal concern was instruction through historical accuracy in language, costumes, and customs, and for this he sought help from experts. Indeed, the historical adviser would characterize the *katsurekishi*. Danjūrō's early advisers were the antiquarian Ichikawa Kumao and then the costume and dress expert for the Arima house, Matsuoka Akiyoshi (1826–1890), who had first assisted him in 1875.[14] More advisers made themselves available to him in 1883, when Danjūrō started a "club," the Antiquarian Society (*kyūkokai*), which was to meet once a month at his own house; it included a number of prominent men, including Yoda Gakkai. When Mokuami retired, Danjūrō was taken up by Fukuchi Ōchi (1841–1906)[15] and appeared in twenty-six of Fukuchi's thirty-six plays.[16]

For the first time, it was permissible to stage authentic martial arts. Yoda wrote of his *Yoshino shui meika no homare* (*Praise of Famous Poems Gleaned at Yoshino*),

> My purpose in having Masatsura shoot an arrow from a horse is to illustrate a style of archery much used by medieval warriors. I have investigated ancient usages carefully, and I have made the actor use a real bow, carry a quiver and other appurtenances modeled exactly on ancient ones, draw his arrow, and shoot from a horse so that the audience can see what warriors did of old.[17]

This new, realistic style of staged combat was called "poodle dog-fight" (*muku-inu kenka*) by the professional fight choreographers, because, like a poodle, it was so foreign.[18]

His efforts were, in fact, in vain. His historically accurate language no one could understand.[19] Ancient customs seemed peculiar if not downright undignified: the depiction of vassals advancing on their knees to receive swords was no doubt highly instructive, but the audience did think it looked a bit queer.[20]

In fact, this historical realism was nothing more than a vague antiquarianism, a collection of old costumes, martial arts, customs, and the like to stage an historical event, to animate the illustrated scrolls Danjūrō had studied as a boy.[21] It was to theater what battle reenactments are to history. Moreover, the narrative was, in its way, just as suspect a rendition of history as the original Kabuki version. The traditional stage was Buddhist; it criticized society by showing the suffering inherent in human experience. In the Meiji "living history" Kabuki play, on the other hand, the morality is Confucian; living-history drama is about filial piety and loyalty to the emperor. For example, in the 1746 play *Sugawara Denju Tenarai Kagami* (*Sugawara's Secrets of Calligraphy*), a couple sacrifice their son to save the son of a man to whom the husband is under obligation. They lament, "'[H]ow hard a thing it is to serve faithfully.'" In October 1870, a change in the script had the husband respond to his wife, "'But this is what faithful service is.'"[22] The Buddhist critique of human values was thereby perverted into a message of the glory of suffering for the sake of loyalty.

Historical Realism in the Period Film

The use of an historically accurate recreation of an historical event as identified with the government and its values was extended in the late 1930s and early 1940s to the period film in the development of the historical film, the *rekishi eiga*. The government wanted these films, demanded them for the war effort, and got them, some better than others. They invested heavily in them, which made possible as never before large, stunning sets, exquisite costumes and wigs, and all-star casting, as in Mizoguchi Kenji's 1941–42 *The 47 Ronin*. In the end, however, these wartime historical films proved not particularly popular as a genre, and too often they turned out the way the directors wanted them to (or, rather, the way directors were used to doing things) rather than the way the government wanted them. The censors knew enough about the traditional rhetoric to ban the *matatabi-mono* during the war; but they never did quite grasp that if they could not use the traditional rhetorical system, there was no effective way to communicate their ideas to the people by using films set in the past. Contemporary war films did much better, films like Tasaka Tomotaka's Best Film for 1938, *Gonin no sekkohei* (*Five Scouts*). Indeed, such films were really so good that, after seeing one, Frank Capra is reported to have said, "We can't beat this kind of thing!"[23]

Typical of the national-policy historical films produced at the time was Marune Sentarō's 1941 *Kakute kamikaze wa fuku* (*Thus Blows the Divine Wind*). Such an important historical event as the defense of southern Japan led by the Kōno clan against the Mongol invasion of 1281 merited careful research: the historical adviser, Ema Tsutomu (1884–1979), a noted specialist in the history of the manners and customs of Japan,[24] had also worked on *The 47 Ronin* and Inagaki Hiroshi's 1941 *Edo saigo no hi* (*The Last Days of Edo* [see below]).[25] It features a full-scale hurricane destroying ships, a cast of thousands to drown, and an all-star cast in the lead roles (our jolly, idle vassal to the shogun as the famed priest Nichiren!)—not to mention a very charming scene depicting the foreman of an arrow-making workshop exhorting his girls to work faster and harder ("Hai!" they enthusiastically reply). It was a strange film for Marune, the director who was supposed to take the place of Yamanaka Sadao in the humanist period film. Perhaps the fact that it was set so far back in time (the present was usually matched with the Tokugawa period, not with anything earlier) put Marune at ease: it is doubtful he had much say in it, anyway.

Historical films might pay lip-service to *bushidō* and the war effort, but most directors managed to work things to their own advantage. Kinugasa Teinosuke's 1941 *Kawanakajima kassen* (*The Battle of Kawanakajima*), too, had a historical adviser who had worked on *The 47 Ronin*, Torii Kiyonobu (1900–1976).[26] It is about the last battle, in 1563, between the great warlords Uesugi Kenshin (1530–1578) and Takeda Shingen (1521–1573). Beautifully made with Eisensteinian montage (lines and lines of horses criss-crossing in different depths of field) and a long, tense build-up to the battle, it is just as much about the peasants killed, looted, and raped as it is about the beauty of death: the final shot is a crane shot of the dead — including a widow (Irie Takako) who had begged her lord for permission to die on the battlefield — lying in mist and smoke and then a pan up to the sky — a shot which echoes the last shot in Kumagai Hisatora's 1938 *Abe ichizoku* (*The Abe Clan*), a tale of proud resistance to arbitrary authority (which I will discuss below).

Most of the film time is actually taken up by a long diversion meant to show the army and the peasantry recently devastated by an army (representing the Japanese army and the Chinese peasantry?) reconciled with each other through the characters played by Hasegawa Kazuo and Yamada Isuzu: Hasegawa and Yamada had already co-starred in several films, including the popular 1938 *Tsuruhachi Tsurujirō* (directed by Mikio Naruse), and would make many more together; moreover, Hasegawa had already made three films with Ri Koran (Yamaguchi Yoshiko, b. 1920) based on the theme of the reconciliation between the Japanese and Chinese.[27] It would be interesting to know just exactly what the audience was responding to in the process of intertextual reading: a growing favorite combination of Hasegawa and Yamada; the theme of the reconciliation of enemies played out by Hasegawa and Yamamoto recalling that played out by Hasegawa and Ri; or the theme of the devastation of the way of the *bushi* played out in the last scene recalling that of *The Abe Clan*.[28] In any case, the viewing of the previous films, and others like them, at least prepared the audience to understand the narrative and to appreciate it as an interesting, indeed spectacular, compilation of well-known themes and scenes done much the way Kabuki and other popular narratives crossed narratives.

Inagaki Hiroshi's 1941 *Edo saigo no hi* (*The Last Days of Edo*) focuses on the Tokugawa naval commander Katsu Kaishū (1823–1899), who, beleaguered on all sides and beset by conflicting loyalties, struggles to negotiate peace between the imperial troops and the shogun before the greedy western powers can take advantage of Japan's vulnerability during the civil war of 1867. The film is about the personal dilemma of a man who puts his country above his personal loyalties to his lord. It is a perfectly reasonable thesis and could even be construed to apply to wartime Japan. But its antipathy toward the West, both in fear of domination by the West and the villains, who are usually dressed in some form of western attire, and the problems incurred in pitting the shogun against emperor in a film set in the final year of the shogunate make it all too susceptible to cooption for government wartime propaganda. Nevertheless, it is a brilliant film, probably the first to use those dominating close-ups which made Kurosawa famous fifteen years later.

The single strongest factor in diluting or resisting a government-approved message was the actor. In two films at least this can be seen at work. The Kabuki bad-boys and crypto-Communist theater group, the Progressive

Edo saigo no hi (*The Last Days of Edo*, 1941), directed by Inagaki Hiroshi. Katsu Kaishū, Lord of Awa and a commissioner of the navy (Bandō Tsumasaburō), tries to reassure his daughters Yae and Teru (Yanagi Emiko and Sawamura Toshiko) as his wife Shizuyo (Tamaki Utako) listens. It is 1867: caught between the restorationists and threat of western incursion, Katsu will persuade the shogun to surrender Edo and the commander of the emperor's forces to allow the shogun to withdraw to his domain. Made during the war against China and released just before the attack on Pearl Harbor, the film was striking both for its meticulous physical realism and its stunning close-ups. However, Inagaki vitiates much of the xenophobia and resentment against the West it was supposed to inflame by focusing on the hero's personal dilemma and scenes such as this, which reveal him as a dedicated father (photograph courtesy of Matsuda Film Productions).

Troupe or Zenshinza, starred in the adaptation of Mori Ōgai's 1913 novella of samurai honor, the 1938 *Abe ichizoku* (*The Abe Clan*), directed by Kumagai Hisatora (1904–1986). The novella is a chronicle of a disorder in a great house (*oiesōdō*) at the beginning of the Tokugawa era: a samurai family stood together to resist their lord and were wiped out. Mori's investigation of the meaning of the way of the *bushi* (*bushidō*) comes to the conclusion that family honor comes before loyalty to lord. In the film, the sets, costumes, and wigs were very authentic, very historical, as was the battle scene, but the historical film was put to use in expressing "anti-feudal" sentiments — family first, blind loyalty last — the real way of the samurai. Even though the film tries to identify the villains as the clan bureaucracy by their insistence on the punctilious application of the law and the good guys as those old-fashioned samurai whose high-minded values have been rendered obsolete (as in Mizoguchi's *The 47 Ronin*), it is hard to imagine that what audiences were reading into the film was somehow totally overridden by what was in the text of the film: Mori's original and the presence of the Zenshinza actors, especially Nakamura Kan'emon and Kawarazaki Chōjūrō in the lead roles. Their film careers had been established by their work in the films of Yamanaka Sadao and in adaptations of their stagings of the works of Hasegawa Shin, neither of whom could be accused of banging the drum for *bushidō*.

Kurosawa and the Didactic Tradition in Period Film

The principal heir of the Confucian or new Kabuki historical tradition initiated by Ichikawa Danjūrō was Kurosawa Akira (1910–1998). With Kurosawa, accuracy in the recreation of time and place was always a prime consideration. Perhaps it is because he was Yamamoto Kajirō's assistant on the 1941 *Uma* (*Horse*), a docu-drama about raising horses for the army for which Kurosawa was principally responsible. However, it must be remembered that the Zenshinza were making their best films at Tōhō at the same time Kurosawa was getting his early training at that same studio.

Kurosawa is famous for the trouble — and expense — he went to in his sets and costumes for period films. It is true that Kurosawa went to museums to research costumes and props for *Seven Samurai* and *Throne of Blood*. The village set in *Seven Samurai* and the Edo set for the 1965 *Red Beard* are famous. Kurosawa showed just as much concern for how things were done as for how things looked; in this, he very much represents the didactic tradition of Danjūrō and the Antiquarian Society. He was just as interested as Danjūrō in showing how samurai advanced on their knees to receive their swords from their lord, as in his 1957 *Kumonosujō* (*Throne of Blood*). The principal function of the combat scenes in *Seven Samurai* is to demonstrate the various martial arts: through Kanbei, the old soldier, Kurosawa demonstrated how to draw a bow; and through the scenes of the peasants fighting off the bandits charging into the village, Kurosawa demonstrated how to fend off an attack by backing a kicking horse into the enemy. Introducing these authentic martial arts into his films set a new precedent in the period film for staged fight scenes (also called "poodle-dog fights"), which, however, never replaced the old style developed out of theater. In the original cut of *Shadow Warrior*, Kurosawa broke the narrative for quite long stretches of time to show how to serve a drink properly, how to load and fire a musket, and what a lord's apartments look like, and to explain the philosophy behind the construction of a garden. He even had his actors speak in the manner of sixteenth century *bushi*, causing much dismay to his modern audiences, who could barely understand what was being said. In this respect, Kurosawa was an old-style Confucian lecturer, who not only demonstrated the ideals of the way of the *bushi* but was accurate in presenting the details he used to do so. Kurosawa was an educator.

In his most famous film, *Seven Samurai*, Kurosawa gave us not only a slice of rural life in the war-torn sixteenth century but also a fairly idealistic portrait of the Confucian *bushi* motivated by benevolence, as a Confucian *bushi* ought to be. The seven accept a job for room and board, pat children on the head, give food to children and the elderly, sacrifice their hair, and share their money; the farmers, on the other hand, are mistrustful, murderous, and mendacious. In this film as in others, Kurosawa over-idealizes his *bushi*, often at the expense of characters of the lower classes. The chamberlain's wife in the 1962 *Sanjuro* is too ladylike (Irie Takako's sister was a lady-in-waiting at court) and too wise for words. On the other hand, in the 1961 *Yojinbo* (*Yojimbo*), the town *saké* merchant and the silk merchant — and their families and henchmen — are too, too gruesome: the witch of a mother, her cowardly son, and the henchman whose fang hangs over his lower lip (Katō Daisuke). In associating idealism with the warrior class and realism — and comedy — with the lower class, Kurosawa was not simply following established conventions of traditional narrative: like Confucian lecturers of old, Kurosawa was clear about the superiority of the *bushi*, but there is little evidence in his work of any ability on the part of commoners either to share the ideals of the *bushi* or to participate in "the same ethical sphere."

Kurosawa as the Heir of the Zenshinza

The Zenshinza brought accuracy of physical details of the historical period to their films, which directly or indirectly opposed authority or ideals representing government policy: *The Abe Clan* (family versus lord), the 1935 *Machi no irezumimono* (*The Village Tattooed Man*/Neighborhood Ex-con; the common man is always trapped), *Kōchiyama Sōshun* (cheating the gang boss as resistance to patriarchal authority), *Humanity and Paper Balloons* (the collusion of the rich against the poor, controlled, again, by patriarchal authority), and the like. The combination of historical event, period detail, and political commitment produced a sense of almost perfect historical realism. However, the historical realism applied to a fictional narrative like that of *The Village Tattooed Man* made for the reconstruction of a period that was historically accurate but referred, through the technique itself, to the present.

This kind of historical realism was inherited by Kurosawa in his passion for physical realism in his sets and costumes. (By the way, he also inherited staff from Yamanaka Sadao, who directed the most famous of the Zenshinza films.) But Kurosawa did not have the political commitment of the Zenshinza. He used the techniques of historical realism to promote the very values the Zenshinza opposed because they were abused: loyalty, benevolence, and paternalism. The techniques of *The Abe Clan*, which was meant to oppose government-promoted social values, were used in *Red Beard* to promote the humanistic self-image of post-war Japan. The techniques associated with historical realism were used to promote idealism. When Kurosawa got "realistic" instead of "idealistic," he tended to go "surrealistic" by turning to the techniques of the stage, most notably the Nō stage. In *Throne of Blood* and *Ran*, for example, both of which are about the evil of the world, Kurosawa used Nō masks, costuming, and musical effects.

It should also be noted that Kurosawa never made a historical film, a film about a specific historical personage or event. *The Abe Clan*, *The Last Days of Edo*, *The Battle of Kawanakajima*, and, yes, even *The 47 Ronin* are about the main characters of famous historical events, even if there are minor characters who might be fictional. Kurosawa's films are, in the main, adaptations of western plays and novels, or of Japanese period novels. *Shadow Warrior*, although it deals with Takeda Shingen, the famous warlord of the sixteenth century, and his brother, focuses on a fictional character, his double. *Ran* is a combination of *King Lear* and the legends of the Mōri house of western Japan, also famous warlords of the sixteenth century. It is difficult to evaluate Kurosawa's historical realism, to determine whether ultimately it has any value other than that of antiquarianism, content without meaning.

8

From Stage Realism to Film Realism

Introduction

The traditional Japanese stage makes for terribly exciting photo essays and terribly slow performances. Most of any Kabuki play consists not of what people are doing, but of people talking about what they have done, are doing, or are about to do. Most action is limited to entrances, exits, and the final murder or fight scene (this does not pertain to dance pieces). The basic element of the Japanese stage is the pose, moving from one pretty picture to the next; the problem is the time it takes to get from one to the other. A good number of the Japanese in the audience wait it out with a nap. (The foreigners — novices — do not yet know which are the good scenes and sit through the entire piece.)

The traditional Japanese stage tends to the static (yes, this is a gross overstatement). Film, on the other hand, is all about movement. It is therefore surprising to note the critical role in the development of Japanese cinema of the Kabuki actor. Japan's first film star was a popular provincial Kabuki actor famous for his flips and somersaults, Onoe Matsunosuke (1875–1926). Makino Shōzō (1878–1929) discovered him in 1909, brought him to Kyoto, and the rest is history.

Inspired by the popularity of ninja stories, Makino and Onoe made ninja films. Ninja were spies believed to have magical powers to disappear, walk through walls, and leap tall buildings in a single bound. Films about them required all sorts of cinematic tricks, tricks like those exemplified in the work of the Georges Méliès (1861–1938). The forms of the Kabuki stage and the pace remained the same, but for the staged combat, *tachimawari*, simple straight cuts (stopping the recording camera and then starting again with Onoe in the same position, in the same place in the frame, but in a different costume or set) made it possible for Onoe to jump magically from place to

Onoe Matsunosuke in two scenes from *Chizakura Okoma* (*Blood-Spattered Okoma*, 1915), directed by Kobayashi Yaroku. The film was based on a Kabuki play about the daughter of a merchant who rejects her rich husband for her lover Saizō, *Koi musume mukashi hachijō* (*The Intrigues of Okoma, Daughter of the Shirokoya*, 1775). Onoe was a small-time Kabuki actor discovered by Makino Shōzō, who made him the first film star. Even so, not until the very end of his career, challenged by Makino's crew of young stars, did he try to move beyond Kabuki-style stage acting. Onoe was the first of a line of low-ranking Kabuki actors, with no hope of a career on the stage, who found success in film.

place, to change characters, form, and roles faster than on stage — where the fast change was an art. Onoe turned himself into a frog and back again, disappeared in and out of his combats, walked on water — there was no end of the possibilities. The principle, however, was the same: everything and anything might move within the frame, but the frame itself, the audience's position — the camera — did not. Moreover, the camera was always far enough to take in the whole body, from the top of the head to the tip of the toe.

The camera was first released in *Serpent.*[1] It was produced by Bandō Tsumasaburō (1901–1953), a former Kabuki actor, who also starred. The big (and long) fight scene at the end features a back-tracking crane shot[2] showing the hero pursued by hordes of police, trapped in the middle of a circle, and fighting his way out. This was the first time a crane shot had been used, indeed, the first time in conjunction with modern fight choreography, or *tate.* The high-angle shot of the hero surrounded by police became the symbol of an age, the passing of the Taishō to the Shōwa, in Ichikawa Utaemon's 1927 *Dokuro* (*Skull*) and Makino Masahiro's *Rōningai* (*Street of Masterless Samurai*, 1928).[3] Not only did the camera, positioned high over the action, move, but through that overhead shot of the hero trapped in the middle of the police, the motif of the circle was established in fight scenes to symbolize "no way out," the theme of the common people in depression-ridden Japan in the 1920s, and the audience was suddenly projected into a three-dimensional rather than merely two-dimensional view of the action.

There was no cutting on Bandō in his combat scenes (cut on action). Bandō was so good and so fast with a sword that cutting, which functions principally to increase the sense of speed, was not necessary. In fight scenes, there was no breaking up of movement into individual shots which were edited together: the action never needed to be faked; the actor and his performance reigned supreme here. Cutting was reserved for expressing emotion. The avant-garde cutting in *Serpent* is not of the fighting itself but of a line of policemen facing the hero: the brief shot has been cut into bits and spliced back together haphazardly to express the hero's near hysteria in the face of his relentless pursuers.

The camera started moving beyond the fight scene with camera-man Karasawa Hiromitsu (1900–1980). He was working for director Nomura Hōtei at the time Itō Daisuke was writing scripts for him. But Itō was unable to get moving until 1926, when Nikkatsu refused to allow Itō to use a new actor, Ōkōchi Denjirō (1898–1962), in *Tsukigata Hanpeita*,[4] but agreed to give him Ōkōchi to film *Chōkon* (*Long Standing Hatred*, 1926). Determined to show off Ōkōchi to the whole studio, he started filming with a scene modeled on one in *Tsukigata Hanpeita*, in which he had the camera track Ōkōchi as he "lurched, staggered, fell, rose, and walked" through an audience hall, all the while giving his lines to correspond in volume to the distance of his counterparts in the corridor (not necessary in a silent film!). Ōkōchi, amazingly, could walk and talk at the same time. Itō made his point and made Ōkōchi a star.[5]

Itō's moving camera earned him the nickname Idō Daisuki ("I love mov-

Abe Ichizoku (The Abe Clan, 1938), directed by Kumagai Hisatora. The Progressive Troupe was critical in the development of western representationalism in the Japanese period film. This scene depicts three Abe brothers who refuse to accept their lord's insults to their house: from the right, second son Yagobei (Nakamura Kan'emon), third son Ichidayū (Ichikawa Shinzaburō) and fifth son Shichinojō (Ichikawa Senshō). A tension between legalism and sincerity (*makoto*) may very well reflect a contemporary tension as it did the tensions of the seventeenth century samurai class making the transition from professional soldier to their new role as government officials. Nevertheless, the real issue, particularly obvious to those who have read Mori Ōgai's original story, is the definition of samurai as the old-fashioned professional and freelancer who would choose family over lord and who could break a contract if the lord did not follow through. One indication of the approval of the rebellion in the film is indicated by the decision to have the family chant Nichiren's *daimoku* (*Namu Myōhō Renge Kyō* [*I Take refuge in the Sutra of the Lotus Flower of the Wonderful Dharma*]) instead of the *nenbutsu* (*Namu Amida butsu* [*I Take refuge in Amida Buddha*]). This is, after all, a Zenshinza (Progressive Troupe) production. It is still performed by them on stage (photograph courtesy of the Kawakita Memorial Film Institute).

ing") and unheard-of full billing with the stars. However, some of the success of Itō and Karasawa has to be credited to Ōkōchi, an actor trained in the second troupe of the New National Theater, founded by Sawada Shōjirō (1892–1929). Sawada had been trained in western techniques and western plays in the new acting program at Waseda University and had been a leading actor of the first Shingeki troupe, the Arts Theater (Geijitsu-za). Sawada, however, made his name staging the first modern sword plays (*kengeki*), such as *Tsukigata Hanpeita*, *Kunisada Chūji*, and, of course, *Great Bodhisattva Pass*. One would expect his disciple, Ōkōchi, like all New National Theater actors trained with one foot solidly on the traditional ground of staged combat, to make his contribution to film development in the fighting scenes. However, the moving camera was initially used to express the psychological state of the protagonist rather than in creating the reality of the fight. In the 1931 *Oatsurae Jirōkichi gōshi* (*Jirōkichi the Ratkid*), Itō moves the camera to track the hero Jirōkichi, played by Ōkōchi, as he walks away from the girl he loves to express the surge of emotion in a man in the very act of renunciation.

One Kabuki troupe that collectively (including their male specialist in female roles, or *onnagata*)[6] made a successful transition to film was the Progressive Troupe, the Zenshinza. In 1933, they made their first film, an adaptation by Inagaki Hiroshi of another Hasegawa Shin work, *Shigure no Danshichi* (*Danshichi in the Mist*). In an interview,[7] one of the two founders of the troupe and co-star of the film, Nakamura Kan'emon (1901–1981), spoke about the trouble they had making the transition from stage to film: things were going so badly that Katō Daisuke, a Zenshinza actor,[8] was dispatched to fetch in Inagaki Hiroshi to help the director. He noted, however, that he eventually got the hang of acting for the camera once he understood how film language corresponded to Kabuki language: an actor who could cut a *mie* (the body freezes into a pose with a roll of the head and one or both eyes crossed (it draws attention to the face) could relate it to the close-up.[9] The Zenshinza went on to make some of the most famous and highly regarded Japanese films of the pre-war period: *The Abe Clan*, *Kōchiyama Sōshun*, *Humanity and Paper Balloons*, and *Genroku Chūshingura*. What is it then about Kabuki that lends itself so well to translation into film?

The Stage

The Kabuki stage is rectangular and the performance area is shallow — even more so when, as in dance pieces, the musicians and chanters are placed behind the actors rather than to the side. The effect is to push the actor toward the audience[10] and for compositions of actors to be two dimensional. Actors playing supporting roles will be arranged to the side or below the main actor,

Meijï period illustration depicting a Kabuki theater.

not to the rear. The flatness of the image has the same effect as the wide screen.

The audience sits either on the floor of the theater (just below the level of the stage) or in the two (or more) levels of balconies on three sides. Depending on where the seat is, an individual is either near to, far from, level with, above, or below the stage. This corresponds to the long and medium shots in film and the angles, straight, high, or low, of film. To achieve an extremely long shot, the adult actor will be replaced by a child actor to make him smaller and thus appear farther away; this is also one of the few occasions that provide the equivalent of deep focus.

To the left, with audience on both sides, is a raised runway (*hanamichi*) leading from the stage to a greenroom at the back of the theater. This is the route by which entrances and exits are made. This creates a three-dimensional space which includes the audience, making the audience participants in the action: not only does the audience face the actors but also other members of the audience. Watching an actor enter or leave the stage forces the audience to twist their heads to follow the actor. This has the same net effect as a panning shot, where the camera swivels to follow the action.

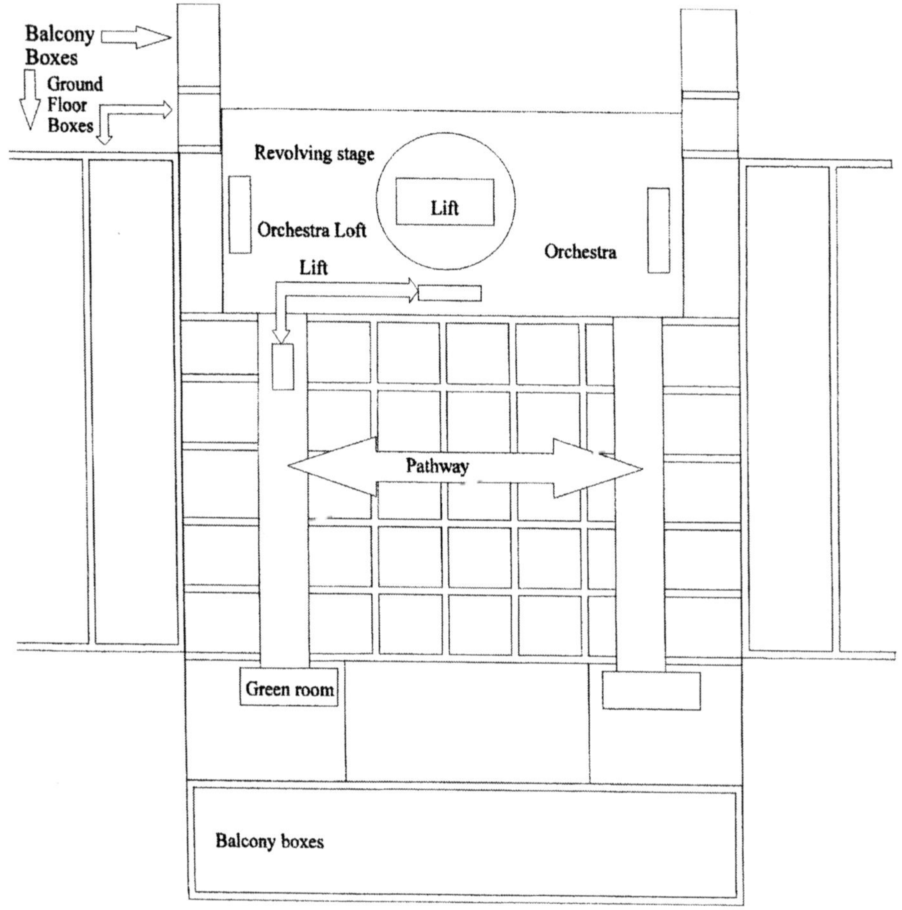

Diagram showing layout of traditional Kabuki theater.

To the right there may also be a second runway (*kari-hanamichi*). It is not always used, but removed to allow for more seats for the audience. One of the uses of both runways is to have two characters, one on each, shouting at each other over the heads of the audience. Those seated between the two actors have to twist their heads from side to side to face the actor speaking; thus, they see two different planes. This has the same effect as alternating shots (reverse-angle shot) of two actors on screen to show one and then the other speaking. Moreover, the audience behind each of the two actors on their runways will see both: one from the rear and the other at some distance facing the first. Depending where the seat is, the audience will look down on both, over the shoulder of one to the other, or even past the feet of one to the other.

This produces the same effect as a high-angle two-shot (two people in the shot), an over-the-shoulder two-shot, or a low-angle two-shot (like the ones used in Westerns, where the sheriff and the villain confront each other to shoot it out).

There are several elevators covered by trap doors. There are two small ones: one at the stage end of the *hanamichi* and one just right of center at the front of the stage. Actors and props appear and disappear through these trap-doors. This effect is usually replicated in film by the dissolve: the blank wall is filmed and then the actor playing, say, a ghost in front of the wall. When processed, the two strips of film are printed to overlap with the light on the first being reduced toward the end of the strip and the light on the second increased from the beginning of the strip so that the ghost seems gradually to appear.[11]

The several elevators in the revolving stage are truly amazing.[12] They are used to greatest effect for scene changes. For instance, a man is pushed off a cliff; we all wait and watch the cliff lifted up until the base of the cliff can be seen and the man who has fallen. Or, the stage lifts, which moves the scene from the roof of a gate to the doors of the gate. This produces the same effect as the crane shot: the camera is mounted on a lift and raised or lowered to follow the action, such as someone going up or down the stairs.

The center stage not only lifts and lowers (in several different sections) but also rotates. Sometimes the stage is rotated from one scene to the next; in the version of Tsuruya Nanboku's *Yotsuya kaidan* (*Yotsuya Ghost Story*) which I saw, the stage revolved to change the scene from Iuemon's hovel to the rich man's mansion. The stage also rotates the scene from one side of a house to another. In film, this is achieved by cutting from one scene to another, sometimes with a dissolve (the two scenes overlap) or a fade-in and fade-out (the screen gradually goes dark at the end of one scene and gradually grows light at the beginning of the next. Particularly in scenes set in mansions, the actors walk as the stage is rotated clockwise so that the audience can follow along as a servant leads a guest along a corridor from one room to another as the stage rotates. Or as in the case of Segawa Joko's 1851 *Martyr of Sakura* (*Sakura gimin den*) staged by the Zenshinza in 1981, the last scene rotates to the right, and we follow the hero from his house, out the gate, out and around the house over a bridge, through the woods, all in the snow and with himself trying to shake off his son who is trying to hold him back. This, of course, corresponds to the tracking or dolly shot: the camera is mounted on a track (or a bicycle or wheelchair, as in the olden days) and pushed along to follow the action.

The actor himself achieves effects that are the equivalent of the close-up in film. As mentioned above, the *mie* correlates to the close-up. In addition, a series of close-ups is anticipated in something I call a sequential articulation. This originated in the movements of puppets and was taken up by Kabuki along with the puppet plays. For example, a hand is raised over the head; however, this is accomplished not in one movement, but by a series of individual movements with the backward flip of the hand last. Or, again, if an actor moves into a pose, the movements of the feet, hands, and head are performed in sequence. If a head is turned to the right, the chin starts moving slightly in the opposite direction before going to the right, and, at the end of the turn, the chin flips slightly to the left. Sequential articulation draws attention to that part of the body being moved and thus functions like the close-up, which also functions to draw attention to one movement or action at a time. The actor does not simply open the door: we see him move to the door; we see his hand move to the doorknob; from the other side of the door we see the knob turn. And so on.

At the time of the Restoration (1867), there were in Japan approximately two thousand Kabuki theaters of various sizes but in general possessing the same equipment. The plays were put on by the local people themselves at festivals and many learned to read from a Kabuki scenario the way Americans learned by reading Shakespeare and the Bible. The permeation of the Kabuki stage throughout Japan may be one reason that it took so long for the Japanese to make the transfer from moving stage to moving camera: film could, in essence, provide nothing more than the stage already could — movement horizontally and vertically, movement from one location to another and back, deep focus, participating in a conversation, being in the middle of a quarrel, even staring into the face of the character and seeing time frozen or fragmented. The fact that the language of the Japanese theater was presentational (not realistic) was no hindrance to conceptualizing in ways that people in the West learned through the process of watching films as they developed over a period of time. In Japan, the experience of watching an early film could not match that of the theater; the Japanese audience and actors were much too sophisticated in their ability to integrate multiple points of view and multiple planes into continuous time and space.

The West, except for the revolving stage, lifts below trap-doors, and tableaux, did not have the advantages of the Japanese stage. Moreover, modern, realistic theater, exemplified by the works of Ibsen and Chekhov, had no need for them. Western stage theorists were less interested in the physical properties of the Japanese stage than in the actor and the actor's relationship to the audience.[13] Therefore, it is natural that westerners should create in film what they did not produce on stage, certainly on the stage of Ibsen and Chekhov. Certainly one reason that the Japanese film took so long to convert its stage language into a corresponding film language is that initially the reform movement in film was in the hands of leaders of Shinpa and especially Shingeki, a direct imitation of the modern western stage, and, of course, of its limitations.

Western Film Realism and Japanese Film Realism

In *To the Distant Observer: Form and Meaning in the Japanese Cinema*, Noël Burch characterizes western film realism as based on depth of field, centering through frame composition, and continuity through the synchronization of sound and image, the focus of the image on a single narrative, a main character, and his action (rather than on observers, reactors, or reactions).[14]

Everything in the Japanese tradition of oral narrative, including film, militates against this rigidity. The story of the hero is always filtered through the reactions of the witnesses to his life, as in the case of Shimizu Jirōchō, who was made famous during his own lifetime by one of his followers.[15] In fact, the life of Jirōchō is the lynchpin connecting the stories of all his famous followers, such as Ōmasa, Komasa, and Mori no Ishimatsu. The story of the revenge of the death of the lord of Akō is the story of nearly fifty men, each one of whose name and role is as well known to the Japanese as that of the leader Ōishi Kuranosuke. In the puppet theater and in Kabuki dance, the function of producing the image belongs to doll or actor, while the function of producing the sound belongs to chanter and musicians. Ozu Yasujirō (1903–1963) breaks the continuity of a character's narrative with shots of laundry or teapots. And finally, Mizoguchi moves his camera to de-center the characters whenever they move or focuses on the faces of those overhearing an argument instead of those involved in the quarrel.

Some of the most interesting effects have been introduced by period film directors who had already made their reputations by mastering and translating western film techniques. After his father's studio failed, Makino Masahiro made newsreels and Naniwa-*bushi* films and thereby became the first major director with full mastery of sound. In fact, he helped several other directors make the transition in the early thirties. Makino continued to experiment with sound. His *Zoku Shimizu minato* (*Shimizu Harbor Continued*, 1940) is the famous story of Mori no Ishimatsu's journey to the Kompira Shrine at Sanuki to present Jirōchō's sword and his death at the hands of rival gamblers. As a film, it violates standard concepts of continuity of time. The film begins with Kataoka Chiezō, the film's starring actor, putting on a record of the story by Hirosawa Torazō (1899–1964) and lying down on a couch to listen. Cut on action[16] as he sits up, and suddenly he is in character and costume as Ishimatsu. Torazō's voice continues as voice-over narration. And then Torazō himself appears as a fellow passenger on the ferry to Sanuki. Not only that, but he starts chanting lines about Ishimatsu to Ishimatsu, and if I remember correctly, the lines about Ishimatsu's death just before his death. All this makes for an extraordinary display of break-in-continuity and time and a violation of the western conventions of narrativity in film. But Makino can afford to play around as much as he likes because the story of Ishimatsu and the position of Torazō as the foremost interpreter of that story are so well known.

Ishida Tamizō's 1938 *Hana chirinu* (*The Flowers Have Fallen*), a story of geisha just before the Restoration, has been highly praised for its innovative continuity. The film, which takes places almost exclusively in a single set, cuts on action constantly. Nevertheless, it is otherwise fairly straightforward except for a couple of shots which telescope time by layering present image with future sound track. Again, the fact that the film was based on a well-known play made innovation possible because the narrative continuity was brought by the audience. Cutting on action was used by Inagaki Hiroshi, and not in the combat scenes, but between two scenes in his 1962 *Chūshingura*. For example, a character moves backwards right to left across the screen; cut to another character in another scene in the same position moving in the same direction. Continuity is based on optics, not narrative (story line). What supports the narrative's continuity is the audience's familiarity with the stories of the forty-seven ronin: the audience is able to identify almost immediately the identity of the successive characters and to provide the logic of continuity.

But note, the conventions of the narrative make possible the playing with film editing conventions. Western film realism was important to those directors working with new narratives. *The Abe Clan* had never been in the repertoire of oral story tellers and was not familiar to mass audiences. There had never been a story like that of *Seven Samurai*. Yamanaka used famous characters, but the stories were borrowed from western films. Playing for effect, performance, is only possible when using material already familiar to the audience. Ichikawa Kon did things in his 1963 *Yukinojō henge* (*Revenge of an Actor*) that would have been impossible had not the story already been filmed at least once before, the first time in 1935 by Kinugasa Teinosuke with the same star, Hasegawa Kazuo.[17] Performance is possible only with familiar material. Japanese film experimentation is, in general, reserved for traditional narratives. Western film realism is used to introduce new narratives.

Why, then, do the top period films, which also tend to be the best examples of the use of "matching past and present" to make a political statement, tend to favor western film realism over Japanese film realism? In films by Itō, Inagaki, Makino, Yamanaka, Kobayashi, and Kurosawa, there is no mistaking that there is one main story supported by one main character, that whom we see is whom we hear, that what we see is a human rather than a nonsentient object, and that, even in wide-screen, characters are centered and depth of field is characteristic of long or even medium shots. Americans have no trouble following one of these Japanese period films because they are such careful deconstructions of American films. Kurosawa is accessible because his presentation style is so American, owing much to John Ford. Although the narratives are traditional Japanese, the mode of representation is western: like Nakazato Kaizan and Hasegawa Shin between 1913 and 1930, the later Japanese film makers and their stage colleagues looked to the West to provide a new political language to state old political grievances.

Part Three

The Scene in Japanese Narrative

9

Thematic Composition, Formulaic Diction and Cinema

Since the 1930s, a variety of theories have been advanced to explain how film works. Certainly, a great deal of theorizing has gone into explaining the American Western. Nevertheless, while a great deal has been said about, for example, myth and archetypes, less has been said about the ability of a director to demonstrate creativity or individuality in the closed narrative system of a genre such as the Western, characterized as it is by its stock characters, conventions, and clichés, or about the value to the director of the closed narrative system itself. Oral tradition studies[1] have a long history of dealing with precisely these issues. However, since the focus has been on the Bible, ancient epic traditions, such as *Gilgamesh* or *Beowulf*, and contemporary folk traditions (aligned with folklore studies), oral tradition studies seem to have had no impact on film studies as a whole, even though individual articles may have come close to it in their methodologies or conclusions.[2]

Standard approaches to traditional and oral or oral-derived narratives have long been provided by analyses based on the original Milman Parry–Albert Lord theory of oral composition.[3] Oral composition is characterized by thematic composition and formulaic diction. In other words, narratives are composed of type scenes, also called themes. The type scene "may be regarded as a recurrent block of narrative with an identifiable structure, such as a sacrifice, the reception of a guest, the launching and beaching of a ship, the donning of armor."[4] For example, the *Odyssey* is made up almost predominantly of hospitality scenes: greeting a guest, bathing him, serving him food and wine.[5] What is critical about the type scene is that it is made up of actions; it demands performance.

The scenes are described conventionally in "formulaic diction" (remember the formula "rosy-fingered dawn"?). *Odyssey* has a high incidence of verbal repetition in the hospitality scenes: the same actions are described in the same formulae, sometimes for many stanzas. Each culture, however, determines the level of rigidity in the relationship between the type scene and its diction, the sequence of actions and the exact words that describe them.

What drives the process of composition in the epic is apparently the need to perform narratives under a time constraint — no long pauses to think about the next line. Meter, formulae, and type scenes are memory aids. They allow a performer to keep performing and at the same time think ahead to what is coming up next. Repeating type scenes and short memorized passages enabled the performer of the *Odyssey*, for example, to keep going and at the same time to keep in mind where Odysseus was going and what he was going to do next.

Similarly, time was an issue in the old Hollywood studio system: with the budgets and time schedules, it was necessary to develop very efficient forms of production. For the director, this meant doing what he knew best: this was usually methods he had perfected by specializing in particular narratives, with corresponding type scenes, and, in certain cases, a corresponding set of actors, sets, and camera techniques. The combination of type scene in composition and diction in filming make up the style of the director; those pressed most for time, directors of the cheapest productions, usually have the same style and their films can scarce be distinguished one from the other.

The size or length of a unit of a narrative is flexible depending on the culture; it can be as short as "white-armed Athena" or as long as a string of sentences describing the arms of a knight. The *Odyssey*, for example, is full of scenes, in nearly identical diction (word for word), of the reception of a guest: bathing him, dressing him, serving him meat and wine. No doubt because it describes action which can be performed, the scene is also a principal narrative unit in cinema. In film, genres have the most easily identified type scenes and formulaic diction. In the American Western, for example, the most easily recognizable units are the scenes: the gunfight, courtin' the schoolmarm (usually in a buggy), the barroom brawl, the chase, the runaway (wagon, train, or cattle), the powwow, etc. Sometimes they are as short as coughing into a handkerchief, which was used to indicate that the character suffered from tuberculosis by John Ford in *My Darling Clementine* (1946) as well as by Phillipe de Broca in *Le Bossu* (*On Guard*, 1997).

In the Western, especially, where this kind of narrative structure predominates, there are actually several different sub-narratives: the pony express, the cattle drive, the cavalry, the railroad, wagons west, the gunfighter, and the big trees — the list is not exhaustive.[6] Even so, they share a common pool of type scenes, those described above. However, the different sub-narratives (sub-genres of the Western) are themselves distinguished in terms of what is in front of the camera — the formulaic diction: depending on the narrative, we see peaceful herds of cattle or of buffalo; the cattle stampede, or the wagon-train horses run away; the Indians chase the wagon-train, or the cavalry, or the stagecoach; or the robbers chase the stagecoach, or the robbers chase the train.

The study of such narrative units is a principal concern of oral tradition studies.[7] Oral tradition studies differs fundamentally from other approaches in its treatment of the narrative unit. The approaches derived from linguistics, for example, posit meaning as derived from the unit's place in a group of other units (context). In oral tradition studies, the meaning of the unit is understood as derived from its function as a referent for an entire body of narrative and narrative practices: there may be variants of the unit, but the meaning of the unit is neither contested nor negotiable.[8]

Take for example the treatment of a narrative unit, the ball scene, which has many variants. In the 1938 William Wyler film *Jezebel*, the Olympus Ball is understood by the usual approaches only as the physical and social setting for Julie's humiliation as a result of her decision to flout social convention by wearing a red dress to embarrass her fiancé Pres and as leading to Pres's decision to end their engagement. The Olympus Ball can only be interpreted according to what is seen, spoken, or narrated in the text or performance itself. However, oral tradition studies would attribute a much wider significance to the ball scene. The very mention of a ball foreshadows doom, that something terrible is about to happen. At a ball, Kitty discovers she has lost Vronsky to Anna Karenina. "It's my party and I'll cry if I want to," because Johnny has gone off with Judy.[9] Finally, the big party at Penelope's place is eventually turned into a bloody massacre by Odysseus. If something terrible is to happen, it will happen at such a celebration. Excitement or tension is created for the audience by putting off the eagerly anticipated and ineluctable catastrophe as late as possible. Needless to say, the use of the ball scene is never an allusion to any one particular text or performance. Rather, the scene and its use are traditional. It is just the way it is done.

A film may have several type scenes. Moreover, variations of a single type scene can make up a considerable proportion of a single film. *Gone with the Wind* (Victor Fleming et al., 1939), for example, is a "fall from paradise" narrative ostensibly about the Civil War and Reconstruction (indicated by the hoop-skirts, singing slaves, and carpet bags); the paradise is that of the old South, the old South of gracious ladies, chivalric gentlemen, and stately mansions — not to mention the loyal family "servants" and contented, well-fed, and ever-euphonious field hands who support them. The fall from paradise narrative has as its variation the narrative of the fall of southern womanhood personified by Scarlett O'Hara. The film is made up principally of variations of one type scene: older woman corrects younger woman. Usually, it is

Mammy scolding Scarlett ("You cain't show yoah bosom 'fo three o'clock."), but India Wilkes, Mrs. Mead and Aunt Pittypat get in their licks, too. Scarlett is constantly in need of correction by the caretakers of the tradition of southern womanhood, black and white, slave and free, something demanding action that can be performed: the women scold, gossip behind their fans, threaten to faint, or just widen their eyes in horror. The multi-forms of the type scene and its diction are created by the change of location, characters, and gestures. Nevertheless, however different they may seem, they are indeed various forms of one type scene.

The type scene was used by John Ford (1894–1973) in his Westerns.[10] In *My Darling Clementine* (1946), he used the chase scene, the cattle drive, the poker game, courtin' the school marm, church raising, the ball, the gunfight, and the barroom brawl in two variations (one very truncated, but nevertheless identifiable as a type scene), among others. In *She Wore a Yellow Ribbon*, Ford used the barroom brawl, a variation of courtin' the schoolmarm (including a truncated buggy ride), the ball, the march, the raid (including the charge), the aftermath of an Indian attack, the chase, on parade, the pow-wow, and others.

Now, Ford used traditional type scenes in traditional ways. In *She Wore a Yellow Ribbon*, Ford used the ball scene traditionally: a retirement party is interrupted by a message and the retiring Captain Nathan Brittles is off to his last military engagement. However, Ford also used the ball scene untraditionally: in *My Darling Clementine*, he used the ball scene as a sign of community because there the hero demonstrates his eligibility for membership by dancing, if awkwardly, with his "lady fair," as he does by his flair with a carving knife at Sunday dinner. Occasionally, a type scene may refer back not only to the tradition of the genre but specifically to films within Ford's own repertoire. For example, that very church-raising dance has Henry Fonda dancing the same high-knee polka he did in Ford's *Young Mister Lincoln* (1939).

Ford also used type scenes which were not necessarily traditional to the Western, such as the Sunday dinner. Where some of them come from, I am not certain. For example, although sermons and funerals are seen often enough in Westerns to be considered traditional, the address to the dead is not. In *She Wore a Yellow Ribbon*, the captain goes to the grave of his wife and children and talks to his wife while watering the flowers. In *My Darling Clementine*, Wyatt Earp visits the grave of his youngest brother, slain by the Clantons, and talks to him. Another type scene peculiar to Ford (and then later a defining motif in the career of Maureen O'Hara) is the violence done to women. In *My Darling Clementine*, Earp dunks the saloon girl into a horse trough. In *She Wore a Yellow Ribbon*, the young niece of the major is subjected to verbal abuse by almost every man in the film, including the sergeant, a clear if new type scene of the narrative of gender hierarchy that substitutes for class hierarchy in the world view of Ford and Americans in general.[11]

In the use of type scenes not traditional to the Western, Ford took advantage of crossing narratives. The crossing of narratives takes a variety of forms; nonetheless, depending on the culture, it is either permitted or it is not. It certainly is a feature of the two films of Ford we have been looking at. For example, *My Darling Clementine* crosses several narratives: the settling-of-the-West narrative, the Victorian death-by-consumption narrative, and the twentieth century hospital romance and sad-drunk narratives. This is accomplished through the character of Doc Holiday, transformed from dentist to Boston surgeon who has fled to the West because of tuberculosis and deals with his problem by drinking and other anti-social behavior. These narratives are identified by their corresponding type scenes and diction. Hospital romance narratives, for example, always include a life-or-death operation: the surgery scene in *Clementine* is complete with the requisite washing of the hands of the god-like surgeon (not to mention the low-angle shot of surgeon against the overhead light) and the adoring nurse.[12] Doc's coughing into a white handkerchief (which the audience knows to be bloodied) is a formulaic motif of the death-by-consumption narrative. Clearly, the real story of the gunfight at the OK Corral was rewritten in terms of clearly established type scenes. *She Wore a Yellow Ribbon* makes use of the happy-drunk narrative in the character of the Sergeant Quincannon, the barroom brawl scene, and the hospital narrative (the surgery in the wagon) as well. Instead of the death-by-consumption narrative, however, the film features the narrative of the old man to be replaced (as in *The Last Laugh*[13] and *King Lear)*, complete with arthritic knee, reading glasses, and the retirement pocket watch. This old man, however, about to ride off into the sunset, is spared the agony of retirement by a commission as a scout.

Despite their reliance on tradition, what has come before in the genre, the films of John Ford stand out in certain ways, certainly in their untraditional use of type scenes. That is, if the Western is a dialect, then Ford's films are recognizably idiolectical in their narrative patterns. This is what makes Ford not just a faithful transmitter of tradition, a role sure to kill any tradition, but a creative force that demonstrates the real flexibility and adaptative qualities of a living tradition. This is what makes Ford an auteur, a recognizable and individual artist in the field of the Western.

Much has been written on the influence of John Ford on the work of Kurosawa Akira (1910–1998).[14] Most of the comparisons emphasize only "strong, general similarities of narrative, image, or characterization."[15] Nevertheless, Ford's influence on Kurosawa is clear enough. We see Nathan Brittles in Kanbei, the middle-aged, oft-defeated professional soldier in *Seven*

Samurai. We see the narrative of the mentor-disciple relationship, a variation of the godfather-godson relationship between Brittles and Lieutenant Cohill in *Yellow Ribbon*, between Kanbei and Katsushirō in *Seven Samurai.* We also see it also in *Sanjuro*, in which the hero (played by Mifune Toshirō) becomes mentor to a troop of perfectly inept young samurai.[16] In *Seven Samurai*, again, we see scenes of samurai being kind to children, as we see in *She Wore a Yellow Ribbon* (as the troopers care for the young survivors of an Indian raid). There is the ball scene, as the traditional Japanese type scene, the festival, which Kurosawa uses conventionally in both the Japanese and western senses, to indicate that something bad is going to happen: the youngest samurai Katsushirō is rejected by the peasant's daughter Shino.

Much of the action is derived from Ford's films. In *Seven Samurai*, we do see a truncated barroom brawl at the inn, we do see the *bushi* bandits run horses through the village (Ford's version of the horse stampede used as a charge on the Indian village at the end of *Yellow Ribbon*), we do see a several versions of the ambush (one with distinctly Japanese diction, a samurai contemplating a flower, and one that clearly parodies the barroom brawl). Of course there is the monumental battle in the rain, truncated to the aftermath of the Clantons' attack on the Earps' camp in *Clementine*. There is even an "on parade" scene, with the peasants lined up like Ford's troopers with their spears at attention.

We can also recognize typical scenes of the Western in general in *Seven Samurai*: the 'round the campfire scene, a sign of community in the Western, in the scene in which Kikuchiyo, the peasant turned soldier, welcomes the others with fish caught and cooking over a fire. Building the defenses round the village can be seen as a functional substitute for circling the wagons. Certainly, the file of *nobushi*, or samurai turned bandits, at the beginning of the film silhouetted against a bright sky and looking down into the valley of the village, are the counterparts of the Indians on the rise, typically a line of fully caparisoned or bonneted warriors lined up on an overlooking ridge.

Although Kurosawa could replicate some of the themes, plot devices, and characters of Ford's films, he found it sometimes difficult to find Japanese correspondences for the Western's type scenes. Difference in culture prevents adaptations of certain type scenes from the Westerns. The courtin' the schoolmarm type scene has no correspondence in Kurosawa's period films. The traditional Western type scene, part of the "up-town girl" narrative of the socially mobile American man, is faithfully followed in *Clementine*: Wyatt Earp courts the lady from Boston who comes in search of Holiday — and who stays in Tombstone to become the schoolmarm. In feudal Japan, a man did not court a woman above his station, certainly not without dreadful consequences, as demonstrated in Mizoguchi's *The Life of Oharu*. The affair between Katsushirō and Shino falls into neither the schoolmarm nor the saloon girl type scenes (saloon girls who fall in love with heroes have to die, as does Chihuahua in the life-or-death operation scene in *Clementine*). Moreover, in Japanese narrative, there are no cattle drives and no herds of cattle because the little pasture land that existed in Japan was used for horses, and in any case, samurai are not drovers. The Japanese version of the poker game belonged conventionally to the Japanese genres devoted to nineteenth and twentieth century gamblers (*matatabi-mono*, *ninkyō*, and yakuza films) and in *Seven Samurai* is truncated in the scene of the transient packhorse drivers playing cards at the inn where the farmers are staying. There are burials but no funerals, no addresses to a higher power, no addresses to the dead.[17]

It is not that Kurosawa is instead particularly interested in traditional Japanese narratives or type scenes. There are indeed traditional Japanese narratives (some older than others) and they, too, are made up of traditional type scenes: the sex scene (*nureba*),[18] the torture scene (*semeba*), the fight scene, (*shuraba*),[19] the death scene, the hero-in-disguise-reveals-himself scene (*jitsuwa*), the lovers-run-away-to-die scene (*michiyuki*),[20] the taking-the-tonsure scene, and others. Some scenes, such as visits to the licensed quarters (*keiseigoto* or prostitute play), are truncations of full plays the performance of which had been forbidden by the government. Like the type scene in the Western, the scene in the traditional Japanese narrative has both denotative and connotative, or traditional, force. When, for example, a man is forced to take up his sword and fight, the scene can be interpreted according to what has happened before: the man has refused to kill a woman and is being attacked by those who demanded the crime of him — simple cause and effect. However, the scene also has a traditional reading: the fight scene is always a Buddhist illustration of hell that proves that the world is evil and that those caught in it suffer. That is how the fight scene, or battle scene, has been used in epic and theater for six hundred years.[21]

Nevertheless, Kurosawa has not shown himself particularly interested in them (except fight scenes, and they are not particularly traditional), just as he has not shown himself to be interested in traditional Japanese narratives — he has made no adaptations of Bunraku or Kabuki, for example, except for a comedy version of a story found in epic, Nō, and Kabuki, the 1945 *Tora no o wo fumu otokotachi* (*The Men Who Tread on the Tiger's Tail*).[22] He has used one type scene from the medieval epic: Kurosawa used variations of the clearly identifiable type scene of the riderless horse as a sign of the fall of the lord in both the 1957 *Throne of Blood* (the bucking horse in the courtyard) and the 1980 *Shadow Warrior* (the horse from which the double falls). As seen in *Throne of Blood* and the 1985 *Ran*, he apparently even created at least one new type scene: the messenger who rides or runs in to bring word to his lord.

What makes Kurosawa an auteur is his combination of historical didactism and his mastery of action: moving camera, multiple cameras and cutting, and scenes of fighting using real martial arts, running, riding horses, and running horses. Despite the break with the tradition of the narratives and their type scenes, even Kurosawa could not escape certain elements of traditional diction. The very antiquarianism that makes for his "poodle fight" scenes, his on-location elaborate sets, and costumes, that commits him to the historical authenticity of physical details, gestures, and speech, also ties him to the iconography of the historical period of the film, the topic with which this book begins. Thus, although the narratives may have been new to the audience, who had always depended on previously seen, traditional forms (even those of American films, like the Western) to interpret what was going on, the iconography, especially that of the Tokugawa period, established clearly the over-arching social context of the individual narrative.

This made the films comprehensible and acceptable to the audience. Their patronage, not the praise of critics, determined whether Kurosawa's period films would contribute to the tradition. Once Kurosawa, as a western-style painter, turned to color, long takes, long shots, and long lectures (as in *Shadow Warrior*), the Japanese audience and producers abandoned him. In the end, the production costs of his period films proved prohibitive to the Japanese film studios; therefore, historical didactism is now just barely preserved in the yearly fictionalized biographical-historical series, the *Taiga Dorama* (*Taiga Drama*), of Japan's public broadcasting company, NHK Television. Of his realistic presentation of fights using real martial arts, little is recognizable except, perhaps, the sound effects.

10

The Japanese Epic as Buddhist Sermon

Of the several hundred surviving examples of Japanese battle literature, including variations, over ninety percent were produced between 1375 and about 1600. Even so, only a handful of texts from the tenth through fourteenth centuries have received significant attention, certainly in the West. And, until the 1970s, only they were generally recognized as war tale or epic, *gunki monogatari* or *senki monogatari*.[1] I am speaking of *Hōgen monogatari* (*Tale of the Disorder in Hōgen*), *Heiji monogatari* (*The Tale of the Heiji Era*), *Heike monogatari* (*The Tale of the Heike*), *Genpei jōsuiki* (*The Chronicle of the Rise and Fall of the Minamoto and Taira*), and *Taiheiki* (*The Chronicle of the Great Pacification*).

A younger wave of Japanese scholars[2] who allied themselves with senior scholars in the field of folklore[3] have identified and added to the list of epics at least five examples from the period after 1375: *Meitokuki* (*Chronicle of the Meitoku Era*), *Ōtō monogatari* (*Tale of the Battle of Ōtō*), *Yūki senjō monogatari* (*Tale of the Battlefield of Yūki*), *Kōnodai senki* (*Chronicle of the Battle of Kōnodai*),[4] *Sasago ochi no sōshi* (*Story of the Fall of Sasago Castle*), and *Nakao ochi no sōshi* (*Story of the Fall of Nakao Castle*).

The principal contribution of these scholars to the study of the epic has been the recognition of the expanded text (rather than the original text) as the object of research and the role of added material, in particular of religious material, in defining the genre.[5] In the epic this religious material is predominantly Pure Land Buddhist.

What sort of material am I referring to? In the *Heike monogatari* and others can be found different kinds of religious material. The first is the motif of invoking the name of Amida Buddha, *Namu Amida Butsu*, the *nenbutsu* motif. The *nenbutsu* is chanted in times of danger or in anticipation of death. For example, in the story of Giō, the dancer replaced by another in the affections of a powerful man, three women in a remote cottage hear a knock at the door at midnight and, anticipating the worst, chant the *nenbutsu* before opening.[6] The *nenbutsu* is often chanted as the *bushi* faces death on the battlefield.[7] The *nenbutsu* motif invokes the Buddhist concept of the Latter Age of Buddhist Teachings, *mappō*, which is used to explain the degeneracy and decline of the social and political sphere or the destruction of a temple.[8]

The second kind of religious material is the sermon. In the *Heike monogatari*, for example, the great Pure Land founder Hōnen (1133–1212) prepares Taira Shigehira for death with a sermon on Pure Land teachings.[9] Sometimes the sermon is indicated in the rhetoric of a descriptive passage. In the *Tale of the Battle of Ōtō*, for example, in describing the battlefield after a slaughter, the narrator exclaims, "Those who have heard what people have seen and heard and have not at this time awakened to religion, [just] what time are they waiting for?"[10]

Stories about religion (*shūkkyō-mono*) were also a category of stories told by professional raconteurs in the nineteenth and early twentieth centuries. This pre-war illustration, part of a series on the life of Shinran (1173–1263), founder of the True Pure Land school of Buddhism, notes that he was the son of Fujiwara Arinori and his wife Kikkōnyo; she had a dream of the Nyoirin Kannon holding five pine branches. When her son was born, she called him Matsumaro (pine boy). I do not think the illustrator knew terribly much about Buddhism: the bodhisattva portrayed is not a typical Nyorin Kannon. Moreover, the iconography of the illustration comes from the extremely common story of the conception of the Buddha as his mother dreamt of an elephant. Taking a type scene from one story and incorporating it into another is extremely common in traditional Japanese narrative.

The third kind is the story of religious awakening (*hosshin-mono),* usually that of a *bushi,* and the story of entering religious life (*shukke-mono*), usually that of a woman. The best known of all *hosshin-mono* is the story of Atsumori, a young member of the Taira family killed in combat. However, the story is not about Atsumori; it is about his slayer, Kumagai Naozane, who entered religious life and became famous as a *nenbutsu* practitioner. Killing Atsumori first opened his eyes to the reality of his life and led to a rejection of it.[11] The best known examples of stories of entering religious life are the stories of the empress Kenreimon'in,[12] Tomoe,[13] and Tora[14] (of the *Soga monogatari* [*The Tale of the Soga Brothers*]), who put on black and devoted their lives to praying for themselves and for the souls of their dead.

The fourth kind of religious material found in epic is the story of rebirth in paradise or *ōjōden.* This is the story of the death of a Pure Land believer, like Kenreimon'in, whose rebirth in paradise is prepared by facing West, tying the hands with a five-colored cord attached to a statue of Amida, and chanting the *nenbutsu.* The attainment of rebirth in paradise is indicated by the scent of incense, the appearance of purple clouds in the sky, the sound of music, and sometimes a rain of flowers, all representing the coming of Amida to welcome to his paradise believers who have died calling on his name (*raigo*).[15]

The fifth and last kind of religious material is the story of the origins of an object of Buddhist worship, usually a temple, the *engi.* Again, in the *Heike monogatari,* a passage is devoted to Zenkōji, the head temple in Nagano of an Amidist cult.[16] However, the antecedents of many people, places, and things are described, including those of the imperial regalia, the sword and the mirror.[17]

Japanese scholars refer to the religious material in the epic as the "sermon" (*shōdō*) aspect and have long recognized the importance of this religious material in defining the epic as a distinct genre of battle literature.[18] Taking the analysis one step further, I would like to demonstrate how this religious material determines the very form and function of the Japanese epic as a Buddhist sermon.

The Japanese epic or war tale is a narrative whose subject is a battle or war in which a great family was destroyed.[19] An epic is never the story of a victory, but of a great tragedy. The key word is *metsubō,* fall or destruction, or a variation.

The epic is usually a compilation of many accounts culled from many sources including diaries, official records, and religious stories about those defeated and killed, about the victors shocked by the horror of battle into leaving the world, and about the servants, lovers, wives, and mothers who entered religious life to pray for the souls of the dead.

The content of the epic falls into three parts. First comes the background, which describes the events leading up to and causing the battle. The second part is the account of the battle itself. Here, victors can shine through their noble exploits on the field, but the focus is on the deaths of the defeated. The third and last part describes the aftermath of the battle. In this section survivors are executed, witnesses of the battle retreat into religious life, and the families and loved ones of the dead devote themselves to their afterlives.[20] Ideally, these three parts fall neatly in succession; however, in longer works with many protagonists, the last two will often be found together in each episode featuring one hero.

The three-part structure of the epic organizes the content as a history. Over this is laid the structure of the Buddhist sermon, itself based on the system of Buddhist logic. There are five parts. The first is the citation of the theme derived from sacred scripture, the sutras, or by extension, the teachings of sectarian founders. The second is the explanation of the citation. The third is a parable which illustrates the citation. The fourth is an example given as a proof of the teachings. And the fifth is a summary or conclusion.[21]

Not all the epics share all the elements of form and content; however, they share enough of them to be classified together.

Now that I have given a general outline of the subject, content, and structure of the Japanese epic, I would like to demonstrate how these three are integrated as a Buddhist sermon by analyzing one example, the *Heike monogatari*. The standard text, the Kakuichi version, was completed in 1371, ending a process of development and expansion begun perhaps around 1200. It is thought that one of the earliest stages in the text's development was produced by the Agui school of Pure Land preachers, to which is attributed the crucial beginning and ending chapters as well as much of the Pure Land material which appears in the text.[22] In the first part of the thirteenth century, the preaching of Pure Land Buddhism was proscribed in the capital (now Kyoto) and the early *Heike* traditions are thought to have been used surreptitiously to preach.[23] Certainly the immediate ancestor of the founder of the Agui school, Fujiwara Michinori Shinzei (1106–1159),[24] is featured prominently in the text as are the Fujiwara and Taira followers of Hōnen. The *Heike* was perfected over a long period of time and, as a perfect example of the genre, came to be the model of the epic, of the epic as sermon.

In the opening chapter of the *Heike* are the first elements of the Buddhist sermon. It opens with lines citing a Buddhist theme. There are references to the Gion temple bell that tolls at the death of a monk and the sala tree that turned color at the death of the Buddha. Then comes the explanation: what flowers withers, and, more importantly, pride goeth before a fall. Then the text cites examples of traitors from the distant pasts of China and Japan, and then it focuses on an example from the recent past, Taira Kiyomori (1118–1181). The entire *Heike monogatari* is the story of Taira Kiyomori and the destruction of the Taira house exacted in retribution for his evil deeds.[25] As set up by the first chapter, the rest of the *Heike* functions as parable and proof of Buddhist teachings. The *Heike monogatari* is in fact a very long, serialized sermon.

The content of the *Heike* between the opening chapter and the closing chapters on the Empress Kenreimon'in (Taira Kiyomori's daughter and mother of the drowned child-emperor Antoku) falls roughly into three sections. Because of the length of the work, these three sections do not fall in strict succession as to form three distinct parts as in a shorter epic — there is considerable overlap.

The function of the first section, the background, is to describe the events leading up to the war and to give the cause for the destruction of the Taira house. In historical — or historiographical terms — the cause is the arrogance of the head of the house, Kiyomori, a cause cited in other epics as well.[26] The background section of the *Heike* is a description of the arrogance of Taira Kiyomori and the suffering he causes: the suffering to the imperial court (in his intervention in the emperor's love affairs and elimination of rivals to his own daughter),[27] the suffering to individuals (such as the two entertainers Giō and Hotoke), the suffering to the religious realm (precedents in ritual broken),[28] and the suffering to himself (he dies of a fever whose heat is equal to that of hell).[29]

In religious terms, the cause of suffering is *mappō*. The idea of the breakdown of both the religious and the sociopolitical realms in the Latter Age of the Buddhist Doctrine is of course a basic tenet of Pure Land Buddhism. In Japan, *mappō* was calculated as beginning in 1052.[30] Taira Kiyomori is presented as a villain, of course, but more importantly as an agent of *mappō* in the disorder he causes to religious, public, and personal life. Again, of those examples of battle literature which have been identified as epics, the Buddhism espoused is predominantly (I will not say exclusively) Pure Land.[31]

The second section is the battle account. Battle accounts, too, have two interrelated functions, the historical and the religious. The first is to describe the battles as they happened: who fought whom, where, when, and how; what were the notable exploits and victories; who was killed. Sometimes an epic will be quite exhaustive in detailing the numbers and types of troops, their weapons, and their deployment.

The second function is to describe the suffering caused in battle to the family and vassals of the head of the house. True to the medieval tradition, the descriptions in epic are explicit and quite horrific. No nice, clean shoulder wounds here. Arms and legs are lopped off; blood soaks the grasses; and the corpses of men lie strewn together with the carcasses of horses.[32] The battlefield has special significance, a particular role in the rhetoric of the sermon in describing suffering as characteristic of the human world. According to Tendai doctrine (from which the Pure Land school derives), existence in this world is divided into six realms or paths of existence (*rokudō*): the realms of hell, of the hungry ghosts, of animals, of the anti-gods, of humans, and of the gods. Normally, one would expect rebirth exclusively in one or the other. But the Tendai concept of the interpenetrability of the realms means that no matter the realm into which one is reborn, one will experience the other realms. This interpenetrability is experienced through the suffering characterizing each of the realms, and the place of this experience is the battlefield, the place of the anti-gods, the *shurajō*.[33] Kenreimon'in relates an account of her own life in terms of the six realms and their interpenetrability: her life in the palace (the realm of the gods), in warfare (that of the anti-gods), on the run without provisions (that of the hungry ghosts), and witness to death by fire (that of hell).[34] The battlefield is representative of the breakdown in the world order, proof of *mappō*, and the place of the fall of the house. Those who should have had everything experience all horror here: Antoku, Kiyomori's grandson, who in a previous life had mastered the ten precepts and been rewarded with rebirth in the estate of emperor, dragged by his grandmother into the sea during a battle[35]; Taira Michimori and his wife Kozaishō—he dead in battle, she, pregnant, a suicide by drowning[36]; Taira Atsumori, young and a gifted musician, slain with a sword through the throat on the beach at Ichinotani.[37]

If the battlefield is replete with suffering, the suffering does not end there but continues into the aftermath of the battle. The children of the defeated are slain, as is twelve-year-old Rokudai.[38] Like the empress Kenreimon'in, the women of the dead survive all only to spend their lives in endless mourning and chanting the *nenbutsu* for their lovers, husbands, and sons as well as for themselves.[39] Even the victors become victims: sooner or later, like Kumagai Naozane, as a result of their battlefield experiences, they retreat into religious life to chant the *nenbutsu* for themselves and the men they killed.[40]

The epic ends with a resolution. In some, the tale ends with the story of a reconciliation: in the *Tale of the Battlefield of Yūki*, the antagonists "met in the suburbs of Kyoto and made peace."[41] In others, in the *Heike* for example, the tale ends with a story of rebirth in paradise (*ōjōden*). The ending must have in the manner of sympathetic magic, shall we say, a salutary effect to counter all the evil produced by the narrative, to pacify the ghosts. The *Heike* ends with the story of Kiyomori's daughter, the empress Kenreimon'in, and her death (accompanied by all the signs of rebirth in paradise). Sending the spirit off to paradise is an effective form of exorcism.

The story of Kenreimon'in's life is the third section, a summary of the *Heike*, a summary of the story of Taira Kiyomori and his house, a summary of the Buddhist doctrine of *mappō* and suffering in the six realms, and a summary of the Pure Land teachings of escape from rebirth in the six realms through belief in the vows of Amida. The story of the life and death of Kenreimon'in is the summary and conclusion of the *Heike monogatari* as Buddhist sermon.

The *Heike monogatari* is probably the most perfect example of Buddhist historiography, the interpretation of history through Buddhist doctrine. The epic, the *Heike* and the others, is informed by the two basic elements of the sermon. The first is the statement of a religious theme — and this can be Taoist, as in the case of the *Taiheiki*, or Confucian as in the case of the *Chronicle of the Meitoku Era*, but most often it is Buddhist. The second is the use of recent history as a proof of that theme. Nevertheless, even if the theme is Taoist or Confucian, the epic is constructed as a Buddhist sermon, and the text will in fact contain a great deal of Buddhist material. The fall of a great house in battle is set in a religious view of history. Thus the epic is a Buddhist sermon.

Realistic Violence in the Japanese Epic

Japanese history between the tenth and seventeenth centuries is punctuated by a series of revolts and palace coups, civil wars and local squabbles which resulted in literally hundreds of accounts of battle, usually of mixed oral and literary provenance. The historical background of the war may be introduced in terms of Taoist concepts of chaos or Confucian ideals of government, but it is Buddhism that lends meaning and significance to the battlefield itself: it is a picture of hell; it is meant to horrify people and turn them to religion. The religious form and function were established by the classic Japanese epic, which resulted from the intersection of a cataclysmic series of disturbances and civil war between 1156 and 1185 and the establishment in Japan of Pure Land Buddhism as an independent school. This is best represented by the Kakuichi version of the *Heike monogatari* (*Tale of the Taira House*), which focuses on the civil war of 1181–1185. The *Heike* casts a long shadow over the accounts of many other battles and wars, which are read against the themes and type scenes established in that version of the *Heike* dictated by its blind composer Kakuichi by 1371, the year of his death.

The reasons for the *Heike*'s preeminence are as much political as religious. The Kakuichi variant of the *Heike* was the monopoly of one guild of epic singers, the Tōdō, blind minstrels who accompanied themselves on a lute (*biwa*). In 1399 control of the guild was transferred to the head of the

Ashikaga military government when a copy of the text was submitted to the third Ashikaga shogun Yoshimitsu (1358–1408; r. 1367–1395).[42] The performance of the *Heike* by the head of the guild became part of the official ceremonies of the shogunal court: at the promotion of each shogun to office and at his funeral.[43]

Ashikaga interest in the *Heike* was based on the shogun's position and function as head of the entire Minamoto clan, transferred to Ashikaga Yoshimitsu in 1483.[44] First, the *Heike* provided the myth legitimating Ashikaga power: the *Heike* describes the fall of the *bushi* family, the Taira, destroyed in 1185 by the Minamoto clan, also called the Genji, who established the first military government or shogunate. The Kakuichi *Heike* is a tale of the transition of *bushi* leadership from the Taira to the Minamoto. The Ashikaga, descendants of the Minamoto, brought down the shogunate which had come under the control of descendants of the Taira, the Hōjō, in 1333 and established a new shogunate in 1336.

Second, winners of battles had pacification rituals performed for the angry spirits of their defeated and dead enemies. Ashikaga Yoshimitsu, then, as chief of the Minamoto, took over the management of the Kakuichi *Heike* as a performance meant to pacify the angry spirits of the Taira family.[45] The *Heike monogatari*, as the version officially authorized by the Ashikaga shogunate, was the dominant, if not the exclusive, version and the one most likely to be heard in *bushi* and court circles. Its influence on later epics was not just strong; it provided the model.

The model used the battlefield for a purpose: "It is the Buddha's work to lead men to enlightenment by showing the reality of suffering, which is the reality of living beings in the world of desire."[46] The description of the battlefield was meant as a way to turn people to Buddhism and abandoning the world by convincing them that in this world suffering, especially suffering in battle, was ineluctable. This is coded by references to or straightforward comparisons with the six realms, especially two of the worst, the realm of the fighting Asuras and hell. This is seen in the *Tale of the Battle of Ōtō*, one of the first (if not the very first) epics to be composed with the *Heike* as a model. It is an account of one very early fifteenth century local uprising in Shinano Province by local magnates against the governor sent by the Ashikaga shogunate. The author identifies the battlefield with the realms of hungry ghosts and animals in his description of a siege, during which the men eat the raw meat of their horses as the blood runs from their mouths. But there is worse:

> Now, the next day, the eighteenth day of the tenth month, in the hour of the tiger (3–5 a.m.) the forces of the vanguard attacked. They raced each other round and round the fort, took the heads of the dead, and dispatched the dying with a blade through the throat. Those fleeing they intercepted and hacked off

their arms and legs. They pursued the dying to the scattered places they had crawled to and took their heads. Their actions were indescribable. Now, the lay priest Kōsaka Munetsugu ... shut his eyes for a time. What he thought in his very heart was that this was nothing more than the Six Realms. There was before his eyes only the fate of those who take up arms. It was in all his own fate. The cause lay solely in greed. All took pride in honor and wealth and failed to reflect on this transient life which disappears so easily. All this because they sought one hundred years of glory and pleasure. As he pondered this deeply, he thought them fools beset by attachments and passions. The agonies of the road to hell were surely like this. Now their desperate situation would make a mountain of gold worthless to them, would make them willingly reject an emperor's throne.... It was the way of an evil destiny, that of arms. Thinking this, he wheeled about and gave an order.

Now, the Tsumado *nenbutsu* practitioners (*jishū*) of Zenkōji and similarly the holy men (*hijiri*) of Jūnenji heard that the men at Ōtō had committed suicide. They hurried there and inspected the miserable state of the battlefield. It was a sight too awful to look upon. Men who only recently had appeared so fine and grand all lay dead upon the moor. The corpses of men lay strewn together with the carcasses of horses. [A carpet of] blood-stained creepers ... resembled red brocade spread out in the sun. Monks and priests who were relatives collected the remains and embraced the dead bodies. They grieved and wept without limit. Such a thing has never been heard of in the past nor seen in our own time.... After hearing what people have seen and heard, those who do not awaken to religion at this time, [just] what time are they waiting for? Those *nenbutsu* practitioners gathered up one by one the corpses lying scattered about. Some they burnt and others they buried. They set up stupas and on each they bestowed *nenbutsu*. Everywhere they raised the hope that Amida would come to lead them to paradise.[47]

Descriptions of battle and the battlefield tend to be sobering, to say the least. They have to be if they are to function as a warning against taking up arms lest one experience such suffering. The *Chronicle of the Battle at Kōnodai*, the account of the death in 1538 of Ashikaga Yoshiaki in his battle with the Hōjō at the first battle of Kōnodai (on the eastern edge of today's Tokyo), too, if briefly, makes reference to this interpretation of the battlefield as a hell picture, a place of suffering, in describing the opening moves of the battle:

In the meantime, as for the noble Prince, seeing this sight, readied the soldiers of the three provinces at the head of his forces and they faced the Hōjō. For just about an hour they fought with words and after that [they began] the battle with the opening volleys of arrows, and, when they were spent, they began to fight with swords; the war cries clashing against each other made this a place none other than the realm of the fighting Asuras.

Later, Yoshiaki's brother and son, also killed in the battle, are described as being in "the hell of the realm of the fighting Asuras."

The description of Yoshiaki's own death was modeled on that of the death of Benkei, the monk attendant of Minamoto Yoshitsune, in the *Gikeiki* (*Yoshitsune*). The theme of the "standing death" (*tachiji*) is used to describe the death of Yoshiaki, who is first allowed to demonstrate his prowess as a *bushi* by cleaving in twain the helmet of an enormous opponent before succumbing to a shower of arrows:

> As for the enemy soldiers, seeing this and, becoming afraid, they did not draw near. From among the great numbers [of men], a man announcing himself as Yokoi Shinsuke took a bundle of thirteen [arrows] to his three-man bow; he fixed [arrow to bow] and he shot for an hour until none remained. These arrows flying across [at Yoshiaki] were what sealed his fate. [They passed] clean through the armor the noble Prince was wearing and stuck right out of his back. Valiant as the prince was, he was fainting, struggling to keep his eyes open, when suddenly he glared at the direct vassals of the Hōjō right in the eyes; [and leaning on] his seven foot three inch sword for support, he died on his feet. "Well!" they said; even so there was no one who would come near him. In such a situation, a Sōshū man announcing himself as Matsuda Yajirō, drawing his three-foot one-inch [sword], came hurrying in front of the lord. He probed under the flap of his armor twice with his sword but, as well you know, [Yoshiaki's] soul had [already] departed, and he suddenly fell down to the bow hand. Matsuda saw this sight and he took his head.[48]

Later texts become even more detailed and gruesome in their descriptions of death in battle. Pulling out one's entrails by the handful is another standard motif in later descriptions of death in battle. In the *Gikeiki*, for example, Yoshitsune decides to die like his vassal Satō Tadanobu:

> With that very dagger he stabbed himself below the left nipple, plunging the blade so deep that it almost emerged through his back. Then he stretched the incision in three directions, pulled out his intestines, and wiped the dagger on the sleeve of his cloak.[49]

This ripping out of the intestines is even worse in the description of the grisly suicide of Tadanobu.[50] Nevertheless, it was apparently a real practice: Father Luis Frois's (1532–1597) description of the suicide of Shibata Katsuie (1530–1583) was considered so indelicate (he cuts his stomach and flings his entrails from the battlements at Toyotomi Hideyoshi) that it was left in the Latin in Murdoch's history of Japan.[51] It was very much like the description of the suicide of a minor warlord who held Sasago Castle in what is now Chiba Prefecture:

> ... he slid out his nine-foot five-inch [sword], cut a cross into his stomach, took out his entrails by the handful, and threw them against the four walls. "This is the end of Eastern Japan," and with these as his last words, he slumped forward on his face.

Not even women and children are spared in the epic. The model was established in the *Heike* in the descriptions of the Heike women dragged out of the sea at the battle of Dannoura (11.11) and the execution of male children (11.16, 12.9). The violence done to Yoshiaki's ladies after the battle of Kōnodai is more than merely reminiscent of the fates of the Heike survivors and, in its violence, is typical of popular stories of the period (such as the sermon ballad, or *sekkyō-bushi, Oguri hangan*), which emphasize sex and violence as the "hell picture" of Buddhist sermons:

> In the meantime the ladies of the Inner Palace, more than two hundred and eighty persons high [ranking] and low, screamed all at once; surely even the shrieks in hell were like this.... [T]hey retreated to their destinations and hurried along on rough stones; the blood flowing from their feet stained the grass on the wayside; this must surely have been like the road to the netherworld. Some were kicked by horses and died; some passed into the hands of the peasants and came to an unhappy end. Indeed, even the retreat from the capital of the Heike general Munemori[52] could not have been worse than this! [445–462].

The horrors of war are never restricted to the battlefield: the *Kōnodai* extends the battle to the headquarters at Oyumi and to Yoshiaki's ladies; the arrogant lord causes suffering not only to his vassals and kinsmen in battle, he also causes suffering to the women and children who survive them. This violence is also a feature of the very first work on the death of Yoshiaki, *Oyumi goshosama onuchiji ikusa monogatari* (*Tale of the Death in Battle of the Prince of Oyumi*, c. 1538): the terrible fate (very likely at the hands of Hōjō soldiers, but this is not said) of the common people of the provinces of Kazusa and Shimōsa and their toddlers lost, trampled and buried on the beach — even the hardened *bushi* wept — in this text has been transferred to the ladies of Yoshiaki's court in *Kōnodai*. The *Oyumi* description of the five- and ten-year-old princes, who "had never even walked on the white sands of the garden," led away in the confusion howling for their nurse and governess has also been transferred to the story in the *Kōnodai* of the fleeing concubines whose torn feet bloodied the paths.[53]

Yoshiaki endangers especially his favorite concubine, who, in the *Kōnodai*, commits suicide out of loyalty (his wife takes refuge in a temple):

> At this time, most moving indeed [was the case of] a person exceedingly beloved of the noble great prince called Aisu no kimi. She had retreated far and away from the gate but remembered it was said, "A wise man does not follow two princes nor a virtuous woman serve two husbands." She withdrew into the Inner Palace, entered her apartments, [and dressed for death]. Next to her skin she put on a white lined garment and over that layered a robe of figured silk and tied on her long crimson culottes. Her disheveled hair she bound high and [then wrote her death poem].... [T]ogether with her tears she folded [the paper on which she had been writing] and put it in her scented sleeve; [then] facing the west, she pressed her hands together and finally in a loud voice she said the invocation of Amida's name, bit off her tongue, and spat it out. [Then] she lay down with her

> head to the north [like the Buddha to die]. The manner of the end of that lady is remembered as truly admirable.[54]

This is a far cry from a typical description of a battlefield death of one hundred and fifty or two hundred years before, the time of the *Heike* and the *Taiheiki*. The c. 1400 *Chronicle of the Meitoku Era* narrates the facts without the sensationalism of the death of Yagi Kurō, who

> bearing wounds deep and slight in five or six places, made a crutch of his sword, and chanted the *nenbutsu*, saying, "Namuamidabutsu, namuamidabutsu." He was walking slowly in the direction of Ōmiya when soldiers of Yamana Gunaisho surrounded him and, in the end, he was killed. How cruel it was![55]

And yet, well before the beginning of the Tokugawa period, the violent and even coarse description of death in battle had been well established. As the production of the epic moved further away from the cultural center of the imperial and shogunal courts, it apparently moved down the scale of delicacy. Nevertheless, the function was still the same and the function, whether directly or indirectly, was passed on to the popular theater of Edo and Osaka.

11

Thematic Composition in the Japanese Epic: On the Type Scene

The Japanese epic or war tale (*gunki monogatari*) is only one of several genres of battle narrative. Of the several hundred surviving written texts of battle literature, perhaps ten and their variants are now accepted as *gunki monogatari*: the best-known include the *Hōgen monogatari* (*Tale of the Disorder in Hōgen*; 1156), *Heiji monogatari* (*Tale of the Heiji Era*; 1159), *Heike monogatari* (*Tales of the Taira House*; twelfth century), and *Taiheiki* (*Chronicle of the Great Pacification*; fourteenth century).

The Japanese epic is recognized as oral narrative (*katarimono*). By this is meant narrative which is orally performed, whether the text is memorized or read from a written source. It is not itself an oral composition: it is not composed, transmitted, and stored in performance. The epic is, however, oral derived: even if written, the text preserves elements of oral composition. The epic is usually the product of a period of development, short or long, which results in several or even many variants. Until fairly recently, research on the development of the epic was focused on the search for the original, written textual source and ignored the usually oral or oral-derived[1] material, which was thought by literature specialists to characterize the later and expanded text of the epic.[2] The folklorists, on the other hand, tried to puzzle out how the expanded text came to be expanded and occupied themselves in identifying oral-derived material as the product of religious propagandists and then, on the basis of that material, on reconstructing contemporary religious practices and beliefs.[3]

A typical object of intense investigation (if not speculation) by folklorists and the folklore wing of specialists in the epic is the religious-awakening story or *hosshin-mono* (also the taking-the-tonsure story [*tonsei-mono*] or entering-religious-life story [*shukke-mono*]). From such stories has been hypothesized

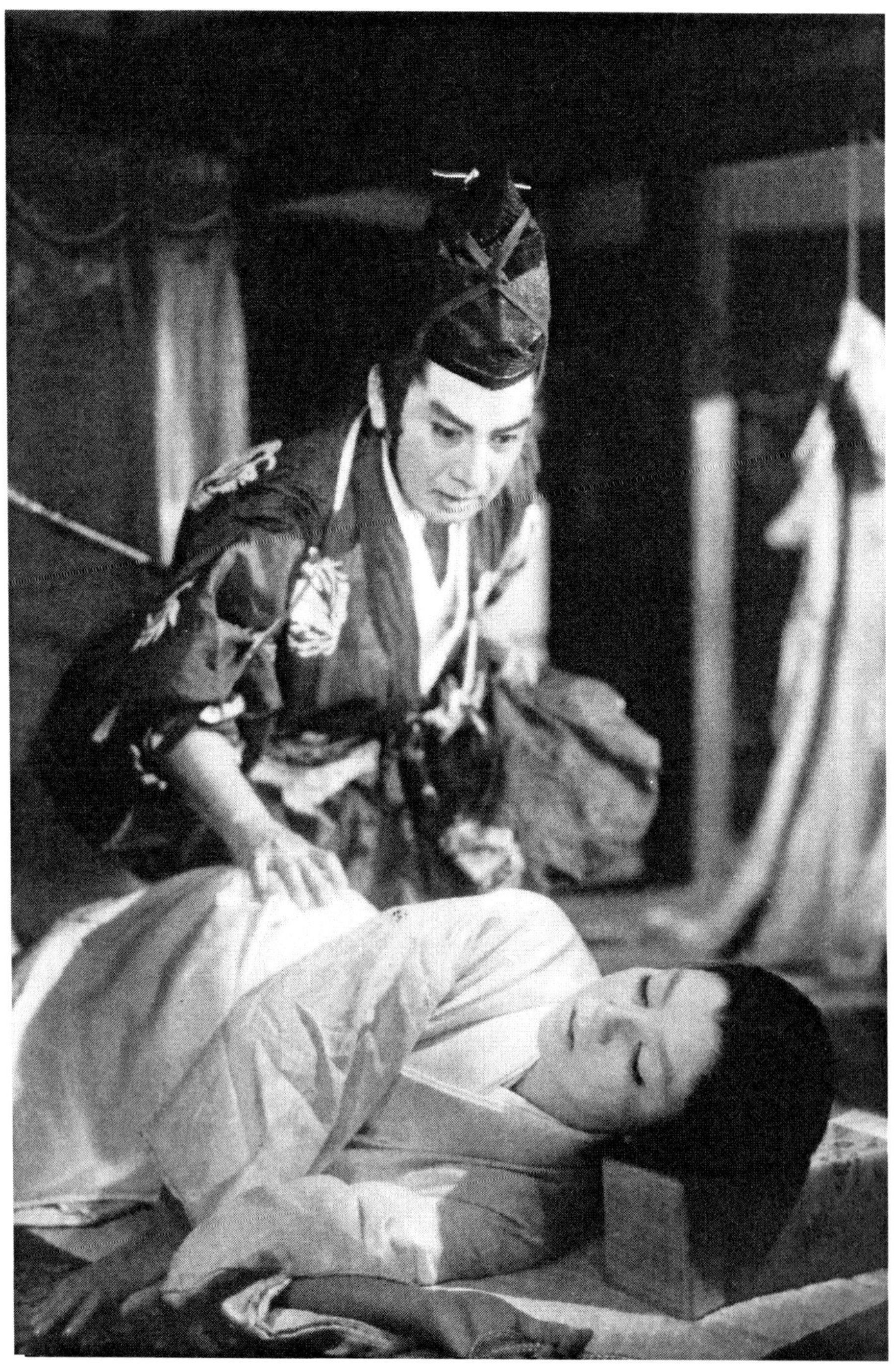

the practice of *bushi*, shocked into religious awakening by experiences in the field, of taking the tonsure and retreating into religious life. Mt. Kōya, the site of the temple Kongōbuji, the headquarters of the Shingon school of Buddhism, has been identified, for example, as a principal center of *bushi* retreatants.[4] A custom has been postulated of getting together and confessing reasons for taking the tonsure.[5] Some see the confessions circulating around Mt. Kōya as religious-awakening stories and as spread throughout the country by fund-raising Kōya retreatants or *hijiri* who repeated the story as confession (*zange*) for oneself or for another as a way to eradicate the sins (*metsuzai*).[6]

One of the most famous of the religious-awakening stories is that of Kumagai Naozane (1141–1208). He was a vassal of Minamoto Yoritomo (1147–1199), founder of the first military dictatorship or shogunate, based in the town of Kamakura (1192–1333). In the campaign against the Taira family (1180–1185), according to the story, he killed a young aristocrat, Taira Atsumori (1169–1184), at the battle of Ichinotani. Shaken by that experience, it is said, he entered religious life. The Naozane narrative in one form or another is carried by epics such as the *Heike monogatari* (including the 1371 Kakuichi variant),[7] the 1390s *Chronicle of the Meitoku Era*,[8] the post–1400 *Ōtō monogatari* (*The Tale of the Battle of Ōtō*),[9] the post–1488 *Yūki senjō monogatari* (*Tale of the Battlefield of Yūki*),[10] and 1570s or later *Kōnodai kōki* (*The Later Chronicle [of the Battle] of Kōnodai*).[11]

The *Heike*,[12] *Ōtō*,[13] and even the *Yūki*[14] versions of the Naozane narrative have been discussed as confirming Mt. Kōya connections with the narratives. To the *Meitokuki*, however, are attributed other propaganda and institutional roots.[15] On the whole, however, when comparing scholarly discussions of similar materials in other epics and other medieval texts, one is left with the ineluctable conclusion that every religious-awakening or taking-the-tonsure story has direct roots in religious institutions and propaganda traditions. This is based on the assumption that medieval texts preserve intact evidence of existing religious practices, institutions, and narratives.

This is not, however, always the case: literary creations are sometimes

***Opposite: Jigokumon* (*Gate of Hell*, 1953), directed by Kinugasa Teinosuke. Endō Moritō (Hasegawa Kazuo) discovers that he has killed Kesa (Kyō Machiko) instead of her husband. He then cuts off his topknot and becomes the famous (and troublesome) monk Mongaku (1139–1203). This story of a fatal attraction is originally a Buddhist propaganda story about how Moritō reached the moment of deciding to enter religious life (*hosshin-mono*), very likely (and typically) a medieval composite of a Chinese story of self-sacrifice and the story of the monk Mongaku, a famous ascetic and thorn in the side of the shogun Minamoto Yoritomo (photograph courtesy of the Kawakita Memorial Film Institute).**

the origins of religious narrative traditions, as in the cases of the Nō plays *Seiganji* (Temple of [Amida's] Vows) and *Yugyō yanagi* (The Itinerant [Saint and] the Willow [Tree]).[16] Furthermore, the process of writing Nō plays, taking a classic as a model and then collating suitable materials from other texts, resembles strongly the suggested process of composing a *Yūki*[17] or a *Kōnodai senki* (*Chronicle of the Battle of Kōnodai*) or the *Kōnodai kōki* (*Later Chronicle of the Battle of Kōnodai*).[18] Thus, one might ask whether the religious propaganda narratives found in epics are subject to the same process of composition that the texts containing them are.

The problem of composition in traditional narrative genres has been addressed in studies of the use of models in writing Japanese sacred biographies. James Foard finds useful the concept "prefiguration"[19] and Shimizu Yoshiaki that of "commemoration."[20] An approach similar to theirs has been taken by William LaFleur in an earlier study of the life of the poet and religious retreatant Saigyō (1118–1190).[21] However, standard approaches to traditional and oral or oral-derived narratives have long been provided by analyses based on the original Parry-Lord theory of oral composition.

Oral composition is characterized by thematic composition and formulaic diction. Narratives are composed of building blocks called themes or type scenes. For example, the *Odyssey* is made up almost exclusively of hospitality scenes: greeting a guest, bathing him, serving him food and drink.[22] The pirate movie always has the taking-the-prize scene. In the Kabuki we can expect, among others, the battle scene (*shuraba*), sex scene (*nureba*), torture scene (*semeba*), and the hero-in-disguise-reveals-himself scene (*jitsu wa*).[23] In Japanese epics, for example, we can expect to see any number of type scenes organized into the background, battle, and aftermath sections.[24] The battle section, for example, contains such well-known type scenes as the description of armor, the declaration of one's name in the challenge, and the invocation of Amida Buddha's name (*nenbutsu*) at death. The aftermath section contains any number of religious-awakening, taking-the-tonsure, and entering-religious-life stories featuring battle survivors or servants and female connections of the slain: wives, mothers, and nurses.

The type scenes are described conventionally in "formulaic diction." *Odyssey* has a high incidence of verbal repetition from scene to scene: the same actions are described in the same formulae, sometimes for many stanzas. In films, the diction is very complex, made up as it is of words, actions, and film techniques: in the pirate-movie taking-the-prize scene, for example, the pirates always board the prize by swinging from halyards from one ship to the other, cutlasses clenched between their teeth, in almost perfect synchronization, and almost always across the screen or into the camera.

As far as I know, there has been very little work on formulaic diction in

Japan. Work by Yamamoto Kichizō[25] on the recorded *goze* (blind, itinerant female entertainers) ballads has been the only serious attempt, as far as I can tell, to analyze formulaic diction in the Japanese oral tradition.[26] Indeed, my general impression of Japanese scholarship is that there has been a strong bias against epics and other texts with a high incidence of formulaic diction.[27] Thus, texts like the *Heike*, the *Ōtō*, and the *Meitokuki*, by virtue of their more literary diction, are treated as having sources in independent religious and historical traditions rather than in popular oral narrative traditions, as are the *Yūki* and *Kōnodai* cycles because of their heavily formulaic diction.[28] More importantly, while scholars seem in general to recognize formulaic diction as a feature of oral narrative, only some have begun to consider the problem of thematic composition and the implications for the analysis of the narrative structure.

Let's begin with the story as carried in the Kakuichi text of the *Heike monogatari* (1371). At the battle of Ichinotani in 1184, Kumagai Naozane, a Minamoto vassal, challenged and slew Taira Atsumori, aged about sixteen or seventeen, on whose body he found a flute. This is supposed to be the reason that Naozane eventually took the tonsure.

Although it is well established that Naozane took the tonsure, was a disciple of Hōnen (1133–1212; he established Pure Land Buddhism as an independent school), and was called Rensei (or Renshō), few of the other details can be ascertained. Neither the biographies of Hōnen nor the *Azuma kagami* (*Mirror of Eastern Japan*),[29] texts we should expect to carry such information, say that Naozane killed Atsumori or that he went to Mt. Kōya.[30]

A different tradition gives another reason for Naozane's entry into religious life. According to the *Sankō Genpei jōsuiki* and *Azuma kagami*, in 1192 (on the 25th day of the third month of the year, in the Kenkyū period), Naozane, frustrated by the shogunate's decision concerning a long dispute with his uncle Kuge Naomitsu over the boundaries between their estates, did in the shogun's palace unsheathe his sword and slice off his topknot, a sign of repudiating the world and therefore his lord and master. And yet, according to a house document dated a year and nine months previous to the incident, Naozane was already calling himself Rensei.[31]

It will avail us little or nothing to seek the historical truth when we consider the kind of sources we have — grab bags of diary entries, documents, gossip, rumors, and other hearsay evidence that would never be admitted in a court of law. But by examining renditions of the story whose process of development is better documented in written sources, we might be able to throw light on the process of the development of the old-*bushi*-slays-young-*bushi* type scene crystallized in the story of Naozane and Atsumori.

If we compare the Kakuichi *Heike* with variants and with the versions of the story in four other *gunki monogatari*, we find that the Kakuichi version does not represent the whole story. In the *Enkyō* version of the *Heike monogatari* (1242–1252),[32] for example, Naozane shaves his head as a disciple of Hōnen, takes the name Rensei, and goes to live at the Rengedani, a center for retreatants at Mt. Kōya. The earliest version of the *Heike*, the *Shibu kassenjō daisanban tōjō* (1218–1222)[33] also mentions his going to Mt. Kōya.[34]

Thus, although the *Kakuichi* text does not state explicitly that Naozane shaved his head, was a disciple of Hōnen, or that his priestly name was Rensei, all this is understood. Any part of the type scene (or the narrative itself) can be abridged or truncated without losing any information; that is provided by the audience according to their experience. We do not have to hear the story of how Will Scarlet was added to Robin's band of Merry Men in any particular telling of the tale to know that he is there and why; at some time, we have heard that story. The *Kakuichi* text needs only to have Naozane describe his feelings for his own son and pity for Atsumori's father or to mention Atsumori's flute: the audience fills in the rest of the story, carried by the *Enkyō* text, of the return of flute and other effects to Atsumori's father and the correspondence also said to have lead to Naozane's tonsure and eventual residence at Mt. Kōya. The narrative, as is common in traditional narrative, is multiform. Any one form can be said to refer to all the others. The operation of this principle of the part standing for the whole, in all its forms,[35] is possible because any one performance resonates all previous performance (versions) known to the audience, singly or collectively: the audience, depending on its experience, have heard one or more versions, play them simultaneously in their heads at any one performance, and thereby compare and evaluate them. The comparison and the effect are possible only where the performer can depend on the audience to know the story, the tradition.

Not only can the performer, such as a writer, depend on the audience as a whole (of course, adults know more than children) to know any one particular narrative tradition well enough to fill in information left out for any number of reasons, but the performer can use any one particular narrative tradition to model others and thus to model the audience's understanding of them. One way is to parallel the story of Naozane and the protagonist in question. The parallel can be made very briefly. The *Tale of the Battlefield of Yūki* features an elaborate description of the execution of two young princes, eleven and thirteen, sons of the Kamakura Deputy Ashikaga Mochiuji (1398–1439). His revolt was crushed and his sons were captured and executed in 1441. Correspondence with the Kakuichi *Heike* version is limited mostly to the depiction of the executioner — only some 5 lines out of 131 as compared with the *Heike* version of 118 lines — where the executioner of the two princes compares himself with Naozane, who killed Atsumori, entered religious life, and achieved rebirth in Amida's paradise (*ōjō*).

> In the past, too, there is an example: Kumagai Naozane took the head of Taira Atsumori and because of this entered religious life (*shukke*) and died easy (*daiōjō*, or "great rebirth in Amida's Pure Land"). Even if I cannot accomplish quite as much, I shall enter religious life (*shukke*), become a retreatant (*tonsei*), and perform services for the consolation of his soul.[36]

The last two details concerning Naozane are not in the Kakuichi *Heike* but belong to the tradition as a whole, as indicated by other texts. Moreover, whereas the *Yūki* makes direct reference to only two things that Naozane did, enter religious life and achieve salvation, the parallel with the executioner suggests more, performing services for Atsumori. The audience can recognize all the motifs which identify the entire Naozane/Atsumori type scene and appreciate both how the performer (writer) has used the type scene to model the audience's understanding of the executioner on the one hand and, on the other, the technique of sharing the elements of the type scene between Naozane and the executioner.

On the other hand, the *Kōnodai kōki*, an account of the second battle at Kōnodai of 1564, makes the parallel through the voice of the narrator: Matsuda Sakyōnosuke Yasuyoshi kills a very young boy in battle and then enters religious life to pray for his afterlife; the narrator parallels the case of Naozane, who experienced religious awakening when he killed Atsumori and "the case of Yasuyoshi, who killed [Satomi] Hirotsugu, entered religious life and became a retreatant (*shukke tonsei*); although the times were different, the impetus was the same."[37]

In addition to the technique of making an overt parallel between Naozane and the protagonist of the individual work is the technique of making the parallel — without mention of the Naozane or Atsumori — by use solely of the form of the type scene, although not with exact verbal correspondence in the diction. In the *Meitokuki*, the shock and entry into religious life of Kawasaki Taitō is described with nearly point-for-point correspondence with the description in the Kakuichi *Heike*— without mention either of Naozane or of Atsumori:

> when he heard faintly the cry of [the lord of] Ōshū's last *nenbutsu* ... he knocked back the adversary facing him and quickly glanced at Ōshū's form. He saw that Ōshū had just been killed, his head taken and impaled. "Now, this is the end (*kore made*)," he thought and, from his horse, threw his great sword away and, unsheathing his [short] sword, jumped down and stood over Ōshū's corpse. "Kojirō is coming, too," he cried and, holding on to the sleeve of Ōshū's armor, was about to cut his stomach. But a soldier of [Isshiki] Sakyō Daibu by the name of Kawasaki Taitō leapt upon Kojirō. He took hold of his helmet and pulled him back. He slipped two swords into the gaps of the face mask [and pried it off]. But when he grasped his hair and pulled his face up, he saw a young warrior of fifteen or sixteen. Charmed by his beauty, even though his

> sword was poised without his knowing it, he grasped his head [by the hair]. "Well, now and who might you be? Declare yourself! Depending on what you say, I may save you." Kojirō said, "Though I declare myself, since I am of low rank, there will be, moreover, no one who will know me. Therefore, take my head, speak to a general from a little distance, and say, 'Here is the head of a person I have killed in battle.' If you enquire in detail of people, there will be a person who knows me by sight." [Taitō] could hear only the sound of chanting the *nenbutsu* faintly under his breath; he said nothing further.[38]

Just as Yamana Kojirō is about to cut his stomach over the body of his father, Kawasaki leaps upon him; the following is the list of correspondences with the Kakuichi *Heike*: Kawasaki pulls off Kojirō's helmet, sees the beautiful face of a young boy of fifteen or sixteen, forgets his raised sword, does not take the head, asks the youth to name himself, hopes to save him; the boy refuses and tells him to take his head to camp where someone will recognize it; Kawasaki wants to save him, sees many of his comrades approaching, takes the boy's head, and at camp finds out who he is and how old. At this point the correspondence ends. The text goes on at length to praise Kojirō's loyalty to his adoptive father and, by comparison, ends by describing those who shamefully abandoned their armor and fled to temples to shave their heads and hide their faces in deep straw hats. Although neither Naozane nor Atsumori are mentioned, it is clear that this description of the killing of Kojirō is the type scene of old *bushi* kills young *bushi*; what is missing is the account of the killer's religious awakening and entry into religious life — that is provided, ironically, by the description of those who ran to temples to shave their heads and hide from the world.

Something of the same is found in the *Kōnodai kōki*. Before mentioning Naozane, the text describes how Matsuda Yasuyoshi killed fifteen-year-old Satomi Hirotsugu. This passage also has the a high incidence of correspondence with the Kakuichi *Heike* version of the death of Atsumori: the description of the youth's horse, armor, and weapon; his identification as a high-ranking general, identification of the old soldier by the formulaic epithet "resident of XX province," galloping alongside, grappling with, and pulling the boy to the ground, seeing his beauty and youth, inability to use his sword, mention of his brothers in arms galloping towards them as thick as a cloud, and his promise to pray for his afterlife. Although the verbal correspondence is high, it is not identical to the Kakuichi *Heike*. Nevertheless, the cluster of the formal narrative elements identify the source as more than likely the Kakuichi *Heike*; their use without making a direct reference to Naozane and Atsumori until some lines later indicates the acknowledgement of both writer and audience of a type scene, the old-*bushi*-slays-young-*bushi* type scene.[39] Clearly, the historical incident was rewritten in terms of a clearly established type scene.

The type scene is usually identified within a single narrative. The *Ōtō monogatari* presents us with a situation[40] in which the functions and motifs of the single type scene are divided up and parceled out to different sets of characters. The *Ōtō* recounts the story of a siege which took place in 1400 near Kawanakajima in Shinano Province when local gentry attacked the train of a very unpopular military governor. Among the defeated is a young, gifted boy of thirteen, who, after chanting the *nenbutsu*, commits suicide with his father and elder brother. On the other side of the battle, the enemy Kōsaka Samanosuke nyūdō Munetsugu, shocked into religious awakening by the savage massacre of starving men, retreats to a temple called Kayadō[41] at Mt. Kōya and becomes a *nenbutsu* practitioner and traveling proselytizer. Now, there is no correspondence with the diction of the *Heike* Naozane/Atsumori story. Nevertheless, the characters and motifs of the broader Naozane story are present: young boy dies in this scene, seasoned *bushi* experiences religious awakening in another. But together they make up a familiar type scene. The author recognized that, if a young boy was killed in battle, tradition demanded that an older, seasoned soldier achieve religious awakening. The audience's traditional expectations of such a narrative have been satisfied; the technique of the author in achieving this by spreading the two parts over two, distinct subnarratives, is also seen in Nō plays written a hundred years later.

The strong influence of tradition in the use of the type scene can lead to unexpected irony. Let's look again at the five versions of the Naozane/Atsumori story and the name Kojirō. According to the *Heike*, the name of Naozane's son was Kojirō, who had indeed been slightly wounded; Naozane's pity for Atsumori's father derives from his love of his own son. In the *Meitokuki*, however, Kojirō is the name of the victim, the adoptive son of Yamana Ujimitsu, the former military governor of Mutsu Province, whom he accompanied in death. In the *Yūki*, it is the executioner of the two boys who is given the name Kojirō, Urushizaki Kojirō.[42] The victim has become the killer. It is possible that by the time the *Yūki* was written, tradition demanded that the name Kojirō had to appear in the text; Naozane and Atsumori are named. In any case, it is clear that a type scene has been used to rewrite the historical incidents in the *Meitokuki* and the *Yūki* and that the use of the type scene was facilitated by the use of a common name, Kojirō.

In the *Kōnodai senki*,[43] another name is used, very obliquely, to indicate a parallel with Naozane and Atsumori by crossing narratives. The *Kōnodai senki* ends not with the death of a young *bushi* and a religious awakening modeled on the Naozane/Atsumori type scene but with a confrontation based on the play *Sumidagawa* (*Sumida River*) between the ghost of the victim and his nurse. This nurse is a stock figure who appears in, among others, *The Tale of Princess Jōruri*, a spin-off of the cycle of stories making up the biography of the great *Heike* hero Minamoto Yoshitsune (1159–1189), younger brother of the first Kamakura shogun: she is the nurse of Yoshitsune's true and abandoned love, Jōruri.[44] Her role, the same as that of the victim's mother in the *Ōtō* and the two princes' nurse in the *Yūki*, is to pray for the afterlife of the youth slain in battle.[45] Her name is Rensei, the same religious name as that of Kumagae Naozane; tradition demands that in the story of a youth killed on the battlefield, someone must take responsibility for praying for his salvation — someone must parallel Naozane.[46] Comparison is made with another man who died young.[47]

While the story of Naozane and Atsumori has been used to emphasize the aspects of death, regret, and religious awakening, the *nenbutsu* motif is also important. Naozane was famed as a follower of Hōnen, founder of Pure Land Buddhism as an independent school, and as a *nenbutsu* practitioner. Although not specifically mentioned in the Kakuichi *Heike* version, the *nenbutsu* is a strong motif in the versions offered by the *Meitokuki* (above) and other epics. In the *Ōtō*, the death of the boy who is the parallel of Atsumori is described, like that of Kojirō in the *Meitokuki*, with the *nenbutsu* motif:

> In all this, especially tragic was the end of the lay priest Tokiwa. Father and two sons, on the point of suicide, joined hands and faced west. In loud voices they earnestly chanted the *nenbutsu*, the promise and the prayer [of Amida] to receive them and not to abandon them. And each blow after blow committed suicide.[48]

The two princes in the *Yūki* also chant the *nenbutsu* before death:

> Lord Haruō saw this and said [to Lord Yasuō], "Oh, this is truly [the end]; since that is so, we must chant the last ten *nenbutsu* (*saigo no nenbutsu*)." Each put hand to hand and changed position to face west. Calmly, they chanted the ten *nenbutsu*, stretched out their necks, [and waited for the sword].[49]

The emphasis on the *nenbutsu* motif in versions of the type scene indicates how important the *nenbutsu* is to the cycle of Naozane stories — the part about killing Atsumori is not the whole story. Both the Kakuichi *Heike* (the

Opposite and above: **These two pre-war postcards illustrate the same famous scene from the *Taiheiki*: before the battle of Minatogawa, Kusunoki Masashige (1294–1336) bids a last farewell to his son, Masatsura (1326–1348). The two scenes are very similar. In both, the boy goes off to the left carrying a memento from his father. His father, dressed in full armor, looks over his right shoulder after the boy. A groom holds his horse. Other soldiers with *naginata* (halberds) are arranged in the rear. At the back to the left is a wing of a cloth enclosure. Other noteworthy elements include the Kusunoki arms and the pennons. However, the two illustrations are otherwise quite different in many details: for example, in the one, the boy is crying, in the other he is not; in one Masashige carries a fan and grasps the reins of his horse, in the other he does not; and in the one, the family crest (*mon*) is on the standards, in the other on the enclosure. In the Japanese traditional type scene, the core elements must be present even though latitude is given to their "performance." On the other hand, the salient points from one story can be used in a completely different story.**

full story)[50] the *Genpei jōsuiki*[51] and the *Taiheiki* (a truncated version) relate a famous incident in the real life of Naozane: that Naozane and Hirayama Sueshige had left camp early to be the first to attack (*sakigake*) the Heike stockade at Ichinotani. In the *Taiheiki*, the two main incidents of the story of Naozane at Ichinotani, the race to be first in the charge and his subsequent rebirth in paradise, can be seen as the basis of the type scene of the *nenbutsu* practitioner who performs bravely and dies well in battle. For example, in the *Taiheiki* is the story of shogunate vassal Hitomi On'a, who in 1331 along with Honma Kurō Suketada slipped early out of camp to attack Akasaka Fort and was killed. Before leaving, he had received the last ten *nenbutsu* from a *jishū* chaplain[52] and thereby apparently achieved a grand rebirth in Amida's paradise in battle.[53] This same chaplain took On'a's head back to his son and told the story of his death. The return of the head and communication to the family are reminiscent of the Enkyō text's description of Naozane's return of Atsumori's head and effects to his father. The text then refers to the similar slipping out ahead of one's comrades to be the first in the attack (*sakigake*) of Naozane and Hirayama at Ichinotani; making the parallel, as we have seen above, indicates that a type scene is being used. The story of On'a (follower of another famous preacher of the *nenbutsu*, Ta'amidabutsu Shinkyō) is modeled on that of Naozane at Ichinotani and his subsequent entry into religious life. There is no corresponding formulaic diction.

The type scene crystallized in the story of Naozane and Atsumori is made up of recognizable if multiform units described in recognizable if multiform diction. If, as indicated in the previous chapter, the epic or *gunki monogatari* has the form and function of the Buddhist sermon, then we should not be surprised to find that component narratives have the form of parables used in sermons, such as the religious-awakening story. What we are seeing here may be the emergence and development of a type scene in the *Heike* cycle and other epics. The fact that this is a feature typical of oral narrative does not necessarily mean that the narrative itself is of exclusively oral provenance, that is, of the preaching of specific, identifiable schools of religious propagandists. Neither can we assume that the traditional compositional rules of narratives such as Nō, *otogizōshi*, *kōwakamai*, or Kabuki do not operate in the *Heike*. Some scholars may not like the direction the traditional process of composition took the *gunki monogatari*, but the truth is that the process was already at work in the *Heike* and it is not functionally different from that of the less-highly esteemed *gunki monogatari* of the latter middle ages.

12

Traditional Narrative and Yamada Yōji

In this book, I have discussed films made up to about 1970, when the two most-representative directors of the early period film, Inagaki Hiroshi and Itō Daisuke, made their last films (*Machibuse* [*Incident at Blood Pass*] and *Bakumatsu* [*The Ambitious*], respectively). I have tried to demonstrate how traditional narratives served as the vehicles for adapting and absorbing foreign narratives and film language. This process kept the narrative tradition current and viable rather than a fossilized museum piece.

What about period films made after 1970? The production rate of period films slowed to a trickle; I can not remember one from that time that impressed me as much as Ichikawa's TV *Tales of Genji*, Inagaki's *Samurai Banners* or Makino's *Jirōchō and the Record of the Three Kingdoms* series. *Anime* has never interested me nor have martial arts. Indeed, the more I researched the precursors of the traditions of the period film, the less I watched film altogether.

It was a great surprise then, to learn that Yamada Yōji (b. 1931), who had based his career on films about contemporary life, had made the 2002 period film *Tasogare Seibei* (*The Twilight Samurai*), nominated for the Oscar in 2004 for Best Foreign Language Film and winner of some thirty and more national and international awards. Equally interesting are the reviews of the film, which point to what is seen as a development in the period film: *The Twilight Samurai* is characterized as "a mature, revisionist" film in which "[t]he genre's battery of traditions takes an evocative, real-world beating,"[1] and as "a fantastic modern samurai flick ... that harkens back to the heyday of *jidai-geki* but does so in a different and unique manner ... by infusing the film with such 'realism' the story gets anchored and becomes more authentic."[2] To those who have seen primarily films like the *Zatoichi* and *Sleepy Eyes of Death* series, the film may indeed seem different, more "real," whatever that means. Nevertheless, the film does more than merely hearken to the past; it has a firm foundation in the Japanese traditions of production, narrative, and realism.

First, *The Twilight Samurai* is a demonstration of the traditional mastery of the craft of filmmaking that comes only from practice, practice, practice. Yamada's training at Shochiku Studios was traditional — characterized by demands for high rates of output. Before *The Twilight Samurai*, he had written or co-written 124 scripts and directed no less than 76 films for Shochiku. These included the 48 films of the Tora-san series between 1969 and 1995. The continuing saga of a family in a traditional, old-fashioned community of Tokyo and a wayward but loveable brother with an itchy foot did make Yamada an expert craftsman as well as the most popular director in Japan. Despite his success, Shochiku made him sweat to earn the other few other films he was permitted to make, such as the 1970 *Kazoku* (*Where Spring Comes Late*) and the 1977 *Shiawase no kiiroi hankachi* (*Yellow Handkerchief*).

In the old studio system, with its budgets and time schedules, it was necessary to develop very efficient forms of production; for the director, this meant doing what he knew best and using the ways he had perfected by practice. For those directors most pressed for time, efficiency was achieved by specializing in particular narratives with corresponding set scenes and a corresponding set of actors, sets, and camera techniques. The combination of set scene in building narratives and formulas in filming establish the style of the director. Those in the cheapest productions and pressed most for time usually have the same style and can scarce be distinguished one from the other.

The studio system was (and is) not much different in Japan. Even a noted director like Yamada was required to grind out films year after year. Only before Tora-san dominated his career was Yamada able to make one period film; yes, despite claims to the contrary, *The Twilight Samurai* is not his first *jidai-geki*. The 1966 *Un ga yokerya* (*Gambler's Luck*) is a light comedy set in the slums of old Edo. Of course, although poor, the characters are human and humane: the young man who collects the waste from the public toilet observes that times are getting hard because the (ahem) "night soil" is getting thinner. Of course, in the end he gets the girl. In many ways, especially in terms of its focus on the quality of human relationships, it anticipates both the Tora-san series and *The Twilight Samurai*. In any case, the requirement to write and direct so many films under severe time constraints forced Yamada to rely on many of the same techniques developed by performers under time constraint at other times and in other places of the world.

Like them or not, the forty-eight films of Yamada's *Tora-san* ("Otoko wa tsurai yo") series provided him the background necessary to create *Twilight Samurai*, on the one hand a perfect representative of the traditional Japanese period film, on the other, a perfect representative of his own style. For Tora-san, he and his team created a narrative formula, a setting, and an ensemble of characters and performers. At the same time, they perfected the art of variation so that for every film they had a set of expectations (formulas) which could be manipulated to create tension (frustration when expectations are not immediately met), surprise (expectations are violated or met in a new way), and pleasure (expectations are met to the satisfaction of the audience): for example, the dream sequence, the unavailable love interest "Madonna," and Tora-san's hometown of Shibamata in Katsushika City.

It would not be far fetched to say that, by concentrating on contemporary films for over forty years, Yamada had been preparing for *The Twilight Samurai*, a film in the tradition of Inagaki's "contemporary films with top-knots attached" and the *nagaya-mono* of Rakugo like Yamanaka Sadao's *Ninjō kamifusen* (*Humanity and Paper Balloons*).

The film is a *nagaya-mono* in the sense that it deals with the trials and tribulations of the poor and oppressed, even if the characters are of the samurai class. The time is about 1865–66: the rule of the shogunate is being challenged; supporters of each side create tension in the Unasaka domain. None of this concerns samurai Iguchi Seibei, a low-ranking, under-paid clerk, recently widowed, up to his neck in debt, and burdened with the care of two beloved daughters and his elderly mother. Into his life reenters a childhood friend, Tomoe, recently divorced from her abusive husband. When her husband comes after her, Seibei defends her and is forced into a duel. Seibei knocks out his opponent with a wooden practice sword. In gratitude, Tomoe comes in regularly to help the girls with housework and homework, but Seibei, because of his poverty, refuses to accept her brother's offer of marriage; she stops coming.

The sudden death of the lord of the domain results in a contest for power and a bloodbath. Only one man is left to kill and Seibei is ordered to do the job. He needs help in getting ready and sends for Tomoe; he then proposes, but she has already accepted another offer. After killing the man, he returns home to find Tomoe still there. They marry, but less than three years later he is killed in the civil war following the abdication of the shogun. The whole film can be seen as a typical contemporary love story set in the past: boy meets girl, boy loses girl, girl finds boy, boy gives up girl, girl comes back to stay. However, the plot is driven by traditional narratives and composition strategies.

Crossing Narratives

The film skillfully employs the tradition of crossing narratives found in Kabuki and Nō plays and in films like Yamanaka's *Humanity and Paper Balloons*. This is done on two levels. First, the script is based on three separate works by Fujisawa Shūhei (1927–1997), Fujisawa's individual performances of traditional narratives, the second level. *The Twilight Samurai* is a combination of three short novels. From *Tasogare Seibei* (1983) came the low-ranking samurai with the wife dying of tuberculosis (no children), who goes home each evening to take care of her and make insect cages for money; he receives an order to kill a high-ranking councilor whose wife has helped his own wife. From *Takemitsu shimatsu* (*The Bamboo Blade*, 1975), set in the seventeenth century, Yamada took an impoverished ronin with two little girls (cancelled the wife), who with his short blade alone kills one Yogo Zen'emon (who intends to return home and take up farming) and receives, as a reward, Zen'emon's income. From *Hoito Sukehachi* (*Sukehachi, the Beggar*, 1988), he took the scruffy clerk who is reproved by the lord, the friend and his sister, the duel with the wooden sword won against her brute of a husband, and the resulting summons to kill a man and their fight to the death.

Even though Yamada's script has drawn heavily on Fujisawa's stories, which have their own formulas, they are not literal adaptations. It is the skillful combination and performance of these narratives that is appreciated by the audience, based on individual experience of these narratives. Moreover, the script, the even more skillful performance by Yamada and Asama Yoshitaka, crosses the main narrative with several sub-narratives.

The film is a *bakumatsu-mono* by virtue of its setting: from the arrival of Perry in 1853 to the abdication from power of the Tokugawa shogun in 1867. When Iinuma Michinojō first meets his friend Seibei, he makes two comments referring to the tumult Japan is experiencing after Perry's arrival in Edo Bay. The first is about all the dirty ronin roaming the streets of the imperial capital and the anti-shogunate assassins whipping out their swords and yelling, "Tenchū!" The other, made against the background of samurai practicing their rifle (musket?) drill, is a snide comment on the domain's timing in securing their defenses. The story takes place as the forces of the pro-restoration domains and the pro-shogunate domains are gearing up for a conclusive confrontation over the issue of opening the country to the West, which the emperor opposes. The background of the *bakumatsu-mono* is an historical interpretation: the restoration will be the death of a class, the samurai, and the substitution of the sword by modern technology. This is a theme articulated in films of the sixties, such as *Yojimbo* and the 1969 *Akage* (*Red Lion*), and in films as recent as the 2003 *The Last Samurai* and the 2003 *Mibu gishi den* (*When the Last Sword Is Drawn*), in which the protagonists are mown down by a machine gun. This theme is referred to in the dialogue several times in the film: by Iinuma, by Yogo Zen'emon, the man Seibei is sent to kill, and by Seibei himself. From the very beginning we know what will ultimately happen to Seibei.

The national political situation obtrudes into domainal politics and provides the background for the plot as an *ōie-sōdō* (disorder in a great house): tension between the reformers and the conservatives explodes when the sudden death of the lord by measles leaves the succession undecided. When the smoke clears, only one samurai of the losing faction remains. In the consultation about what to do about Yogo, Seibei's name comes up; the tale of his match with Tomoe's former husband Kōda Toyotarō has apparently spread. Seibei is an accomplished swordsman, a skill he more or less abandoned when life got in the way: his wife's illness and funeral, the household chores, and the side job. But the officials have found out that he was more than just a fencing student: he had been an instructor at the school which specialized in the short sword (convenient for fighting in close quarters, since Yogo has barricaded himself in his house). Seibei is in no position to refuse. He reluctantly accepts a mission he barely survives. The inexorable fate of those who, because of their fidelity to their identity as samurai, submit to the control of their superiors is not so much avoided as simply postponed for Seibei. The next time he submits to domainal commands, he is not so lucky. When war finally does break out, the Unasaka domain joins a northern coalition led by Aizu to back the shogunate, and Seibei is killed, as his daughter relates.

The film's main narrative is that of the poor samurai, a variation of the poor ronin narrative seen in films like *Humanity and Paper Balloons* and *Seppuku* (*Harakiri*). Here we have a poor clerk in the quartermaster's office. Seibei's troubles are compounded by the fact that he has two small daughters to care for. The narrative of the impoverished samurai with children to raise alone except for the help of a kind neighborhood woman goes back at least to 1885 with *Suitengu megumi no Fukagawa* (*Kōbei, the Brush Maker*), a play by Kawatake Mokuami: in this case, the story of an impoverished former samurai takes place after the Restoration.[3]

The narrative of the impoverished soldier is usually indicated by the scene of the ronin pasting paper on the ribs of an umbrella: taking in piecework. In addition to working a garden, Seibei also takes in piecework, in this case making cricket cages to supplement his income. This one scene is divided up and spread throughout the film. The entire process is demonstrated, from the delivery of supplies to the pickup and payment by the contractor's agent. Here, again, a traditional scene is reinvigorated by a variation.

However, this narrative is made up of (or crossed with) several sub-narratives, each indicated by shorter and longer type or set scenes. They are sub-narratives not because they are minor, but because they support the main narrative rather than being main narratives themselves.

The first is the tuberculosis narrative, represented here (as a type scene rather than the voice-over monologue) by only the two short funeral scenes at the beginning of the film: laying out the dead and the procession through a stark, winter landscape to the crematorium. We do not see the first signs, coughing and spattered blood. We do not see the months of suffering, the wasting, or the visits of the doctor. We see only the end. However, the entire narrative and all its possible scenes are invoked by the very mention of tuberculosis; they are all well known in popular media.

The second sub-narrative is the selling of the sword (or "the bamboo blade"). To help pay for his debt, Seibei is forced to sell his long sword, a good weapon inherited from his father. We do not see this: we do not see the man disappear into a pawn shop, sit, and watch as the pawnbroker carefully examines the sword; we do not see him take far less than what it is worth and then leave. The audience only learns this when Seibei tells the man he has been ordered to kill, Yogo Zen'emon, and pulls the bamboo blade three or four inches out of the scabbard. We do see the scorn of Tomoe's former husband when Seibei proposes to take him on with the wooden practice piece; indeed, Yogo goes nearly mad with fury at the insult of being challenged with a bamboo blade.

The narrative of the impoverished samurai or ronin has a parallel in the rebellion and tendency films of the 1920s such as *Orochi* (*Serpent*) and *Nikkō no Enzō* (*Enzō from Nikkō*), in which the downtrodden fight back. The real vehicle for these narratives is the man Seibei is ordered to kill, Yogo Zen'emon. He refuses to commit suicide when ordered. He kills a police inspector come to kill him. He gets drunk. He attacks Seibei, representing the domain, for insulting him by trying to kill him with a bamboo blade and a short sword — adding oil to the fire. Even his costume harkens back to the rebellion film: among the military, only a samurai off-duty or a ronin wears a kimono without the over-culottes (*hakama*). Zen'emon's rejection of the clan is indicated by wearing only a robe; as he is fighting, his kimono falls apart to reveal his underwear: this was the trademark in the 1920s of the ronin who fights back, such as Heisaburō in *Serpent*. In keeping with the tradition of the narrative, Zen'emon is being abused by the domain for serving the domain, simply because his superior was eliminated in the contest for power. Just as he is expected to kill himself as ordered, Seibei is expected to kill him on orders. Seibei is summoned at night (not a good sign); the clan officials bring enormous pressure to bear on Seibei, from bribery to threats of expulsion, in order to force his submission. This, too, is the narrative of the upper samurai abusing the lower in the manner of *Serpent*, *Gero* (*Servant*), and even *Samurai* (*Samurai Assassin*). Both Yogo and Seibei are equally subjected to the not-so-very-tender mercies of the domain.

The third and final sub-narrative, that of the master swordsman, is the old *bugei-mono* or martial arts story of Kōdan. To all appearances, Seibei is nothing more than a grimy, minor clerk in the office of the castle quartermaster. However, hints of something more are given early in the film: his friend Iinuma wants to recommend him for a position in the imperial capital as a palace guard. And the night before the duel, Iinuma is truly worried that Seibei will really kill his former brother-in-law: fighting for any reason was forbidden, even in self-defense (Kira was not prosecuted by the shogunate because he did not draw his sword to defend himself against Asano's attack). Before the fight with Kōda, Seibei tries to warm up but nearly collapses: he is out of shape. Even so, he manages to dodge Kōda and knock him out with his wooden practice sword.

Seibei now enters the ranks of legendary (whether real or fictional) swordsmen like Araki Mataemon, Tsukue Ryūnosuke, and Miyamoto Musashi. Tomoe is pleased. Yogo comes to ask for a match. His colleagues are a bit nervous about the nickname they have given him. He has already been identified with Zen: he eats breakfast, fills his bowl with hot water, picks up a pickle to scrub out the bowl, pops the pickle in his mouth, drinks down the water, and puts bowl and chopsticks into their box. The manners of the samurai come from the discipline of the monastery. He is shown examining his blade (with the pin connecting tang to hilt in his mouth to prevent breathing on it; usually it is a piece of paper) and sharpening it on a whetstone as a true professional and expert should. He practices his moves (as Kyūzō does in *Seven Samurai*). In the great tradition of the medieval epic, he is dressed and armed for combat (Tomoe gets him ready as Ōishi's wife dresses him in Mizoguchi's *Genroku Chūshingura*).

The traditionality of the narratives can be examined by comparing their use in *Harakiri*. First comes the narrative of poverty as a result of losing one's lord to suicide and the disbanding of the domain's samurai; Tsugumo is shown pasting paper to the ribs of an umbrella, a well-known convention. He refuses an offer for his daughter, not of marriage, but of concubinage; instead, he chooses an honorable marriage to a poor man. Poverty and hard work result in the tuberculosis of Tsugumo's delicate daughter (she coughs blood onto the paper of the fans she is making) and his grandson's illness. Then his son-in-law sells his sword and is later forced to commit *seppuku* with the bamboo blade. Tsugumo's daughter and grandson die, although the audience does not see the funeral. In revenge, the old soldier, the master swordsman, by virtue of practice in the field, gets his own back by taking the top-knots of the three who had brought home the body of his son-in-law and then by assaulting the icon of the founder of the house in a massed combat scene. The main and sub-narratives of the two films are the same, if variations. However, the sequencing and setting make for completely different stories if for the same interpretation: internalization of the identity of the samurai leads to death and destruction. It is important to note that *The Twilight Samurai* is not making direct allusions to *Harakiri*. They both emerge as different performances of the same narratives.

Thematic Composition

Each narrative is made up of a number of conventional type or set scenes (also called themes). One of my favorite set scenes is the ball scene. It appears in all genres in different forms: birthday parties, wedding parties, cocktail parties, even the opera — in Japanese films, it is the festival scene. Traditionally, bad things happen at the ball. In *Jezebel* (1938), set in ante-bellum New Orleans, high-handed Julie wears a red dress to the Olympus Ball and loses both her respectability and her man. In *Anna Karenina*, it is at a ball that Kitty realizes that she has lost the man she loves. In *Gone with the Wind*, Scarlett causes a scandal (and heart palpitations for Aunt Pittypat) by appearing in her widow's weeds at a fund-raising ball and, even worse, dancing with Rhett Butler. The audience always knows as soon as the scene starts that something bad is about to happen and waits in suspense to find out what. This use of a technique often dismissed as conventional and formulaic persists because it has its uses in the narrative. Tolstoy used the ball scene. So did William Wyler — twice in *Wuthering Heights* (1939), although such a scene is not in the original novel. Of course, it was used to great effect in *Dangerous Liaisons* (1988): it is at an evening social gathering, during the concert, that the Marquise de Mertueil realizes that the great love of her life, the Vicomte de Valmont, is in love with Madame de Tourvel.

Japanese period films have their own set scenes. *The Twilight Samurai* has not only the requisite fight scenes, but many other scenes. One, for example, is the brief scene in which the hero looks in on his two sleeping daughters after he has decided to accept the dangerous mission. This is a variation of a scene found in other plays and films: for example, in Shinoda Masahiro's adaptation of a Chikamatsu play, *Yari no Gonza* (*Gonza the Spearman*), a

***Opposite*: Another *kata* (formula) representing parental love and portending ill as well. Here, Seibei (Sanada Hiroyuki) checks in on his daughters Kayano (Itō Miki, center) and Ito (Hashiguchi Erina) before settling down to sharpen the blade of his short sword in preparation for his assignment to kill another samurai. The extensive use of traditional formulas and other narrative techniques in a film praised for its atypical realism and emotional depth confirms the viability of traditional Japanese narrative strategies as a perdurable source of creativity. (Still from *The Twilight Samurai*, directed by Yōji Yamada, 2002, Shōchiku Co., Ltd., Nippon Television Network Corporation, Sumitomo Corporation, Hakuhōdō, Inc., Nippon Shuppan Hanbai, Inc., Eisei Gekijo Co., Ltd. All Rights Reserved.)**

woman takes a last look at her sleeping children before, forced by circumstance, running away with a man. Another is a scene based on the Chūshingura cycle: the arrival from Edo of a messenger by palanquin to the home domain to report on the death of the lord of the domain. In *The Twilight Samurai*, too, a major councilor arrives by palanquin to report the death of the lord in Edo. The very appearance of (or reference to) the palanquin always portends trouble.

The set scene is usually performed with its own conventions: smaller building blocks of formulas of actions and film techniques. Take the pirate film of the thirties and forties as an example: pirate films almost always have the "taking the prize" scene: almost always, the pirates clench their cutlasses between their teeth, grab a halyard, and swing from one ship to the other. Not only is this scene usually performed the same way, it is also usually filmed in the same way using formulas more specific to film techniques: the pirates are seen *en masse* in a long shot swinging across the screen from right to left; less often, a pirate in the far distance swings from his perch right into the audience's lap (from a long shot to a close-up)!

The Twilight Samurai is composed of such scenes, shorter and longer. For example, the scene of the arrival of the messenger from Edo is staged conventionally by Yamada: the palanquin bearers, followed by lower-ranking samurai, run up the street calling out the pace in exhaustion, "Hey, ho! Hey, ho!" As soon as they park the palanquin, they drop, heaving and gasping, to the ground. The chief councilor crawls out, stands, and begins to falter, when he is caught and dragged down the hall by his retainers. This scene signals that something dreadful has happened — trouble in the house of a warlord, an *oie-sōdō*.[4]

Narrative Strategies

Several techniques are used to string the scenes together. The first technique is framing. In a narrative, the "plot" is arranged as a series of scenes and then the order of the scenes is reversed: a graph describing the process would look like a series of squares one inside the other. The structure of *The Twilight Samurai* demonstrates features of this pattern.

The first frame is created by the rituals performed for the dead. The film begins with a funeral: a wake of wailing women and muttering men shot indoors and in the dark ends with a shot of little Ito's face; then there is the procession to the crematorium in the bright, blinding snow. The film ends with the ritual that continues after death: a visit to the grave (*ohaka-mairi*) made by the elderly Ito. The frame also crosses narratives as this *bakumatsu-mono* makes its transition from the Tokugawa period to the Meiji period.

A second frame again involves Ito. Seibei is shown for the first time at the office and walking home from work. As he nears his house, Ito, who is playing outside, runs to him. He picks her up and walks to his gate. Near the end of the film, he walks out of the house in which he has finished his "job" of killing Yogo and, receiving a bandage, stands at the gate; he comes through his own gate, hands his "sword" to Naota, picks up Ito, and moves to the door of his house.

It is also possible to frame a scene. For example, as Seibei sharpens his sword in preparation for dealing with Yogo, the rasp of the stroke is heard loud enough to wake Ito; after practice in the early dawn, Seibei is grating bonito (dried fish used for soup stock), which makes somewhat the same sound. Again, when his superior Kusaka Chōbei arrives at Seibei's house to fetch him to the officials, he takes a seat and sees Ito for the first time when she peeks around the corner. He makes a face to make her laugh. After the grueling interview with the officials, as they exit the gate, Kusaka tries to encourage Seibei and promises to take care of his family. Kusaka is a good man, and, according to convention, good men are nice to little children; both scenes are variations of the scene of being kind to children.

The second technique is repetition. In the *Odyssey*, for example, Odysseus goes from place to place, but at each place where he is welcomed, the welcoming scene is described almost word for word in the same way.

The first example in the film, and most obvious, is the repetition of the scenes of the office at the end of the day: "Thank you, gentlemen. That will be all for today." The second is the repetition of Seibei's mother's question, "Who are you?" to Seibei, to her brother, and even to Tomoe, whom she has recognized before.

An important example of repetition involves the dueling scenes. In both there is almost the same sequence. The first one begins with a challenge by the drunken Kōdo; the second with the order from the domainal officials (divided into two scenes, the arrival of Kusaka and the interview with the officials). The next two parts are reversed: in the first, Seibei eats breakfast and then goes outdoors to practice; in the second, Seibei practices in the dark and then helps prepare breakfast. In both, Seibei walks to the appointed place and humiliates his opponent by failing to arrive with proper long sword. In the first duel, he knocks out his opponent; in the second, he kills him. The repetition is not exact (the scene of Seibei sharpening his sword had to be added to the second because this time he was to use a real weapon) but more than close enough to be recognized as such. Variation is also germane to traditional narrative.

Another form of this repetition is a kind of parallelism. For example, Seibei's relatives have given him a lot of trouble by demanding a funeral that will not shame the family. His uncle, especially, is a fearsome and unpleasant personality who bellows at the door, scolds Seibei for stinking in the presence of the lord (for which he had to go to and apologize), reproves Kayano for studying Confucius's *Analects*, and tries to force Seibei into a marriage with the daughter of a village headman he knows — still at home (we can guess) because of her (lack of) looks. He is a dreadfully sexist man who tells Seibei's daughter Kayano that Confucius (by which he means Chinese characters) is a waste for women. He is so mean to his sister, Seibei's mother, that she cries herself to sleep that night. Tomoe also has trouble: her sister-in-law keeps her from running off to catch Seibei after he has left the house and gives her a fine lecture on the propriety of a "returned bride" threatening her prospects for marriage by being seen with a samurai on the street (like Seibei's uncle, she is very concerned about the family's reputation).

The most poignant parallel, however, is between Seibei and Yogo. When Yogo first comes to see Seibei, he puts himself on Seibei's side by telling him, with some contempt, that Kōda, his erstwhile drinking buddy, whined to him and begged him to take on his enemy.

Another technique is to create tension by stretching out a scene and delaying the next part of it. The entire process of making insect cages is demonstrated. However, the entire "scene" is broken up into sequential parts and distributed throughout the film: the cages are collected by the contractor's agent and an apprentice only just as Kusaka, on orders from the domain officials, arrives to fetch Seibei. Another example is the tension created between the time of Yogo's challenge to a match and that of the expected match itself, when Seibei is sent to kill him. A third example is the insertion of a short scene of Kayano telling Ito to go buy tofu between the scene of Seibei passing through Yogo's gate and the scene of arriving at his own.

A one-time reference may be made to the overall tradition outside the film itself. For example, at one point in the confrontation between Seibei and Yogo, they are seated and seen as if back to back: being seated back to back is a stage convention for indicating lovers, who are so shy and overcome that they can not look at each other. This motif is used unconventionally to indicate the similarity between Seibei and Yogo: two master swordsmen, two men who have suffered terrible poverty, two husbands and fathers who have lost family to tuberculosis, and two men sent to their deaths by their superiors. At another point, Tomoe helps Seibei dress and then she arranges his hair. In reality, she should have cut the band tying up his hair, combed it (as Kayano did for Ito earlier in the film) and retied it; that, however, is not so easy to do on a wig. Nevertheless, this is a scene that resonates intimacy: in Kabuki, it can be seen as far back as the 1809 *Sekitori Senryō Nobori* (*The Pride of a Sumo Wrestler/The Rise of a 1000 Ryō Wrestler*), where it indicates the unspoken intimacy between a sumo wrestler, who has to throw a match, and his wife, who is dressing his hair.[5]

Tomoe (Miyazawa Rie) combs the hair of Seibei (Sanada Hiroyuki) before he sets out on the mission charged to him by his domainal superiors. The scene of combing the hair of another is a *kata* (formula) for intimacy, whether between a mother and child (as in Makino Masahiro's 1942 version of Izumi Kyōka's *Onna keizu* [*Genealogy of Women*]) or between man and wife (as in the 1809 Kabuki *Sekitori Senryō Nobori* [*The Pride of a Sumo Wrestler/The Rise of a 1000 Ryō Wrestler*]). Earlier in the film, Seibei's elder daughter Kayano is seen combing her sister's hair before school. A variant of the scene can be seen in Inagaki's 1928 *Hōrō zanmai* (*Wanderlust*), in which a samurai returning from Edo imagines his wife trimming his son's bangs, and even as far back as Murasaki Shikibu's *Genji monogatari*, in which Genji is reported as trimming Murasaki's ends. The formula may portend ill: Seibei confesses his feelings and asks Tomoe to marry him; unfortunately, she has already accepted a very good offer. The samurai finally arrives home to find his wife dead. And Genji ends up forcing himself on Murasaki. (Still from *The Twilight Samurai*, directed by Yōji Yamada, 2002, Shōchiku Co., Ltd., Nippon Television Network Corporation, Sumitomo Corporation, Hakuhōdō, Inc., Nippon Shuppan Hanbai, Inc., Eisei Gekijo Co., Ltd. All Rights Reserved).

Mitate by Crossing Narratives

In the thirties, especially for those in the Narutaki study group (Inagaki, Yamanaka, Mimura and others), the idea was to make the period film virtually indistinguishable — except for the wigs — from films about contemporary life. Directors like Ozu Yasujirō and Shimizu Hiroshi were the models. These filmmakers were almost exclusively specialists in the period film. However,

Yamada has made his career on light comedies set in the present, especially the Tora-san series (forty-eight before the star, Atsumi Kiyoshi, died in 1996). He was already a widely-acclaimed expert in the genre, the only director to have a national audience, when he made *The Twilight Samurai*.

Tasogare Seibei is a traditional *jidai-geki* that combines three main narratives: the impoverished soldier, tuberculosis, and the martial arts story of the master swordsman. However, what makes a *jidai-geki* a *jidai-geki* and not a simple re-enactment of some incident of the past is the reference to the present. This is accomplished by crossing narratives which are identified with contemporary pieces. There are several, but I will limit analysis to just a few.

The first to appear in the film is the salary-man narrative set in the modern period. It is not entirely unusual to see samurai performing duties of a kind less than martial. In his *Genroku chūshingura*, Mizoguchi shows the accountants of the domain checking the facts and figures on all supplies, weapons, and cash before handing over the castle to the new lord. However, the film does not tell the story from the perspective of one of those accountants. *Tasogare Seibei* does. Four times we are shown the office where he works — eight desks in two rows facing each other with the quartermaster at the top end; three times the ritual ending the day, including the friendly chatter after and the same curt but civil reply to invitations to go drinking. Three times the day ends as usual and the scene is shot the same way each time. The fourth time, the shot is reversed at the end, because this day is not as usual: the lord's death has been reported and the day is cut short. Twice we are shown the storehouse for the supplies: once when Yogo comes to ask him for a match as supplies are being delivered and once when the lord comes on inspection and Seibei is the one to report on the kinds, amounts, and shelf-life of the provisions. Whereas, in the twenties or sixties period films had attracted the young and disaffected, the film apparently resonated with male, middle-class, salaried office workers in Japan:

> Ordinary male office workers are reported to have responded viscerally to the film: a lot of middle class workers found many things that were familiar to them in this film and thus, became very emotionally attached to the story. The film made the aged, yet experienced, male cry in a similar way as some other documentary shows do in Japan, such as *Project X*, which deals with various historic constructions and scientific projects done by skilled men that greatly contributed to modern technological society. *The Twilight Samurai*, on the other hand, is about a lower class samurai, which resembles the lives of every other man today who goes to work and raises his children, and whose pay is low. This film caught the hearts of the middle aged male audience.[6]

The second is the childhood friendship narrative, which may be more familiar to western audiences from acquaintance with modern literature and stories about contemporary life. What is significant here is the understanding shared between filmmakers and audience of the importance of childhood and the relationships formed in childhood. This is seen in the scene where Seibei's mother asks Tomoe who she is and the only way she can express her feelings for Seibei is to identify herself as Seibei's childhood friend. In the beginning of the film, Seibei's only friend appears to be Iinuma Michinojō, a man of some importance in domainal affairs. Why would the son of a 400 *koku* house bother with the son of a 50 *koku* house? Because they met and became friends in school, of course, most likely fencing school, from the particular warning he gives Seibei with his duel with Kōda. They have stayed friends even though it is evident that Seibei has the upper hand here: although he nearly breaks Iinuma's arm pushing him out of the way of the duel with Kōda, he is big brother and protector.

The most important scene representing Seibei's intimate relationship with Michinojō is the fishing scene. Scenes of fishing together have been used a long time in films about contemporary life to perform the idea of a close relationship. Ozu, for example, uses the fishing scene to illustrate the intimacy of father and son in *Chichi ariki* (*There Was a Father*; 1942). More recent is a popular series of films, *Tsuribaka nisshi* (seventeen since 1988), about a salaryman (Nishida Toshiyuki) and his boss (Mikuni Rentarō), his devoted student of the fine art of fly fishing. Yamada has been a co-writer of the scripts since the beginning.

The third is the "uptown girl" narrative. This is an American success narrative that often appears in film: *Laura*'s (1944) lower-middle class detective got a silver shin in breaking a case and he gets the classy career woman working in a publishing company; in *The Best Years of Our Lives* (1946), the soda jerk (the same actor, Dana Andrews [1909–1992], by the way) returns from World War II an air force captain decorated for courage under fire and he gets the daughter of a banker. This is not the narrative I have found in Japanese period films; more likely, the man who aspires to love his social superior gets killed: in the Tokugawa period, seducing the wife or daughter of one's employer was punishable by death. Mizoguchi's 1954 *A Story from Chikamatsu* is an adaptation of *Daikyōji mukashi goyomi* (1715) and Ihara Saikaku's story "Osan Mouemon" from *Koshoku gonin onna* (*Five Women Who Loved Love*; 1686): an employee of the calendar maker to the emperor has loved his employer's wife only from afar, but eventually they are executed for adultery. In the 1960 *Senhime goten* (*Princess Sen in Edo*), the hero loves the widowed and wanton daughter of the former shogun, but dies in order to protect her (she finally shapes up and becomes a nun to pray for him). Inagaki's 1943 *Muhōmatsu no isshō* (*The Live of Muhomatsu the Untamed*) was censored and cut because it suggested the less-than-pure love of a rickshaw man for an officer's widow.

Nevertheless, there is a tradition of narratives about love between people of different rank. Michinojō has a sister, Tomoe. When she was little Seibei made dolls for her; when she fell out of a tree, he carried her to the doctor's (a scene familiar from both *The Life of Muhomatsu the Untamed* and the 1995 *Persuasion*). She is the vehicle for the battered wife narrative, although she is lucky that her brother cares enough for her to secure a divorce. (This is less a film about the evils of *bushidō* than a story about ordinary people, a *nagaya-mono*; if a cranky, old uncle tries to run Seibei's life, then it is equally credible that a brother would protect his sister.) However, now that she is home, she moves into the horrible in-laws narrative: her sister-in-law puts her to work weaving and to escape she visits Seibei, her childhood friend and protector. When he accompanies her home from this first visit, her recently-divorced husband, drunk as usual, is throwing his weight around. He pushes her brother down; he slaps her. Seibei moves in to control the situation and effectively pins the man down. This tussle with Kōda is the first visual sign that Seibei has skills other than of toting up figures. He is then forced into a duel. Despite being creaky and out of shape, Seibei easily beats Kōda with a wood practice sword. This earns him her gratitude; by the time he returns from the fight with Yogo, having kept up the pretense of normality for the girls by doing housework with them (her sleeves are tied back), Tomoe has decided to stay with him.

If, in American films, bravery in the line of duty (for policeman or soldier) is rewarded by winning a woman of a higher rank or class, in Japanese films, the reward for expertise with the sword is rewarded by adoption and marriage into a higher-ranking family. This does not always lead to happiness; as seen in Kobayashi's 1967 *Jōi-uchi: hairyō tsuma shimatsu* (*Samurai Rebellion*), the hero endures the scorn of his wife. Seibei's marriage with the daughter of a one hundred and twenty *koku* house was very likely made possible by his early promise with the sword; his failure to rise was a constant source of friction with his nagging wife, especially during her illness, as he confides to Michinojō when they are out fishing.

The final two narratives concern mental handicaps. The first, the narrative of the senile parent, found usually in films about contemporary life, is represented by variations of one scene: Seibei's mother keeps asking, "Who are you?" In film, this narrative goes back at least to 1973 with Toyoda Shirō's film based on Ariyoshi Sawako's ground-breaking novel, *Kōkotsu no hito* (*The Twilight Years*). Yamada's own experience with directing the elderly goes back to 1969, at least, with the Tora-san series: Chishū Ryū appeared regularly in the series as priest of the local Buddhist temple, from the age of sixty-five to eighty-seven.

The second is that of the mentally handicapped. Inagaki Hiroshi made the first two films in Japan about mentally-handicapped children based on novels by Kamura Tazuji: the 1948 *Te o tsunagu kora* (*Children Holding Hands*) and 1949 *Wasurareta kora* (*Forgotten Children*). In *Tasogare Seibei*, the mentally-handicapped character is Naota, Seibei's one and only servant (samurai, like their European counterparts, were not allowed to carry anything; the hands had to be kept free to fight). With wood sword (or stick) tucked into his sash at the back, he waits for Seibei at the castle gate to carry his lunch box home or accompanies him on calls. He performs various simple tasks: drawing water from the well, carrying water, watering the garden, working in the kitchen, and waiting at the gate to receive "visitors." The most important task he performs is to go to Tomoe with a message to go to Seibei's house; delivering the message leaves him gasping. What is interesting about this scene is its similarity to (adaptation of) one in the 1941 *Little Foxes*, in which Horace Giddens (Herbert Marshall) sends his servant Harold (Henry "Hot Shot" Thomas) to the bank: Harold has to repeat the message over and over to remember; Naota, too, has to repeat the message over and over.

The narratives of the senile parent and the mentally-handicapped serve as the main moral compass in this film. We know that Seibei, his daughters, and Tomoe are good because of the way they treat Seibei's mother, Kinu: Seibei is always courteous, the little girls take her to bed and to the bathroom, and Tomoe, too, is respectful in that she formally asks after her health. We know that her brother Tōemon (Tamba Tetsurō [1922–2006]) is a truly mean old man because he tells Seibei to take her out of the room and tie her to a pillar — she is not someone he wishes the neighbors to see.

Finally, the narrative of the enormous changes wrought by the end of the shogunate and subsequent modernization of Japan are invoked by the whistle of a steam engine and the sight of a rickshaw pulled by a man in western-style uniform — Ito on the way to her parents' grave. The whistle invokes not only the steam engine but also the ash in the eye, the hard, wood seats, and the sandals left on the platform by those entering the cars and tossed in after them — all well-known motifs of this Meiji-period narrative. The rickshaw is self-explanatory: a western invention exported to Japan.

Ito has benefited from the modernization. Seibei has kept the girls in school despite his poverty and despite his uncle's obvious displeasure — will Confucius get a girl married? Even the schoolteacher knows that times are changing and girls will need an education: learning the *Analects* is getting an education. Tomoe carries out Seibei's responsibilities to his daughters when she takes them to Tokyo to be educated. Indeed, the Japanese have traditionally considered the education of girls of importance. The position of girls in the transitional period and after is a narrative of its own. Five girls were sent by the new government to study in the United States in 1871. Another girl was sent from the far north to be educated in Tokyo: Inagaki Etsuko (1873–1950), who became an instructor of Japanese at Columbia University, was educated in the Chinese classics at home and then sent to school in Tokyo to prepare for marriage with a businessman in the United States. Of course, not every girl fared so well. In the 1953 film version of *Yoake mae* (*Before Dawn*), the hero is sympathetic to the plight of the peasants but will not allow his daughter to go Tokyo to study: she cuts her throat but survives and wears a scarf to hide the scar as she paces between her pupils in the little school she runs. Still, many Japanese cared about women's education: every higher school and college built for girls during the Meiji period was built with private funds. As the heroine of the 1966 version of *Ki no kawa* (*The River Ki*) tells her daughter, "Being a woman is no excuse for being ignorant!"

One of the most interesting references to the present is the casting of Tanaka Min (b. 1945) as Yogo. A dancer with an international reputation, he trained with Butoh master Hijikata Tatsumi. The most recognizable image of Butoh is that of all-but-naked men caked in white and writhing in slow motion across the floor and up the wall. Tanaka's background in avant garde performance dance and Butoh informs the *shuraba* scene at the end of the film. His face is made up in grey green (more visible in stills than in the film itself) and his long, drawn-out death scene, from the last slash to falling over and reaching for Seibei, is choreographed in a way I have not seen in period film — with a full knowledge of how the body works.[7]

Mitate and Women as the Link to the Present

The women in the film, as usual, make the strongest reference to the present. Their make-up and costumes are very crisp. At the time, women, once married, at least blackened their teeth and shaved off their eyebrows. Both Tomoe and her sister-in-law are made up to look "not made up"; their teeth are white and their eyebrows are still there. The hair is modern: the style is traditional (but look carefully at the sister-in-law's ponytail), yet caters to modern taste and dispenses with the heavy camellia oil. The two women's kimonos are of modern length; the hems hit the toes. The sashes (*obi*) are typically stiffened in front with a piece of plastic for the smooth pouter-pigeon line of modern women with modern figures. The toes could point in more, as they do if women normally sit on their heels (no one can sit properly any more). At least the actresses are all Japanese; no one makes a grotesque faux pas like that in *Memoirs of a Geisha*, when a supposedly gracious and well-trained geisha, climbing into a room, exposes her leg up and over the knee![8]

Realism

Linguistic Realism

Most period films seem to have followed the rules of linguistic realism established in the 1930s by Inagaki Hiroshi and Mimura Shintarō: the dialect of the civil servants and businessmen of the Marunouchi district in Tokyo for samurai and the local working-class accent for the commoners — no matter where the film took place. *Tagosare Seibei* takes place in what is now Yamagata Prefecture, and most of the characters speak in the strong dialect of the area which is distinguished by its pronunciation: *kudaharu* instead of *kudasaru*, *gozans* instead of *gozuimas,' nei* instead of *nai*, *seppatsu* instead of *shuppatsu*, *watase* instead of *watashi*, *gara* instead of *kara*, *shizure* instead of *shitsure*, *sa* instead of *e*, etc.

The characters not using the local dialect fall into two groups, good and evil. The good are, first, the lord of the domain, who lives half the time in Edo and was probably raised there. The second is the elderly Iguchi Ito, raised and educated in modern Tokyo, whose voice-over narrates the entire film. The evil include the drunken lout and wife-beater Kōdo Toyotarō as well as the upper-ranking officials who force him to take up the commission to kill the man who will not commit suicide on orders. The Warden (*gokaro*) of the clan we know is evil; he cannot look Seibei quite fully in the face and he is conventionally made up to look evil with a sickly, pale skin, circles 'round the eyes, and almost no eyebrows. He plays good cop–bad cop as bad-cop with the lower-ranking samurai who does most of the talking.

The last to speak conventionally "standard" Edo Japanese is Yogo Zen'emon, whom Seibei is ordered to kill. He slips from "good" to "evil" in the flicker of an eye. When Seibei arrives on his mission, Yogo offers a long *monogatari* (monologue) on his past life, losing a job and losing wife and child to consumption, and the trials of paying for a funeral. The story, so like Seibei's own, wins Seibei's sympathy and elicits his own confession, that he was forced to sell his long sword. Insulted, like his drinking buddy Kōda, because Seibei has shown such arrogance in bringing a wood sword to a fight, as drunk as he is, he seizes his sword and goes after Seibei.

Whereas the difference in dialect had been used to indicate only class difference, difference in dialect in *The Twilight Samurai* has more ambiguous functions because their uses are historically grounded rather than grounded in an agreed-upon convention. First, characters who come from or spend a great deal of time out of the domain speak standard, upper-class Edo dialects — the lord, Ito, the domainal officials, and Yogo. Seibei's friend Iinuma Michinojō speaks something in between because he spends time in the capitals and his domain (*keeru* instead of *kairu*). Yogo is clearly an outsider only recently employed by the domain (as master of the watch).

Ito's case is interesting. Her accent changes both in terms of geography and of time. As a girl in the domain, she speaks with the local accent. As an elderly lady educated (and most likely married and living) in Tokyo, she speaks standard Japanese in her voice-over narration. This change of residence is made possible only by a historical change in regime and Japan's transition to the modern period.

However, it is clear that all the men of Seibei's class, except his colleagues in the quartermaster's office, are above him in income and therefore above him in rank. Rank is determined by hereditary stipends. Seibei earns a salary in addition to his because he actually has a job as an accountant in the quartermaster's office: without the job he would have been much worse off. Nevertheless, his rank is determined by the amount of his total stipend or *kokudaka* of rice rations for fifty men a year. His wife's family had 150. His friend Iinuma has 400. The Kōda have 1,200. His lord has 70,000, out of which he pays the stipends and the salaries. He is also, in all probability, "borrowing" up to fifty percent of Seibei's income. All, including the high officials, both outrank him and speak something other than the local dialect. In this case, the men who give him trouble are indicated by their accents — even Iinuma gives Seibei trouble when he tries to convince him to marry his sister.

Yogo's case is especially problematic. He does apparently outrank Seibei (he addresses him as *onushi*, used for social inferiors). However, in the beginning, despite the fact that he does not speak in the local dialect, which would indicate a "villain," he is a sympathetic character even in the end. He first appears to ask Seibei for a match and wins sympathy by calling a spade a spade and Kōda a whiner. Yogo again wins Seibei's sympathy when he asks him to let him go and when he tells his story. Only when he finds out that Seibei has come with a wood sword does he change character and attack Seibei. Therefore, he is played against type (iconography) and then returned to type, villain. Even then, he is a sympathetic character because of all the misery he has experienced.

The film is not breaking with the tradition of linguistic realism, but going back to an older tradition in Kōdan and Rakugo of exactly reproducing local dialects, geographical and occupational; the principle is the same. Even so, in important scenes, the duels and his interview with the clan officials, Seibei's low position in his social group and the rank of those who put pressure on him coincide generally with difference in dialect as far as I can tell.

Photographic Realism

A brief comment should be made about the cinematography by Naganuma Mutsuo, who has worked with Yamada on six other films (including *The*

Hidden Blade). The film is meant to look as if shot in available light and is shot almost exclusively against the light. The indoor shots are dark; the outdoor shots bright. This makes for the illusion of reality if for no other reason than that most films are shot, if not in high key lighting, at least lit from the front. It certainly makes for the same impression of oppressiveness as the chiaroscuro in some of the early period films, especially *Humanity and Paper Balloons*.

Didactism

Didactism, whether in terms of exhortations to morality or a lesson in how to do something, has a long history in Japanese performing arts. In film, it is best represented in the films of Kurosawa Akira: in *Seven Samurai* were several demonstrations of martial techniques: how to test a soldier, how properly to draw a bow, and how to use a horse, not to mention how to be a compassionate warrior by accepting a commission to defend those in need.

In *Tasogare Seibei*, instruction is given on a variety of matters. The first example is the funeral scene, in which Seibei's uncle shows how to lay out the dead properly and, especially, in which direction to point the fan that is placed upon the body. Another is how to make cricket cages, where the materials come from, and how to sell them and for how much.

Another is how properly to eat. At breakfast, Seibei finishes his meal, scrubs out his bowl with hot water and a pickle, tosses it all down, and places bowl and chopsticks in a box for the purpose.

The longest scene of this type demonstrates how to dismantle, examine, and sharpen a sword. One knocks out the pin that connects the tang to the hilt (and puts it in the bucket of water to avoid losing it), grasps the hilt and thumps on the hand holding it until it is loosened. Always hold the blade with paper or a cloth. To sharpen, wet the whetstone, lay the blade flat on it facing away, and then draw the blade back and forth with pressure on the edge of the blade and the outward push.

One scene demonstrates how to fire a gun and what happens when one misfires. Another informs the audience of the contents of castle stores, how much, shelf life, and turnover rates. Yet another shows the morning ritual of going to school: kneeling before the teacher to say good-morning, fetching a desk, and sitting down to read and recite lessons at the same time as the other students. In one scene we see the performance of a real lion dance and a comedy skit: this is the Yutagawa *kagura* performed at the shrine festival in July in Yutagawa Shrine in Tsuruoka.[9] Two scenes show a technique for warming up with a wood sword and a routine for practicing with a real sword. For westerners, the film affords a glimpse into everyday life, especially the greetings for coming, going, and going to bed at night: for those who think that all women are deferential to all men, it may come as a surprise to see Seibei so formal and respectful to his mother, even if she is senile.

The *Monogatari* as Complaint

Tasogare Seibei maintains the form and function of the *monogatari* as complaint of suffering. There are actually several *monogatari*. The first is that of the voice-over narrator, Seibei's daughter Ito as an elderly woman. The entirety of the story is related by her: the major part of the story, from her mother's death to Seibei's return from his killing of Yogo, is told in flashback; the part from the end of the shogunate and Seibei's death in the Bōshin War to his former colleagues' assessment of Seibei's life is continued seamlessly as an asynchronous voice-over to the visuals of Ito's visit to her parents' grave. Seibei's victory over Yogo and Tomoe's decision to stay to await his return notwithstanding, he was in the end killed by gunfire in the Bōshin War and left Tomoe a widow with two children to raise without even his paltry salary. Even though this part of the story is told succinctly, it is still there and counts toward generating the interpretation of the whole story as a *monogatari* of suffering.

The first part of the story, the death of Seibei's wife, his poverty, his burden of two children and a senile mother is told thrice more in contracted form. First, at their favorite drinking hole, his colleagues discuss his smell, raggedness, and even their own attempts to find him a wife, who would have to take in work. Next, after bawling him out for causing such shame to the family by appearing before the lord in rags and stinking like a fish, Seibei's uncle proposes a marriage and lets him know what he has told the headman about Seibei's predicament: his poverty and other burdens. And finally, Seibei relates part of his story to Yogo as they commiserate their similar fates: Yogo initiates by asking questions about his wife's illness, and Seibei continues with his *monogatari* of his poverty, his wife's death, the main family's demand of a funeral he could not afford, and his selling of his sword, the soul of a samurai.

Yogo tells a parallel tale of woe. He lost his job when his lord was ordered to commit suicide. Seven years he was on the road trying to survive as a farmhand, a porter, a beggar. His wife died of tuberculosis before he was taken on by the Unasaka domain. Then his daughter died. And now the domain wants him to commit suicide. Even Tomoe tells a tale heavy with nostalgia for her childhood that only amplifies the pain of her more recent troubles. She played with the boys. Seibei used to tease her. Seibei took her to the doctor when she fell out of a tree. But when she got to be nine, her mother told her not to play with the boys anymore. It is no fun to be a female.

None of the *monogatari* is about happiness. They are about death, poverty, and the problems of life after childhood. The ultimate source of unhappiness is their status (or lack thereof) as samurai. Yogo has lost his status; that has led to his poverty and the deaths of his wife and daughter. Regaining status means that when ordered to commit suicide, he should commit suicide. Seibei is all too willing to let him escape; but Yogo's pride as a swordsman prevents him. Seibei himself takes up his sword when ordered because, ultimately, he is a samurai even if not an important one (*hashikure no samurai*); ultimately he will be killed because of his status and what that status demands. The only one not particularly concerned about status seems to be Tomoe: she bucks the system in taking Seibei's daughters to a commoners' festival, with its scary dragon and its ribald skit; this prepares the audience for her willingness to trade in a position as daughter of a 400 *koku* house for a position as wife in a 50 *koku* house.

The confrontation with Yogo, however, is a different affair: neither of the fights are in the style of Sawada Shōjirō, but are "poodle fights"; the fight with Yogo is especially drawn-out and gruesome, to say the least. The scene is set up as a *shuraba* like those of epics where the battlefield is presented as a collapse of the (religious) universe. The official waiting for Seibei warns him that Yogo is no longer human, but a beast (*kedamono*). Yogo munches on the bones of his daughter; he has become a *gakki*, a hungry ghost — a characterization reinforced by his white makeup. The two battling it out inside the house are now Asura, the titans engaged in eternal battle with the gods. Screens are slashed. A tea kettle is knocked into the brazier. Blood is heard dripping onto the floor and Seibei's final slash produces a terrifying squelch; the fight scene is a true *shuraba* in the tradition of *Serpent* and *Street of the Masterless Samurai*. Seibei emerges limping and covered in blood like a ghost out of hell; as he approaches his house, women scream, men scuttle by, and even his daughter runs from him.

The Hidden Blade

The same narrative appears in both *The Twilight Samurai* and *The Hidden Blade*: the settings in the provinces, the suffering of lower-ranking samurai at the hands of their superiors (representing salarymen and corporate bosses), the "impossible" marriage, and the price of being a samurai. Not only are the narratives of the two films the same, but so are the scenes. Prominent are the abused bride and her rescue by the hero, abuse at the hands of elder (elderly) relatives, abuse of lower-ranking samurai by upper-ranking samurai, the super-*sensei* (seen or merely referred to), the funeral, the duel, the revenge, women who cook and clean for the men they love, refurbishing a sword, being kind to children, children who work, the swordsman killed by modern weaponry — to name but a few. The scenes, however, are not identical; they are variants.

For example, in *The Twilight Samurai*, the abused bride rescued is a woman of samurai rank, a childhood friend, and a divorcée. Her husband comes to her brother's house looking for her, slaps her to the ground, and is pinned down by Seibei as she is hustled indoors by her brother. Challenged to a duel, Seibei knocks the man out with a wood practice sword. In *The Hidden Blade*, the abused bride rescued is a farmer's daughter, formerly a trusted family servant, and exhausted by overwork and a miscarriage, whose witch of a mother-in-law neither pays for a doctor for her nor allows anyone, including her father, to see her. When her former master hears she has not been seen in the shop for two months, he forces his way into the freezing corridor where she is lying (under a ragged quilt, under the stairway, and hidden by a screen), orders her husband to leave a writ of divorce for him to pick up the next day, gives the mother-in-law a piece of his mind, and then stalks out of the shop with the girl on his back.

Yamada and Asama also create a variation of the scene "bad news comes by palanquin." The convention, of course, is to show the palanquin being carried to its destination. In *The Hidden Blade*, mention is made that the inspector had arrived by palanquin the day before. However, the scene is used for Hazama's return by the Ōshū Highway in his prisoner's cage.

The scene "being nice to children" is also a component of the narrative. In *The Twilight Samurai*, there are two variants. In the first, Seibei's immediate superior, the commissioner in charge of stores, Kusaka Chōbei, comes late at night to fetch Seibei to the chief councilor. As he sits waiting in the entry, Seibei's five-year-old daughter Ito peeks round a corner to look at him. He talks to her, asks her age, calls her a cute kid, and makes a funny face. After Seibei receives his order to kill Yogo Zen'emon, Kusaka offers, to Seibei's great relief, to take responsibility for his family should anything happen to him. In *The Hidden Blade*, the younger sister of the abused bride Kie is sent by her worried father to travel on foot alone all the way from the farm to see how she is doing. While she is wiping down the floor, the master of the house Munezō comes through the door; when she drops to a full kowtow, he says, trying to raise her up, she need not do *that*. Later, Kie and Munezō laugh at the servant Naota's enormous yawn and Munezō turns to the little girl to point out that Kie is laughing, a sign that she is on the mend.

Yamada also uses different parts of a scene in the two films. For example, in refurbishing a blade, one checks the edge, takes it apart, grinds the edge on a whetstone, and then reassembles it, including retying the straps on the hilt. In *The Twilight Samurai*, Seibei examines the edge, takes the sword apart, and grinds the edge. In *The Hidden Samurai,* we see Munezō examine the edge (by dipping the blade in ashes to bring out the irregularities) and then tying the straps. Although only part of the process is actually shown in each film, the entire process is invoked. Although in each film the scene is truncated, the entire scene is understood as a whole.

Again, there is a sequence of events that follows death including laying out the corpse, the wake, placing the corpse in a coffin and processing to the crematorium, a Buddhist funeral at which a posthumous Buddhist name is conferred, interment of the ashes in the grave, and then a series of formal memorial services within forty-nine days, at the first, third, and later anniversaries, and regular visits to the grave.[10] In *The Twilight Samurai,* we see the laying out of the corpse and family who have already arrived, the procession to the crematorium, and Ito's visit to her parents' grave (*ohaka-mairi*) when she is an elderly woman. In *The Hidden Blade,* when they meet three years after her marriage, Kie apologizes to Munezō for not being able to attend the memorial service on the first anniversary of his mother's death. However, we get a glimpse of the Buddhist memorial service held on the third anniversary, just as the priest finishes chanting and right before refreshments are served. As they wait during the interim, Munezō's uncle and Samon's blind father light into the young men for their abandonment of the samurai way, i.e., learning to use western military technology and defending it, too. An out-and-out row is averted only when Shino arrives, just in time, to announce that the saké is being served. Toward the end of the film, Munezō makes a visit to the grave of Hazama and his wife and to bury the weapon with which he has avenged them.

Finally, both films contain variants of the swordsman-killed-by-a-gun scene. In *The Twilight Samurai,* Seibei's daughter Ito, now an old woman on a visit to her parents' grave, relates in the voice-over that her father, the master swordsman, was killed in battle by a gun. The death is related, not enacted. On the other hand, in *The Hidden Blade,* Munezō wounds his opponent — his former friend and escaped prisoner Hazama Yaichirō — with a dangerous move taught by his former fencing master. Yaichirō, infuriated by such a dirty trick, raises his sword to attack when a shot from a rifle blows his hand from his wrist (medium shot) and the following shot kills him (long shot). Munezō is horrified: he had meant to kill a fellow swordsman with his own sword. He drops to his knees and apologizes.

There are more comparisons to be made. In *The Hidden Blade,* as in *The Twilight Samurai,* scenes frame the narrative, but differently. The film begins with a departure scene and a comment that Edo is so far away and life will be hard without a wife; just before the end of the film there is a departure with the comment that Ezo (Hokkaidō) is so far away and if only Munezō had a (new) wife to go with him. The second frame overlaps the first rather than being placed inside it: Munezō "orders" Kie to sing an ancient poem; as they sit on a bluff overlooking the sea, Munezō orders Kie to return to her home; as they sit on a hill on the edge of the farm, Munezō "orders" Kie to marry him.

Many of the motifs are the same. A knock at the door at night means trouble: Samon brings news that Hazama is being brought back for imprisonment and Hazama's wife comes to ask Munezō not to kill her husband, to offer her body, and to leave to offer her body to the evil councilor for her husband's sake. The treatment of women here, as in *The Twilight Samurai*, serves as a moral compass in the film: Munezō teases his sister Shino mercilessly, but apologizes when scolded by Kie; he rescues Kie, but never takes advantage of her; he takes her to see the sea, and sends her home to her father; he is truly shocked by Hazama's wife and truly distressed by her situation. Hazama's husband, on the other hand, shows nothing but contempt for her: at his send-off, Samon, Munezō's friend and later his brother-in-law, remarks how hard it will be without his wife. "In Edo you can have as many girls as you want as long as you have the money!" replies Hazama. His friends are embarrassed; Hazama's wife is standing only a few yards away, close enough to hear him. She gets a curt nod as he boards. She sacrifices her honor in a futile attempt to save his life. When Munezō tries to get Hazama to commit suicide like a samurai and to think about his wife, that she will have to live down the shame the rest of his life unless he does so, Hazama lets Munezō know that he has told his wife to commit suicide. Finally, the councilor is shown at his worst when he makes jokes about "enjoying" her in the next room of the geisha house where Munezō has found him.

The scene in *The Twilight Samurai* of the samurai practicing their rifle drill and others laughing at their hapless attempts is stretched out in *The Hidden Blade* as a sub-narrative: an instructor all the way from Edo comes to teach artillery and modern military methods to Usanaka samurai. There are scenes of the instructor explaining artillery, trying to teach the men to march, to snap to orders, to run English style, and a demonstration before the young lord. Despite the humor of the scenes, one thing is clear: the lower-ranking foot-soldiers (*ashigaru*) gradually displace the samurai from the center of the action. The last shot of training is of a column of foot-soldiers wielding rifles with bayonets fixed, practicing modern drills such as thrusting with the bayonet and rifle butt as well as the stationary infantry square to repel cavalry.

What is not in *The Twilight Samurai* but in *The Hidden Blade* is the scene of the successful revenge of the samurai. The meaning of the Devil's Claw (*oni no tsume*) of the original Japanese title, *Kakushiken: oni no tsume*, is not revealed until almost the end of the film although it is referred to by the inspector questioning him about his relationship to Hazama and, when he is wounded by Munezō, by Hazama himself. It was taught by fencing master, the eccentric former samurai Yamamoto Kansai, to Munezō rather than to the better swordsman Hazama and apparently is deeply resented by Hazama. But Munezō is the better man and Toda knew it, indeed, expected that the two would come to blows some day; that is why he teaches Munezō how to provoke Hazama (who we know, by the way he treats his wife, is not very nice) into making a move that will get him killed. Despite Munezō's efforts, Hazama is shot by snipers armed with the newest in rifles, and his wife is deceived. Munezō is an upright man and does the right thing: he avenges Hazama and his wife by using the Devil's Claw, the technique of driving a *kogai* (a small, ornamented blade attached to the sword) straight into the heart, to kill the wicked councilor.

The Social Construction of Narrative

People learn to understand and tell narratives the same way they learn a language: they hear other people, they try to speak, they are corrected, they try again. Children, for example, are very prescriptive about the way bedtime stories are supposed to be told and will correct the inexperienced story-teller: fairy tales always begin "once upon a time," the magic word is always "abracadabra," and we always look first at Papa Bear's bed. Grown-ups are no different: the man in the white hat is the good guy, the good guy always outdraws the bad guy (who wears a black hat), and the good guy always gets the girl. This we learn by the experience of seeing the same pattern over and over — and not only in film — and we expect this pattern to be followed. American films are accused of being formulaic (as though this were truly wicked); and it is true — they are, and they are because the formula works. This is rarely questioned by filmmakers themselves; a gentleman's agreement requires that the moving-image industry always give the public what the public wants and the public wants formulas. Only social scientists, film scholars, and artists bother to offer a challenge (however, they do not make the same money, which means that they do not receive the same public approval as the film industry).

The form and content of narratives are determined by society; they are socially constructed. In preliterate society, approval of the narrative (or the narrative unit) was expressed by preservation through remembering and repeating. In modern society, approval of the narrative is expressed as box office returns. Narratives, old and new, work because they are useful to society (or, as is more frequent, a segment of society) in identifying and analyzing issues that are of concern to society: good, evil, the individual, class, race, how to get ahead in the world, technology vs. nature. A narrative without significance to society will be abandoned if old or rejected if new: where has the Western gone? Why was *Jefferson in Paris* such a failure with critics and audiences alike? Why was *Tasogare Seibei* so immensely successful? What significance does the *bakumatsu-mono* still have for the contemporary Japanese audience?

The Japanese have had a rough time in the last fifteen years. The spectacular economic growth in the fifties and sixties was cut in half by the 1973 Arab oil embargo, although the economy continued to do comparatively well. The economic bubble of 1986–1990 burst and left Japan in recession for ten years. In 1994–1995, Japan was traumatized by Aum Shinrikyō subway attacks and assassinations and in 1995 by the Kobe Earthquake. Throughout the nineties and since, the Japanese have worried about historical revisionism in school textbooks, the discovery of the role of the military in organizing brothels and the coercive recruitment of women during the war, whether to send troops abroad and in what capacity, fewer opportunities for employment for the young, the aging of Japan, teenage disaffection and prostitution, parasite singles, the falling birthrate, and a perceived increase in numbers of foreigners and crime. Unease has been reflected in cinema by the increasing popularity of the escape mechanisms of inurement and denial: pornography, violence, crime, horror, fantasy, futurism, and historical revisionism. The modern period piece rose as a response to political repression, rice riots (especially those of 1918), the depression (which began earlier in Japan), and finally the Tokyo earthquake of 1923. Yamada's turn to the period film is a confirmation of the viability of the period film as a traditional response to unease in Japanese society. His Tora-san may have tapped into a nostalgia for a Japan that never existed except in Tōei period films: a smaller, cozier, more secure and less hierarchical Japan. But *Tasogare Seibei* and *The Hidden Blade* resonate with an anxiety in a modern and globalized Japan that is almost palpable.[11] The world of these films is awful because the present is awful.

Narrative as Myth and as Ideology

Myths have three functions: they explain why things are the way they are (such as natural phenomena); they argue for one side or the other in a contest over rights (as over land); they are also the assumptions people have about how things work in the world (as I believe Barthes uses the word)[12]; they are in and of themselves ideologies. The narratives promote ideologies in the sense that they work if the audience (individually or as a whole) accepts the basic premises on which the plot is based.

Take the ideology of the Tora-san series. Our hero never finds true happiness because, for example, he always falls in love with an unattainable woman. This is a Buddhist critique of society, which emphasizes that suffering characterizes the human experience. The films preach the benefits of good social and family relationships (represented by the inhabitants of Tora-san's old neighborhood and his family — old-fashioned, working people) in an otherwise cold world. This is the method of the Confucian critique of society: to set up high standards of behavior that implicitly denounce those of the present reality of society by force of the gap between them. Yamada is a critic of modernity in that his hero, with his flip-flops and woolen tummy band, represents a nostalgia for the (idealized) past that is, at the same time, a rejection of the present.[13]

Yamada's films give the broad outline of the basic Fujisawa narrative, which is itself a variant of the period narrative established in the 1910s and 1920s by Nakazato Kaizan and Hasegawa Shin: the world of the soldier is evil; one is destroyed by remaining in it, but saved by leaving, physically or ethically, for real or fictive familial relationships. Although Fujisawa's stories are set in various time periods and places, *The Twilight Samurai* and *Hidden Blade* (which takes place in the years before and after 1861, the only date given) are set in the Unasaka domain (as is the yet-to-be released *Bushi no ichibun*) and in the *bakumatsu* (end-of-the-shogunate) period of 1853–1867. The *bakumatsu* background not only allows opportunity for much serious sword play in the recreation of the events of this period in history, but also provides the context of the domainal politics that sets up the climactic duels in the films. *The Twilight Samurai*'s hero is ordered to take out the last surviving member of the reform party in the domain; the hero of *The Hidden Blade* is ordered to take out a former friend who was arrested and imprisoned for his connections with reformers in the shogunate. The Unasaka are *fudai*, shogunal vassals of long standing (i.e., before the decisive battle of Sekigahara in 1600) and yet, at the same time, fearful of the shogunate's wrath should the role of Unasaka men in reformist politics become known — they prefer to handle the traitors by themselves, whatever it takes.

Those who do not comply with orders do not remain. Either way, the result is death: loss of position in society or loss of life. The films are about highly skilled killers, samurai of low position and skill with the sword incommensurate with their rank. The hero of *The Twilight Samurai* loses his happy family and is destroyed by his commitment to his status; the hero of *The Hidden Blade* is saved by giving up his status — he never has to kill again and he is able to marry the girl he loves.

Yamada's two *bakumatsu-mono* are not nostalgic for the past. In using the *bakumatsu* background and the low-ranking samurai paralleling the outsider ronin of the 1920s and 1930s, Yamada is taking up the same themes and the same critical stance of modern Japan taken up by the 1960s in the films of Kobayashi, Shinoda, and Okamoto. *The Twilight Samurai* and *The Hidden Blade* are without doubt Yamada's finest films and rank with the very best of the Japanese period films I have seen: the performances are exquisite, the pacing deliberate, the *dénouement* inexorable. Yamada and his long-time colleague Asama Yoshitaka have demonstrated in these films both a mastery of a national narrative tradition and the continuing viability of that tradition.

Chapter Notes

Introduction

1. The film has since been lost. Despite what the Internet Movie Database (www.imdb.com) says, the film is not an animated film, and, according to the *Nihon eiga kantoku zenshū* (*Complete Anthology of Japanese Film Directors*), it was released in 1965. *Nihon eiga kantoku zenshū, Kinema junpō* sōkan no. 698 (December 24, 1976), s.v. "Ichikawa Kon."

2. Donald Richie, "Introduction to the Michigan Electronic Reprint," *Japanese Cinema: Film Style and National Character* (2004, reprint of 1971), *University of Michigan Center for Asian Studies Electronic Publications*, http://www.umich.edu/%7Eiinet/cjs/publications/cjsfaculty/ filmrichie.html (accessed November 22, 2005).

3. Aaron Gerow, "Subject: Suzaku and Zen," May 20, 1997, *Memorable Threads from Kine-Japan*, http://pears.lib.ohio-state.edu/Markus/ (accessed December 22, 2005). In regard to this tendency, he notes, "Noël Burch's work has been both provocative and problematic in this regard: see his *To the Distant Observer: Form and Meaning in the Japanese Cinema*, ed. Annette Michelson (Berkeley: University of California Press, 1979)." "Swarming Ants and Elusive Villains: Zigomar and the Problem of Cinema in 1910s Japan," *Asian Film Connections*, http://www.asianfilms.org/japan/ (accessed December 26, 2004).

4. Letter from Inabata Katsutaro to Tanaka Jun'ichirō, Dec. 27, 1924, cited in Toki Akihiro and Mizoguchi Kaoru, "A History of Early Cinema in Kyoto, Japan (1896–1912): Cinematographe and Inabata Katsutaro," *CineMagazine Net!* 1 (Autumn 1996), online journal September 17, 1996, http://www.cmn.hs.h.kyoto-u.ac.jp/NO1/SUBJECT1/INAEN.HTM (accessed October 30, 2005). Inabata's equipment was passed on to Yokota Einosuke (1973–1943), later head of Nikkatsu, who, in 1907, contracted Makino Shōzō (1878–1929) to start making films for him.

5. This idea is more palatable to specialists in popular literature. Scott Langton emphasizes two characteristics of popular period literature 1913–1939 argued here for the period piece in general: its roots in traditional performing arts and the use of the past to express the concerns of the present. See his "A Literature for the People: A Study of the *Jidai Shōsetsu* in Taishō and Early Shōwa Japan," Ph.D. dissertation, Ohio State University, 2000 (Ann Arbor, MI: University Microfilms, 2001). The idea of "tradition" has not been abandoned by the Japanese themselves: the titles of the seventh and eighth annual public lectures by film professionals sponsored by the National Museum of Modern Art, Tokyo, Film Center were titled "Satsuei gijutsu — dentō no katachi (The craft of filming — traditional forms)," and "Heisei 15 [sic] nendo eiga seisaku senmonka yōsei kōza" (*National Film Center*, March 10–13, 2004, http://www.momat.go.jp/FC/ yoseikouza2003.html [accessed January 1, 2006]), and "Heisei 16 [sic] nendo eiga seisaku senmonka yōsei kōza" (*National Film Center*, March 9–12, 2005, http://www.momat.go.jp/FC/yoseikoza2004.html [accessed January 1, 2005]).

6. See Hori Ichirō, *Folk Religion in Japan: Continuity and Change*, ed. Joseph M. Kitagawa and Alan L. Miller, Haskell Lectures on History of Religions new series 1 (Chicago: University of Chicago Press, 1968), and H. Neill McFarland, *Rush Hour of the Gods: A Study of New Religious Movements in Japan* (New York: Macmillan, 1967).

7. See, for example, Wilbur M. Fridell, *Japanese Shrine Mergers, 1906–1912: State Shinto Moves to the Grassroots* (Tokyo: Sophia University, 1973).

8. For a recent articulation of this, see Eric C. Rath, "From Representation to Apotheosis: Nō's Modern Myth of Okina," *Asian Theatre Journal* 17, no. 2 (Fall 2000): 253–68.

9. The use of the flashback as a form of legitimation is seen most clearly in Hashimoto's

Rashōmon and in the scenario for Kobayashi Masaki's 1962 *Seppuku* (*Harakiri*). It is used also in Shinoda Masahiro's 1964 *Ansatsu* (*Assassination*).

10. First published in *Asian Cinema* 7, no. 2 (Winter 1995): 46–57.

11. As in the video series narrated by Jane Seymour and directed by Peter Spry-Leverton, *Japan* (*The Electronic Tribe, The Sword and the Chrysanthemum, The Legacy of the Shogun* and *A Proper Place in the World*), produced by WTTW Chicago, 1988 (Northbrook, Ill.: Coronet Film and Video), VHS, 4 hours.

Chapter 1

1. Joseph L. Anderson and Donald Richie, *The Japanese Film: Art and Industry* (Tokyo and Rutland, Vermont: C.E. Tuttle Co., 1959), p. 48.

2. Yoda Yoshikata, to an audience at the Pacific Film Archive, 1979.

3. Located at Ofuna, outside Kamakura.

4. Nihon Kindai Bungku-kan, ed., *Nihon kindai bungaku daijiten*, 6 vols. (Tokyo: Kodansha, 1977), I:332–335, s.v. "Osanai Kaoru"; *Nihon eiga kantoku zenshū* (Tokyo: Kinema Junpōsha, 1976), s.v. "Itō Daisuke" and "Nomura Hōtei."

5. It is difficult to know whether to use "caste" or "class"; caste is status based on birth, class on wealth. "Caste" is how the *bushi* like to view themselves; "class" indicates the economic and social reality of Japan after about 1700. The word "warrior" is often used; nevertheless, they were soldiers, professional fighting men. Some had positions; others did not.

6. Arashi Kanjūrō appeared in at least thirty-two Kurama Tengu films. "Arashi Kanjūrō," *Japan Movie Database*, http://www.jmdb.ne.jp/person/p0369750.htm (accessed April 13, 2005). Hereafter *JMDb.*

7. For Japanese costume through the ages, see "Costume in Japan," *The Costume Museum*, http://www.iz2.or.jp.english/index.htm (accessed January 12, 2006).

8. Ruth Shaver, *Kabuki Costume* (Tokyo and Rutland, Vermont: Charles E. Tuttle Company, Inc., 1966).

9. In China, precedence was taken by the class of literati providing the bureaucrats to the imperial government.

10. Makino Masahiro, *Rōningai*; Itō Daisuke, *Chūji tabi nikki*; *Hatamoto Taikutsu Otoko* series, featuring Ichikawa Utaemon (1904–1999) from the thirties to the fifties (e.g., the 1959 *Hatamoto taikutsu otoko* or *Vassal to the Shogun, Gentleman at Leisure, Bored Vassal to the Shogun*, or *Idle Vassal*). Between 1930 and 1963, Utaemon played the role about twenty-eight times. *JMDb*, "Ichikawa Utaemon," http://www.jmdb.ne.jp/person/p0152640.htm (accessed April 12, 2005).

11. Hono Eijiro, "The Commoner Class of the Edo Period," *Kyoto University Economic Review* 8 (1933): 44–45, http://www.econ.kyoto-u.ac.jp/review/10000100.pdf (accessed April 13, 2005), and Donald Shively, "Sumptuary Regulation and Status in Early Tokugawa Japan," *Harvard Journal of Asiatic Studies* 25 (1964–1965): 128, http://links.jstor.org/sici?sici=0073-0548%281964%2F1965%2925%3C123%3ASRASIE%3E2.0.CO%3B2-2 (accessed April 13, 2005).

12. See the following chapter.

13. I find both Kinjirō and Kinshirō in titles. Tōyama Kinshirō Kagemoto was Edo magistrate in the late Tokugawa period.

14. As in the 1960 *Gozonji irezumi hangan*, starring Kataoka Chiezō. The earliest I could find in the Japan Movie Database was for 1924. But there are many. One TV series of twenty-two episodes, *Tōyama no Kinsan: Sakura bugyō vs. onna nezumi*, subtitled in English and broadcast on KIKU-TV (Hawaii), ended 6/10/99. "Toyama no Kinsan," KIKU TV: Multicultural Television, http://www.kikutv.com/shows/Japanese_Programs/toyama_no_kinsan/ (accessed April 11, 2005). The Toei Web site, for example, lists the series *Tōyama no Kinsan torimonochō* (173), *Gozonji Tōyama no Kinsan* (188), *Tōyama no Kinsan* (243), *Tōyama no Kinsan 2* (278), *Tōyama no Kinsan* (379), and *Meibugyō Tōyama no Kinsan* (493). "Library/English Titles," Toei TV Website, http://www.toei.co.jp/tv/library/series-title.html (accessed April 11, 2005).

15. I found listings back to 1910 for this film in the Japan Movie Database (accessed April 10, 2005). There was at least one — if not two or more — made each year. It is standard fare on TV.

16. Bitō Masahide, "Society and Social Thought in the Tokugawa Period," *Japan Foundation Newsletter* 9 (June–September 1981): 4–6.

17. Part of Yamaga Sokō's *Shidō* is translated as "The Way of the Samurai" in Tsunoda Ryusaku et al., *Sources of Japanese Tradition* (New York: Columbia University Press, 1958), pp. 389–91. See also *Great Thinkers of the Eastern World: The Major Thinkers and the Philosophical and Religious Classics of China, India, Japan, Korea, and the World*, ed. Ian P. McGreal (New York: HarperCollins Publishers, 1995), s.v. "Yamaga Sokō."

Chapter 2

1. In addition, during the desperately hard times of the 1830s, as part of reforms and retrenchment, the government forbade comedy.

See, for example, Engeki Hakubutsukan (Kawatake Shigetoshi et al.) ed., *Geinō jiten* (Tokyo: Tōkyōdō, 1953) and Manabe Motoyuki, ed, *Taishū bungaku jiten* (Tokyo: Seiabo, 1967), s.v. "Kōdan" and "Rakugo"; and see also Sekiyama Kazuo, *Sekkyō no rekishi*, Iwanami Shinsho 64 (Tokyo: Iwanami Shoten, 1978), pp. 106–115, 129–144.

2. 1659–1660, according to *Geinō jiten*, p. 393, and Inagaki Shisei, *Oiesōdō* (Tokyo: Bunkei Shunshū, 1979), pp. 90, 93; and 1671, according to Inoura Yoshinobu and Kawatake Toshio, *The Traditional Theater of Japan*, 2 vols. (New York and Tokyo: Weatherhill, 1971), II:159.

3. The definitive stage version, *Meiboku Sendai hagi* (*The Famous Tree at Sendai*) was written in 1785. Kawatake, *Geinō jiten*, p. 139. See the play in James R. Brandon, trans., *Kabuki: Five Classic Plays* (Cambridge, Mass. and London: Harvard University Press, 1975). For a comparison of the Kabuki and Kōdan versions as well, see Inagaki, *Oiesōdō*, pp. 90–133.

4. Takahashi Hiroshi, *Taishū geinō: sono ayumi to geijintachi* (Tokyo: Kyōiku Shiryō Shuppan-kai, 1980), passim. See also Sekiyama, *Sekkyō*, pp. 129–144. By the end of the Tokugawa period, several genres of stories were being told by both Kōdan and Rakugo specialists, even Shōrin Hakuen and Sanyūtei Enchō. During the Meiji period, Rakugo included comic stories, true stories about people, stories of human feeling (*ninjō-banashi*), tragedies, ghost stories and adaptations of foreign works, much the same as Kōdan, which, however, did not include short stories whose sole object was the joke or punchline. Takahashi, *Taishū geinō*, pp. 44–45. Police continued to attend all public performances, all of which were subject to the same constraints of government censorship, especially the demand for "rewarding good and punishing evil."

5. Bunraku is the name of a troupe; Jōruri is the style of chant.

6. Sekiyama, *Sekkyō*, p. 131.

7. For the general acceptance of shamanic practices as the background of Kabuki, see, for example, Benito Ortolani, *The Japanese Theater: From Shamanistic Ritual to Contemporary Pluralism* (Princeton: Princeton University Press, 1995 rev. of 1990), pp. 172–174. This theme will be continued in the following chapters.

8. *The Actors' Analects* (*Yakusha Rongo*), edited, translated and with an introduction and notes by Charles J. Dunn and Bunzō Torigoe (New York: Columbia University Press, 1969), p. 23.

9. For a list of fourteen narrative subgenres in Kōdan in the 1890s, see Kurata Yoshihiro, *Meiji Taishō no minshū goraku*, Iwanami Shinsho 114 (Tokyo: Iwanami Shoten, 1980), p. 132.

10. In the Tokugawa period, Kōdan specialists also told stories out of the contemporary scandal sheets. By 1881, the popular order of the program was the martial arts (*buyū*) piece, followed by pieces about thieves or other commoner criminals and historical battle pieces. Kurata, *Meiji Taishō*, pp. 35–36, citing the *Chōya shinbun* (September 11, 1881).

11. Plays of this type came under government pressure but managed to survive as individual scenes in longer plays. In January 1664, Shimabara plays (Shimabara was a fashionable pleasure quarter in Kyoto) and courtesan roles were banned, but they managed to survive in *oie-mono*. Brandon, *Kabuki*, p. 7, quoting Ihara Toshirō, *Kabuki Nenpyō*, 8 vols. (1956–1963), I:93.

12. The word *shinjū* was first used for a Kabuki play, now lost, of 1662. Brandon, *Kabuki*, p. 7, citing Ihara, *Nenpyō*, I:87–89. Suicide plays had been performed in Osaka since 1683 when the courtesan Yamato Ichinojō and her patron Goze Chōemon committed suicide and plays based on the incident ran in three Osaka theaters. But Chikamatsu Monzaemon established the love-suicide play as a form of high tragedy and established its conventions and thematic structure.

13. Like *shinjū-mono*, they involve prostitutes.

14. The previously mentioned *sewa-mono* were developed in the Kyoto-Osaka area. But the fourth type was developed in Edo during the Kasei period (1804–1830) by Tsuruya Nanboku (1755–1829). The *kizewa-mono* (living true-life stories) were about Edo low-life: thieves, murderers, pimps, and renegade priests. Brandon, *Kabuki*, p. 7, citing Ihara, *Nenpyō*, I:87–89.

15. *Ōchō-mono* or *ōdai-mono* are plays set in the imperial court through the Heian period. They were established in Edo by actor Ichikawa Danjūrō (1660–1704), who wrote his own plays. His style of acting was called *aragoto* (rough stuff) and was distinguished by its characteristic *mie* (rolls of the head followed by a freeze) and *kumadori* (heavy, symbolic make-up). The plays were very similar to local folk-religious plays with their content of myth, contests, and display of martial prowess. Examples of *ōchōmono* are *Sugawara denju tenarai kagami* (*The Secret of Sugawara's Calligraphy*, 1746 by Takeda Izumo [1691–1756], Namiki Senryū [1695–1751], and Miyoshi Shōraku [1696–1775]), set in the ninth century, and *Imoseyama onna teikin* (*An Example of Noble Womanhood*, 1771, Chikamatsu Hanji et al.), about the overthrow of Soga Iruka in the seventh century. They are best represented by plays written for Kabuki such as *Narukami Fudō Kitayamazakura* (*Narukami*, 1684 by Tsuda Hanjūrō for Danjūrō) or Danjūrō's own *Shibaraku* (*Wait a Moment!*, 1697). Brandon, *Kabuki*, pp. 9–10.

16. Set in the late Heian, Kamakura, and Ashikaga periods, they are sometimes fanciful treatments of historical events. Examples include *Yoshitsune senbon zakura (Yoshitsune and a Thousand Cherry Trees,* 1757, by Takeda, Namiki, and Miyoshi). Inoura and Kawatake, *Traditional Theater,* p. 180. Others include *Ichinotani futabunki* (*The Chronicle of the Battle of Ichinotani,* 1755, by the same three), and *Ehon taikōki* (*Picture Book of the Taikō,* 1799) about Akechi Mitsuhide's assassination of Oda Nobunaga. Brandon, *Kabuki,* pp. 158–159.

17. They concern the political maneuverings and scandals in the houses of the great domainal lords, *daimyō,* and direct vassals of the shogun, *hatamoto.* Already to be seen in young men's Kabuki (*yarō kabuki,* 1653–1688), from the period around 1716–1735, they were featured in the fall performances (*aki kyōgen*) and were very popular in the Kansai area with the rise of revenge novels (*adauchi-mono*). From about 1830–1843, staged *oiesōdō-mono* paralleled the rise in the popularity of books discussing real events, contemporary or historical (*jitsuroku-bon*) and lectures (Kōdan) often on the same material. Engeki Hakubutsukan, ed., Waseda Daigaku Engeki Hakubutsukan (Kawatake Shigetoshi et al.) ed., *Engeki hyakka daijiten,* 6 vols. (Tokyo: Heibonsha, 1960), I:376. There were more than twenty different incidents which were dramatized in several different versions. Among the best known are the Daté (already mentioned) and the Kaga incidents. The Kaga incident involved a revenge story: a domainal court lady, Sawano, abused a concubine, Michi, for using her sandal, or *zori,* by mistake. Michi killed herself, and her serving woman stabbed Sawano in revenge. This 1725 incident, often called the "Woman's Chūshingura," was given the definitive stage treatment in the 1782 Jōruri by a doctor formerly in the service of the shogun's harem, Yo Yōdai, *Kagamiyama kokyō no nishikie* (*Mirror Mountain*). Kawatake, *Geinō jiten,* p. 139. See also Inagaki, *Oiesōdō,* pp. 162–196.

18. *Engeki hyakka daijiten,* I:376.

19. Brandon, *Kabuki,* p. 5.

20. It can be an earlier play which provides the basic characters and plots which are worked over and over: the Yūgiri-Izaemon world was established in 1678 and went through twenty versions and more. Brandon, *Kabuki,* p. 215. The entire world can be truncated to a single motif which is used for special effect: the striking with a sandal, or *zori uchi,* motif from *Mirror Mountain* was used in 1853 by the third Sakurada Jisuke in a play about the Sengoku household disturbance, but it was done between men and called "men's striking with a sandal" or *otoko zori uchi.* Kawatake, *Geinō jiten,* p. 346.

21. "In time, a whole system of conventional parallels between places, situations, people, and events from past and present developed." Brandon, *Kabuki,* p. 5.

22. This date follows the modern, western calendar. Keene, *Chūshingura,* p. 1.

23. One apparently escaped sentencing because he had been sent to Akō to report.

24. The now-lost *Akebono Soga no Youchi* (*Night Attack at Dawn by the Soga*). Donald Keene, trans., *Chūshingura (The Treasury of Loyal Retainers): A Puppet Play by Takeda Izumo, Miyoshi Shōraku, and Namiki Senryū* (New York: Columbia University Press, 1971), p. 3. It was apparently meant as a third act to his *Kenkō hōshi monomiguruma (The Sight-seeing Carriage of the Priest Kenkō),* a standard *jidai-mono* about how the author of the *Tsurezuregusa* (*Essays in Idlemess*) helped a court lady by persuading her unwanted suitor, Kō no Moronao (d. 1351) to turn to Kaoya, the wife of Enya Hangan Takasada (d. 1338). She refused him and Moronao assassinated Takasada. *Goban Taiheiki* concerns the revenge of Enya's vassals. The two plays were never performed together.

25. Keene, *Chūshingura,* p. 3. *Akenobono Soga no Youchi* tried *mitate*; either the references were too broad, or the timing wrong. But the idea of using *mitate* existed at that point, and the advantages, both political and artistic, increased in importance with the years. Chikamatsu may have gotten away with his version because three years had elapsed or because censorship was less severe in the Kansai than in Edo. Keene, *Chūshingura,* p. 6, citing Matsushima Eiichi, *Chūshingura: sono seiritsu to tenkai,* Iwanami shinsho 541 (Tokyo: Iwanami Shoten, 1964).

26. *Sukeroku Yukari no Edo Zakura* (*Sukeroku: Flower of Edo*), written in 1713 by Tsuuchi Jihei II and Tsuuchi Hanemon, is a contemporary play (*sewa-mono*) set within a period play (*jidai-mono*): the world of the courtesan Agemaki and her lover Sukeroku, presented as a love-suicide play (*shinjū-mono*) since 1675, is set within the world of the twelfth century Soga brothers. Brandon, *Kabuki,* p. 51.

27. Brandon, *Kabuki,* p. 5. In 1193, Soga Jūrō Sukenari (1172–1193) and Soga Gorō Tokimune (1174–1193) invaded the hunting party of the shogun Minamoto Yoritomo to avenge themselves on the man who had killed their father eighteen years before. Jūrō's death and Gorō's execution were the culmination of an inheritance dispute that had lasted three generations.

28. "Although it is part of a 'history' play, Japanese consider the *sandan no kiri* (final section of the third act) suicide or family sacrifice a *sewa,* or 'domestic,' scene." Brandon, *Kabuki,* p. 17. Examples include *The Secret of Sugawara's Calligraphy, The Famous Tree at Sendai,* and *The Chronicle of the Battle of Ichinotani.*

29. "[T]he unnatural human relationships that were enforced by feudalism stand out in glaring form." Inoura and Kawatake, *Traditional Theater*, p. 170.

30. Inasmuch as the *jidai-mono* represents the commoner's attitude toward Tokugawa society (rather than the samurai's) that it is not a place for humans or their feelings (at least, not those of commoners) just as it does in *sewa-mono*, the *jidai-mono* can rightly be called a *jidai-sewa-mono*. *Engeki hyakka daijiten*, III:90.

31. Komiya, *Music and Drama*, pp. 28, 184, 188.

32. Komiya, ed., *Music and Drama*, p. 23.

33. For developments in Kabuki, see the chapter "Realism in the Japanese Period Film."

34. It is considered the book that initiated popular literature (*taishū bungaku*), but the author, who never considered himself part of the movement, called his work a Mahayana novel. Nihon Kindai Bungakukan, ed., *Nihon Kindai bungaku daijiten*, 6 vols. (Tokyo: Kōdansha, 1977–78), II:489, s.v. "Nakazato Kaizan." From here on, cited as *NKBD*.

35. His family had been wiped out financially by the restoration and subsequent problems in the rural areas, and, as a young man, he had been a strong supporter of the party.

36. Lack of finances and fear of the draft kept Nakazato at home as a schoolteacher instead of going on to university. During the Russo-Japanese War, he became noted for his anti-war poetry in the socialist newspaper *Heimin shinbun*. He was famous as a traveler, both for his trips all over Japan (one, at least, with the folklorist Yanagida Kunio) to research locations for his great novel, as well as for his trips to China and Korea in 1931. In 1939, he came back from his trip to the United States and reported on conditions; he warned, like the other still-Christian followers of Uchimura Kanzō, that Japan could never win a war with America.

37. Including heroic treatments of a peasant rebellion and of the Shimabara insurrection.

38. See Matsumoto Kenichi, *Nakazato Kaizan*, Asahi Hyōdensen 18 (Tokyo: Asahi Shinbunsha, 1978) for a complete study of Nakazato and his work. See also *NKBD*, II:489–491.

39. There is an English translation of the first part: C.S. Bavier, trans., *The Great Bodhisattva Pass* (Tokyo: Shunjūshakan, 1929).

40. Kikuchi Kan and Akutagawa Ryūnosuke also helped him get it serialized 1921–22 in the *Tōkyō nichinichi shinbun* and the *Osaka mainichi shinbun*, the biggest in mass media at the time. Tanizaki and others also published on the work. *NKBD*, II:491, citing Tanizaki Junichirō et al., "Nakazato Kaizan Daibosatsu toge tokuhon," *Bungei*, April 1956.

41. Manabe, *Taishū bungaku*, p. 120.

42. Discussion based on Emmanuel Sarkisyanz, *Rußland und der Messianismus des Orients: Sendungsbewußtsein und politischer Chiliasmus des Ostens* (Tubingen: J.C.B. Mohr, 1955).

43. For a somewhat different characterization of the Buddhism behind the work, see Ozaki Hotsuki, "Kaisetsu," in *Nakazato Kaizan-shū*, Shōwa kokumin bungaku zenshū 1 (Tokyo: Chikuma Shobō, 1978), pp. 492–496.

44. Manabe, *Taishū bungaku*, p. 122ff. for a discussion of the political background and development of the *bakumatsu-mono*.

45. At this time, *furigana*, syllabary written alongside the Chinese characters, enabled the less educated to read the pronunciation of the words.

46. "Hasegawa Shin," *Japanese Literature Publishing Project*, http://www.jlpp.jp/english/list/works18/main.html (accessed 30 June 2004). This text has been selected for translation.

47. Included in Hasegawa Shin, *Kutsukake Tokijirō hoka gohen* (Tokyo: Ryūa Shobō [Shinkokugeki jimusho nai], 1928), pp. 57–98, a collection of Hasegawa's plays published by the New National Theater or Shinkokugeki.

48. It was written for Sawada Shōjirō and the theater group Shinkokugeki and performed May 1928 at the Teikokugekijō.

49. The word *matatabi* appears in famed Rakugo-specialist Sanyūtei Enchō's *Shiobara Tasuke ichidaiki* and seems to have been derived from the expression, "Tabi kara tabi o mata ni kakeru" (leg it from one journey to the next; wander). There seems to have been an expression for traveling geisha, *matatabi geisha*. Otherwise, it was used by Hasegawa for the first time in the title of a play written in 1929, *Matatabi waraji* (*Straw Sandals for Traveling Shoes*). Manabe, *Taishū bungaku*, p. 289, quoting Hasegawa Shin, *Shinpen goroku* (*Oral Record of One's Person*).

50. See, for example, Joseph L. Anderson and Donald Richie, *The Japanese Film* (New York: Grove Press, Inc., 1960 of 1959), p. 47.

51. The story of Jirōchō, who controlled all the gambling on the Tōkaido highway between Edo and Kyoto, was first written by Amada Gorō and published in 1879 as *Tōkaido yūkyakuden*. "Shimizu no Jirōchō," April 20, 2005, *Shizuoka chasenmonten Komatsuen*, http://www3.tokai.or.jp/komatsuen/jirotyou%20.htm (accessed April 27, 2005). The stories were taken up by Kōdan specialist Kanda Hakuzan and became the forte of Naniwa-*bushi* performer Hirosawa Torazō II (1899–1964). Torazō sings the voiceover narrative and even appears as a character who sings snippets from the life of Mori no Ishimatsu (Ishimatsu of the forest) in Makino Masahiro's 1949 *Zoku Shimizu minato*, which stars Kataoka Chiezo.

52. Satō Tadao, *Hasegawa Shin-ron: giri ninjō*

to wa nani ka (Tokyo: Chūōkōronsha, 1975), chapter 2, "Isshuku ippan to iu koto."

53. Satō Tadao, *Kimi wa jidaigeki o mita ka* (Tokyo: Jakometei Shuppan, 1977).

54. In the late seventies and early eighties, Yamamoto Kikuo wrote a series of articles ("Rensen ronbun: hikaku eiga kenkyū") in the organ of the Tokyo Modern Museum of Art Film Center, *Firum senta–*, 1979–1980, which were published in one volume as *Nihon eiga ni okeru gaikoku eiga no eikyō* (*The Influence of Foreign Films on Japanese Film*) (Tokyo: Waseda Daigaku Shuppan-bu, 1997).

55. See, for example, Anderson and Richie, *Japanese Film*, pp. 69–71, 99, 128ff. For the processes involved in film censorship, see Peter B. High, *The Imperial Screen: Japanese Film Culture in the Fifteen Years' War, 1931–1945* (Madison: University of Wisconsin Press, 1995).

56. In English, see High, *Imperial Screen*, p. 60, citing Iwasaki Akira, "An Outline History of the Japanese Cinema," in *Cinema Yearbook of Japan 1936–1937* (Tokyo: Sanseidō), pp. 8–9.

57. Married to one of their actresses, Benizawa Yōko, star of Thomas Kurihara's *Amateur Club* (*Amachua Kurabu*, 1920) and *Lasciviousness of the Viper* (*Jasei no in*, 1921).

58. Kinema Junpōsha, ed., *Nihon eiga kantoku zenshū*, Kinema junpō supplementary issue 688 (Tokyo: Kinema Junpōsha, December 24, 1976), s.v. "Furumi Takuji." From here on, cited as *NEKZ*.

59. *NEKZ*, s.v. "Itō Daisuke."

60. *NEKZ*, s.v. "Makino Masahiro."

61. Although variously titled in English as *Adverse Current* or *Back Current*, the literal translation is closer to the English "countercurrent," with the meaning of "repercussion."

62. Specifically, the eight-headed serpent or dragon killed by the god Susanoō.

63. See Yamamoto Kikuo, "Rensai ronbun: hikaku eiga kenkyū (19); America eiga no eikyō, museiki; hiro [sic] no keifu 3," *Firum senta–*39 (March 30, 1977): 39.

64. Again, based on Sarkisyanz's discussion in *Messianismus*, passim. In Russian nihilism, committing the crime necessary to bring about the creation of paradise on earth results in losing one's place there.

65. For his life and career, see *NEKZ*, s.v. "Furumi Takuji." There are also interviews with Furumi and Benizawa in Takenaka Tsutomu, *Keikō eiga no jidai* (Tokyo: Shirakawa Shoten, 1974), pp. 57–96.

66. In this case, not the city, but the Tendai sect temple Nikkō-zan Rinnōji, the site of the mausoleum of Tokugawa Ieyasu. In the Meiji period, it was split from the mausoleum.

67. Takenaka, *Keikō*, pp. 82–83.

68. Takenaka, *Keikō*, pp. 83–84.

69. Kinema Junpōsha, ed. *Nihon eiga haiyū zenshū: danyū-hen, Kinema Junpō* supplementary issue 772 (Tokyo: Kinema Junpōsha, October 23, 1979), s.v. "Ōkōchi Denjirō." From here on, cited as *NEHZ*.

70. According to Yamamoto Kikuo, the film was based on John Ford's 1926 *Three Bad Men*. Yamamoto, "Amerika eiga no eikyō, p. 41.

71. In three parts.

72. Yamamoto Kikuo, "Rensei ronbun: hikaku eigashi kenkyū (26): Amerika eiga to jiyūshugi jidai-geki, Inagaki Hiroshi kantoku sakuhin o megutte," *Firum senta–*56 (March 6, 1980): 34.

73. *NEKZ*, s.v. "Inagaki Hiroshi."

74. The *Internet Movie Database* gives the English title as *Peace on Earth*, but not the Japanese title under Inagaki Hiroshi. "Hiroshi Inagaki," http://www.imdb.com/name/nm0408348/ or "*Sengoku gunto-den*," http://www.imdb.com/title/tt0019260/ (accessed 21 July 2004). Hereafter, *IMDb*.

75. *Currents in Japanese Cinema* (Tokyo, New York, San Francisco: Kōdansha, 1982), pp. 42–43.

76. Yamamoto, "Inagaki Hiroshi kantoku," p. 31.

77. Yamamoto, "Inagaki Hiroshi kantoku," p. 31, citing Inagaki Hiroshi, *Nihon eiga wakaki hibi* (Tokyo: Mainichi Shinbun-sha, 1978), p. 124.

78. Inagaki, *Nihon eiga*, p. 124. Narutaki was the area of Kyoto in which Inagaki then lived. The other members of the group were Yamanaka Sadao, Takizawa Eisuke, Fuji Yahiro, Mimura Shintarō, Hagiwara Ryō, Doi Seiken, and Fujii Shigeji. Twenty-six films resulted from the collaboration.

79. There are two parts: *Zenpen tora okami* (*First Volume Tiger [and] Wolf*) and *Kōhen akitsuki no zenshin* (*Last Volume Advance at Dawn*).

80. Yamamoto Kikuo, "Rensei ronbun: hikaku eigashi kenkyū (28): Amerika eiga to jiyūshugi jidai-geki, Yamanaka Sadao no nagaya-mono o megutte," *Firum senta–*60 (May 7, 1980): 37–38.

81. For a film-by-film, shot-by-shot analysis of the relationship between Yamanaka's films and those of American directors and Ozu, see Yamamoto Kikuo, "Rensai ronbun: hikaku eigashi kenkyū (27) Amerika eiga to jiyūshugi jidai-geki, Yamanaka Sadao no matatabi-mono o megutte," *Firum senta–*59 (March 6, 1980): 33–40 and "(28) Yamanaka Sadao no nagaya-mono o megutte," *Firum senta–*60 (May 7, 1980): 37–44.

82. Yamamoto, "Yamanaka Sadao no nagaya-mono," pp. 39–40.

83. Yamamoto, "Yamanaka Sadao no nagaya-mono," p. 42.

84. For a summary in French, see "Tsuyu

Kosode Mukashi Hachijō/Kamiyui Shinza," *Le Kabuki dans la Langue de Molière,* http://kabuki.ifrance.com/kabuki/kamiyui_shinza.htm (accessed 23 July 2004). For a translation, see Faith Bach, tr., "Shinza the Barber/Kamiyui Shinza," in James R. Brandon and Samuel L. Leiter, eds., *Kabuki Plays on Stage: Restoration and Reform, 1872–1905* (Honolulu: University of Hawaii Press, 2003), *Kabuki Plays on Stage,* 4 vols., IV:82–119.

85. Yamamoto, "Yamanaka Sadao no nagayamono," p. 44.

Chapter 3

1. Ichiro Hori, *Folk Religion in Japan: Continuity and Change,* ed. Joseph M. Kitagawa and Alan L. Miller (Chicago: Chicago University Press, 1968), pp. 23–24.

2. The shrine built to their memory became an international fascist shrine as Germany and Italy erected memorial monuments there. For the Byakkotai, see Armen Bakalian, "The Battle of Aizu," 2003, http://www.shinsengumihq.com/aizubattlebf.htm (accessed April 30, 2005). For the fall of Aizu, see *Remembering Aizu: The Testament of Shiba Gorō,* ed. Ishimitsu Mahito and translated with introduction & notes by Teruko Craig (Honolulu: University of Hawaii Press, 1999).

3. By 863, there were five officially recognized angry spirits of the dead (*goryōshin*): two dismissed crown princes, the real mother of one of them, and two ministers, including Sugawara Michizane. Hori, *Folk Religion,* pp. 112 and, for Michizane, 115. The first official services, held in 803, soothed those spirits with a combination of Shintō and Daoism (*onmyō-dō*). Hori, p. 115. These spirits, identified by magicians or shamans and shamanesses, were enshrined in Goryō-jinja and Kitano-jinja, established especially for the souls of the vengeful dead. Ibid., p. 43. Unlike the Roman senate, which conferred deification upon emperors whose policies the senate approved and intended to maintain, the Japanese secular-religious officialdom conferred deification upon political failures.

4. The scenario is based on Chikamatsu's 1715 *Daikyōji mukashi goyomi* and Ihara Saikaku's "Osan Mōemon," in the 1686 *Kōshoku gonin onna* (*Five Women Who Loved Love*).

5. The film is based on the 1706 *Horikawa nami no tsuzumi* (*Drum of the Waves of Horikawa*).

6. This is a version of Tsuruya Nanboku's 1825 Kabuki play, *Yotsuya kaidan* (*Yotsuya Ghost Story*).

7. The story is based on Kikuchi Kan's, which is based ultimately on stories about the famous monk Mongaku and the reason he took religious vows. See, for example, "Mongaku hosshin no koto," *Shintei genpei jōsuiki,* 6 vols., ed. Mizuhara Hajime, book 19.1 (Tokyo: Shinjin Oraisha, 1988–1991), III:19–29. Thanks to Michael Watson, January 13, 2000, Premodern Japanese Studies discussion archive, for "Gate of Hell," *PMJS,* http://www.meijigakuin.ac.jp/~pmjs/ archive/2000/jigokumon.html (accessed 5 July 2004). Kesa is most likely a fictional character based on a Chinese model and attached to the famous monk Mongaku (1139–1203).

8. For a translation, see *The Tale of the Heike,* translated, with an introduction, by Helen Craig McCullough (Stanford, Calif.: Stanford University Press, 1988).

9. Helen Craig McCullough has titled her partial translation *The Taiheiki: A Chronicle of Medieval Japan* (New York: Columbia University Press, 1959). Taihei means "great peace" even though a better translation would be "great pacification."

10. For a translation, see *Yoshitsune: A Fifteenth-century Japanese Chronicle,* translated and with an introduction by Helen Craig McCullough (Stanford, Calif.: Stanford University Press; Tokyo: University of Tokyo Press, 1966).

11. *The Tale of the Soga Brothers,* translated, with an introduction and notes, by Thomas J. Cogan (Tokyo: University of Tokyo Press, 1987).

12. The film is based on a short story by Tanizaki Junichirō.

13. The film is based on the 1953 novel by Inoue Yasushi.

14. For New Year's ceremonies for the purification of ancestors who appear first as devils (*oni*), see the following for examples: Kobayashi Kazushige, "On the Meaning of Masked Dances in Kagura," *Asian Folklore Studies* 11, no. 1 (1981): 1–22; Hayakawa Kōtarō, *Hana matsuri,* Minzoku mingei sōsho 2 (Tokyo: Iwasaki Bijutsusha, 1966); and Anne Marie Bouchy, "Kagura to shugendō," *Matsuri* 31 (1978): 65–76.

15. Tokugawa Mitsukuni (1628–1700); grandson of Ieyasu, patron of the history *Dainihonshi.*

16. Tōyama Kagemoto, shogunal official in Edo: *metsuke,* 1840 Kita-machi *bugyō, Saemon-nojō*; retired 1852; d. 1855.

17. Ōoka Tadasuke (1677–1751), shogunal official, including *machi-bugyō* (1717); raised to *daimyō* status in 1748. Famed for administration and legal decisions, recounted in *Ōoka meiyo seidan.* Search the antiquarian book shops for I.G. Edmonds, *Solomon in Kimono: Ooka, a Wise Judge of Old Yedo* (Tokyo: Stars and Stripes, 1956) and its sequel *Ooka: More Tales of Solomon in Kimono* (1957). Those who read Dutch will find a series of detective novels by Bertus Aafjes (1914–1993) based on Ōoka stories. See Johan

W. Konig, "Bertus Aafjes: 1914–1993," July 2, 2002, *Konig Johan's Huispage*, http://home.hcc-net.nl/jw.koning/aafjes/ba-bron-uitleg.htm (accessed July 10, 2004).

18. Shiobaraya Tasuke (1743–1816) left his home in what is now Gunma Prefecture and made good in Edo. He was celebrated in the Rakugo specialist Sanyūtei Enchō's *Shiobara Tasuke ichidaiki* (*A Record of the Life of Shiobara Tasuke*), performed, serialized, and published first between 1876 and 1885.

19. Edo gang leader killed 1650 (1657?) in a fight by Mizuno Jūrōzaemon, leader of a gang of shogunate vassals, himself ordered to commit suicide in 1664; hero of many Kabuki plays.

20. He was a gang leader (1820–1893) based in the port of Shimizu (now Shizuoka City in Shizuoka Prefecture) who controlled the highway between Edo and the old capital and was later renowned as a humanitarian, promoter of westernization, and developer of the town. His story, based on the memoirs of Amada Gorō (*Tōkaido yūkyōden: ichimei Jirōchō monogatari* [*Stories of Chivalry on the Tōkaido: Tales of One Also Known as Jirōchō*] [Tokyo: Yorinsha, 1884]), was taken up by the Kōdan specialist Kanda Hakuzan III (1872–1932) and then by the Naniwa-*bushi* specialist Hirozawa Torazō II (1899–1964), who performs the voice-over Naniwa-*bushi* narration for Makino Masahiro's 1940 film *Zoku Shimizu minato* (extant). For a complete chronology of his life in Japanese, see "Shimizu no Jirōchō," *Komatsuen*, April 20, 2005, http://www3.tokai.or.jp/komatsuen/ (accessed April 30, 2005).

21. Hori, *Folk Religion*, p. 11.

22. Hori, *Folk Religion*, p. 72.

23. Plays were produced as memorial services for the protagonists of plays based on real people. Chikamatsu wrote his Jōruri *Yūgiri and the Straits of Narutō* in honor of the thirty-third anniversary of Yūgiri's death. James R. Brandon, trans., *Kabuki: Five Classic Plays* (Cambridge, Mass. and London, 1975), pp. 32–33. "January 1720: first Kabuki adaptation of Chikamatsu Monzaemon's puppet theater *shinjū-mono* 'Shinjū Kasane Izutsu,' which was written in 1707. The same play is simultaneously produced in the three Edo theaters and commemorates the 16th anniversary (17th memorial service) of the suicide of the couple Tokubei and Ofusa, whose roles are played by Ôtani Hiroji I and Sanogawa Mangiku at the Nakamuraza." Shōriya Aragōrō, "Nakamuraza," *Kabuki 21*, latest update April 23, 2005, http://www.kabuki21.com/nakamuraza.php (accessed May 2, 2005). A more recent example is the Byakkotai Kenbu, a yearly reenactment, with sung narration (*chigin*, or Chinese poetry), of the death of the nineteen boys of the White Tiger Brigade before their graves. This has been a tradition since 1888, the seventeenth anniversary of their deaths.

24. Hajime Nakamura, *Ways of Thinking of Eastern Peoples: India, China, Tibet, Japan* (Honolulu: East-West Center Press, 1964), p. 386.

25. For the commonness of this idea, see for example Ayao Okumura, "A Cherry Blossom Picnic," *Food Forum*, 2005, online journal, http://www.kikkoman.com/ forum/021/ff021.html (accessed May 2, 2005). Gary L. Ebersole, "The Buddhist Ritual Use of Linked Poetry in Medieval Japan," *Eastern Buddhist* 16, no. 2 (Autumn 1983): 50–71, for the pacification of falling cherry blossoms through linked poetry and the use of linked poetry to secure victory in battle.

26. See, for example, Lafcadio Hearn, "In a Japanese Garden, V," *Atlantic Monthly* 70, no. 417 (July 1892): 20; *Cornell University Library Making of America*, http://cdl.library.cornell.edu/cgi-bin/moa/moa-cgi?notisid=ABK2934-0070-4 (accessed May 2, 2005).

27. *Soga monogatari*, XI, "Hinjo ga ittō no koto," p. 404, in *Gikeiki, Soga monogatari*, Nihon koten bungaku taikei 88, ed. Ichiko Teiji and Ōshima Tatehiko (Tokyo: Iwanami Shoten, 1966), p. 404.

28. Frank Hoff, *Song, Dance, Storytelling: Aspects of Performing Arts in Japan*, Cornell University East Asia Papers 15 (Ithaca, New York: Cornell University China-Japan Program, 1978), pp. 154–156. Hoff relies heavily on Honda Yasuji's *Kagura: Nihon no minzoku geinō I* (Tokyo: Kibunsha, 1966), *Yamabushi kagura bangaku* (1971 reprint of 1942), *Okina sono hoka: nō oyobi kyō genkō no ni* (Tokyo: Meizendō Shoten, 1958), *Ennen: Nihon no minzoku geinō III* (Tokyo: Kibunsha, 1969), and *Katarimono/furyū II: Nihon no minzoku geinō IV* (Tokyo: Kibunsha, 1970).

29. The gods as "wandering person" or *marebito* coming seasonally include "guardian spirits, ancestor spirits, kami of the rice field, and spirits of the dead." Hori, *Folk Religion*, p. 69.

30. This scene is based on an incident in the life of the famous swordsman, Kamiizumi Ise no kami Hidetsuna, which is related in Daisetz T. Suzuki, *Zen and Japanese Culture*, Bollingen Series 64 (Princeton, New Jersey: Princeton University Press, 1970 of 1959), pp. 128–129.

31. For examples in the nineteenth century, see Carmen Blacker, "Millenarian Aspects of the New Religions in Japan," in Donald H. Shively, ed., *Tradition and Modernization in Japanese Culture*, Studies in the Modernization of Japan 5 (Princeton: Princeton University Press, 1971) and Emily Groszos Ooms, *Women and Millenarian Protest in Meiji Japan: Deguchi Nao and Ōmotokyō*, Cornell East Asia Series 61 (Ithaca, New York: Cornell East Asia Program, 1993). See also Hori, *Folk Religion*, p. 78.

32. See Blacker's works cited above and those cited in note 10.

33. One of the translations of the Japanese word for story, tale, or narrative, *monogatari*, could be "ghost story." The word *mono* is also used to refer to supernatural beings such as buddhas, gods, spirits, and devils of all sorts.

34. For the play in English, see Donald Keene, trans., *Major Plays of Chikamatsu* (New York: Columbia University Press; reprint edition 1961), pp. 57–90.

35. See note 19.

36. Alison Tokita, "The Reception of the Heike Monogatari as Performed Narrative: The Atsumori Episode in Heikyoku, Zatō Biwa and Satsuma Biwa," *Japanese Studies* 23, no. 1 (May 2003): 61, http://0-search.epnet.com.library.lib.asu.edu:80/login.aspx?direct=true&db=aph&an=9930258 (accessed May 15, 2005), citing Suganuma Hiroshi, "Biwa hōshi," in *Heike monogatari ga wakaru*, Aera Mook 31 (Tokyo: Asahi Shinbunsha, 1997), pp. 104–119, 108. In 1985, I had the opportunity to see a documentary, funded by the Toyota Foundation, on a contemporary *biwa hōshi* who performed an exorcism for the building of a new house.

37. The idea of the sermon as pacification of the violent spirit of the dead is to be seen in, for example, Fukuda Akira, *Chūsei katarimono bungei: Sono keifu to tenkai*, Miyai sensho 8 (Tokyo: Miyai Shoten, 1981), especially pp. 9–15, 140–148.

38. Suffering as the way to deification is the theme of many of the propaganda stories of the fourteenth century *Shintō-shū*. For a discussion, see D.E. Mills, "*Soga Monogatari*, *Shintōshū* and the Taketori Legend," *Monumenta Nipponica* 30, no. 1 (Spring 1975): 46–47, http://links.jstor.org/sici?sici=0027-0741%28197521%2930%3A1%3C37%3ASMSATT%3E2.0.CO%3B2-L (accessed May 15, 2005).

39. This is a product of Tendai Buddhist thought which permeates, for example, the *Heike monogatari*: one may be born into the highest realm, likened to that of the angels, but because of the interpenetration of the realms, one can never escape suffering, even that of hell.

40. For examples of the belief that those who die in battle will be reborn as *shura*, see Mills, "*Soga Monogatari*," pp. 46–47, where, according to the *Bosatsu reigenki*, the ghosts of the Soga brothers are portrayed as wielding bloody swords, and Sybil A. Thornton, "*Kōnodai senki*: Traditional Narrative and Warrior Ideology in Sixteenth-Century Japan," *Oral Tradition* 15, no. 2 (2000): 376–377.

41. For the *matatabi-mono* and militarism, see Satō Tadao, *Hasegawa Shin-ron: giri ninjō to wa nani ka* (Tokyo: Chūō Kōronsha, 1975). For *Daibosatsu toge*, Ozaki Hideki refers to a song in the novel for "the journey of death," to a poem by novelist Miyazawa Kenji (1896–1933) for the "journey of a *shura*," and shamanism in characterizing the novel. Ozaki Hideki, "Kaisetsu," *Nakazato Kaizan-shū*, Shōwa kokumin bungaku zenshū 1 (Tokyo: Chikuma Shobō, 1978), pp. 495–496. This is fairly standard in writings on the novel.

42. The most famous example is the mother of the child-emperor Antoku, drowned in the battle of Dannoura in 1185, the empress Kenreimon'in (1155–1213): rescued from the sea and brought to the capital, she removed to a retreat at Ohara, the Jakkō'in, to spend the rest of her days in prayer. See, *The Tale of the Heike*, 2 vols., translated by Hiroshi Kitagawa and Bruce T. Tsuchida (Tokyo: University of Tokyo Press, 1975), II:763–782. This sort of story is typical of the epic. See Thornton, "*Kōnodai senki*" for a complete analysis of the epic.

43. "The Death of Atsumori," in *Heike*, II:561–563.

44. Brandon, p. 33. See also Fukuda Akira, *Gunki monogatari to minkan denshō* (Tokyo: Iwasaki bijitsusha, 1974), p. 217, and Origuchi Shinobu, "Yashima katari no kenkyū," in *Origuchi Shinobu zenshū* (Tokyo: Chūōkōronsha, 1956), XVII:209.

45. Directed by Mizoguchi Kenji and released in 1954, it is based on a story by Mori Ōgai.

46. Shizuka is featured in Nō and Kabuki plays. For the others, see *The Tale of the Soga Brothers*, trans. Thomas G. Cogan (Tokyo: University of Tokyo Press, 1987); James S. de Benneville, *Tales of the Samurai: Oguri Hangwan Ichidaiki* (Tokyo: Fukuin Printing Company, Limited, 1916).

47. Hori, p. 78. Oracles at shrines were ended in A.D. 812. Haruko Okano, *Die Stellung der Frau im Shintō: Eine Religionsphänomenologische und Soziologische Untersuchung* (Bonn: Rheinische Friederich-Wilhems-Universität, 1975), p. 80. All priests were men, although women gradually reasserted themselves here and there. Ibid., p. 65. Shamanic functions and their practitioners moved out of the shrine system, which had been taken over by the government. The secularization of the women serving in the shrines, *jinja uneme*, is posited as the beginning of secular prostitution in Japan. For a discussion of the transition of initiation rites for women as a kind of marriage to a deity into prostitution, see ibid., pp. 138–139.

48. See, for example, Susan Matisoff, review of *The Tale of the Soga Brothers*, translated by Thomas J. Cogan, *Monumenta Nipponica* 43, no. 1 (Spring, 1988): 101–103, http://links.jstor.org/ sici?sici=0027-0741%28198821%2943%3A1%3C101%3ATTOTSB%3E2.0.CO%

3B2-M (accessed February 7, 2006). See also Robert Borgen, review of *Avatars of Vengeance: Japanese Drama and the Soga Literary Tradition*, by Laurence R. Kominz, *Journal of Japanese Studies* 25, no. 2. (Summer 1999): 450, http://links.jstor.org/sici?sici=0095-6848%28199922%2925%3A2%3C448%3AAOVJDA%3E2.0.CO%3B2-7 (accessed February 7, 2006).

49. The 1958 remake, including scenes censored during the war, won the Venice Gold Lion.

50. Supreme Commander of Allied Powers, or General Douglas MacArthur.

51. Literally, "pictures of the floating world," the term was used primarily to refer to woodblock prints portraying the pleasure quarters as well as illustrations of popular books, plays, and even landscapes.

52. Kobayashi Kazushige, "On the Meaning of Masked Dances in Kagura," *Asian Folklore Studies* 11, no. 1 (1981): 10; Geinō Kenkyūkai, ed., *Kagura: kodai no kabu to matsuri*, Nihon no koten geinō 1 (Tokyo: Heibonsha, 1969), p. 13; Hayakawa Kōtarō, *Hanamatsuri*, Minzoku mingei sōsho 2 (Tokyo: Iwasaki Bijutsusha, 1966), p. 100.

53. The title is taken from the title of the Chinese work concerning the disintegration of the Han empire, *Romance of the Three Kingdoms.* A version is available at www.ThreeKingdoms.com.

54. Sato Tadao, *Currents in Japanese Cinema: Essays by Tadao Sato*, trans. Gregory Barrett (Tokyo : Kodansha International; New York : Kodansha International/USA : distributed by Harper & Row, 1982), p. 43.

55. Tokugawa Ieyasu, first shogun of the Edo period, is enshrined in the Tōshōgu at Nikkō. The peasant economist Ninomiya Sontoku (1786–1856) is enshrined in the Hotoku Ninomiya Jinja shrine established in Odawara in 1894 (http://www.asahi-net.or.jp/~QM9T-KNDU/Ninomiya.htm [accessed May 24, 2005]); for his own accomplishments, Matsudaira Sadanobu worshipped himself in effigy 1812–1829. Herbert Ooms, *Charismatic Bureaucrat: A Political Biography of Matsudaira Sadanobu 1758–1829* (Chicago: University of Chicago Press, 1975).

56. Ichikawa Utaemon obliged me with an interview October 29, 1981, and invited me to dinner a week or two later, when he told me about the *kimono.*

57. The film, *Ōkubo Hikozaemon dai ippen* (*Ōkubo Hikozaemon*, Part One), the first listing "Isshin Tasuke" in a film with Ōkubo, was based on an original story by Osaragi Jirō. *JMDb*, http://www.jmdb.ne.jp/1936/bl000500.htm (accessed May 24, 2005).

58. Later, he took the name Yorozuya Kinnosuke (1932–1997).

59. For *bun* and *yaku*, see Bitō Masahide, "Society and Social Thought in the Tokugawa Period," *Japan Foundation Newsletter* 9 (June–September 1981): 4–6.

60. This is the basic thrust of Neo-Confucianism, the school that culminated in the work of Chu Hsi/Zhu Xi (1130–1200).

61. Sato, *Currents*, p. 42.

62. For example, moved by the suffering caused by famines and the failure of the government to respond adequately, Ōshio Heihachirō (1793–1837), former magistrate in Osaka, raised a rebellion which ended in the destruction of one quarter or more of the city and his own death by suicide. He was a follower of the Chinese Confucianist and bureaucrat Wang Yangming (1472–1529), who taught that to know was to act. See Najita Tetsuo, "Oshio Heihachiro (1793–1837)," in Albert M. Craig and Donald H. Shively, eds., *Personality in Japanese History* (Berkeley, CA: University of California Press, 1970).

63. The best sources in English are Henry D. Smith II, "Rethinking the Story of the 47 Ronin: Chūshingura in the 1980s" (2003 revision of 1990), *Henry Smith's Home Page*, http://www.columbia.edu/~hds2/47ronin/47ronin_rev.htm (accessed May 27, 2005), and "The Trouble with Terasaka: The Forty-Seventh Rōnin and the Chūshingura Imagination," *Japan Review* 16 (2004): 3–65. They can both be accessed from Prof. Smith's homepage at http://202.231.40.34/jpub/pdf/jr/IJ1601.pdf (accessed may 27, 2005).

64. In *The Incident at Sakai and Other Stories*, ed. David Dilworth and J. Thomas Rimer; additional contributions by Richard Bowring (Honolulu: University of Hawaii Press, 1977). One of the incidents related in the work concerns a samurai family that walked out on their lord with their matchlocks primed and the fuses lit.

65. See, among others, "Yamaga Sokō," in *Great Thinkers of the Eastern World*, edited by Ian P. McGreal (New York: HarperCollins Publishers, Inc., 1995), pp. 359–362.

66. Yamaga Sokō, "The Way of the Samurai," in *Sources of Japanese Tradition*, 2 vols. (New York: Columbia University Press, 1958), 1:389–91.

67. "Ogyū Sorai," in *Great Thinkers of the Eastern World*, edited by Ian P. McGreal (New York: HarperCollins Publishers, Inc., 1995), pp. 371–374.

Chapter 4

1. In 1874, Itagaki Taisuke (1837–1919) and others touched off this movement when they petitioned for a representative government. The

national assembly, or Diet, composed of a house of representative and a house of peers, was first convened in 1890, the year after the promulgation of the constitution. Itagaki survived an assassination attempt in 1882 and went to France; there he met Hugo, who advised him to popularize the movement through novels.

2. Written originally for the puppet theater in 1748 by Takeda Izumo II, Miyoshi Shōraku, and Namiki Sōsuke. For a translation, see *Chushingura (The Treasury of Loyal Retainers): A Puppet play by Takeda Izumo, Miyoshi Shōraku, and Namiki Senryū*, translated by Donald Keene (New York, Columbia University Press, 1971).

3. The topics seem to focus for the most part on the rise of Oda Nobunaga and Toyotomi Hideyoshi and the fall of Osaka Castle.

4. One famous example is the reception of Tang poet Bo Juyi's "Song of Everlasting Sorrow" (*Chōgonka* in Japanese), Emperor Xangzong's lament on the death of his concubine Yang Guifei, in *Genji monogatari*, the tale of Kogō in versions of the *Heike monogatari*, and Zenchiku's play *Kogō*. Michael Watson, "Modes of Reception: *Heike monogatari* and the Nō play *Kogō*," *International and Regional Studies* (*Kokusaigaku kenkyū*) 16 (March 1997): 275–303, October 14, 2000, http://www.meijigakuin.ac.jp/~watson/heike/kogo.html (accessed July 13, 2005).

5. Examples include Itō Daisuke's 1927 *Gerō* (*Servant*), 1928 *Shinpan Ōoka seidan* (*Tange Sazen*), and even 1961 *Hangyakuji* (*Conspirator*). A later example is Imai Tadashi's 1963 *Bushidō zankoku monogatari* (*Cruel Stories of the Samurai's Way*).

6. Even in Kobayashi Masaki's *Seppuku* (*Harakiri*), the old ronin seeking vengeance for the cruel death of his son-in-law must confront his own collusion in the fate of the young man.

7. He figures in Kinugasa Teinosuke's *Kawanakajima kassen* (*The Battle of Kawanakajima*), Inagaki Hiroshi's *Furin kazan* (*Samurai Banners*, 1969), and Kadokawa Hiroki's *Ten to chi* (*Heaven and Earth*, 1990).

8. Such epics include the famous *Heike monogatari* (thirteenth century) as well as the not-so-famous *Kōnodai senki*. See Sybil Thornton, "*Kōnodai senki*: Traditional Narrative and Warrior Ideology in Sixteenth-Century Japan," *Oral Tradition* 15, no. 2 (2000): 306–376.

9. The film is based on the novel of the same name by Inoue Yasushi.

10. The film is based on the novel of the same name by Fukasawa Shichirō.

11. The film is based on the novel of the same name by Muneta Hiroshi.

12. The armies of the Shimazu in Kyushu expanded as they took over most of the island in the sixteenth century. When Hideyoshi suppressed them, he substantially reduced the domain of the Shimazu; the size of the domain was not great enough to support all the soldiers of his armies and so many were assigned land to farm and earn their living rather than be supported by the domain's treasury.

13. This occurred as more land was reclaimed for cultivation, more rice was produced, and the value of rice decreased. By 1700, most of the samurai class was up to its collective neck in debt to the merchants who converted their rice to money and also controlled the rate of exchange.

14. Both based on the novel by Kon Tōkō, the first was directed by Tanaka Kinuyo and the second by Kumai Kei. I had the opportunity to visit Kumai's set as the scene of Ogin's suicide was being filmed.

15. The film, based on a novel by Inoue Yasushi, was directed by Kumai Kei.

16. The film, based on the novel *Hideyoshi to Rikyū* (*Hideyoshi and Rikyū*) by Nogami Yaeko, was directed by Teshigahara Hiroshi.

17. Beatrice M. Bodart, "Tea and Counsel: The Political Role of Sen Rikyū," *Monumenta Nipponica* 32, no. 1 (Spring 1977): 49–74, http://links.jstor.org/sici?sici=0027–0741%2819 7721%2932%3A1%3C49%3ATACTPR%3E2.0.CO%3B2-C (accessed July 15, 2005).

18. They are often portrayed as making hand gestures (*mudra*) associated with the esoteric schools of Buddhism.

19. Paul Schrader, "Yakuza Eiga: A Primer," *Film Comment* 10, no. 1 (February 1974): 8–17.

20. Also translated as *Big Gambling Ceremony*. See Mark Schilling, *The Yakuza Movie Book: A Guide to Japanese Gangster Films* (Berkeley: Stone Bridge Press, 2003), pp. 162–163.

21. 1954 *Miyamoto Musashi*; 1955 *Zoku Miyamoto Musashi: Ichijōji no kettō* (*Duel at Ichijoji Temple)*; and *Miyamoto Musashi kanketsuhen: kettō Ganryūjima* (*Duel on Ganryu Island*). All three are based on the novel by Yoshikawa Eiji.

Chapter 5

1. Like the term "samurai film," the term "yakuza film" is used for more films than it technically covers either in terms of time or in terms of content. The word *yakuza*, like gypsy, is not a nice word. It means "eight-nine-three," a bad throw of the dice — worthless. The earliest use I found (in a quick search in IMDb and JMDb) in a film title was for Suzuki Seijun's 1962 *Hai tiin yakuza* (*High Teen Yakuza*); the term came into more general use for titles in the 1960s and 1970s. *Kyōkaku*, from the late-Tokugawa period, is the earliest favorable word used for these gamblers. In the mid- or late-Meiji period, the term *sanjaku-mono* was used for the genre; "sanjaku"

refers to the length of the sword (three *shaku*) and therefore to the sword itself. "Matatabi-mono" was first used for the works of Hasegawa Shin and should be used specifically for those films about "wandering gamblers" that reject militarism, killing in exchange for a meal and place to stay the night (*isshoku ippan*).

2. One was *kuchiire*: recruiting workers for various businesses and standing guarantee for them. This put the worker under certain obligations to his "boss."

3. Mark Schilling gives it the name *Big Gambling Ceremony*. Mark Schilling, *The Yakuza Movie Book: A Guide to Japanese Gangster Films* (Berkeley, California: Stone Bridge Press, 2003), s.v. "*Bakuchiuchi Socho Tobaku.*"

4. As reported in the diary of Yamashina Tokitsugu (1507–1576). *Tokitsugu kyōki*, cited in "Ishikawa Goemon no nakamatachi," *Nakahara Chūya to dadaizumu* (September 20, 2005?), http://www.ten-f.com/goemon.html (accessed October 13, 2005).

5. The book was written or edited by Hayashi Razan (1583–1657), founder of the orthodox school of Confucianism endorsed by the Tokugawa regime. Ibid.

6. According to Worldcat (www.worldcat.org), the full title is *Relación del Reino de Nippon a que llaman corruptamente Jappon*. It was first published in *Archivo Iberoamericano*, v. 36–38, 1933–35.

7. "Ishikawa Goemon," *Wikipedia*, http://en.wikipedia.org/wiki/Ishikawa_Goemon (accessed June 10, 2006).

8. "Kataoka Nizaemon I," *Kabuki 21: All About Japan's Traditional Theatre Art of Kabuki!*, http://www.kabuki21.com/nizaemon1.php (accessed August 6, 2005).

9. Shōriya Aragorō, "Sanmon Gosan no Kiri," *Kabuki 21*, http://www.kabuki21.com/sanmon.php (accessed August 6, 2005), citing Kawatake Toshio, *Kabuki: Baroque Fusion of the Art* (Tokyo: International House of Japan, 2003).

10. Sekka Sanjin, *Sarutobi Sasuke: Sanada sanyūshi ninjutsu meijin*, Tachikawa Bunko series 40 (Osaka: Tachikawa Bunmeidō, 1914; reprint: Tokyo: Horupu Shuppan, 1975, Meicho Fukkoku Nihon Jidō Bungakkan 6).

11. Richard Torrance, "Literacy and Literature in Osaka, 1890–1940," *The Journal of Japanese Studies* 31, no. 1 (2005), pp. 55–56, http://0-muse.jhu.edu.library.lib.asu.edu/journals/journal_of_japanese_studies/v031/31.1torrance.pdf (accessed August 6, 2005), citing Scott Langton, "A Literature for the People: A Study of Jidai Shōsetsu in Taishō and Early Shōwa Japan," Ph.D. diss. (Ohio State University, 2000). The NACSIS Webcat site lists a 1910 *Sarutobi Sasuke* by Tamada Gyokushūsai and Yamada Tadao, published in Osaka. *Sarutobi Sasuke*, http://webcat.nii.ac.jp/cgi-bin/shsproc?id=BA72827352 (accessed October 5, 2005).

12. *Shinobi no mono*, directed by Yamamoto Satsuo and released in 1963.

13. *Zoku shinobi no mono* (*The Ninja Part II*), directed by Yamamoto Satsuo, script by Takaiwa Hajime, 1963.

14. "Kunisada Chūji (Nagaoka Chūjirō)," April 13, 2004, *Jōshū Kunisada Chūji chaya honbo*, http://www5.wind.ne.jp/fisherman/ch/chuji/kunisada.htm (accessed August 8, 2005).

15. More usually called Geki; also Yōkyū and Kandō.

16. "Kaei Suikoden," *Shirandō*, http://homepage1.nifty.com/sira/tyuuji/ index.html (accessed August 8, 2005).

17. "Kaei Suikoden gendaigoyaku," *Shirandō*, http://homepage1.nifty.com/sira/tyuuji/index.html (accessed August 8, 2005). There are at least three official monuments.

18. Satoshi Takahashi, "The Water Margin (Suikoden) in Japan around the End of the Edo Period," *Rekihaku* (*Witness to History*) no. 117 (March 2003), National Museum of Japanese History, http://www.rekihaku.ac.jp/e-rekihaku/117/index.html (accessed August 8, 2005).

19. "Kabuki Play Titles Dictionary," *Kabuki 21: All about Japan's Traditional Theatre Art of Kabuki!*, http://www.kabuki21.com/dic.php (accessed August 6, 2005).

20. Takahashi, "The Water Margin."

21. "Popular Culture and Invented Heroes," 2004, National Museum of Japanese History, http://www.rekihaku.ac.jp/e_news/index82/index.html (accessed on August 8, 2005).

22. Part of the text is rendered into modern Japanese. "Kaiei Suikoden," *Shirandō*, http://homepage1.nifty.com/sira/tyuuji/index.html (accessed August 8, 2005). Which came first, the chicken or the egg (identification with the pantheon of the Chinese bandits on his grave marker or the illustrations and popular texts), is not clear.

23. Takahashi, "The Water Margin," http://www.rekihaku.ac.jp/koohoo/journal/no117/pic7.jpg (accessed August 9, 2005). The author's name as writer of the text is clearly seen on the right below the titles against red and yellow rectangles.

24. "Kichō shiryō gazō de-tabesu," *Tōkyō tōritsu tōshokan* (*Tokyo Metropolitan Library*), http://metro.tokyo.opac.jp/tml/tpic/cgi-bin/detail.cgi?Kbseqid=7944&S ryparam=001&Backpage=/tml/tpic/resprint_d/all/isbn001_0_100/isbn001_001_036.html&Srhfname=/resprint_d/all/isbn001_0_100/isbn001&Rp_kind=8&Prtype=0&Displmt=100 (accessed August 9, 2005).

25. "Nineteenth Century 1801–1900," *Kabuki 21: All about Japan's Traditional Theatre*

Art of Kabuki!, http://www.kabuki21.com/hist_19.php (accessed August 6, 2005).

26. These include *Sannin Kichisa Tomoe no shiranami* (1860), *Shiranami gonin otoko* or *Benten Kozō* (1862), and *Koharunagi Okitsu shiranami* (1864). One of the plays of Nanboku III, *Tsuki no En Tsuki no Shiranami* (*Circle of the Moon, White Waves of the Moon*; 1821), is one of the very earliest to use the word *shiranami* in the title. "Nineteenth Century 1801–1900," *Kabuki: All about Japan's Traditional Theatre Art of Kabuki!,* http://www.kabuki21.com/hist_19.php (accessed August 6, 2005). Early titles included *Tōtōmigata koi no shiranami* (1819). "Asao Kuzaemon I," *Kabuki,* http://kabuki.ifrance.com/kabuki/kuzaemonl_gf.htm (accessed October 10, 2005).

27. Under the record for Emperor Ling (r. 168–189), second month.

28. J. Scott Miller, "Japanese Shorthand and Sokkibon," *Monumenta Nipponica* 49, no. 4. (Winter, 1994), pp. 474–476, http://links.jstor.org/sici?sici=0027-0741%28199424%2949%3A4%3C471%3AJSAS%3E2.0.CO%3B2-8 (accessed August 18, 2005). Japanese shorthand was developed by Takasaki Kōki (1854–1938) between 1878 and 1881.

29. 1914, 1918, 1921, 1925, compared with Ishikawa Goemon films in 1912 and 1922. "Onoe Matsunosuke," *JMDb,* http://www.jmdb.ne.jp/person/p0330730.htm (accessed August 18, 2005).

30. "Yukitomo Rifu," *JMD.,* http://www.jmdb.ne.jp/person/p0109110.htm (accessed August 18, 2005).

31. This is a film I was not able to see in the early eighties, when I was in Tokyo doing research. Part of the three-part series was discovered in the early nineties and is now in the Tokyo Museum of Modern Art Film Center.

32. Yamoto Kikuo, "Rensai ronbun: hikaku eigashi kenkyū (28): Amerika eiga to jiyūshūgi jidaigek, Yamanaka Sado no nagaya-mono o megutte," *Firum senta*-60 (May 7, 1980): 38. This article goes into depth on the influence of Edmund Goulding's 1932 *Grand Hotel,* which stars Greta Garbo and John Barrymore.

33. Directed by Taniguchi Senkichi (b. 1912) from a script by Shindō Kaneto (b. 1912).

34. "Japanese warship Kanrin Maru," *Wikipedia,* http://en.wikipedia.org/wiki/Kanrin_Maru (accessed August 19, 2005).

35. Katō Sadahito, "Bakumatsu Tōhoku yowa 9: Jirōchō to Guan (ge), *Nda Nda gekijō* 74 (February 2005), http://www.mumyosha.co.jp/ndanda/05/bakumatu02.html (accessed August 19, 2005), citing Fumikura Heijirō, *Bakumatsu gunkan Kanrinmaru,* 2 vols. (Tokyo: Chūōkōronsha, 1993; first published in 1938).

36. *Matsuhiro: Shimizu minato funayado kinenkan* (official homepage of the Matsuhiro: Shimizu harbor shipping agent memorial hall), http://www.portwave.gr.jp/suehiro/index.html (accessed August 19, 2005). Jirōchō rebuilt this in 1886. For Tesshū, see "Yamaoka Tesshū," 2004, *Rekishikan,* http://www.geocities.jp/str_homepage/ rekishi/bakumatsu/jinbutsu/meikan/tesshu.html (accessed August 19, 2005). Yamaoka Tesshū (1836–1888) was a fencing master, leader in the early pro-shogunate militia, the Shinsengumi, the representative of the shogunate naval commander Katsu Kaishū (1823–1899) to Saigō Takamori (1827–1877) for the negotiation of the surrender of Chiyoda Castle of Edo — he is credited with the peaceful handover — and escort of the shogun back to Shizuoka. The Shinsengumi (1863–1868) was a private force permitted by the lord of Aizu to police Kyoto to counter pro-imperialist revolutionaries. After services to the shogun and shogunal retainers and the new government, he was in 1872 appointed chamberlain to the emperor and served in various but important capacities on the imperial household staff. He was granted lower-third rank. "Yamaoka Tessyu [sic] to wa," *Yamaoka Tessyu,* http://www.tessyuu.jp/yamaoka.htm (accessed August 19, 2005).

37. He was the son of a vassal of the Iwakidaira domain. Separated from his family by the civil war, he wandered up and down the country looking for them until he became a student of Yamaoka Tesshū. He became a monk Guan at thirty-four and took the name Tetsugen the year before his death. See, for example, Fukushima Prefectural Board of Education, *Fukushima bungaku no furusato hyakusen* (2001–2002), http://www.db.fks.ed.jp/txt/47000.1994fukushima_bungaku100/html/00014.html (accessed August 19, 2005).

38. Katō, "Jirōchō to Guan."

39. Kikuchi Shin'ichi, "Kanda Rozan, Shimizu Jirōchō," March 30, 1962, *Kikuchi Shin'ichi kenkyūshitsu; Nihon bungaku, kōdan, kanji, http://www.konan-wu.ac.jp/~kikuchi/kodan/rozan.htm* (accessed September 27, 2005); Aritake Shūji, "Shimizu Jirōchō ni tsuite."

40. "Kanda Hakuzan," *JMDb,* http://www.jmdb.ne.jp/person/p0203730.htm (accessed September 27, 2005).

41. "*Chūji to Oman,*" *JMDb,* http://www.jmdb.ne.jp/1936/bl000890.htm (accessed September 27, 2005). It was directed by Tsuji Kichirō for Nikkatsu. In 1929, Tsuji had directed Ōkōchi Denjirō in the first *matatabimono, Kutsukake Tokijirō* (*Tokijirō from Kutsukake*).

42. "Hirosawa Torazō," *JMDb,* http://www.jmdb.ne.jp/person/p0105320.htm (accessed September 27, 2005).

43. "Shimizu minato," *JMDb,* http://www.

jmdb.ne.jp/1939/bo002920.htm (accessed September 27, 2005). The original script was written by Oguni Hideo, who also co-wrote Kurosawa's *Ran*.

44. A third part starring Sano Shūji was released by Tōei in 1954, *Shin jinsei gekijō: bōkyōhen* (*New Theater of Life: Volume on Nostalgia*).

45. "*Jinsei gekijō: seishunhen* (1958)," *Goo eiga*, 2005, http://movie.goo.ne.jp/movies/PMVWKPD25989/index.html (accessed October 13, 2005).

46. In his article on the yakuza film (including chivalry films), Paul Schrader described the formulaic scenes of the genre and the production conditions responsible for them. Paul Schrader, "Yakuza-eiga: A Primer," *Film Comment* 10, no. 1 (January–February, 1974): 8–17. In his chapter in a book on yakuza films, Kusumoto Kenkichi has an interesting diagram of the situation in which the typical hero of the chivalry film finds himself. Kusumoto Kenkichi, "Yakuza eiga no gendai teki kōsai," in *Ninkyō eiga*, ed. Kusumoto Kenkichi (Tokyo: Araji Shuppansha, 1969), pp. 7–28.

47. In Katō Tai's 1971 *Hibotan bakutō: oinochi itadakimasu* (*Woman Gambler: Death to the Wicked*). The pollution of farmlands by a factory recalls the Ashio copper mine case of the 1880s.

48. *Jingi* is a term coined by the philosopher Itō Jinsai (1627–1705). "Humanity and righteousness or duty" was opposed to *giri* (righteousness and principle) just as his philosophy of the ability of human beings to grow and develop in morality was opposed to the orthodox Confucian concept that morality coincided directly with caste and status. "Do the right" was not the same as "do your duty."

49. "Category 9: Drama Programs/Other Major Presentations," *50 Years of NHK Television: A Window on Japan and the World*, http://www.nhk.or.jp/digitalmuseum/nhk50years_en/categories/p52/ (accessed October 23, 2005).

50. *Nihon keizai shinbun* August 1981.

51. In some films, as in this film and the versions of *Jinsei gekijō*, the hero loses his woman because he is in the world of the gambler; he has killed. Whether killing results in his losses or his losses lead to his killing, the point is ultimately the same; the plots of the films simply focus on different parts of the cycle.

Chapter 6

1. James Brandon, *Kabuki: Five Kabuki Classic Plays* (Cambridge: Harvard University Press, 1975), p. 5. Between about 1700 and 1870, the popular stage, or Kabuki, perfected a rhetorical system dependent on historical events and historical characters and on contemporary sentiments, language and costuming to indicate the current event under discussion, a "disturbance in a great house" of the upper-ranking samurai or nobility.

2. Nihon Kindai Bungku-kan, ed., *Nihon kindai bungaku daijiten* (Tokyo: Kodansha, 1977), IV:228–229, s.v. "Shinkokugeki." From here on, *NKBD*.

3. *NKBD*, II:139, s.v. "Sawada Shōjirō." See also *Nihon eiga haiyū zenshū: danyū-hen* (Tokyo: Kinema Junpōsha, 1980), pp. 257–259, s.v. "Sawada Shōjirō." From here on, *NEHZDH*.

4. *NKBD*, II:407–410, s.v. "Tsubouchi Shōyō." For a discussion of the development of modern theater in Japan at this time, including the relationships among Tsubouchi, Sawada, the Art Theater, Ichikawa Sadanji, and Osanai Kaoru as discussed below, see Toita Kōji, "The New-Theatre Movement," in Toyotaka Komiya, *Japanese Music and Drama in the Meiji Era*, translated by Donald Keene (Tokyo: Toyo Bunko, 1956), pp. 285–303.

5. Most of the Art Theater joined Sawada's New National Theater after the sudden deaths of Hōgetsu and Matsui. Toita, "New-Theatre Movement," p. 298.

6. See, for example, Mifune Toshirō's performance of the role created by Sawada in Taniguchi Senkichi's 1960 *Kunisada Chūji* (*The Gambling Samurai: Kunisada Chūji*).

7. At the center of this development was a group of fight choreographers in Nagoya, including Sawada's own, Sawamura Denpachi, and that of future stars Bandō Tsumasaburō and Ichikawa Utaemon, Ichikawa Momokuri. Nagata Tetsurō, *Tate* (Tokyo: San'ichi Shobō, 1974), pp. 33–35.

8. Two were made with Makino Shōzō in 1924–25: *Kunisada Chūji* and *Onshū no kanata ni* (*Beyond Love and Hate*, based on the work by Kikuchi Kan). His last, the 1925 *Tsukigata Hanpeita*, was similarly the filming (this one by Kinugasa Teinosuke) of a current stage production. The other two were the 1921 *Natsukashiki chikara* or *Chikara yo hibike* (the second according to *JMDb*, "Sawada Shōjirō," http://www.jmdb.ne.jp/person/p0262830.htm (accessed 14 August 2004) and the 1924 *Yagaigeki Takadanobaba*.

9. *Nihon eiga kantoku zenshū* (Tokyo: Kinema Junpōsha, 1976), pp. 42–45, s.v. "Itō Daisuke." From here on, *NEKZ*.

10. This gets a bit complicated. In 1919, former Art Theater member, co-founder of the New National Theater, and good friend of Sawada, Kurahashi Sentarō, left the company because of illness and moved to the Osaka area. Upon regaining his health, he started a theater

training school soon after the 1923 Tokyo earthquake (the New National Theater research institute had been destroyed in the fire) and this developed into the Second New National Theater, directed by himself but chaired by Sawada from afar. Training was in all the stage arts, including the classical. In 1925, the New National Theater and the Second New National Theater appeared together on the same stage. The same year, Makino produced a film version of their stage production, the 1925 *Midagahara no satsujin* (*Slaughter at Midagahara*), directed by Kinugasa Teinosuke, whose last film had been the New National Theater's *Tsukigata Hanpeita. NEHZDH*, p. 98, s.v. "Ōkōchi Denjirō."

11. Most camera development would take place in planning the fight scenes. That is where they were used in American Westerns, and that is where the possibilities were in the period film.

12. These outsider actors were condemned to a lifetime of minor roles in Grand Kabuki, or they performed old-style Kabuki in the little theaters. Some even joined up with the "outlaws" of theater, the New School or Shinpa, contemporary, popular Japanese theater. Ichikawa Sadanji's father had been a member of the clique of top Kabuki actors, but, when he died, his son found himself out in the cold. Luckily, he had his own theater, the Meijiza, and the help and support of the Shinpa leaders, who frequently rented his theater for their own performances.

13. Koita, "New Theatre Movement," pp. 299–300 and *NKBD*, II:127, s.v. "Ichikawa Sadanji."

14. Koita, pp. 301–303, and *NKBD*, IV:190–191, s.v. "Jiyūgekijō."

15. Koita, p. 301, and *NKBD*, IV:190–191, s.v. "Jiyūgekijō."

16. *NKBD*, I:332–335, s.v. "Osanai Kaoru."

17. Koita, p. 304.

18. *NKBD*, IV:190, "Jiyūgekijō."

19. *NEHZDH*, pp. 180–181, s.v. "Kawarazaki Chōjūrō."

20. For Kawarazaki, whose family had been prominent in Kabuki a long time, the discrimination against those outside the Ichikawa-led clique was unendurable.

21. Kinugasa Teinosuke's 1925 *Nichirin* (*The Sun*).

22. A very low-ranking actor, Kan'emon, like his father, had preferred the little theaters to the humiliation and discrimination of upper-ranking actors. In 1925, he formed a troupe to help Kabuki apprentices and young actors where their masters gave them none. In 1929, Kan'emon began publishing his magazine *Gekisen* (*Theater War*), in which he blasted the official Kabuki world and brought it down on his head: his own teacher Nakamura Utaemon disowned him. In 1931 he too joined Ennosuke before eventually forming the Progressive Troupe. *NEHZDH*, p. 415, s.v. "Nakamura Kan'emon."

23. They were lucky in having Kawarazaki in establishing a new Kabuki troupe, for he had the right to grant professional names and the right, as hereditary manager of the defunct Kawarazaki Theater, to produce the Eighteen Favorites of the Ichikawa family (although *they* disputed it). See Sakamoto Tokumatsu, *Zenshinza* (Tokyo: Kōdosha, 1953), pp. 66–67, 69.

24. See *NKBD*, III:61–63, s.v. "Hasegawa Shin."

25. In an interview October 20, 1980.

26. See the chronology of productions in Sakamoto, *Zenshinza*, pp. 3–41 (from the end of the book). There were four in the first year including *Tobitchō* and *Seki no Yatappe*. Other plays included *Machi no irezumimono* and *Shigure no Danshichi*.

27. *NEKZ*, pp. 46–48, s.v. "Inagaki Hiroshi." The following discussion on Inagaki and the liberal/liberalism film is taken from Yamamoto Kikuo, "Rensai ronbun: hikaku eigashi kenkyū (26) Amerika to jiyūshūgi jidaigeki, Inagaki Hiroshi kantoku sakuhin o megutte," *Firum senta*–56 (Oct. 17, 1979): 30–36. See also *NKBD*, III:304, s.v. "Mimura Shintarō."

28. Literally, "Danshichi in the rain" ("Danshichi in the drizzle" does not sound quite right). In the interview cited above, Kan'emon said that it was a terrible film.

29. Zenshinza member Katō Daisuke (the short, stocky one in *Seven Samurai*) got his brother, an actor at Nikkatsu, to persuade Inagaki to come and help the director, Kimura Keigo (interview with Kan'emon).

30. The literal translation is "Journey under blue skies"; also known as *Travels under the Blue Skies* and *My Blue Heaven*.

31. Yamamoto, "Inagaki Hiroshi," p. 31.

32. On stage, in addition to updating Kabuki plays, much work was done with a scenarist from the Shingeki world, Murayama Tomoyoshi, in modern comedies using the most up-to-date language.

33. See Satō Tadao, *Currents in Japanese Cinema: Essays by Tadao Sato*, trans. Gregory Barrett (Tokyo: Kodansha, 1982), pp. 41–43.

34. *NEHZDH*, p. 415, s.v. "Nakamura Kan'emon."

35. For a complete discussion, see Katō Tai, "Machi no irezumimono," *Kinema junpō*, extra number, May 30, 1982, *Music and Drama* pp. 78–79. Katō (1916–1985), a famed director himself, was Yamanaka's nephew.

36. Takizawa Eisuke's 1937 *Sengoku guntō den* (*Story of a Bandit Band in the Country at War*, Part One: *Tiger and Wolf*; Part Two: *Advance at Dawn*) and 1938 Ōma no tsuji *(Cross-*

roads at Twilight, o.s. Osaragi Jirō, the Geijutsu Prize to Kan'emon), and finally Hagiwara Ryō's 1939 *Sono zenya* (*The Night Before*, Yamanaka's last script).

37. *NEHZDH*, p. 181, s.v. "Kawarazaki Chōjūrō."

Chapter 7

1. The period of the establishment of the Tokugawa government (especially the discussion of Toyotomi Hideyoshi and his heir Hideyori) was still considered sensitive.

2. The term of address is used in the Zen schools, while the Risshū, Shingon, and Shinshū schools will also pronounce it "wajō." The Tendai school uses the term *kashō*. This use of a clerical form of address links Rakugo to the Buddhist sermon.

3. For a review of the change of the audience's experience through the change of theater reform, see Rachel M. Payne, "Meiji Theatre Design: From Communal Participation to Refined Appreciation," Nissan Occasional Paper Series 34 (2003), Oxford University Nissan Institute of Japanese Studies, http://www.nissan.ox.ac.uk/nops/nops34.pdf (accessed June 15, 2005).

4. *The Actors' Analects* (*Yakusha Rongo*), edited, translated and with an introduction and notes by Charles J. Dunn and Bunzō Torigoe (New York: Columbia University Press, 1969), p. 23.

5. Ōzasa Yoshio, *Nihon gendai engeki-shi: Meiji Taishō-hen* (Tokyo: Hakusuisha, 1985), pp. 19–20. The petition by Zenzaemon was made in 1708.

6. Komiya Toyotaka, ed., *Japanese Music and Drama in the Meiji Era*, trans. Edward G. Seidensticker and Donald Keene (Tokyo: Toyo Bunko, 1956), p. 195.

7. Komiya, *Music and Drama*, p. 230. Danjūrō VII wore Nō robes in *Shakkyō* in 1813 and *Kanjinchō* in 1840. Ibid., p. 435. Later, Danjūrō was able to buy costumes from the Sekioka family when Nō lost its government patronage and hereditary stipends, and he received more or bought from the last *daimyō* of Tosa, Yamanouchi Yōdō (1827–1872) and other patrons. Ibid., p. 230.

8. Komiya, *Music and Drama*, pp. 78–79. The head of the Hōshō school was permitted a public performance in 1848. The only time ordinary people had the opportunity to see a Nō play was at such a public performance.

9. Kawatake Shigetoshi, *Nihon engeki zenshi* (Tokyo: Iwanami Shoten, 1959), p. 667.

10. Komiya, *Music and Drama*, p. 28. For a more detailed analysis, including direct quotes from original sources, see Kawatake, *Engeki zenshi*, pp. 757–759.

11. In March 1879, he supervised the annexation of the Ryūkyū Islands.

12. Komiya, *Music and Drama*, pp. 30–31, 190–191.

13. Kawatake, *Engeki zenshi*, p. 793. For translations, see Komiya, *Music and Drama*, p. 198 and Jean-Jacques Tschudin, "Danjūrō's *Katsureki-geki* (Realistic Theatre) and the Meiji 'Theatre Reform' Movement," *Japan Forum* 11, no. 1 (April 1991): 83–94, 84, http://0-search.epnet.com.library.lib.asu.edu:80/login.aspx?direct=true&db=aph&an=6695057 (accessed June 11, 2005). Danjūrō, on the other hand, paid him the compliment of using the term *katsureki* in 1884 at the opening of a new theater. Komiya, *Music and Drama*, p. 198.

14. For the *Kibi-daijin Shina monogatari* (*The Tale of the Minister Kibi in China*) in May 1875 at Morita's original theater, the Morita-za. Komiya, *Music and Drama*, pp. 196–197.

15. He was a former official of the shogunate sent abroad, journalist, and politician.

16. Komiya, *Music and Drama*, p. 236.

17. Komiya, *Music and Drama*, pp. 223–224. On October 17, 1886, the play was read by coauthor Kawajiri Hōgin before the Society for Theater Reform (Engeki Kairyōkai), organized in August 1886. Morita Kanya and Danjūrō were also present.

18. Nagita Tetsurō, *Tate* (Tokyo: San'ichi Shobō, 1974), p. 11.

19. Komiya, *Music and Drama*, p. 197, citing the *Zokuzoku kabuki nendaiki*, comments on Kawatake Mokuami's 1876 *Shigemori kangen* (*Shigemori's Admonition*), taken bodily from the *Heike monogatari* and "'filled with antique expressions which quite mystified the audience.'" See also Tschudin, "Danjūrō," p. 92.

20. Komiya, *Music and Drama*, p. 198.

21. "'I was in my thirteenth year when I hit upon the idea of reforming the theatre. At that time, I was studying the Tosa style of painting, examining the illustrated scrolls, and even trying my hand at painting. As a result, I started to wish I could play on stage according to what I was seeing, not only as regards the costumes but for everything else as well. I understood then that everything we were putting on stage was just a lie.'" Tschudin, "Danjūrō," p. 84, quoting Enomoto Torahiko, *Ōchi Koji to Danjūrō* (Tokyo: Kokkōsha, 1903), p. 17.

22. Komiya, *Music and Drama*, p. 189.

23. Joseph L. Anderson and Donald Richie, *The Japanese Film: Art and Industry* (New York: Random House, Inc., 1960 of 1959), p. 132.

24. *Iwanami Shoten Kojien*, 5th edition (Tokyo: Iwanami Shoten, 1998).

25. "Ema Tsutomu," available at *JMDb*, http://www.jmdb.ne.jp/person/p0106970.htm/1

941/bq002510.htm (accessed June 14, 2005).

26. "Torii Kotondo," *Hanga Gallery and Torii Gallery*, http://www.hanga.com/bijin-ga/kotondo/ (accessed June 14, 2005).

27. Peter B. High, *The Imperial Screen: Japanese Film Culture in the Fifteen Years' War*, 1931–1945 (Madison, WI: University of Wisconsin Press, 2003), pp. 271–275.

28. For an analysis of *The Battle of Kawanakajima*, see Darrell William Davis, *Picturing Japaneseness: Monumental Style, National Identity, Japanese Film* (New York: Columbia University Press, 1996), pp. 94–104.

Chapter 8

1. Directed by Futagawa Buntarō (1899–1966), who had previously worked with Thomas Kurihara. The film was severely censored, since the Law for the Maintenance of Public Order had been passed that year.

2. The camera is mounted high on a crane which is pulled backwards to follow the action.

3. The sense of excitement in this film's big fight scene is achieved with the choreography, the "rugby style" of massed staged combat. Makino played rugby in school.

4. *Tsukigata Hanpeita*, named for a fictional Restoration supporter created by Yukitomo Rifu for Sawada Shōjirō and the New National Theater, was first filmed in 1925 with Sawada in the title role and Kinugasa Teinosuke as director. It was subsequently filmed fifteen times between 1926 and 1961; Itō finally made the film with Ōkōchi in 1933. *JMDb*, www.jmdb.ne.jp (accessed June 20, 2005).

5. Fuji Masaharu, *Ōkōchi Denjirō* (Tokyo: Chūokōronsha, 1981), pp. 128–130.

6. Kawarazaki Kunitarō played a woman in Yamanaka Sadao's 1935 film version of Hasegawa Shin's *Machi no irezumimono* (*Village Tattooed Man* [Neighborhood Ex-con]), which the Progressive Troupe had been performing since 1932.

7. October 20, 1980, Tokyo.

8. 1910–1975. He played the short, stocky samurai Shichirōji in Kurosawa's *Seven Samurai.*

9. Interestingly, Kan'emon said nothing about modern, western stage techniques in which he was equally proficient.

10. Earlier, the stage had actually projected into the audience. This was abandoned in the Meiji period to provide for more seats.

11. The most notorious use of this technique occurs in the 1940 German film *Jud Süss* (*Jew Suess*), directed by Veidt Harlan. An analysis of the techniques exposed the film as anti-Semitic even though Veidt managed to swing a light sentence from American judges in 1945. See Marc Ferro, "Dissolves in Jud Süss," in his *Cinema and History*, translated by Naomi Greene (Detroit, Michigan: Wayne State University Press, 1988), pp. 139–141.

12. For a description of the twelve lifts in the main revolving stage of a theater in Kanazawa City, Ishikawa Prefecture, see "Hougaku Hall: The Stage," *Ishikawa Ongakudo*, http://www.ongakudo.pref.ishikawa.jp/english/set_japanese.html (accessed June 22, 2005).

13. See Erika Fischer-Lichte, "The Reception of Japanese Theatre by the European Avant-Garde (1900–1930)," in *Japanese Theatre and the International Stage*, Brill's Japanese Studies Library 12, edited by Stanca Scholz-Cionca and Samuel L. Leiter, 27–42 (Leiden, Boston, and Köln: Brill, 2001).

14. Review of *To the Distant Observer: Form and Meaning in Japanese Cinema*, by Noël Burch, *Cinema Journal* 21, no. 1 (Autumn 1981): 59–64.

15. Amada Gorō Guan, whose *Tōkai yūkyaku den: Ichimei Jirōcho monogatari* was published in 1884 by Tōkyō Yōron. A modern version of the text is included in Takahashi Satoshi, *Shimizu no Jirōchō to bakumatsu isshin: "Tōkai yūkyō den" no sekai"* (*Shimizu Jirōchō and the End of the Shogunate and the Restoration: The World of Tales of Chivalry*) (Tōkyō: Iwanami Shoten, 2003).

16. Cutting on action means editing together two shots taken from different angles or distance at a point where the movement is exactly the same. For example, in a first shot we see a woman extend her hand; in the next we see a close-up of her hand touching her partner's hand. It is used frequently in action movies, for example, where we see from the front a horse leap a fence and see it hit the ground from the rear.

17. Versions—sometimes more than one—were filmed in 1935–36, 1939, 1954, 1957, and 1959.

Chapter 9

1. The field of study begins with the work on Serbo-Croatian epic by Milman Parry (d. 1935) and his student Albert Bates Lord (1912–1991). The leader of the field now is John Miles Foley, director of the Center for Oral Tradition at the University of Missouri, Columbia, and founder of the journal *Oral Tradition.*

2. The best example of the approach is Paul Schrader, "Yakuza Eiga: A Primer," *Film Comment* 10, no. 1 (February 1974): 8–17.

3. For a basic introduction, see Albert Bates Lord, *The Singer of Tales* (Cambridge: Harvard University Press, 1960).

4. Mark W. Edwards, "Homer and Oral Tradition: The Type Scene," *Oral Tradition* 7, no. 2 (October 1992): 286. Some, like Edwards, distinguish between type scene and theme; others do not. Ibid., pp. 285–287, for a review. See also John Miles Foley, *Traditional Oral Epic: The "Odyssey," "Beowulf," and the Serbo-Croatian Return Song* (Berkeley, Los Angeles, Oxford: University of California Press, 1990), pp. 331–335.

5. See, for example, Edwards, "Homer and Oral Tradition," pp. 284–330.

6. In truncated form, they often appear as type scenes. For example, *She Wore a Yellow Ribbon* begins with a scene of a pony express rider bringing the news of Custer's defeat at the Little Big Horn (1876): the rider gallops in, transfers pouch and self to another horse, and rides off again. The story of the pony express could be a narrative of its own. In this case, it functions as a type scene in a cavalry narrative.

7. In oral tradition studies, the narrative is broken down into scene, formula, and motif.

8. See John Miles Foley, *Immanent Art: From Structure to Meaning in Traditional Oral Epic* (Bloomington and Indianapolis: Indiana University Press, 1991). Foley's concept of "traditional referentiality" means that the use of a traditional unit "entails the invoking of a context that is enormously larger and more echoic than the text or work itself, that brings the lifeblood of generations of poems and performances to the individual performance or text." Ibid., p. 7. In other words, a single performance (even a written one) is not the whole text but merely a version that, even in truncated form, invokes the entire text; for example, any telling of the story of Robin Hood and Friar Tuck invokes the entire Robin Hood cycle of stories.

9. "It's My Party," lyrics by Lesley Gore, 1963.

10. This technique has been noted by other critics who were not aware of oral tradition methodologies and their diction.

11. Poor Maureen O'Hara spent her career in the Western getting spanked; her punishment, no doubt, for breaking the gender rules as a female pirate!

12. The type scene brilliantly lampooned in another film, *The Secret Life of Walter Mitty* (Norman C. McLeod, 1947).

13. *Der letzte Mann* (F.W. Murnau, 1924).

14. For a summary, see Stephen Prince, *The Warrior's Camera: The Cinema of Akira Kurosawa*, revised and expanded edition (Princeton, New Jersey: Princeton University Press, 1999 [1991]), pp. 12–18.

15. Prince, *Warrior's Camera*, p. 13.

16. We also recognize it when he himself is counseled by an elderly and high-ranking lady, who, disturbed by the amount of blood-letting, tells him gently that really good blades are kept in their scabbards. The scene here may be ironic; nevertheless, the narrative purpose is clear.

17. In *Seven Samurai*, the god is Kanbei: to him is offered rice; to him is offered the gesture of worshipping a bodhisattva (in Buddhism, the supernatural being working for the salvation of others in this world) as the peasants press palm to palm when he accepts their rice. With both Ford and Kurosawa, god is the father. But that is another paper.

18. In Kabuki and Bunraku, again, the seduction can take place between a princess and a monk, as in *Narukami Fudō Kitayama zakura* (*Narukami*; 1742 by Tsuuchi Hanjurō et al.) but more usually it is occurs between commoners or low-ranking samurai (as in Chikamatsu's 1717 *Yari no Gonza kasane katahira* or *Gonza the Spearman*).

19. A commoner may murder his father-in-law (*Natsu matsuri Naniwa kagami* [*Summer Festival: Mirror of Osaka*], 1745 by Namiki Sōsuke et al.) or the wife of his master (Chikamatsu's 1721 *Onna goroshi no abura jigoku* or *Woman Killer and the Hell of Oil*); a high-ranking woman may try to kill a young lord (*Meiboku Sendai hagi*).

20. For a list of fourteen narrative subgenres in Kōdan in the 1890s, see Kurata Yoshihiro, *Meiji Taishō no minshū goraku*, Iwanami Shinsho 114 (Tokyo: Iwanami Shoten, 1980), p. 132. In Kabuki and Bunraku, the road-to-death scene usually appears in the love-suicide play about commoners strapped for money, such as Chikamatsu Monzaemon's 1703 *Sonezaki shinjū* (*The Love Suicides at Sonezaki*); yet, in the end-of-the-shogunate piece, the road to death can be the narrative itself and the chief protagonist a sword for hire, as in *The Great Bodhisattva Pass*.

21. See S.A. Thornton, "*Kōnodai senki*: Narrative and Warrior Ideology in Sixteenth-Century Japan." *Oral Tradition* 15 (2000): 306–77. Not every account of a battle is an epic. See chapter 11.

22. The plays are *Ataka* by Kanze Nobumitsu Kojirō (1435–1516) and the 1840 Kabuki dance piece *Kanjinchō* (*The Subscription Roll*), whose text was written by Namiki Gohei III. I make a distinction between what he himself has directed and what he has written or helped write for others.

Chapter 10

1. See, for example, Sugimoto Keizaburō, Kami Hiroshi, Kajihara Masaaki, Fukuda Akira, et al., "Gunki monogatari jiten," *Kokubungaku kaishaku to kanshō* 28, no. 4 (March 1963): 80–126. It lists and discusses fully and individ-

ually seven *gunki monogatari* through the *Taiheiki*, and lumps together the production of the next two hundred years in a four-page review before discussing the *Gikeiki* (*Chronicle of Yoshitsune*) and *Soga monogatari*. Even Tomikura Tokujirō admits that the c. 1393 *Meitokuki* (which he edited) is not considered to rank with either the *Heike monogatari* or the *Taiheiki*. See his "Kaimon" in *Meitokuki*, Iwanami bunko 2899–2900 (Tokyo: Iwanami Shoten, 1941), p. 180. Kajihara states that the *Meitokuki* does not have the scale of the other two. Kajihara Masaaki, "Ikusa monogatari no henbō: 'Yūki senjō monogatari' no keisei o megutte," *Bungaku* 38, no. 8 (August 1970): 41–42. Ichiko Teiji states explicitly that the *Meitokuki*, *Kakitsuki*, *Ōninki*, and *Yūki* are not to be ranked with the *Heike* or the *Taiheiki*. See his article on the *gunki monogatari* in *Zusetsu Nihon bunkashi taikei 7: Muromachi jidai* (Tokyo: Shogakukan, 1957), p. 232.

2. For example, Kajihara Masaaki (article cited above) and Kami Hiroshi ("'Ōtō monogatari' shoron: Muromachi gunki kenkyū no tegakari," *Bungaku* 38, no. 8 (August 1975).

3. Fukuda Akira, Kadokawa Gen'yoshi, etc.

4. Kajihara, "Chūsei gōki no shogunki," in "Gunki monogatari jiten," p. 17, and Kami Hiroshi, *Gunsho kaimon* dai 14 kan (Tokyo: Kabushiki Kaisha Zoku Gunsho Ruijū Kanseikai, 1960), pp. 32–34 (*Sasago/Nakao*) and 52–53 (*Kōnodai*). *Yūki senjō monogatari* (written after 1488, the variant of a text composed soon after 1455) and *Sasago ochi no sōshi* and *Nakao ochi no sōshi* (presumed 1543) in Hanawa Hokinoichi, *Gunsho ruijū* dai 20 shū (Tokyo: Kabushiki Kaisha Zoku Gunsho Ruijū Kanseikai, 1940), vol. 383 and dai 21 shū, vol. 386; *Ōtō monogatari* (written soon after 1400) and *Kōnodai senki* (1575) in Hanawa Hokinoichi, *Zoku gunsho ruijū* dai 21 shū ge (Tokyo: Kabushiki Kaisha Zoku Gunsho Ruijū Kanseikai, 1940), vols. 619 and 613; and *Meitokuki* (1393), ed. by Tomikura Tokujirō, Iwanami bunko 2899–2900 (Tokyo: Iwanami Shoten, 1941).

5. Kami, "'Ōtō,'" pp. 73 and 76. Kajihara, "'Yūki,'" pp. 49–53. Kajihara uses the term, but not as a category, preferring a different term for each kind of religious story discussed.

6. *Heike monogatari*, I.6.

7. Ibid., IV.12, describing the death of Minamoto Yorimasa or IX.14, describing the death of Tadanori. See also IX.19, X.5, X.10–12, XI.9, XI.18, and Epilogue.5 describing executions and other deaths.

8. *Heike monogatari*, II.12 (the fate of Zenkōji), II.13 (the squabbling on Mt. Hiei), IV.9 (fate of Miidera), IV.15 (of Kōfukuji). Imperial edicts accuse Kiyomori of destroying both Buddha's Law and the Imperial Law. Ibid., IV.7, IV.8, V.10, and VII.10.

9. *Heike monogatari*, X.5.

10. *Ōtō*, p. 371.

11. *Heike monogatari*, IX.6.

12. *Heike monogatari*, "Epilogue" (five chapters).

13. Mizuhara Hajime, "Tomoe densetsu-setsuwa," *Kokugungaku kaishaku to kanshō* 32, no. 8 (July 1937): 202–204.

14. Fukuda Akira, *Chūsei katarimono bungei: sono keifu to tenkai* (Tokyo: Miyai Shoten, 1981), pp. 54–60.

15. *Heike monogatari*, Epilogue.5.

16. *Heike monogatari*, II.13.

17. *Heike monogatari*, XII.11 and 14.

18. See note 5.

19. See Tomikura Tokujirō, "Gunki monogatari no honshitsu," in *Gunki monogatari no bodai to kanryō (tokushū)*: *Kokubungaku kaishaku to kanshō* 28, no. 4 (March 1963):10; Takagi Ichinosuke, "Gunki monogatari," *Nihon bungakushi jiten*, ed. Fujimura Tsukuru and Nishio Minoru (Tokyo: Nihon Hyōron Shinsha, 1960), p. 235; and Takagi Takeshi, "Senki monogatari," in *Nihon bungaku daijiten* vol. 4 (Tokyo: Shinchōsha, 1936), p. 194.

20. This three-part structure is taken from Kami, "'Ōtō,'" p. 73.

21. Sekiyama Kazuo, *Sekkyō no rekishi*, Iwanami shinsho 64 (Tokyo: Iwanami Shoten, 1978), pp. 24–25.

22. Sekiyama, *Sekkyō*, p. 69, citing the *Hossokushū*, collected in the *Tendaishū zensho*.

23. For the development of the epic, see Butler, Kenneth Dean, "The Textual Evolution of the Heike monogatari," *Harvard Journal of Asiatic Studies* 26 (1966): 5–51.

24. *Heike monogatari*, I.12, I.13, II.4, and IV.1. The founder was Jōken (1126–1203), seventh son of Shinzei, whose name also appears in I.12, III.15, and III.18.

25. See *Heike monogatari*, Epilogue.5, for the sins of Kiyomori and the sins paid for by his descendants.

26. *Heike monogatari*, I.1. Such are also the cases of Yamana Ujikiyo in the *Meitokuki*, of Ogasawara Nagahide in the *Ōtō*, and Ashikaga Mochiuji in the *Yūki*, all of whose actions precipitate the destructions of their families.

27. *Heike monogatari*, VI.4.

28. *Heike monogatari*, I.8, for example.

29. *Heike monogatari*, VI.7.

30. Hori Ichiro, "The Appearance of Self-Consciousness in Japanese Religion and Its Historical Transformations," in *The Japanese Mind: Essentials of Japanese Philosophy and Culture*, ed. Charles A. Moore (Honolulu: University of Hawaii Press, 1967), p. 210.

31. The *Meitokuki* contains one reference to a Zen priest and the *Nakao ochi no sōshi* describes the chanting of the invocation of the title of the

Lotus Sutra (*daimoku*) ten times at death.

32. As in the *Ōtō*.

33. The characters for this word are also read *shuraba*, which means both *shurajō* and the battle or fight scene in Kōdan and theater.

34. *Heike monogatari*, Epilogue.4.

35. *Heike monogatari*, XI.9.

36. *Heike monogatari*, IX.18 and 19.

37. *Heike monogatari*, IX.16.

38. *Heike monogatari*, XII.9.

39. *Heike monogatari*, Epilogue.1.

40. This is a pattern from Mt. Kōya propaganda traditions. It is also seen in the *Ōtō* and the *Yūki*.

41. *Yūki*, p. 734.

42. Hyōdō Hiromi, "Kakuichi-bon *Heike monogatari* no denshō o megutte: Muromachi ōken to geinō," in *Heike biwa: katari to ongaku*, ed. Kamisangō Yūkō (Tokyo: Hitsuji Shōbō, 1993), pp. 62–63.

43. Hyōdō Hiromi, "*The Tale of the Heike* as Warrior Mythology: The Fictional Basis of Genji Political Power," an unpublished paper presented at the 1977 Cornell Symposium in Early Japan Studies: Presenting Tales of the Heike in Medieval Japan.

44. Hyōdō, "Kakuichi-bon," *Heike monogatari*, pp. 64–65.

45. Hyōdō, "Kakuichi-bon," *Heike monogatari*, pp. 65, 77.

46. Kyōko Motomochi Nakamura, trans. and ed., *Miraculous Stories from the Japanese Buddhist Tradition: The "Nihon Ryōiki of the Monk Kyōkai,"* Harvard Yenching Institute Monograph Series 20 (Cambridge: Harvard University Press, 1973), p. 160.

47. *Ōtō monogatari*, in *Zoku gunsho ruijū* 21/2, ed. Hanawa Hokinoichi (Tokyo: Zoku Gunsho Ruijū Kanseikai, 1933; first edition 1924), pp. 355–376. For a translation of the section, see Sybil Thornton, "Epic and Religious Propaganda from the Ippen School of Pure Land Buddhism," in *Religions of Japan in Practice*, ed. George J. Tanabe, Jr. (Princeton, New Jersey: Princeton University Press, 1999), pp. 185–192.

48. *Kōnodai senki*, in *Zoku gunsho ruijū* 21/2, ed. Hanawa Hokinoichi (Tokyo: Zoku Gunsho Ruijū Kanseikai, 1977), pp. 165–176.

49. Helen Craig McCullough, trans., *Yoshitsune: A Fifteenth-Century Japanese Chronicle* (Stanford: Stanford University Press, 1966), p. 290. For the Japanese text, see Okami Masao, ed., *Gikeiki*, Nihon koten bungaku taikei 37 (Tokyo: Iwanami Shoten, 1959), p. 383.

50. McCullough, *Yoshitsune*, pp. 205–206.

51. Murdoch, James, *A History of Japan*, 3 vols. (Yokohama: Asiatic Society of Japan; London: K. Paul, Trübner, 1910–1949).

52. Taira Munemori (1147–1185), second son of Kiyomori and head of the Taira when, in 1183 after a disastrous defeat, they retreated from Kyoto to escape an advancing Minamoto army.

53. *Kōnodai*, pp. 453–455. Bōsō Sōshō Kankōkai, ed., *Oyumi gosho-sama onuchiji ikusa monogatari*, in Bōsō sōsho vol. 1 (Chiba, Japan: Bōsō Sōsho Kankōkai, 1912), p. 193.

54. *Kōnodai*, pp. 463–501.

55. Tomikura Tokujirō, ed., *Meitokuki*, Iwanami bunko 2899–2900 (Tokyo: Iwanami Shoten, 1941), p. 89.

Chapter 11

1. For "oral-derived," see John Miles Foley, *Traditional Oral Epic: The "Odyssey," "Beowulf," and the Serbo-Croatian Return Song* (Berkeley, Los Angeles, Oxford: University of California Press, 1990), pp. 5–10.

2. Extreme examples are Kenneth Dean Butler, "The Textual Evolution of the *Heike monogatari*," *Harvard Journal of Asiatic Studies* 26 (1966): 5–51 and Helen McCollough's abridgement in her translation of the *Taiheiki* on the basis of those principles. Analysis of the process of developing a *gunki monogatari*, for example, presumes that one starts out with a purely historical or documentary account to which legends or *setsuwa* are added. See Butler; Kajihara Masaaki, "Ikusa monogatari no henbō: 'Yūki senjō monogatari' no keisei o megutte," *Bungaku* 38, no. 8 (August 1970): 41–53; and Kanai Kiyomitsu, "Zenkōji no katarimono," in *Jishū bungei kenkyū* (Tokyo: Fukan Shobō), pp. 189–190.

3. For example, Sugimoto Keizaburō, "Heike monogatari ni okeru shi no shosō," in *Gunki monogatari no sekai* (Tokyo: Meichō Kankōkai, 1985): 82–101; Fukuda Akira, *Chūsei katarimono bungei: sono keifu to tenkai* (Tokyo: Miyai Shoten, 1981); and Kami Hiroshi, "*Kōnodai senki* shōkō," *Kōnan kokubun* 24 (1977): 93–94 for the work of Usuda, Morogi, and Fukuda.

4. See Gorai Shigeru, *Kōya hijiri no yūraiki*, published in installments in *Seiai* (Kōyasan Shuppansha) from January 1957 to July 1959. See December 1957 for samurai including Kumagai Naozane at Mt. Kōya, March 1958 for Rengedani *hijiri*, April 1958 for Kurodani Ren'amidabutsu, July and August 1958 for Kayadō *hijiri*, and April 1959 for Kōya *hijiri* and *jishū*.

5. Fukuda Akira, *Gunki monogatari to minkan denshō* (Tokyo: Iwasaki Bijitsusha, 1972), p. 217.

6. "Yashima katari no kenkyū," in *Origuchi Shinobu zenshū* vol. 17 (Tokyo: Chūōkōronsha, 1956), p. 209.

7. *Heike monogatari*, 2 vols., Iwanami

bunko 413–415 (Tokyo: Iwanami Shoten, 1939, 12th reprint of 1929). For a translation of the section, see "The Death of Atsumori," in *The Tale of the Heike*, translated by Hiroshi Kitagawa and Bruce T. Tsuchida, with a foreword by Edward Seidensticker (Tokyo: University of Tokyo Press, 1975), II:561–563.

8. *Meitokuki*, Iwanami bunko 2899–2900, ed. Tomikura Tokujirō (Tokyo: Iwanami Shoten, 1941). For a translation of the section (in "Yamana Kojirō uchijini su, ibid., pp. 94–97"), see Sybil Thornton, "From Warrior to Holy Man," *Parabola* 12, no. 1 (Spring 1987):43–49.

9. *Ōtō monogatari*, in *Zoku gunsho ruijū* 21/2, ed. Hanawa Hokiichi (Tokyo: Zoku Gunsho Ruijū Kanseikai, 1933, first edition 1924), pp. 355–376. For a translation of the section, see Sybil Thornton, "Epic and Religious Propaganda from the Ippen School of Pure Land Buddhism," in *Religions of Japan in Practice*, ed. George J. Tanabe, Jr. (Princeton, New Jersey: Princeton University Press, 1999), pp. 185–192.

10. *Yūki senjō monogatari*, in *Gunsho ruijū* 20, Hanawa Hokiichi (Tokyo: Zoku Gunsho Ruijū Kanseikai, 1940), pp. 712–734.

11. *Kōnodai kōki*, in *Zoku gunsho ruijū* 21/2, ed. Hanawa Hokiichi (Tokyo: Zoku Gunsho Ruijū Kanseikai, 1940), pp. 176–183.

12. See Gorai, Kōya *hijiri*, December 1957, and Kanai, *Jishū bungei kenkyū*, p. 129.

13. Kami Hiroshi, "'Ōtō monogatari' shoron: Muromachi gunki kenkyū no tegakari (gunkimono)," *Bungaku* 38, no. 8 (August 1975), pp. 74–75, and Kanai, *Jishū bungei kenkyū*, pp. 129, 189–190.

14. Mizuhara Hajime, "Geinō gunki zakkan: *Yūki senjō monogatari* nado kara," *Gunki to katarimono* 11 (October 1974): 3.

15. See Kadokawa Gen'yoshi, "Meitokuki no seiritsu," *Dentō bungaku kenkyuū* 2, no. 5 (April 1962): 1–13 and Ōshima Tatehiko, "Gunkimono," *Kokubungaku kaishaku to kanshō* 26, no. 5 (April 1961): 92–96.

16. See Sybil Thornton, "The Propaganda Traditions of the Yugyō ha: The Campaign to Establish the Jishū as an Independent School of Japanese Buddhism (1300–1700)," Ph.D. dissertation (University of Cambridge, 1990).

17. See Kajihara Masaaki, "'Ikusa monogatari' no henbō: 'Yūki senjō monogatari' no keisei o megutte," *Bungaku* 38, no. 8 (August 1970): 41–53.

18. Kami, "*Kōnodai senki* shokō," pp. 83–97.

19. See James Foard, "Prefiguration and Narrative in Medieval Hagiography: *The Ippen hijiri-e*," in *Flowing Traces: Buddhism in the Literary and Visual Arts of Japan*, ed. James H. Sanford, William R. LaFleur, and Masatoshi Nagatomi (Princeton: Princeton University Press, 1992), 86–92, citing John J. White, *Mythology in the Modern Novel: A Study of Prefigurative Techniques* (Princeton: Princeton University Press, 1971).

20. See Yoshiaki Shimizu, "Multiple Commemorations: The Vegetable Nehan," in *Flowing Traces: Buddhism in the Literary and Visual Arts of Japan*, ed. James H. Sanford, William R. LaFleur, and Masatoshi Nagatomi (Princeton: Princeton University Press, 1992), pp. 206–207, citing Eugene Vance, "Roland and the Poetics of Memory," in *Textual Strategies*, ed. Josué Harari (Ithaca: Cornell University, Press, 1979), pp. 374–375.

21. William R. LaFleur, "The Death and 'Lives' of the Poet-Monk Saigyō: The Genesis of a Buddhist Sacred Biography," in *The Biographical Process: Studies in the History and Psychology of Religion*, ed. Frank E. Reynolds and Donald Capps (The Hague. Mouton, 1976), pp. 343–361.

22. See, for example, Mark W. Edwards, "Homer and Oral Tradition: The Type-Scene," *Oral Tradition* 7, no. 2 (October 1992): 284–330.

23. Discussion on Kabuki taken from James R. Brandon, trans., *Kabuki: Five Classic Plays* (Cambridge: Harvard University Press, 1975).

24. Kajihara, "'Ikusa,'" p. 41.

25. Yamamoto Kichizō, "'Kuchigatari' no ron (jō) Goze uta no baai," part 1, *Bungaku* 44, no. 10 (October 1976): 1364–1386 and "Kuchigatari no ron (ge) Goze uta no baai," part 3, *Bungaku* 45, no. 1 (January 1977): 89–107. *Goze* were blind, itinerant females who played the three-stringed samisen and performed a variety of folk and religious songs.

26. Konishi has done some work on formulae in the *Manyōshū*. See Konishi, Jin'ichi, *A History of Japanese Literature*, Volume 1, *The Archaic and Ancient Ages*, tr. Aileen Gatten and Nicholas Teele, ed. Earl Miner (Princeton: Princeton University Press, 1984).

27. I base this on the fact that texts with high formulaic density are not included in the list of *gunki monogatari*, which tend to be praised for their literary quality. Kajihara Masaaki also notes the bias in favor of literary texts or *yomi-mono*. "'Ikusa,'" p. 41.

28. I suspect that the high incidence of formulaic diction in the *Yūki* and the *Kōnodai kōki* caused researchers to classify them as "performing arts *gunki*" or "fiction" and thereby to discredit them as reliable documentation of religious practice. Mizuhara, "Geinō gunki," and Kami, "*Kōnodai senki* shokō."

29. A history produced by the Kamakura shogunate which includes eighty-seven years' worth of documents from 1180 as well as legendary material.

30. Kameyama Sumio, "Chūsei shoki tōkoku

bushi no seikatsu ishiki to seishin no saikōsai: Kumagai Naozane o chūshin ni," *Tōkyō nōkō daigaku ippan kyōikubu kiyō* 27 (March 31, 1991): 37, 43.

31. Shida Itaru, "Naozane no shojō—Tsunemori no henpō: *Heike monogatari* ni okeru Kumagai Rensei no katari o megutte," *Kokugo kokubun* 52, no. 6 (June 1983): 34–35.

32. Sugimoto Keizaburō, Kami Hiroshi, Kajihara Masaaki, Fukuda Akira, et al, "Gunki monogatari jiten," *Kokubungaku kaishaku to kanshō* 28, no. 4 (1963): 80–126.

33. Butler, p. 36.

34. In the Kakuichi *Heike*, Atsumori refuses to reveal his identity. In the Shibu and the Enkyō texts, Atsumori identifies himself after Naozane promises to perform services for him. In the Kakuichi text, raillery and badinage (*kyō gen kigo*) are connected with praising Buddhism and teaching people (*sanbutsujo*). In the Shibu text, Naozane shaves his head and goes to Mt. Koya. Shida, "Naozane," pp. 27–19.

35. John Miles Foley, *Immanent Art: From Structure to Meaning in Traditional Oral Epic* (Bloomington and Indianapolis: Indiana University Press, 1991), pp. 9–10.

36. *Yūki senjō monogatari*, pp. 728–729.

37. "*Kōnodai senki* shokō," p. 180.

38. *Meitokuki*, pp. 95–96. The passage goes on to relate that the old *bushi* killed Kojirō and found out who he was; the passage ends with praise of Kojirō, the only one of Ujikiyo's forty or so children to die with him.

39. Delaying the mention of Naozane and Atsumori plays with the tradition: the audience expects to hear the direct parallel; tension is present until the audience gets what it wants.

40. One that I find taking place in later Nō plays, such as *Benkei in the Boat*.

41. This is the chapel of the Karukaya Dōshin story.

42. In the *Ashikaga jiranki*, partially derived from the *Yūki*, the name given is Kakizaki Kojirō. He has completely different names in the *Kamakuradono monogatari*, the immediate precursor and in the *Uesugi Norizane-ki*. Kajihara, "'Ikusa,'" p. 44.

43. *Kōnodai senki*, in *Zoku gunsho ruijū* 21/2, ed. Hanawa Hokinoichi (Tokyo: Zoku Gunsho Ruijū Kanseikai), pp. 165–176. For a translation and study, see S.A. Thornton, "*Kōnodai senki*: Traditional Narrative and Warrior Ideology in Sixteenth-Century Japan," *Oral Tradition* 15, no. 2 (2000): 306–376.

44. Kami, "*Kōnodai senki*," pp. 93–94: Yoshitsune cycle, *Morokado monogatari* (same Princess Jōruri and Rensei), *Shimizu kanja monogatari* (Daihime), etc.

45. Kami, "Yūki," p. 94.

46. Many people took the name Rensei/Renshō on entering religious life. There were besides Naozane Utsunomiya Saburō Yoritsuna Jisshinbō Rensei and the founder of the temple Kōmyōji in Kyoto, Hara Shigeyuki nyūdo Rensei. We might also look to the line of Kōya *hijiri* apparently called Ren'amidabutsu established at the Renge valley by Myōhen (Yanagita Kunio, "Ario to Shunkan sozū," *Bungaku*, January 1940, cited by Kanai Kiyomitsu, *Jishū bungei kenkyū* [Tokyo: Kazama Shobō, 1967], p. 16), uncle of Seikaku of the Agui school of preaching, which had a major role in the production of the *Heike monogatari* (Butler, pp. 35–36 for the Hiramatsuke text, produced by 1242), who introduced Naozane to Hōnen (Miyazaki Fumiko, "Religious Life of the Kamakura Bushi: Kumagai Naozane and his Descendants," *Monumenta Nipponica* 47, no. 4 [1992], p. 458, citing Harper H. Coates and Ryugaku Ishizuka, *Honen the Buddhist Saint: His Life and Teaching* [New York and London: Garland, 1981 reprint], p. 488).

47. Kami, "*Kōnodai senki* shokō," p. 88, describing the death of Ashikaga Yoshiaki, is based on that of the death of Benkei in the *Gikeiki*, and the horse motif (Yoshiaki's horse with empty saddle runs home) is compared with the horse Tayūkuro by recounting an alternate version of that in the *Heike monogatari* XI. 3, "Death of Tsuginobu."

48. *Ōtō monogatari*, in *Zoku gunsho ruijū* 21/2, ed. Hanawa Hokinoichi (Tokyo: Zoku Gunsho Ruijū Kanseikai, 1933, first edition 1924), pp. 355–376. For a translation of the section, see Sybil Thornton, "Epic and Religious Propaganda from the Ippen School of Pure Land Buddhism," in *Religions of Japan in Practice*, ed. George J. Tanabe, Jr. (Princeton, New Jersey: Princeton University Press, 1999), pp. 185–192.

49. *Yūki*, p. 728.

50. *Heike monogatari*, book 9, chapter 10, II:542–546.

51. *Genpei jōsuiki*, volume 36 (2004), http://etext.virginia.edu/etcbin/ot2www-japanese?specfile=/web/data/japanese/search/japanese.o2w&act=surround&lang=en&offset=6544720&id=AnoGpsj&query=%B7%A7%C3%AB%C4 %BE%BC%C2 (accessed August 4, 2005).

52. A chaplain from the Ippen (1139–1189) school of Pure Land Buddhism.

53. *Taiheiki*, I:201. Shinkyō was the disciple of Ippen and second founder of the Jishū, or Time Sect, of Pure Land Buddhism. To receive the ten *nenbutsu* means to repeat the *nenbutsu* after a monk or nun ten times.

Chapter 12

1. Michael Atkinson, "Codes Unknown: In

a Revisionist Samurai Epic, Tough Financial Realities Trump the Warrior Myth of Honor," a review of *Tasogare Seibei,* directed by Yamada Yōji, *The Village Voice* (April 20, 2004), http://www.villagevoice.com/film/0416,atkinson,52812,20.html (accessed July 26, 2006).

2. Nicholas Rucka, review of *Tasogare Seibei,* directed by Yamada Yōji, *Midnight Eye,* March 10, 2004, http://www.midnighteye.com/reviews/twilsamu.shtml (accessed July 26, 2006).

3. "Enjoy Kabuki & Bunraku in English," *Iyafon gaido,* http://www.eg-gm.jp/eg/e_joho/e_kb_dic/bun_eep.htm (accessed July 28, 2006). The play was presented at the Kabuki-za Theater March 3–27, 2006.

4. Even a single actor, such as John Wayne or Bruce Willis, can code an entire narrative through the audience's experience of seeing an actor build a career through specific kinds of roles in specific genres. As for coding an entire narrative, the casting of Sanada Hiroyuki means that the film is going to be more than a tale of the everyday trials and tribulations of a scruffy clerk: this is the narrative of a master swordsman.

5. Shōriya Aragorō, "Arashi Kitsusaburō," *Kabuki 21* (Sept. 9, 1999–July 31, 2006), http://www.kabuki21.com/kitsusaburo1.php (accessed August 3, 2006). It played at the National Theatre in Tokyo February 6–18, 2006. "Enjoy Kabuki & Bunraku," *Iyafonu gaido,* http://www.eg-gm.jp/eg/e_joho/e_kb_dic/bun_eep.htm (accessed July 29, 2006).

6. Nakayama Takeshi, review of *The Twilight Samurai, Asahi Shinbun,* translated by Fumie Nakamurai, cited in Minnie Chi, "Japan's 'The Twilight Samurai' Nominated for Best Foreign Language Film," *Asia Pacific Arts,* Jan. 23, 2004, UCLA Asia Institute, http://www.asiaarts.ucla.edu/article.asp?parentid=6861 (accessed August 1, 2006).

7. See his Web site at *Tanaka Min,* 2003, http://www.min-tanaka.com/ (accessed August 1, 2006).

8. I do have to mention one thing: in this film, in the scene where she is listening to Seibei's proposal, Tomoe does not sit with her feet under her; she is balanced on her toes and leaning forward. I have never seen this in a period film before. Again, in *The Hidden Blade,* the hero's sister is first kneeling with her posterior on the floor and between her feet; the feet should be tucked under. I am not certain what is going on; perhaps the position indicates her childishness, perhaps modern Japanese women are not comfortable in the formal position. Baisho Chieko, who played the hero's mother, seemed to have no trouble.

9. "Annual Events Calendar," 2006, Shōnai, http://shonai.wikispaces.com/Annual+Events+Calendar (accessed August 8, 2006).

10. For descriptions of full Japanese funeral services, see "Japanese Funeral Style 1," http://www.osoushiki-plaza.com/eng/eng1.html (accessed September 22, 2006), and Billy Hammond, "Japanese Funeral Customs," 2001, A.E.L.S., Inc. (TanuTech), http://tanutech.com/japan/jfunerals.html (accessed September 22, 2006).

11. For nostalgia in Japan in the nineties, see Iwabuchi, Koichi, "Nostalgia for a (Different) Asian Modernity: Media Consumption of 'Asia' in Japan," *positions: east asia cultures critique* 10, no. 3 (2002): 547–573, http://muse.jhu.edu.ezproxy1.lib.asu.edu/journals/positions/v010/10.3iwabuchi.html#endnoteposition:3 (accessed August 14, 2006).

12. Roland Barthes, *Mythologies,* selected and translated from the French by Annette Lavers (New York: Hilland Wang, 1972).

13. The entire studio set, props, and costumes have been donated to a museum in the city. See The Tokyo Chamber of Commerce and Industry, "Katsushika Shibamata Tora-san Museum," A Guide to Technical Visits and Industrial Museums in Tokyo, 2006, http://www.tokyo-cci.or.jp/sangyokanko/english/055.html (accessed September 12, 2006).

Filmography

Films are listed under both their original title and their translated title.

Abare Goemon (*Rise Against the Sword*, aka *Wild Goemon*). Inagaki Hiroshi, dir. 1966. Tōhō.

The Abe Clan (*Abe ichizoku*). Kumagai Hisatora, dir. 1938. Tōhō Eiga, Tokyo Studio, and Zenshinza.

Abe ichizoku (*The Abe Clan*). Kumagai Hisatora, dir. 1938. Tōhō Eiga, Tokyo Studio, and Zenshinza.

An Actor's Revenge (*Yukinojō henge*). Ichikawa Kon, dir. 1963. Daiei, Kyoto Studio.

Akahige (*Red Beard*). Kurosawa Akira, dir. 1965. Tōhō/Kurosawa Productions.

Akutō (*Scoundrel*). Kaneto Shindō, dir. 1965. Tōkyō Eiga and Kindai Eiga Kyōkai.

The Ambitious (*Bakumatsu*). Itō Daisuke, dir. 1970. Nakamura Productions.

Ambush at Blood Pass (*Machibuse*). Inagaki Hiroshi, dir. 1970. Mifune Productions.

Andrei Ryublov, aka *The Passion According to Saint Andrew*, aka *Andrei Roublev*. Andrei Tarkovsky, dir. 1969. Mosfilm.

Ansatsu (*Assassination*). Shinoda Masahiro, dir. 1964. Shōchiku, Kyoto Studio.

Assassination (*Ansatsu*) Shinoda Masahiro, dir. 1964. Shōchiku, Kyoto Studio.

Bakuchiuchi: sōchō tobaku (*The Gambler: The Game to Be Chairman*). Yamashita Kōsoku, dir. 1968. Tōei, Kyoto Studio.

Bakumatsu (*The Ambitious*, aka *The Restoration of Meiji*). Itō Daisuke, dir. 1970. Nakamura Productions.

Ballet. Frederick Wiseman, dir. 1995.

Band of Assassins (*Shinobi no mono*). Yamamoto Satsuo, dir. 1962. Daiei, Kyoto Studio.

The Battle of Kawanakajima (*Kawanakajima kassen*). Kinugasa Teinosuke, dir. 1941. Tōhō Eiga, Kyoto Studio.

Beheading Place (*Kubi no za*). Makino Masahiro, dir. 1929. Makino Production, Omuro Studio.

The Best Years of Our Lives. William Wyler, dir. 1946. Samuel Goldwyn Company.

The Black Swan. Henry King, dir. 1942. Twentieth Century Fox.

Bloody Spear at Mount Fuji (*Chiyari Fuji*). Uchida Tomu, dir. 1955. Tōei, Kyoto Studio.

Capricious Young Man (*Sengoku kitan: Kimagure kanja*). Itami Mansaku, dir. 1936. Chiezō Productions.

Chikamatsu monogatari (*A Story from Chikamatsu*). Mizoguchi Kenji, dir. 1954. Daiei, Kyoto Studios.

Chikamatsu Monzaemon Yari no Gonza (*Gonza the Spearman*). Shinoda Masahiro, dir. 1986. Hyōgensha and Shōchiku.

Chiyari Fuji (*Bloody Spear at Mount Fuji*). Uchida Tomu, dir. 1955. Tōei, Kyoto Studios.

Chōkon (*Long-Standing Hatred*). Itō Daisuke, dir. 1926. Nikkatsu, Daishōgun Studio.

Chūji tabi nikki (*A Journal of Chūji's Travels*). Three parts. Itō Daisuke, dir. 1927–1928. Nikkatsu, Daishōgun Studio.

Chūshingura: hana no maki; yuki no maki (*Chushingura*). Inagaki Hiroshi, dir. 1962. Tōhō.

Chushingura, aka *The 47 Ronin*; *The 47 Samurai*; *Chushingura: 47 Samurai*; and *The Loyal 47 Ronin* (*Chūshingura: hana no maki; yuki no maki*). Inagaki Hiroshi, dir. 1962. Tōhō.

Citizen Kane. Orson Welles, dir. 1941. Mercury Productions, Inc., and RKO Radio Pictures, Inc.

Culloden. Peter Watkins, dir. 1964. BBC.

Dangerous Liaisons. Stephen Frears, dir. 1988. Lorimar Film Entertainment, NFH Productions, and Warner Bros. Pictures.

Danshichi in the Rain (*Danshichi shigure*). Koishi Eiichi, dir. 1933. Dainihon Jiyū Eiga Productions.

Danshichi shigure (*Danshichi in the Rain*). Koishi Eiichi, dir. 1933. Dainihon Jiyū Eiga Productions.

Death of a Tea Master (*Sen no Rikyū*). Kumai Kei, dir. 1989. Seiyu Production, Shōchiku Films Ltd., Teshigahara Productions, and Tōhō.

Double Suicide (*Shinjū ten Amijima*). Shinoda Masahiro, dir. 1969. Art Theatre Guild and Hyōgensha.

Dragnet Girl (*Hijōsen no onna*). Ozu Yasujirō, dir. 1933. Shōchiku Kinema, Kamata Studio.

Du Barry Was a Lady. Roy Del Ruth, dir. 1943. Loew's, Inc. (as Loew's, Incorporated) and Metro-Goldwyn-Mayer.

Edo saigo no hi (*The Last Days of Edo*). Inagaki Hiroshi, dir. 1941. Nikkatsu, Kyoto Studio.

Emma. Douglas McGrath, dir. 1996. Haft Entertainment, Matchmaker Films, and Miramax.

The English Patient. Anthony Minghella, dir. 1996. Miramax.

Enzō from Nikkō (*Nikkō no Enzō*). Furumi Takuji, dir. 1929. Ichikawa Utaemon Productions.

Fatal Attraction. Adrian Lyne, dir. 1987. Paramount Pictures.

Festival across the Sea (*Umi o wataru sairei*). Inagaki Hiroshi, dir. 1941. Nikkatsu, Tokyo Studios.

Firefly Light (*Hotarubi*). Gosho Heinosuke, dir. 1958. Kabukiza Eiga.

Five Men of Edo (*Ōedo gonin otoko*). Itō Daisuke, dir. 1951. Shōchiku, Kyoto Studio.

Five Women Around Utamaro, aka *Utamaro and His Five Women* (*Utamaro o meguru gonin no onna*). Mizoguchi Kenji, dir. 1946. Shōchiku, Kyoto Studio.

Flash of a Sword, Swirl of Cherry Blossoms (*Kenkō sakura fubuki*). Suganuma Kanji, dir. 1941. Nikkatsu, Kyoto Studios.

The Flowers Have Fallen (*Hana chirinu*). Ishida Tamizō, dir. 1938. Tōhō Eiga, Kyoto Studio.

The 47 Ronin: Parts 1 and 2, aka *The Loyal 47 Ronin of the Genroku Era* (*Genroku chūshingura*). Mizoguchi Kenji, dir. 1941–2. Kōa Eiga, Shōchiku, Kyoto Studio.

Front Line Street (*Sensengai*). Furumi Takuji, dir. 1930. Ichikawa Utaemon Productions.

Fuefukigawa (*The River Fuefuki*). Kinoshita Keisuke, dir. 1960. Shōchiku, Ōfuna Studio.

Fukuro no shiro (*Owls' Castle*). Shinoda Masahiro, dir. 1999. *Fukuro no shiro* Seisaku Iinkai.

Furin kazan (*Under the Banner of the Samurai*, aka *Samurai Banners*). Inagaki Hiroshi, dir. 1969. Mifune Productions.

The Gambler: The Game to Be Chairman (*Bakuchiuchi: sōchō tobaku*). Yamashita Kōsoku, dir. 1968. Tōei, Kyoto Studio.

Gambler's Luck (*Un ga yokeriya*). Yamada Yōji, dir. 1966. Shochiku, Ofuna Studio.

Gate of Hell (*Jigokumon*). Kinugasa Teinosuke, dir. 1953. Daiei, Kyoto Studio.

Genealogy of Women (*Onna keizu*). Makino Masahiro, dir. 1942. Tōhō Eiga.

Genji monogatari (*The Tales of Genji*), directed by Ichikawa Kon, 1965.
Genroku Chūshingura. Mizoguchi Kenji, dir. 1941. Kōa Eiga, Shōchiku, Kyoto Studio.
Gero (*Servant*). Itō Daisuke, dir. 1927. Nikkatsu, Daishōgun Studio.
Die Geschichte vom weinenden Kamel (*The Story of the Weeping Camel*). Byambasuren Davaa and Luigi Falorni, dir. 2003. Hochschule für Fernsehen und Film Munchen (HFF) and Bayerischer Rundfunk (BR).
Glory. Edward Zwick, dir. 1989. TriStar Pictures.
Go Champion (*Ōshō*). Itō Daisuke, dir. 1948. Daiei, Kyoto Studio.
The Godfather (aka *Mario Puzo's The Godfather*). Francis Ford Coppola, dir. 1972. Paramount Pictures.
Gone with the Wind. Victor Fleming et al., dir. 1939. Selznick International Pictures.
Gonza the Spearman (*Yari no Gonza*). Shinoda Masahiro, dir. 1986. Hyōgensha, Shōchiku.
Gyakuryū (*Retaliation*). Futagawa Buntarō, dir. 1924. Tōa Kinema, Tōjiin Studio.
Hana chirinu (*The Flowers Have Fallen*). Ishida Tamizō, dir. 1938. Tōhō Eiga, Kyoto Studio.
Harakiri (*Seppuku*). Kobayashi Masaki, dir. 1962. Shōchiku, Kyoto Studio.
Hatamoto taikutsu otoko (*Idle Vassal* series). 22 films starring Ichikawa Utaemon, 1930–1963. Ichikawa Utaemon Productions/Tōei, Kyoto Studio.
The Heiress. William Wyler, dir. 1949. Paramount Pictures.
The Hidden Blade (*Kakushiken: oni no tsume*). Yamada Yōji, dir. 2004. Shochiku, Nippon Television Network Corporation, Sumitomo Corporation, et al.
High School. Frederick Wiseman, dir. 1968. Osti Productions.
Hijōsen no onna (*Dragnet Girl*). Yasujirō Ozu, dir. 1933. Shōchiku Kinema, Kamata Studio.
Hōrō zanmai (*Wanderlust*). Inagaki Hiroshi, dir. 1928. Chiezō Productions.
Horse (*Uma*). Yamamoto Kajirō, dir. 1941. Tōhō Eiga and Gōshigaisha Eiga Kagaku Kenkyūsho.
Hotarubi (*Firefly Light*). Gosho Heinosuke, dir. 1958. Kabukiza.
Humanity and Paper Balloons (*Ninjō kamifusen*). Yamanaka Sadao, dir. 1937. P.C.L.
Idle Vassal series. 22 films starring Ichikawa Utaemon, 1930–1963. Ichikawa Utaemon Productions/Tōei, Kyoto Studio.
Illusion of Blood (*Yotsuya kaidan*). Toyoda Shirō, dir. 1965. Tōkyō.
Isshin Tasuke (*Single-minded Tasuke*). Inagaki Hiroshi, dir. 1930. Chiezō Production.
Japan (*The Electronic Tribe, The Sword and the Chrysanthemum, The Legacy of the Shogun* and *A Proper Place in the World*), Peter Spry-Leverton, dir. 1988. Produced by WTTW Chicago. Coronet Film and Video, VHS, 4 hours.
Jefferson in Paris. James Ivory, dir. 1995. Merchant Ivory Productions and Touchstone Pictures.
Jezebel. William Wyler, dir. 1938. Warner Brothers.
Jigokumon (*Gate of Hell*). Kinugasa Teinosuke, dir. 1953. Daiei, Kyoto Studio.
Jinsei gekijō: Zankyaku hen (*Theater of Life: Cruel Chivalry*). Uchida Tomu, dir. 1936. Nikkatsu, Tamagawa Studio.
Jinsei gekijō (*Theater of Life*). Saburi Shin, dir. 3 films: *Jinsei gekijō dai ichibu seishun aiyoku* (*Theater of Life Part One: Passion of Youth*). 1952. *Jinsei gekijō dai nibu fūunhen* (*Theater of Life Part Two: Out of the Tempest Cruel Chivalry*). 1953. *Jinsei gekijō bōkyōhen Sanshū Kira no minato* (*Theater of Life, Nostalgia: The Harbor of Kira in Mikawa*). 1954. Tōei, Tokyo Studio.
Jinsei gekijō: Hishakaku (*Theater of Life: Hishakaku's Story*). Sawashima Tadashi, dir. 1963. Tōei, Tokyo Studio.
Jinsei gekijō: Hishakaku to Kiratsune (*Theater of Life: Hishakaku and Kiratsune*). Uchida Tomu, dir. 1968. Tōei, Tokyo Studio.
Jinsei gekijō seishunhen (*Theater of Life*). Sugie Toshio, dir. 1958. Tōhō.
Jinsei gekijō: Shin Hishakaku (*Theater of Life: A New Story of Hishakaku*). Sawashima Tadashi. 1964. Tōei, Tokyo Studio.

Jinsei gekijō: Zankyaku hen (*Theater of Life: The Volume on the Last of Chivalry*). Chiba Yasuki, dir. 1938. Nikkatsu, Tamagawa Studio.

Jinsei gekijō: Zoku Hishakaku (*Theater of Life: Hishakaku's Story Continued*). 1963. Tōei, Tokyo Studio.

Jirōchō and the Record of the Three Kingdoms (*Jirōcho Sangokushi*). Nine parts. Makino Masahiro, dir. 1952–54. Tōhō.

Jirōchō and the Record of the Three Kingdoms (*Jirōchō Sangokushi*). Four parts. Makino Masahiro, dir. 1963–1965. Tōei, Kyoto Studio.

Jirōchō from Shimizu (Shimizuno Uirōchō). Ikeda Tomiyasu, dir. 1935. Uzumasa Hassei Eiga.

Jirōcho Sangokushi (*Jirōchō and the Record of the Three Kingdoms*). Nine parts. Makino Masahiro, dir. 1952–54. Tōhō.

Jirōchō Sangokushi (*Jirōchō and the Record of the Three Kingdoms*). Four parts. Makino Masahiro, dir. 1963–1965. Tōei, Kyoto Studio.

Jirōkichi the Ratkid, aka *Made to Order Cloth* (*Oatsurae Jirōkichi kōshi*). Itō Daisuke, dir. 1931. Nikkatsu, Daishōgun Studio.

Jissetsu Kunisada Chūji: kari no mure (*The True Story of Chūji from Kunisada: A Flock of Wild Geese*). Nomura Hōtei, dir. 1923. Shōchiku Kinema, Kamata Studio.

Jōiuchi: Hairyō tsuma shimatsu (*Samurai Rebellion*). Kobayashi Masaki, dir. 1967. Mifune Productions and Tōhō.

A Journal of Chūji's Travels (*Chūji tabi nikki*). Three parts Daisuke, dir. 1927–1928. Nikkatsu, Kyoto Studio.

The Journey (*Otokotachi no tabiji*). 13 parts. Yamada Taichi, scenarist. Starring Tsuruta Kōji. 1976–1982. NHK.

Journey of a Thousand and One Nights (*Matatabi sen-ichiya*). Inagaki Hiroshi, dir. 1936. Nikkatsu, Kyoto Studio.

Kagemusha (*Shadow Warrior*, aka *Kagemusha [The Shadow Warrior]*, *Kagemusha the Shadow Warrior*, and *The Double*). Kurosawa Akira, dir. 1980. Kurosawa Productions, Tōhō, and Twentieth Century Fox.

Kaidan (*Kwaidan*). Kobayashi Masaki, dir. 1964. Bungei Productions and Ninjin Kurabu.

Kaidō ichi no abarenbō (*Last of the Wild One* [*Jirōchō and the Record of the Three Kingdoms*, part 8]). Makino Masahiro, dir. 1954. Tōhō.

Kakushiken: oni no tsume (*The Hidden Blade*). Yamada Yōji, dir. 2004. Shochiku, Nippon Television Network Corporation, Sumitomo Corporation, et al.

Kakute kamikaze wa fuku (*Thus Blows the Divine Wind*). Marune Sentarō, dir. 1941. Daiei, Kyoto Studio.

Kawanakajima kassen (*The Battle of Kawanakajima*). Kinugasa Teinosuke, dir. 1941. Tōhō Eiga, Kyoto Studio.

Kazoku (*Where Spring Comes Late*). Yamada Yōji, dir. 1970. Shochiku, Ofuna Studio.

Ken (*Sword*). Furumi Takuji, dir. 1930. Ichikawa Utaemon Productions.

Kenkō sakura fubuki (*Flash of a Sword, Swirl of Cherry Blossoms*). Suganuma Kanji, dir. 1941. Nikkatsu, Kyoto Studio.

Kettō Ganryūjima (*Samurai III: Duel on Ganryu Island*, aka *Bushido*, *Duel on Ganryu Island*, and *Musashi and Kojiro*). Inagaki Hiroshi, dir. 1955. Tōhō.

Kōchiyama Sōshun. Yamanaka Sadao, dir. 1936. Nikkatsu and Uzumasa Hassei Eiga.

Kokushi musō (*Peerless Patriot*). Itami Mansaku, dir. 1932. Chiezō Productions.

Kozure Ōkami (*Lone Wolf and Cub*, aka *Sword of Vengeance* series). Six films. Starring Wakayama Tomisaburō. 1972–1974. Katsu Productions.

Kubi no za (*Beheading Place*). Makino Masahiro, dir. 1929. Makino Productions, Omuro Studio.

Kumonosujō (*Throne of Blood*, aka *Cobweb Castle*, *Macbeth*, *Spider Web Castle*, and *The Castle of the Spider's Web*). Akira Kurosawa, dir. 1950. Tōhō.

Kutsukake Tokijirō (*Tokijirō from Kutsukake*). Tsuji Kichirō, dir. 1929. Nikkatsu, Uzumasa Studio.
Kwaidan (*Kaidan*). Kobayashi Masaki, dir. 1964. Bungei Productions and Ninjin Kurabu.
Lady and Gent. Stephen Roberts, dir. 1932. Paramount.
Lady Ogin (*Ogin-sama*). Kumai Kei, dir. 1978. Takarazuka Eiga Seisakusho.
The Last Days of Edo (*Edo saigo no hi*). Inagaki Hiroshi, dir. 1941. Nikkatsu, Kyoto Studio.
The Last of the Mohicans. George B. Seitz, dir. 1936. Edward Small Productions as Reliance Pictures, Inc.
The Last Laugh (*Der letzte Mann*). F.W. Murnau, dir. 1924. Universum Film A.G. (UFA).
The Last Samurai, aka *The Last Samurai: Bushidou*. Edward Zwick, dir. 2003. Warner Bros. Pictures, The Bedford Falls Company, Cruise/Wagner Productions, and Radar Pictures Inc.
Last of the Wild One (*Kaidō ichi no abarenbō*). Makino Masahiro, dir. 1954. Tōhō.
Der Letzte Mann (*The Last Laugh*). F.W. Murnau, dir. 1924. Universum Film A.G. (UFA).
The Life of Muhōmatsu the Untamed (*Muhōmatsu no isshō*). Inagaki Hiroshi, dir. 1943. Daiei, Kyoto Studio.
Life of Oharu (*Saikaku ichidai onna*). Mizoguchi Kenji, dir. 1952. Shintōhō and Koi Productions.
The Little Foxes. William Wyler, dir. 1941. Samuel Goldwyn Company.
Little House on the Prairie. Michael Landon et al., dir. 1964–1973 (nine seasons). Ed Friendly Productions and NBC.
Lone Wolf and Cub, aka *Sword of Vengeance* (*Kozure Ōokami*). Six films. Starring Wakayama Tomisaburō. 1972–1974. Katsu Productions.
Long Standing Hatred. Itō Daisoke, dir. 1926. Nikkatsu, Daishōgun Studio.
Love under the Crucifix (*Ogin-sama*). Tanaka Kinuyo, dir. 1960. Ninjin Kurabu.
Machi no irezumimono (*The Village Tattooed Man*). Yamanaka Sadao. 1935. Nikkatsu, Kyoto Studio.
Machibuse (*Ambush at Blood Pass*, aka *Incident at Blood Island*, *Incident at Blood Pass*, *The Ambush*, and *The Ambush: Incident at Blood Pass*). Inagaki Hiroshi, dir. 1970. Mifune Productions.
Man of Aran. Robert J. Flaherty, dir. 1934. Gainsborough Pictures and Gaumont British Picture Corporation, Ltd.
Man-slashing, Horse-piercing Sword (*Zanjin zanba ken*). Itō Daisuke, dir. 1930. Shōchiku Kinema, Kyoto Studio.
Matatabi sen-ichiya (*Journey of a Thousand and One Nights*). Inagaki Hiroshi, dir. 1936. Nikkatsu, Kyoto Studio.
Miyamoto Musashi (*Samurai 1: Musashi Miyamoto*, aka *Master Swordsman*, *Musashi Miyamoto*, *Samurai*, and *The Legend of Musashi*). Inagaki Hiroshi, dir. 1954. Tōhō.
Muhōmatsu no isshō (*The Life of Muhōmatsu the Untamed*, aka *Muhomatsu, the Rikshaw Man*, and *The Rickshaw Man*). Inagaki Hiroshi, dir. 1943. Tōhō.
My Darling Clementine (aka *John Ford's My Darling Clementine*). John Ford, dir. 1946. Twentieth Century Fox.
Nanook of the North, aka *Nanouk l'esquimau*. Robert J. Flaherty, dir. 1922. Les Frères Revillon and Pathé Exchange, Inc.
Nemuri Kyōshirō (*Sleepy Eyes of Death*, aka *Nemuri Kyoshiro* series). Starring Ichikawa Raizō. Twelve films. 1963–1969. Daiei, Kyoto Studio.
A New Edition of Tales of Ōoka's Administration (*Shinpan Ōoka seidan*). Three parts. Itō Daisuke, dir. 1928. Nikkatsu, Daishōgun Studios.
New Theater of Life (*Shin jinsei gekijō*). Yuge Tarō, dir. 1961. Daiei, Tokyo Studio.
Night Drum (*Yoru no tsuzumi*). Imai Tadashi, dir. 1958. Gendai Productions.
Night Mail. Harry Wall and Basil Wright, dir. 1936. GPO (General Post Office) Film Unit.

Nihon kyōkaku den (*Tales of Chivalry in Japan* series). Eight films. 1965–69. Tōei, Kyoto Studio.
Nikkō no Enzō (*Enzō from Nikkō*). Takumi Furuji, dir. 1929. Ichikawa Utaemon Productions.
Ninjō kamifusen (*Humanity and Paper Balloons*). Yamanaka Sadao, dir. 1937. P.C.L.
Oatsurae Jirōkichi kōshi (*Jirōkichi the Ratkid*). Itō Daisuke, dir. 1931. Nikkatsu, Daishōgun Studio.
Ōedo gonin otoko (*Five Men of Edo*). Itō Daisuke, dir. 1951. Shōchiku, Kyoto Studio.
Ogin-sama (*Lady Ogin*, aka *Lady Ogin, Love and Faith, Love and Faith of Ogin, Love and Faith: Lady Ogin*, and *Ogin: Her Love and Faith*). Kumai Kei, dir. 1978. Takarazuka Seisakusho.
Ogin-sama (*Love under the Crucifix*). Tanaka Kinuyo, dir. 1960. Ninjin Kurabu.
The Old Maid. Edmund Goulding, dir. 1939. First National Pictures Inc. and Warner Bros. as Warner Bros. Pictures Inc.
Onna keizu (*Genealogy of Women*). Makino Masahiro, dir. 1942. Tōhō Eiga.
Onna Taikōki (*Women's Taikōki*). Hashida Sugako, scenarist. 1981. NHK.
Onnatachi no Chūshingura–inochi moyuru made (*Women's Chūshingura: Unto Death*). Hashida Sugako, scenarist. 1979. TBS.
Orochi (*Serpent*). Futagawa Buntarō, dir. 1925. Bandō Tsumasaburō Productions.
Ōshō (*Go Champion*). Itō Daisuke, dir. 1948. Daiei, Kyoto Studio.
Otokotachi no tabiji (*The Journey*). 13 parts. Yamada Taichi, scenarist. Starring Tsuruta Kōji. 1976–1982. NHK.
The Outrage. Martin Ritt, dir. 1964. February Harvest, KHF Productions, Kayos, Martin Ritt Productions, and MGM.
Owls' Castle (*Fukuro no shiro*). Shinoda Masahiro, dir. 1999. *Fukuro no shiro* Seisaku Iinkai.
Peace on Earth (*Tenka Taiheiki*). Inagaki Hiroshi, dir. 1928. Chiezō Productions.
Peerless Patriot (*Kokushi musō*). Itami Mansaku, dir. 1932. Chiezō Productions.
Pension Mimosas. Jaques Feyder, dir. 1935. Films Sonores Tobis.
Persuasion. Roger Michell, dir. 1995. BBC, France 2 Cinéma, Millésime Productions, Mobile Masterpiece Theatre, and WGBH Boston.
Pride and Prejudice. Robert Z. Leonard, dir. 1940. MGM.
Princess Sen in Edo (*Senhime goten*). Misumi Kenji, dir. 1960. Daiei, Kyoto Studio.
La Prise de pouvoir par Louis XIV (*The Rise of Louis XIV*). Roberto Rosselini, dir. 1966. Office de Radiodiffusion Television Francaise (ORTF).
Ran (*Ran*). Kurosawa Akira, dir. 1985. Herald Ace Inc., Greenwich Film Productions, and Nippon Herald Films.
Rashōmon (aka *In the Woods, Rasho-Mon*, and *Rashomon*). Kurosawa Akira, dir. 1950. Daiei, Kyoto Studio.
Red Beard (*Akahige*). Kurosawa Akira, dir. 1965. Kurosawa Productions.
Retaliation (*Gyakuryū*). Futagawa Buntarō, dir. 1924. Tōa Kinema, Tōjiin Studio.
Revenge of an Actor (*Yukinojō henge*). Ichikawa Kon, dir. 1963. Daiei, Kyoto Studio.
Riding Grounds at Sōzen Temple (*Sōzenji-baba*). Itō Daisuke, dir. 1928. Makino Masahiro, dir. 1928. Makino Productions, Omuro Studio.
Rikyū (*Rikyu*). Teshigagara Hiroshi, dir. 1989. Teshigahara Productions, Shōchiku Eizō, Itōchū Shōji, (Corporation) and Hakuhōdō (Inc.).
Rise Against the Sword (*Abare Goemon*). Inagaki Hiroshi, dir. 1966. Tōhō.
The Rise of Louis XIV (*La Prise de pouvoir par Louis XIV*). Roberto Rosselini, dir. 1966. Office de Radiodiffusion Television Francaise (ORTF).
The River Fuefuki (*Fuefukigawa*). Kinoshita Keisuke, dir. 1960. Shōchiku, Ōfuna Studio.
Rojō no reikon (*Souls on the Road*). Murata Minoru, dir. 1921. Shōchiku Kinema Kenkyūsho.
Rōningai (*Street of Masterless Samurai*), 3 parts. Makino Masahiro, 1928–1929.
Saikaku ichidai onna (*Life of Oharu*, aka *Diary of Oharu*). Mizoguchi Kenji, dir. 1952. Koi Productions, Shintōhō.

Sakamoto Ryōma. Edamasa Yoshirō, dir. 1928
Samurai (*Samurai Assassin*). Okamoto Kihachi, dir. 1965.
Samurai Assassin (*Samurai*). Okamoto Kihachi, dir. 1965. Mifune Productions and Tōhō.
Samurai I: Musashi Miyamoto (*Miyamoto Musashi*), Inagaki Hiroshi, dir. 1954.
Samurai II: Duel at Ichijoji (*Zoku Miyamoto Musashi: Ichijōji no kettō*). Inagaki Hiroshi, dir. 1955.
Samurai III: Duel on Ganryu Island (*Miyamoto Musashi kanketsuhen: kettō Ganryūjima*, aka *Kettō Ganryūjima*). Inagaki Hiroshi, dir. 1956. Tōhō.
Samurai Rebellion (*Jōiuchi: Hairyō tsuma shimatsu*). Kobayashi Masaki, dir. 1967. Mifune Productions and Tōhō.
Sanjuro (*Tsubaki Sanjūrō*). Kurosawa Akira, dir. 1962. Mifune Productions and Tōhō.
Sanshō Dayū (*Sansho the Bailiff*, aka *Legend of Bailiff* and *The Bailiff*). Mizoguchi Kenji, dir. 1954. Daiei, Kyoto Studio.
Sansho the Bailiff (*Sanshō Dayū*). Mizoguchi Kenji, dir. 1954. Daiei, Kyoto Studio.
Sazen Tange and the Pot Worth a Million Ryo (*Tange Sazen yowa: Hyakuman ryō no tsubo*). Yamanaka Sadao, dir. 1935. Nikkatsu, Kyoto Studio.
Scoundrel (*Akutō*). Shindō Kaneto, dir. 1965. Tōkyō Eiga and Kindai Eiga Kyōkai.
The Secret Life of Walter Mitty. Norman Z. McLeod, dir. 1947. Samuel Goldwyn Company.
Seki no Yatappe (*Yatappe from Seki*). Hasegawa Shin, original story. Seven versions 1930–1963.
Sengoku guntōden (*Story of a Bandit Band in the Country at War*, Part One: *Tiger and Wolf*; Part Two: *Advance at Dawn*). Takizawa Eisuke, dir. 1937. Two parts. P.L.C. Seisakusho and Zenshinza.
Sengoku kitan: Kimagure kanja (*Capricious Young Man*). Itami Mansaku, dir. 1936. Chiezō Productions.
Senhime goten (*Princess Sen in Edo*). Misumi Kenji, dir. 1960. Daiei, Kyoto Studio.
Sen no Rikyū Hongakubō ibun (*Death of a Tea Master*). Kumai Kei, dir. 1989. Seiyu Production, Shōchiku Films, Ltd., Teshigahara Productions, and Tōhō.
Sensengai (*Front Line Street*). Furumi Takuji, dir. 1930. Ichikawa Utaemon Productions.
Seppuku (*Harakiri*). Kobayashi Masaki, dir. 1962. Shōchiku, Kyoto Studio.
Serpent (*Orochi*). Futagawa Buntarō, dir. 1925. Bandō Tsumasaburō Productions.
Servant (*Gero*). Itō Daisuke, dir. 1927. Nikkatsu, Daishōgun Studio.
Seven Samurai (*Shichinin no samurai*). Kurosawa Akira, dir. 1954. Tōhō.
Shadow Warrior (*Kagemusha*). Kurosawa Akira, dir. 1980. Kurosawa Productions, Tōhō, and Twentieth Century Fox.
She Wore a Yellow Ribbon. John Ford, dir. 1949. Argosy Pictures Corporation.
Shiawase no kiiroi hankachi (*The Yellow Handkerchief*, aka *The Yellow Handkerchief of Happiness*). Yamada Yōji, dir. 1977. Shochiku.
Shichinin no samurai (*Seven Samurai*). Kurosawa Akira, dir. 1954. Tōhō.
Shimizu no Jirōchō (*Jirōchō from Shimizu*). Ikeda Tomiyasu, dir. 1935. Uzumasa Hassei Eiga.
Shimizu minato (*Harbor of Shimizu*). Makino Masahiro, dir. 1939. Nikkatsu, Kyoto Studio.
Shin Heike monogatari: Shizuka to Yoshitsune (*The Warrior and the Dancer*). Shima Kōji, dir. 1956. Daiei, Kyoto Studio.
Shin jinsei gekijō (*New Theater of Life*). Yuge Tarō, dir. 1961. Daiei, Tokyo Studio.
Shinjū ten no Amijima (*Double Suicide*). Shinoda Masahiro, dir. 1969. Hyōgensha and ATG.
Shinobi no mono (*Band of Assassins*, aka *Ninja 1*; *Ninja, a Band of Assassins*; *The Ninja*; and *Those That Are Unseen*). Yamamoto Satsuo, dir. 1962. Daiei, Kyoto Studio.
Shinpan Ōoka seidan (*A New Edition of Tales of Ōoka's Administration*). Three parts. Itō Daisuke, dir. 1928. Nikkatsu, Daishōgun Studios.
Single-minded Tasuke (*Isshin Tasuke*). Inagaki Hiroshi, dir. 1930. Chiezō Productions.
Sleepy Eyes of Death series (*Nemuri Kyōshirō*). Twelve films. Starring Ichikawa Raizō. 1961–1969. Daiei, Kyoto Studio.

The Sorrow and the Pity (*Le Chagrin et la pitié*). Marcel Ophüls, dir. 1969. Norddeutscher Rundfunk (NDR), Television Rencontre, and Television Suisse-Romande (TSR).
Sōzenji-baba (*Riding grounds at Sōzen temple*, aka *The Racing Track at Sozenji*). Makino Masahiro, dir. 1928. Makino Productions, Omuro Studio.
Souls on the Road (*Rōjō no reikon*). Murata Minoru, dir. 1921. Shōchiku Kinema Kenkyūsho.
A Star Is Born. William A. Wellman, dir. 1937. Selznick International Pictures and United Artists.
The Story of Adele H (*Histoire d'Adéle H., L'*). François Truffaut, dir. 1975. Les Films du Carrosse and Les Productions Artistes Associés.
Story of a Bandit Band in the Country at War, Part One: *Tiger and Wolf*; Part Two: *Advance at Dawn* (*Sengoku guntōden zenpen tora Ōkami; kōhen akatsuki no zenshin*). Takizawa Eisuke, dir. 1937. Two parts. P.L.C. Seisakusho and Zenshinza.
The Story of the Weeping Camel (*Die Geschichte vom weinenden Kamel).* Byambasuren Davaa and Luigi Falorni, dir. 2003. Hochschule für Fernsehen und Film München (HFF) and Bayerischer Rundfunk (BR).
Street of Masterless Samurai (*Rōningai*). Three parts. Makino Masahiro, dir. 1928–1929. Makino Productions, Omuro Studio.
Sword (*Ken*). Furumi Takuji, dir. 1930. Ichikawa Utaemon Productions.
Tabi wa aozora (*Travels under the Blue Sky*). Inagaki Hiroshi, dir. 1932. Chiezō Productions, Sagano Studio.
Tange Sazen yowa: Hyakuman ryō no tsubo (*Sazen Tange and the Pot Worth a Million Ryo*). Yamanaka Sadao, dir. 1935. Nikkatsu, Kyoto Studio.
Tasogare Seibei (*The Twilight Samurai*). Yamada Yōji, dir. 2002. Shochiku, Nippon Television Network Corporation, Sumitomo Corporation, et al.
Tenka Taiheiki (*Peace on Earth*). Inagaki Hiroshi, dir. 1928. Chiezō Productions.
Theater of Life (*Jinsei gekijō*). Three parts. 1952–54. Saburi Shin, dir. Tōei, Tokyo Studio.
Theater of Life (*Jinsei gekijō*). Uchida Tomu, dir. 1936. Nikkatsu, Tamagawa Studio.
Theater of Life (*Jinsei gekijō seishunhen*). Sugie Toshio, dir. 1958. Tōhō.
Theater of Life: Hishakaku and Kiratsune (*Jinsei gekijō: Hishakaku to Kiratsune*). Uchida Tomu, dir. 1968. Tōei, Tokyo Studio.
Theater of Life: Hishakaku's Story (*Jinsei gekijō: Hishakaku*). Sawashima Tadashi, dir. 1963. Tōei, Tokyo Studio.
Theater of Life: Hishakaku's Story Continued (*Jinsei gekijō: Zoku Hishakaku*). Sawashima Tadashi, dir. 1963. Tōei, Tokyo Studio.
A Theater of Life: A New Story of Hishakaku (*Jinsei gekijō: Shin Hishakaku*). Sawashima Tadashi, dir. 1964. Tōei, Tokyo Studio.
Theater of Life, Part Two: *Cruel Chivalry* (*Jinsei gekijō zankyōhen*). Chiba Yasuki, dir. 1938. Nikkatsu, Tamagawa Studio.
The Thin Man. W.S. Van Dyke, dir. 1934. Cosmopolitan Films and Metro-Goldwyn-Mayer.
The Three Musketeers. Fred Niblo, dir. 1921. Douglas Fairbanks Pictures Corp.
Throne of Blood (*Kumonosujō*). Akira Kurosawa, dir. 1950. Tōhō.
Thus Blows the Divine Wind (*Kakute kamikaze wa fuku*). Marune Sentarō, dir. 1941. Daiei, Kyoto Studio.
Titicut Follies. Frederick Wiseman, dir. 1967.
Tokijirō from Kutsukake (*Kutsukake Tokijirō*). Tsuji Kichiro, dir. 1929. Nikkatsu. Uzumasa Studio.
Too Hot to Handle. Jack Conway, dir. 1938. Loew's, Inc., and MGM.
Tora no o wo fumu otokotachi (*The Men Who Tread on the Tiger's Tail*). Kurosawa Akira, dir. 1945 (released 1952). Tōhō.
The True Story of Chūji from Kunisada: A Flock of Wild Geese (*Jissetsu Kunisada Chūji: kari no mure*). Nomura Hōtei, dir. 1923. Shōchiku Kinema, Kamata Studio.
Tsubaki Sanjūrō (*Sanjuro*). Kurosawa Akira, dir. 1962. Kurosawa Productions.

Tsukigata Hanpeita (*Tsukigata Hanpeita*). Kinugasa Teinosuke, dir. 1925. Rengō Eiga Geijutsuka Kyōkai, Tōjiin Studio.

Tsuruhachi Tsurujirō (*Tsuruhachi [and] Tsurujiro*). Mikio Naruse, dir. 1938. Tōkyō Eiga, Tokyo Studio.

The Twilight Samurai (*Tasogare Seibei*). Yamada Yōji, dir. 2002. Shochiku, Nippon Television Network Corporation, Sumitomo Corporation, et al.

Ugetsu (*Ugetsu monogatari*). Mizoguchi Kenji, dir. 1953. Daiei, Kyoto Studio.

Ugetsu monogatari (*Ugetsu*). Mizoguchi Kenji, dir. 1953. Daiei, Kyoto Studio.

Uma (*Horse*). Yamamoto Kajirō, dir. 1941. Tōhō Eiga, Tokyo Studio and Gōshigaisha Eiga Kagaku Kenkyūsho.

Umi o wataru sairei (*Festival across the Sea*). Inagaki Hiroshi, dir. 1941. Nikkatsu, Kyoto Studio.

Un ga yokeriya (*Gambler's Luck*). Yamada Yōji, dir. 1966. Shochiku, Ofuna Studio.

Under the Banner of the Samurai (*Furin kazan*). Inagaki Hiroshi, dir. 1969. Mifune Productions.

Utamaro o meguru gonin no onna (*Five Women around Utamaro*, aka *Utamaro and His Five Women*). Mizoguchi Kenji, dir. 1946. Shōchiku, Kyoto Studio.

Wakaki hi no Jirōchō (*The Early Days of Jirōchō*). Makino Masahiro, dir. Three parts, 1960–1962. Tōei.

Wanderlust (*Hōrō zanmai*). Inagaki Hiroshi, dir. 1928. Chiezō Productions.

The Warrior and the Dancer (*Shin Heike monogatari: Shizuka to Yoshitsune*). Shima Kōji, dir. 1956. Daiei, Kyoto Studio.

Where Spring Comes Late (*Kazoku*). Yamada Yōji, dir. 1970. Shochiku, Ofuna Studio.

Women's Taikōki (*Onna Taikōki*). Hashida Sugako, scenarist. 1981. NHK.

Wuthering Heights. William Wyler, dir. 1939. Samuel Goldwyn Company.

The Yellow Handkerchief (*Shiawase no kiiroi hankachi*). Yamada Yōji, dir. 1977. Shochiku.

Yoake mae (*Before Dawn*). Yoshimura Kōzaburō, dir. 1953. Kindai Eiga Kyōkai and Mingeiza.

Yojimbo (*Yōjinbō*). Kurosawa Akira, dir. 1961. Tōhō and Kurosawa Productions.

Yōjinbō (*Yojimbo*, aka *Yojimbo the Bodyguard* and *The Bodyguard*). Kurosawa Akira, dir. 1961. Tōhō and Kurosawa Productions.

Yoru no tsuzumi (*Night Drum*). Imai Tadashi, dir. 1958. Gendai Productions.

Yotsuya kaidan (*Illusion of Blood*). Toyoda Shirō, dir. 1965. Tōkyō Eiga.

Young Mister Lincoln. John Ford, dir. 1939. Cosmopolitan Productions and Twentieth Century Fox.

Yukinojō henge (*An Actor's Revenge*, aka *The Revenge of an Actor*, *Revenge of a Kabuki Actor*, *The Revenge of Ukeno-Jo*, and *The Revenge of Yuki-No-Jo*). Ichikawa Kon, dir. 1963. Daiei, Kyoto Studio.

Zanjin zanba ken (*Man-slashing, Horse-piercing Sword*). Itō Daisuke, dir. 1930. Shōchiku Kinema, Kyoto Studio.

Zatōichi series. Twenty-six films. 1962–1989. Starring Katsu Shintarō. Daiei, Kyoto Studio and Katsu Productions et al.

Zoku Miyamoto Musashi: Ichijōji no kettō (*Samurai II: Duel at Ichijoji*), Inagaki Hiroshi, dir. 1955. Tōhō.

Bibliography

The Actors' Analects (*Yakusha Rongo*). Edited, translated and with an introduction and notes by Charles J. Dunn and Bunzō Torigoe. New York: Columbia University Press, 1969.

Amada Gorō. *Tōkai yūkyōden: ichimei Jirōchō monogatari.* Tokyo: Yorinsha, 1884.

Anderson, Joseph L., and Donald Richie. *The Japanese Film: Art and Industry.* Tokyo and Rutland, Vermont: C.E. Tuttle Co., 1959.

"Annual Events Calendar." 2006. Shōnai. http://shonai.wikispaces.com/Annual+Events+Calendar (accessed August 8, 2006).

Atkinson, Michael. "Codes Unknown: In a Revisionist Samurai Epic, Tough Financial Realities Trump the Warrior Myth of Honor." A review of *Tasogare Seibei*, directed by Yamada Yōji. *The Village Voice*, April 20, 2004, http://www.villagevoice.com/film/0416,atkinson,52812,20.html (accessed July 26, 2006).

Bach, Faith, trans. "Shinza the Barber/Kamiyui Shinza." In *Kabuki Plays on Stage*, ed. James R. Brandon and Samuel L. Leiter. Vol. 4, *Restoration and Reform 1872–1905*, 82–119. Honolulu: University of Hawaii Press, 2003.

Barthes, Roland. *Mythologies.* Trans. Annette Lavers. New York: Hill and Wang, 1984.

Benneville, James S. de. *Tales of the Samurai: Oguri Hangwan Ichidaiki* (*Being the Story of the Lives, the Adventures, and the Misadventures of the Hangwan-dai Kojiro Sukeshige and Terute-hime, his Wife*). Tokyo: Fukuin Printing Company, Limited, 1916.

Bitō Masahide. "Society and Social Thought in the Tokugawa Period." *Japan Foundation Newsletter* 9 (June–September, 1981): 4–6.

Blacker, Carmen. "Millenarian Aspects of the New Religions in Japan." In *Tradition and Modernization in Japanese Culture*, ed. Donald H. Shively, 563–600. Studies in the Modernization of Japan 5. Princeton: Princeton University Press, 1971.

Bodart, Beatrice M. "Tea and Counsel: The Political Role of Sen Rikyū." *Monumenta Nipponica* 32, no. 1 (Spring 1977): 49–74. http://links.jstor.org/sici?sici=0027-0741%28197721%2932%3A1%3C49%3ATACTPR%3E2.0.CO%3B2-C (accessed July 15, 2005).

Borgen, Robert. Review of *Avatars of Vengeance: Japanese Drama and the Soga Literary Tradition*, by Laurence R. Kominz. *Journal of Japanese Studies* 25, no. 2 (Summer 1999): 448–453. http://links.jstor.org/sici?sici=0095-6848%28199922%2925%3A2%3C448%3AAOVJDA %3E2.0.CO%3B2-7 (accessed February 7, 2006).

Bouchy, Anne Marie. "Kagura to shugendō." *Matsuri* 31 (1978): 65–76.

Brandon, James R., trans. *Kabuki: Five Classic Plays.* Cambridge, Mass., and London: Harvard University Press, 1975.

Butler, Kenneth Dean. "The Textual Evolution of the *Heike Monogatari.*" *Harvard Journal of Asiatic Studies* 26 (1966): 5–51.

"Category 9: Drama Programs/Other Major Presentations." 2003. *50 Years of NHK Television: A Window on Japan and the World.* http://www.nhk.or.jp/digitalmuseum/nhk50years_en/categories/p52/ (accessed October 23, 2005).

Chi, Minnie. "Japan's 'The Twilight Samurai' Nominated for Best Foreign Language Film." *Asia Pacific Arts*, Jan. 23, 2004). http://www.asiaarts.ucla.edu/article.asp?parentid=6861 (accessed August 1, 2006).

Chikamatsu Monzaemon. *Major Plays of Chikamatsu.* Trans. Donald Keene. Records of Civilization, Sources and Studies, 66. New York: Columbia University Press, 1961; reprint 1990.

"Costume in Japan." 1998. *The Costume Museum.* http://www.iz2.or.jp.english/index.htm (accessed January 12, 2006).

Davis, Darrell William. *Picturing Japaneseness: Monumental Style, National Identity, Japanese Film.* New York: Columbia University Press, 1996.

Ebersole, Gary L. "The Buddhist Ritual Use of Linked Poetry in Medieval Japan." *Eastern Buddhist* 16, no. 2 (Autumn 1983): 50–71.

Edmonds, I.G. *Ooka: More Tales of Solomon in Kimono.* Tokyo: Stars and Stripes, 1957.

_____. *Solomon in Kimono: Ooka, a Wise Judge of Old Yedo.* Tokyo: Stars and Stripes, 1956.

Edwards, Mark W. "Homer and Oral Tradition: The Type Scene." *Oral Tradition* 7, no. 2 (October 1992): 284–330.

Engeki Hakubutsukan, Waseda Daigaku Engeki Hakubutsukan, Kawatake Shigetoshi et al., eds. *Engeki hyakka daijiten.* 6 vols. Tokyo: Heibonsha, 1960.

Engeki Hakubutsukan, Kawatake Shigetoshi et al., eds. *Geinō jiten.* Tokyo: Tōkyōdō, 1953.

"Enjoy Kabuki & Bunraku in English." *Iyafon gaido.* http://www.eg-gm.jp/eg/e_joho/e_kb_dic/bun_eep.htm (accessed July 28, 2006).

Fischer-Lichte, Erika. "The Reception of Japanese Theatre by the European Avant-Garde (1900–1930)." In *Japanese Theatre and the International Stage*, ed. Stanca Scholz-Cionca and Samuel L. Leiter, 27–42. Brill's Japanese Studies Library 12. Leiden, Boston, and Köln: Brill, 2001.

Foard, James. "Prefiguration and Narrative in Medieval Hagiography: *The Ippen Hijiri-e.*" In *Flowing Traces: Buddhism in the Literary and Visual Arts of Japan*, ed. James H. Sanford, William R. LaFleur, and Masatoshi Nagatomi, 76–92. Princeton: Princeton University Press, 1992.

Foley, John Miles. *Immanent Art: From Structure to Meaning in Traditional Oral Epic.* Bloomington and Indianapolis: Indiana University Press, 1991.

_____. *Traditional Oral Epic: The "Odyssey," "Beowulf," and the Serbo-Croatian Return Song.* Berkeley, Los Angeles, Oxford: University of California Press, 1990.

Fridell, Wilbur M. *Japanese Shrine Mergers 1906–1912: State Shinto Moves to the Grassroots.* Tokyo: Sophia University, 1973.

Fuji Masaharu. *Ōkōchi Denjirō.* Tokyo: Chūokōronsha, 1981.

Fukuda Akira. *Chūsei katarimono bungei: Sono keifu to tenkai.* Miyai sensho 8. Tokyo: Miyai Shoten, 1981.

_____. *Gunki monogatari to minkan denshō.* Tokyo: Iwasaki Bijitsusha, 1974.

Fukushima Prefectural Board of Education. Fukushima bungaku no furusato hyakusen. 2001–2002. http://www.db.fks.ed.jp/txt/47000.1994fukushima_bungaku100/html/00014.html (accessed August 19, 2005).

Genpei jōsuiki. Vol. 36. *Japanese Text Initiative.* April 6, 2004. http://etext.lib.virginia.edu/japanese/texts/AnoTaih/f-vertical-frame-36.html (accessed August 4, 2005).

Gerow, Aaron. "Subject: Suzaku and Zen." May 20, 1997. *Memorable Threads from KineJapan.* http://pears.lib.ohio-state.edu/Markus/ (accessed December 22, 2005).

_____. "Swarming Ants and Elusive Villains: Zigomar and the Problem of Cinema in 1910s Japan." *Asian Film Connections.* http://www.asianfilms.org/japan/ (accessed December 26, 2004).

Gikeiki Soga monogatari. Nihon koten bungaku taikei 88. Ed. Ichiko Teiji and Ōshima Tatehiko. Tokyo: Iwanami Shoten, 1966.

Great Thinkers of the Eastern World: The Major Thinkers and the Philosophical and Religious Classics of China India Japan Korea and the World. Ed. Ian P. McGreal. New York: HarperCollins Publishers, 1995.

Gunsho kaidai 14: *Shōsokubu, kassenbu* 2. Tokyo: Kabushiki Kaisha Zoku Gunsho Ruijū Kanseikai, 1961.

Hammond, Billy. "Japanese Funeral Customs." 2001. A.E.L.S., Inc. (TanuTech). http://tanutech.com/japan/jfunerals.html (accessed September 22, 2006).

"Hasegawa Shin." *Japanese Literature Publishing Project.* http://www.jlpp.jp/english/list/works18/main.html (accessed June 30, 2004).

Hasegawa Shin. *Kutsukake Tokijirō hoka gohen.* Tokyo: Ryūa Shobō (Shinkokugeki jimusho-nai), 1928.

Hayakawa Kōtarō. *Hana matsuri.* Minzoku mingei sōsho 2. Tokyo: Iwasaki Bijutsusha, 1966.

Hearn, Lafcadio. "In a Japanese Garden V." *Atlantic Monthly* 70, no. 417 (July 1892): 20. *Cornell University Library Making of America.* http://cdl.library.cornell.edu/cgi-bin/moa/moa-cgi?notisid=ABK2934-0070-4 (accessed May 2, 2005).

Heike monogatari. 2 vols. Iwanami bunko 411–415. Ed. Yamada Yoshio. Tokyo: Iwanami Shoten, 1929; 12th reprint 1939.

"Heisei 16 (*sic*) nendo eiga seisaku senmonka yōsei kōza." March 9–12, 2005. *National Film Center.* http://www.momat.go.jp/FC/yoseikoza2004.html (accessed January 1, 2005).

High, Peter B. *The Imperial Screen: Japanese Film Culture in the Fifteen Years' War 1931–1945.* Madison: University of Wisconsin Press, 1995.

Hoff, Frank. *Song, Dance, Storytelling: Aspects of Performing Arts in Japan.* Cornell University East Asia Papers 15. Ithaca, NY: Cornell University China-Japan Program, 1978.

Hono, Eijiro. "The Commoner Class of the Edo Period." *Kyoto University Economic Review* 8 (1933): 44–45. http://www.econ.kyoto-u.ac.jp/review/10000100.pdf (accessed April 13, 2005).

Hori Ichiro (Ichirō). "The Appearance of Self-Consciousness in Japanese Religion and Its Historical Transformations." In *The Japanese Mind: Essentials of Japanese Philosophy and Culture,* ed. Charles A. Moore, 201–280. Honolulu: University of Hawaii Press, 1967.

_____. *Folk Religion in Japan: Continuity and Change.* Ed. Joseph M. Kitagawa and Alan L. Miller. Haskell Lectures on History of Religions new series 1. Chicago: University of Chicago Press, 1968.

"Hougaku Hall: The Stage." *Ishikawa Ongakudo.* http://www.ongakudo.pref.ishikawa.jp/english/set_japanese.html (accessed June 22, 2005).

Hyōdō Hiromi. "Kakuichi-bon *Heike monogatari* no denshō o megutte: Muromachi ōken to geinō." In *Heike biwa: katari to ongaku,* ed. Kamisangō Yūkō, 55–82. Tokyo: Hitsuji Shobō, 1993.

Hyōdō Hiromi. "*The Tale of the Heike* as Warrior Mythology: The Fictional Basis of Genji Political Power." An unpublished paper presented the 1977 Cornell Symposium in Early Japan Studies: Presenting Tales of the Heike in Medieval Japan.

Iwabuchi, Koichi. "Nostalgia for a (Different) Asian Modernity: Media Consumption of 'Asia' in Japan." *positions: east asia cultures critique* 10, no. 3 (2002): 547–573. http://muse.jhu.edu.ezproxy1.lib.asu.edu/journals/positions/v010/10.3iwabuchi.html#endnoteposition:3 (accessed August 14, 2006).

Ichiko Teiji. "Gunki monogatari." In *Zusetsu Nihon bunkashi taikei 7: Muromachi jidai,* ed. Kodama Kōta. Tokyo: Shogakukan, 1957.

Inagaki Shisei. *Oiesōdō.* Tokyo: Bunkei Shunshū, 1979.

Inoura, Yoshinobu and Toshio Kawatake. *The Traditional Theater of Japan.* 2 vols. New York and Tokyo: Weatherhill, 1971.

"Ishikawa Goemon." May 1, 2006. *Wikipedia.* http://en.wikipedia.org/wiki/Ishikawa_Goemon (accessed June 10, 2006).

Iwanami Shoten Kojien. 5th edition. Tokyo: Iwanami Shoten, 1998.
"Japanese Funeral Style 1." *Osoushiki Plaza.* http://www.osoushiki-plaza.com/eng/engl.html (accessed September 22, 2006).
"Japanese warship Kanrin Maru." July 8, 2005. *Wikipedia.* http://en.wikipedia.org/wiki/Kanrin_Maru (accessed August 19, 2005).
"*Jinsei gekijō: seishunhen* (1958)." *Goo eiga.* 2005. http://movie.goo.ne.jp/movies/PMVWKPD25989/index.html (accessed October 13, 2005).
Kadokawa Gen'yoshi. "Meitokuki no seiritsu." *Dentō bungaku kenkyuū* 2, no. 5 (April 1962): 1–13.
"Kaei Suikoden." *Shirandō.* http://homepagel.nifty.com/sira/tyuuji/index.html (accessed August 8, 2005).
"Kaei Suikoden gendaigoyaku." *Shirandō.* http://homepagel.nifty.com/sira/tyuuji/index.html (accessed August 8, 2005).
Kajihara Masaaki. "Chūsei gōki no shogunki." In "Gunki monogatari jiten," by Sugimoto Keizaburō, Kami Hiroshi, Kajihara Masaaki, Fukuda Akira et al. *Kokubungaku kaishaku to kanshō* 28, no. 4 (March 1963): 80–126.
_____. "Ikusa monogatari no henbō: 'Yūki senjō monogatari' no keisei o megutte." *Bungaku* 38, no. 8 (August 1970): 41–53.
Kameyama Sumio. "Chūsei shoki tōkoku bushi no seikatsu ishiki to seishin no saikōsai: Kumagai Naozane o chūshin ni." *Tōkyō nōkō daigaku ippan kyōikuhu kiyō* 27 (March 31, 1990): 1–51.
Kami Hiroshi. "*Kōnodai senki* shōkō." *Kōnan kokubun* 24 (March 1977): 83–97.
_____. "'Ōtō monogatari' shoron: Muromachi gunki kenkyū no tegakari (gunkimono)." *Bungaku* 38, no. 8 (August 1975): 65–77.
Kanai Kiyomitsu. *Jishū bungei kenkyū.* Tokyo: Kazama Shobō, 1967.
Katō Sadahito. "Bakumatsu Tōhoku yowa 9: Jirōchō to Guan (ge)." *Nda Nda gekijō* 74 (February 2005). http://www.mumyosha.co.jp/ndanda/05/bakumatu02.html (accessed August 19, 2005).
Katō, Tai. "*Machi no irezumimono.*" In *Nihon eiga besto 200 shiryō* (*Kinema junpō* sōkan), 78–79. Nihon eiga besto 200 shiri-zu. Tokyo: Kinema Junpōsha, 1982.
_____. "*Ninjō kamifusen.*" In *Nihon eiga besto 200 shiryō* (*Kinema junpō* sōkan), 102–103. Nihon eiga besto 200 shiri-zu. Tokyo: Kinema Junpōsha, 1982.
Kawatake Shigetoshi. *Nihon engeki zenshi.* Tokyo: Iwanami Shoten, 1959.
Kawatake Toshio. *Kabuki: Baroque Fusion of the Art.* Tokyo: International House of Japan, 2003.
Keene, Donald, trans. *Chūshingura. The Treasury of Loyal Retainers: A Puppet Play by Takeda Izumo, Miyoshi Shōraku and Namiki Senryū.* New York: Columbia University Press, 1971.
Kikuchi Shin'ichi. "Kanda Rozan *Shimizu no Jirōchō.*" March 30, 1962. *Kikuchi Shin'ichi kenkyūshitsu: Nihon bungaku kōdan kanji.* http://www.konan-wu.ac.jp/~kikuchi/kodan/rozan.htm (accessed September 27, 2005).
Kinema Junpōsha, ed. *Nihon eiga besto 200 shiryō* (*Kinema junpō* sōkan). Nihon eiga besto 200 shiri-zu. Tokyo: Kinema Junpōsha, 1982.
_____. *Nihon eiga kantoku zenshū Kinema junpō* sōkan 688. Tokyo: Kinema Junpōsha, 1976.
_____. *Nihon eiga haiyū zenshū: danyū-hen Kinema junpō* sōkan 772. Tokyo: Kinema Junpōsha, 1979.
Kobayashi Kazushige. "On the Meaning of Masked Dances in Kagura." *Asian Folklore Studies* 11, no. 1 (1981): 1–22.
Komiya, Toyotaka, ed. *Japanese Music and Drama in the Meiji Era.* Trans. Edward G. Seidensticker and Donald Keene. Tokyo: Toyo Bunko, 1956.
Konishi Jin'ichi. *A History of Japanese Literature.* Volume 1, *The Archaic and Ancient Ages.* Trans. Aileen Gatten and Nicholas Teele. Ed. Earl Miner. Princeton: Princeton University Press, 1984.

Kōnodai kōki. In *Zoku gunsho ruijū* 21/2, ed. Hanawa Hokinoichi, 176–183. Tokyo: Zoku Gunsho Ruijū Kanseikai, 1940.

Kōnodai senki. In *Zoku gunsho ruijū* 21/2, ed. Hanawa Hokinoichi, 165–176. Tokyo: Zoku Gunsho Ruijū Kanseikai, 1940.

"Kunisada Chūji, Onoue Kikugorō." *Tōkyō tōritsu tōshokan: Kichō shiryō gazō de–tabesu*. http://metro.tokyo.opac.jp/tml/tpic/cgi-bin/detail.cgi?Kbseqid=7944&Sryparam=001&Backpage=/tml/tpic/resprint_d/all/isbn001_0_100/isbn001_001_036.html&Srhfname=/resprint_d/all/isbn001_0_100/isbn001&Rp_kind=8&Prtype=0&Displmt=100 (accessed August 9, 2005).

"Kunisada Chūji (Nagaoka Chūjirō)." April 13, 2004. *Jōshū Kunisada Chūji chaya honbo*. http://www5.wind.ne.jp/fisherman/ch/chuji/kunisada.htm (accessed August 8, 2005).

Kurata Yoshihiro. *Meiji Taishō no minshū goraku*. Iwanami Shinsho 114. Tokyo: Iwanami Shoten, 1980.

Kusumoto Kenkichi. "Yakuza eiga no gendai teki kōsai." In *Ninkyō eiga no sekai*, ed. Kusumoto Kenkichi, 7–28. Tokyo: Araji Shuppansha, 1969.

LaFleur, William R. "The Death and 'Lives' of the Poet-Monk Saigyō: The Genesis of a Buddhist Sacred Biography." In *The Biographical Process: Studies in the History and Psychology of Religion*, ed. Frank E. Reynolds and Donald Capps, 343–361. The Hague: Mouton, 1976.

Langton, Scott. "A Literature for the People: A Study of the *Jidai Shōsetsu* in Taishō and Early Shōwa Japan." Ph.D. dissertation, Ohio State University, 2000. Ann Arbor, MI: University Microfilms, 2001.

"Library/English Titles." Toei TV Website. http://www.toei.co.jp/tv/library/series-title.html (accessed April 11, 2005).

Lord, Albert Bates. *The Singer of Tales*. Cambridge: Harvard University Press, 1960.

McFarland, H. Neill. *Rush Hour of the Gods: A Study of New Religious Movements in Japan*. New York: Macmillan, 1967.

Manabe Motoyuki, ed. *Taishū bungaku jiten*. Tokyo: Seiabo, 1967.

Matisoff, Susan. Review of *The Tale of the Soga Brothers*, trans. Thomas J. Cogan. *Monumenta Nipponica* 43, no. 1 (Spring 1988): 101–103. http://links.jstor.org/sici?sici=0027–0741%28198821%2943%3A1%3C101%3ATTOTSB %3E2.0.CO%3B2-M (accessed February 7, 2006).

Matsuhiro: Shimizu minato funayado kinenkan. http://www.portwave.gr.jp/suehiro/index.html (accessed August 19, 2005).

Matsumoto Kenichi. *Nakazato Kaizan*. Asahi Hyōdensen 18. Tokyo: Asahi Shinbunsha, 1978.

Meitokuki. Ed. Tomikura Tokujirō. *Iwanami bunko* 2899–2900. Tokyo: Iwanami Shoten, 1941.

Miller, J. Scott. "Japanese Shorthand and *Sokkibon*." *Monumenta Nipponica* 49, no. 4 (Winter 1994): 471–487. http://links.jstor.org/sici?sici=0027–0741%28199424%2949%3A4%3C471%3AJSAS%3E2.0.CO%3B2–8 (accessed August 18, 2005).

Mills, D.E. "*Soga Monogatari, Shintōshū* and the Taketori Legend." *Monumenta Nipponica* 30, no. 1 (Spring 1975): 37–68. http://links.jstor.org/sici?sici=0027–0741%28197521%2930%3A1%3C37%3ASMSATT%3E2.0.CO%3B2-L (accessed May 15, 2005).

Miraculous Stories from the Japanese Buddhist Tradition: The "Nihon Ryōiki of the Monk Kyōkai." Translated and edited by Kyōko Motomochi Nakamura. Harvard Yenching Institute Monograph Series 20. Cambridge: Harvard University Press, 1973.

Miyazaki Fumiko. "Religious Life of the Kamakura Bushi: Kumagai Naozane and his Descendants." *Monumenta Nipponica* 47, no. 4 (Winter 1992): 435–467.

Mizuhara Hajime. "Geinō gunki zakkan: *Yūki senjō monogatari* nado kara." *Gunki to katarimono* 11 (October 1974): 1–3.

_____. "Tomoe densetsu-setsuwa." *Kokubungaku kaishaku to kanshō* 32, no. 8 (June 1967): 202–204.

"Mongaku hosshin no koto." In *Shintei genpei jōsuiki*. 6 vols. Ed. Mizuhara Hajime. III:19–29. Tokyo: Shinjin Oraisha, 1988–1991.
Mori Ōgai. *The Incident at Sakai and Other Stories*. Ed. David Dilworth and J. Thomas Rimer with additional contributions by Richard Bowring. Honolulu: University of Hawaii Press, 1977.
Murdoch, James. *A History of Japan*. 3 vols. Yokohama: Asiatic Society of Japan; London K. Paul Trübner, 1910–1949.
Nagata Tetsurō. *Tate*. Tokyo: San'ichi Shobō, 1974.
Najita, Tetsuo. "Oshio Heihachiro (1793–1837)." In *Personality in Japanese History*, ed. Albert M. Craig and Donald H. Shively. Berkeley, CA: University of California Press, 1970.
Nakamura, Hajime. *Ways of Thinking of Eastern Peoples: India, China, Tibet, Japan*. Revised English translation. Ed. Philip P. Wiener. Honolulu: East-West Center Press, 1964.
Nakao ochi no sōshi. In *Gunsho ruijū* 21, ed. Hanawa Hokinoichi, 34–40. Tokyo: Kabushiki Kaisha Zoku Gunsho Ruijū Kanseikai, 1940.
Nakazato Kaizan. *The Great Bodhisattva Pass*. Trans. C.S. Bavier. Tokyo: Shunjūshakan, 1929.
Nihon Kindai Bungaku-kan, ed. *Nihon kindai bungaku daijiten*. 6 vols. Tokyo: Kōdansha 1977–1978.
Okano, Haruko. *Die Stellung der Frau im Shintō: Eine Religionsphänomenologische und Soziologische Untersuchung*. Bonn: Rheinische Friederich-Wilhems-Universität, 1975.
Okumura, Ayao. "A Cherry Blossom Picnic." *Food Forum*. 2005. http://www.kikkoman.com/forum/021/ff021.html (accessed May 2, 2005).
Ooms, Emily Groszos. *Women and Millenarian Protest in Meiji Jajpan: Deguchi Nao and Ōmotokyō*. Cornell East Asia Series 61. Ithaca, New York: Cornell East Asia Program, 1993.
Origuchi (Orikuchi) Shinobu. "Yashima katari no kenkyū." In *Orikuchi Shinobu zenshū* 17, 194–212. Tokyo: Chūōkōronsha, 1956.
Ortolani, Benito. *The Japanese Theater: From Shamanistic Ritual to Contemporary Pluralism*. Princeton: Princeton University Press, 1990; revised 1995.
Ōshima Tatehiko. "Gunkimono." *Kokubungaku kaishaku to kanshō* 26, no. 5 (April 1961): 92–96.
Ōtō monogatari. In *Zoku gunsho ruijū* dai 21/2, ed. Hanawa Hokinoichi, 355–376. Tokyo: Kabushiki kaisha soku Gunsho Ruijū Kanseikai, 1940.
Oyumi gosho-sama onuchiji ikusa monogatari. In *Bōsō sōsho* vol. 1, ed. Bōsō Sōshō Kankōkai, 189–195. Chiba, Japan: Bōsō Sōsho Kankōkai, 1912.
Ozaki Hideki. "Kaisetsu." In *Nakazato Kaizan-shū*, 492–496. Shōwa kokumin bungaku zenshū 1. Tokyo: Chikuma Shobō, 1978.
Ōzasa Yoshio. *Nihon gendai engeki-shi: Meiji Taishō-hen*. Tokyo: Hakusuisha, 1985.
Payne, Rachel M. "Meiji Theatre Design: From Communal Participation to Refined Appreciation." Nissan Occasional Paper Series 34. 2003. Oxford University Nissan Institute of Japanese Studies. http://www.nissan.ox.ac.uk/nops/nops34.pdf (accessed June 15, 2005).
"Popular Culture and Invented Heroes." 2004. *National Museum of Japan*. http://www.rekihaku.ac.jp/e_news/index82/index.html (accessed on August 8, 2005).
Prince, Stephen. *The Warrior's Camera: The Cinema of Akira Kurosawa*. Princeton: Princeton University Press, 1991; revised and expanded 1999.
Rath, Eric C. "From Representation to Apotheosis: Nō's Modern Myth of Okina." *Asian Theatre Journal* 17, no. 2 (Fall 2000): 253–68.
Remembering Aizu: The Testament of Shiba Gorō. Ed. Ishimitsu Mahito; edited and translated with introduction and notes by Teruko Craig. Honolulu: University of Hawaii Press, 1999.
Richie, Donald. "Introduction to the Michigan Electronic Reprint [of *Japanese Cinema:*

Film Style and National Character]." 1971; reprint 2004. University of Michigan Center for Asian Studies Electronic Publications. http://www.umich.edu/%7Eiinet/cjs/publications/cjsfaculty/filmrichie.html (accessed November 22, 2005).

Romance of the Three Kingdoms. 1997–2005. http://www.ThreeKingdoms.com (accessed Feb. 6, 2006).

Rucka, Nicholas. A review of *Tasogare Seibei*, directed by Yamada Yōji. *Midnight Eye*, March 10, 2004. http://www.midnighteye.com/reviews/twilsamu.shtml (accessed July 26, 2006).

Sakamoto Tokumatsu. *Zenshinza.* Tokyo: Kōdosha, 1953.

Sarkisyanz, Emmanuel. *Rußland und der Messianismus des Orients: Sendungsbewußtsein und politischer Chiliasmus des Ostens.* Tubingen: J.C.B. Mohr, 1955.

Shida Itaru. "Naozane no shojō—Tsunemori no hempō: *Heike monogatari* ni okeru Kumagai Rensei no katari o megutte." *Kokugo kokubun* 52, no. 6 (June 1983): 26–38.

Sasago ochi no sōshi. In *Gunsho ruijū* 21, ed. Hanawa Hokinoichi, 24–33. Tokyo: Kabushiki Kaisha Zoku Gunsho Ruijū Kanseikai, 1940.

Sato (Satō) Tadao. *Currents in Japanese Cinema: Essays by Tadao Sato.* Translated by Gregory Barrett. Tokyo: Kodansha International; New York: Kodansha International/USA, distributed by Harper and Row, 1982.

Satō Tadao. *Hasegawa Shin-ron: giri ninjō to wa nani ka.* Tokyo: Chūōkōronsha, 1975.

_____. *Kimi wa jidaigeki o mita ka.* Tokyo: Jakometei Shuppan, 1977.

"Satsuei gijutsu-dentō no katachi." 1 and 2. *Heisei 15* [*sic*] *nendo eiga seisaku senmonka yōsei kōza.* March 10–13, 2004. National Film Center. http://www.momat.go.jp/FC/yoseikouza2003.html (accessed January 1, 2006).

Schilling, Mark. *The Yakuza Movie Book: A Guide to Japanese Gangster Films.* Berkeley: Stone Bridge Press, 2003.

Schrader, Paul. "Yakuza Eiga: A Primer." *Film Comment* 10, no. 1 (February 1974): 8–17.

Sekiyama Kazuo. *Sekkyō no rekishi.* Iwanami shinsho 64. Tokyo: Iwanami Shoten, 1978.

Sekka Sanjin. *Sarutobi Sasuke: Sanada sanyūshi ninjutsu meijin.* Tachikawa Bunko 40. Osaka: Tachikawa Bunmeidō 1914; reprint: Tokyo: Horupu Shuppan, 1975, Meicho Fukkoku Nihon Jidō Bungakkan 6.

Shaver, Ruth. *Kabuki Costume.* Tokyo and Rutland, Vermont: Charles E. Tuttle Company, Inc., 1966.

Shimazu Masayoshi. "The Battle of Aizu." *Shinsengumi.* 2003. http://www.shinsengumihq.com/aizubattlebf.htm (accessed April 30, 2005).

Shimizu, Yoshiaki. "Multiple Commemorations: The Vegetable Nehan." In *Flowing Traces: Buddhism in the Literary and Visual Arts of Japan*, ed. James H. Sanford, William R. LaFleur and Masatoshi Nagatomi, 201–233. Princeton: Princeton University Press, 1992.

"Shimizu no Jirōchō." *Shizuoka chasenmonten Komatsuen.* April 20, 2005. http://www3.tokai.or.jp/komatsuen/jirotyou%20.htm (accessed April 27, 2005).

Shively, Donald. "Sumptuary Regulation and Status in Early Tokugawa Japan." *Harvard Journal of Asiatic Studies* 25 (1964–1965): 123–164. http://links.jstor.org/ sici?sici=0073-0548%281964%2F1965%2925%3C123%3ASRASIE%3E2.0.CO%3B2-2 (accessed April 13, 2005).

Shōriya (Aragorō). *Kabuki: Le Kabuki dans la Langue Molière.* http://kabuki.ifrance.com/kabuki/kuzaemon1_gf.htm (accessed October 10, 2005).

Shōriya Aragōrō. *Kabuki 21.* September 9, 1999 (revised April 23, 2005). http://www.kabuki21.com (accessed May 2, 2005).

Shōriya Aragorō. "Arashi Kitsusaburō." *Kabuki 21* (September 9, 1999–July 31, 2006). http://www.kabuki21.com/kitsusaburo1.php (accessed August 3, 2006).

Smith II, Henry D. "Rethinking the Story of the 47 Ronin: Chūshingura in the 1980s." 1990; revised 2003. Henry Smith's Home Page. http://www.columbia.edu/~hds2/47ronin/47ronin_rev.htm (accessed May 27, 2005).

_____. "The Trouble with Terasaka: The Forty-Seventh Rōnin and the Chūshingura Imagination." *Japan Review* 16 (2004): 3–65. http://202.231.40.34/jpub/pdf/jr/IJ1601.pdf (accessed May 27, 2005).
Suganuma Hiroshi. "Biwa hōshi." In *Aera Mook: Heike monogatari ga wakaru.* Tokyo: Asahi Shinbunsha, 1997.
Sugimoto Keizaburō, Kami Hiroshi, Kajihara Masaaki, Fukuda Akira et al. "Gunki monogatari jiten." *Kokubungaku kaishaku to kanshō* 28, no. 4 (March 1963): 80–126.
_____. "Heike monogatari ni okeru shi no shosō." In *Gunki monogatari no sekai*, 82–101. Tokyo: Meichō Kankōkai, 1985.
Suzuki, Daisetz T. *Zen and Japanese Culture.* Bollingen Series 64. Princeton: Princeton University Press, 1959; reprint 1970.
The Taiheiki: A Chronicle of Medieval Japan. Translated and with an introduction and notes by Helen Craig McCullough. New York: Columbia University Press, 1959.
Takagi Ichinosuke. "Gunki monogatari." In *Nihon bungakushi jiten*, ed. Fujimura Tsukuru and Nishio Minoru. Tokyo: Nihon Hyōron Shinsha, 1960.
Takagi Takeshi. "Senki monogatari." In *Nihon bungaku daijiten*, vol. 4. Tokyo: Shinchōsha, 1936.
Takahashi Hiroshi. *Taishū geinō: sono ayumi to geijintachi.* Tokyo: Kyōiku Shiryō Shuppankai, 1980.
Takahashi Satoshi. *Shimizu no Jirōchō to bakumatsu isshin: "Tōkai yūkyō den no sekai."* Tokyo: Iwanami Shoten, 2003.
Takahashi Satoshi. "The Water Margin (Suikoden) in Japan around the End of the Edo Period." *Rekihaku* 117, March 2003. http://www.rekihaku.ac.jp/e-rekihaku/117/index.html (accessed August 8, 2005).
The Tale of the Heike. Translated and with an introduction by Helen Craig McCullough. Stanford California: Stanford University Press, 1988.
The Tale of the Heike. 2 vols. Trans. Hiroshi Kitagawa and Bruce T. Tsuchida. Tokyo: University of Tokyo Press, 1975.
The Tale of the Soga Brothers. Translated and with an introduction and notes by Thomas J. Cogan. Tokyo: University of Tokyo Press, 1987.
Takenaka Tsutomu. *Keikō eiga no jidai.* Tokyo: Shirakawa Shoten, 1974.
Tanaka Min. 2003. http://www.min-tanaka.com/ (accessed August 1, 2006).
Thornton, S.A. (Sybil Anne). "Epic and Religious Propaganda from the Ippen School of Pure Land Buddhism." In *Religions of Japan in Practice,* ed. George J. Tanabe Jr., 185–192. Princeton: Princeton University Press, 1999.
_____. "From Warrior to Holy Man." *Parabola* 12, no. 1 (Spring 1987): 43–49.
_____. "*Kōnodai senki*: Traditional Narrative and Warrior Ideology in Sixteenth-Century Japan." *Oral Tradition* 15, no. 2 (2000): 306–377.
_____. "Ogyū Sorai." In *Great Thinkers of the Eastern World*, ed. Ian P. McGreal, 371–374. New York: HarperCollins Publishers, Inc., 1995.
_____. "The Propaganda Traditions of the Yugyō ha: The Campaign to Establish the Jishū as an Independent School of Japanese Buddhism (1300–1700)." Ph.D. thesis [*sic*], University of Cambridge, 1990.
_____. Review of *To the Distant Observer: Form and Meaning in Japanese Cinema*, by Noël Burch. *Cinema Journal* 21, no. 1 (Autumn 1981): 59–64.
_____. "The Shinkokugeki and the Zenshinza: Western Representational Realism and the Japanese Period Film." *Asian Cinema* 7, no. 2 (Winter 1995): 46–57.
_____. "Yamaga Sokō." In *Great Thinkers of the Eastern World*, ed. Ian P. McGreal, 359–362. New York: HarperCollins Publishers, Inc., 1995.
Toita, Kōji. "The New-Theatre Movement." In *Japanese Music and Drama in the Meiji Era*, ed. Toyotaka Komiya and trans. Donald Keene, 285–303. Tokyo: Toyo Bunko, 1956.
Toki Akihiro and Mizoguchi Kaoru. "A History of Early Cinema in Kyoto Japan 1896–1912:

Cinematographe and Inabata Katsutaro." *CineMagazineNet!* 1, Autumn 1996 (September 17, 1996). http://www.cmn.hs.h.kyoto-u.ac.jp/NO1/SUBJECT1/INAEN.HTM (accessed October 30, 2005).

Tokita, Alison. "The Reception of the *Heike Monogatari* as Performed Narrative: The Atsumori Episode in Heikyoku Zatō Biwa and Satsuma Biwa." *Japanese Studies* 23, no. 1 (May 2003): 59–85.

The Tokyo Chamber of Commerce and Industry. "Katsushika Shibamata Tora-san Museum." *A Guide to Technical Visits and Industrial Museums in Tokyo*. 2006. http://www.tokyo-cci.or.jp/sangyokanko/english/055.html (accessed September 12, 2006).

Tomikura Tokujirō. "Gunki monogatari no honshitsu." In *Gunki monogatari no bodai to kanryō (tokushū): Kokubungaku kaishaku to kanshō* 28, no. 4 (February 1963): 10–16.

Torrance, Richard. "Literacy and Literature in Osaka 1890–1940." *The Journal of Japanese Studies* 31, no. 1 (2005): 27–60. http://0-muse.jhu.edu.library.lib.asu.edu/journals/journal_of_japanese_studies/v031/31.1torrance.pdf (accessed August 6, 2005).

"Torii Kotondo." *Hanga Gallery and Torii Gallery*. http://www.hanga.com/bijin-ga/kotondo/ (accessed June 14, 2005).

"Toyama no Kinsan." KIKU TV: Multicultural Television. http://www.kikutv.com/shows/Japanese_Programs/toyama _no_kinsan/ (accessed April 11, 2005).

Tschudin, Jean-Jacques. "Danjūrō's *Katsureki-geki* (Realistic Theatre) and the Meiji 'Theatre Reform' Movement." *Japan Forum* 11, no. 1 (April 1991): 83–94. http://0-search.epnet.com.library.lib.asu.edu:80/login.aspx?direct=true&db=aph&an=6695057 (accessed June 11, 2005).

"Tsuyu Kosode Mukashi Hachijō/Kamiyui Shinza." *Le Kabuki dans la Langue de Molière*. http://kabuki.ifrance.com/kabuki/kamiyui_shinza.htm (accessed July 23, 2004).

Watson, Michael. "Modes of Reception: *Heike monogatari* and the Nō play *Kogō*." *Kokusaigaku kenkyū* 16 (March 1997): 275–303. October 14, 2000. http://www.meijigakuin.ac.jp/~watson/heike/kogo.html (accessed July 13, 2005).

Yamaga Sokō. *The Way of the Samurai*. In *Sources of Japanese Tradition*, 398–400, ed. Ryusaku Tsunoda et al. Introduction to Oriental Civilizations 54. New York: Columbia University Press, 1958; 4th reprint 1960.

Yamamoto Kichizō. "Kuchigatari no ron (ge) Goze uta no baai." *Bungaku* 45, no. 1 (January 1977): 89–107.

_____. "Kuchigatari no ron (jō) Goze uta no baai." *Bungaku* 44, no. 10 (October 1976): 1364–1386.

Yamamoto Kikuo. "Rensai ronbun: hikaku eiga kenkyū (19): America eiga no eikyō museiki, hi-ro-no keifu 3." *Firumu senta-* 39 (March 30, 1977): 35–42.

_____. "Rensai ronbun: hikaku eigashi kenkyū (26): Amerika eiga to jiyūshugi jidai geki, Inagaki Hiroshi kantoku sakuhin o megutte." *Firumu senta-* 56 (March 6, 1980): 30–40.

_____. "Rensai ronbun: hikaku eigashi kenkyū (27): Amerika eiga to jiyūshugi jidai geki, Yamanaka Sadao no matatabi-mono o megutte." *Firumu senta-* 59 (March 6, 1980): 33–40.

_____. "Rensei ronbun: hikaku eigashi kenkyū (28): Amerika eiga to jiyūshugi jidai geki, Yamanaka Sadao no nagaya-mono o megutte," *Firumu senta-* 60 (May 7, 1980): 37–44.

"Yamaoka Tesshū." 2004. *Rekishikan*. http://www.geocities.jp/str_homepage/rekishi/bakumatsu/jinbutsu/meikan/tesshu.html (accessed August 19, 2005).

"Yamaoka Tessyu [*sic*] to wa." *Yamaoka Tessyu*. http://www.tessyuu.jp/yamaoka.htm (accessed August 19, 2005).

Yamashina Tokitsugu (1507–1576). *Tokitsugu kyōki*. Cited in "Ishikawa Goemon no nakamatachi." *Nakahara Chūya to dadaizumu*. September 20, 2005. http://www.ten-f.com/goemon.html (accessed October 13, 2005).

Yoshitsune: A Fifteenth-century Japanese Chronicle. Trans. and with an introduction by

Helen Craig McCullough. Stanford, California: Stanford University Press; Tokyo: University of Tokyo Press, 1966.

Yūki senjō monogatari. In *Gunsho ruijū* 20, ed. Hanawa Hokinoichi, 712–734. Tokyo: Kabushiki Kaisha Zoku Gunsho Ruijū Kanseikai, 1940.

Index